THE COLLECTED WORKS OF
TIAN XUEYUAN

4.

田雪原
文集

社会科学文献出版社
SOCIAL SCIENCES ACADEMIC PRESS (CHINA)

目　录
CONTENTS

英文论文

附　录

导　　论

《田雪原文集》（四）分为两部分：第一部分，为笔者所作绪论、总论、前言和序，共选录 19 篇；第二部分，为公开发表的英文论文，选录 13 篇。此外，同前三卷一样，选录网络直播、访谈、采访、报道、书评、书讯等 11 篇。内容涉及人口、经济、社会、资源、环境等诸领域，时间跨度近 30 年，反映笔者以人口研究为主并与相关学科相结合，积极推动边缘和交叉研究的特点。

第一部分，绪论、总论、前言和序。选入本《文集》的 19 篇中，包括绪论 7 篇，其中 5 篇列在笔者担任主编或主笔的专著篇首，2 篇列在好友主编的专著篇首。总论 2 篇，位列笔者主编或主笔的专著首篇。绪论和总论，主要阐述该专著的撰著背景、核心内容、框架结构、创新之处、理论和应用价值、需要讨论的问题和不足之处。举如下二例说明。

"《改革开放中的人口问题研究》绪论"，为收入本《文集》7 篇绪论之一，列在沙吉才研究员主编的同名专著首篇，分（一）、（二）、（三）三个部分。（一）阐述对改革开放背景的认识，从世界的改革浪潮到中国经济体制改革的提出和发展，影响所及，波及经济生活、政治生活、社会生活、家庭生活各个方面，人口的变动和发展，也必然为改革开放大潮所左右。（二）设计出经济体制改革、政治体制改革影响人口变动与发展框架结构，提出并阐发：（1）对人口数量控制的影响。基于市场经济体制改革和孩子成本—效益发生的变动，在改革前期经济发展水平不高的条件下，由于家庭生产和经营职能的恢复，孩子劳动—经济效益、养老—保险效益等重新得到恢复和强化，从而提高了人们生育孩子的预期效益和积极性。相反，在改革力度较大和经济比较发达地区，孩子成本特别是教育成本显著提高，高收入和社会保障事业的发展削减了孩子的劳动—经济效益和养老—保险效益，诱导人们从多生多育向少生优育优教转变，遂使生育率下降。（2）对人口素质主要是文化教育素质的影响。关键是追加的孩子智力投资能否带来相应的效益，针对当时"花钱念书不如挣钱跑运输"、"拿手术刀的不如拿剃头刀的"新的"读书无用论"，提出和阐发按劳分配要体现复杂劳动是简单劳动倍加原则，适当向脑力劳动倾斜、提高人口智力投资积极性的建议。（3）对人口结构的影响。随着改革开放的深入和经济的发展，男孩子效益的提升更为显著，使得一部分人偏爱男性孩子的性别偏好有所滋长。1990年人口普查0~4岁组性别比上升到110以上，已处于严重偏高状态，需要引起重视和着力解决。（三）鉴于改革开放上述深刻而深远的影响，人口必须置于这一大环境背景之下，如何兴利却弊地驾驭未来人口变动和发展的趋势，是摆在我们面前必须回答的问题。"绪论"具体分析了未来中国人口变动和发展的八大趋势，即人口数量继续增长、人口素质不断提高、生产年龄人口所占比例上升、人口老龄化、人口城市化、人口迁移新变动、人口流动增强、婚姻和家庭变动新趋势，颇值得重视。需要将这些趋势放到改革开放之中，寻求解决的路径和决策。

"《21世纪中国人口发展战略研究》总论"，为收入本《文集》2篇总论之一，列在笔者主持的同名国家社科基金重大项目最终成果的专著首篇。"总论"关于国际背景的阐述，重点分析了信息化和经济全球化，指出：立足于人口学视角，信息化推进了人的现代化，促进了就业结构的调整；经济全球化带动全球市场的进一步形成，金融体制接轨为大势所趋，以跨国公司为主体的国际合作组织日益扩大，发展不平衡和财富不均越来越严重。经济全球化和中国加入世贸组织，给人口、就业带来新的机遇和挑战，是21世纪中国人口发展战略必须考虑的国际背景。国内背景重点阐发经济转轨，包括：由计划经济体制转变到市场经济体制，发展方式由外延为主转变到内涵为主；社会转型，由政府主导型转变到社会服务型；人口转变，由高出生、低死亡、高增长转变到低出生、低死亡、低增长，进入"转变后"人口阶段。在国际"两化"、国内"三转"大背景下，提出和阐述21世纪中国人口发展战略"三步走"宏观思路。第一步，把高生育率降下来，降到更替水平以下，实现人口再生产由高出生、低死亡、高增长向低出生、低死亡、低增长类型的转变。第二步，稳定低生育水平，直至实现人口的零增长；同时注重人口素质的提高和结构的调整。第三步，零增长以后，由于人口的惯性作用将呈一定程度的减少趋势，再依据届时的经济、社会发展状况以及资源、环境状况，作出理想适度人口的抉择。这样的理想适度人口是全方位的，不仅数量是适当的，而且素质是比较高的，年龄、性别等的结构也是合理的。如此"三步走"人口发展战略目标，第一步已于20世纪90年代中期达到，第二步也已经走过10年的路程，预计可在2030年前后完成，第三步则是实现人口零增长以后的事情，现在能够做到的是测算出其后的人口变动和发展趋势，为最终实现全方位适度人口目标奠定基础。当前的人口发展战略，应锁定在以人口零增长为主要目标，包括人口数量、素质、结构的全面发展上，并且有利于向下一步全方位适度人口过渡。

一般情况下，绪论和总论篇幅不很长，力求对全书作出提纲挈领的概括，起到画龙点睛的作用。与之相比，前言和序更要短一些，目的是起一点儿"提神"的作用。选入本《文集》的前言一篇是"《中国人口政策60年》前言"。该"前言"开始，摆出对中国人口政策持不同观点的5本论著，接着1980年从本人作为首次中国人口学家代表团成员出席在美国举行的国际会议的争论起笔，说明不同观点由来已久。然而事实胜于雄辩，真理总是可以说服人的。中国人口生育政策特别是30年来提倡一对夫妇生育一个孩子，赢得国际社会越来越多的理解和赞同；当然，不赞同者和反对者，至今仍然有之。大千世界，无奇不有，无碍大局。开展不同观点的讨论和争论是必要的，但是最重要的是实事求是地阐发中国人口政策提出和制定的社会背景、理论依据、主导思想、基本要求和实施的效果。《中国人口政策60年》，就是本人亲历1980年人口政策出台和30年走过的不平道路，加以人口学、经济学、社会学等理论方法诠释的一部实证研究专著。说它是实证研究专著，是因为研究的实体内容是社会的客观存在；而具体的阐述，不是经验式的总结，而是学术性质的讨论。提出要用发展的眼光，用"30年河东、30年河西"发展和辩证的眼光分析，开展与时俱进的研究。

选入本《文集》的9篇序，以"《人力资本开发研究》序"为例说明。该"序"着眼于信息化、经济全球化视野，在概述自古典学派人力资本主要代表人物主要观点，近年来的主要发展，立足货币资本获取与投资由单一竞争向多元竞争转变的基础上，着力阐释强化人力资本、提高人力资本利用效率的重要意义。改革开放以来，我国人力资本研究取得长足进步。面对全面建设小康社会的艰巨任务，破解当前发展方式转变、缩小城乡差距和地区发展差距、消除贫困、合理利用资源、落实科学发展观等难题，在某种意义上，开发利用好人力资源、不断增强人力资本积聚的能力、变人口大国为人力资源大国和人力资本强国是关键。从这样的意义上说，李玉江教授主持的列入国家自然科学基金"人力资本时空结构及对区域可持续发展支撑能力研究"课题，同时获得与该课题接近且与之形成交叉研究的教育部和山东省支持的两项课题，最后完成《人力资本开发研究》专著，很有现实意义和实际应用价值。"序"介绍了该专著有关内容，包括：我国东部与中西部区域人力资本变动、"极化效应"显著、人力资本存量区域差距呈倒 U 型趋势、对可持续发展构成逆向变动，以及方法论等的创新之处，该专著具有一定的学术价值和实际应用价值。

第二部分，英文论文。新中国成立 60 年特别是改革开放 30 年来，人口科学同其他许多社会科学一样，加快了走出国门、交流切磋和融入世界的步伐。然而同自然科学、社会科学不少学科相比，还处于相对落后状态，从而妨碍学科的建设和发展。笔者作为新中国成立后第一批成长起来的知识分子，20 世纪 50 年代笔者所在的初中、高中，外语一律开设俄语，进到大学仍然学习俄语，因而总共学了 8 年俄语。转入人口研究以后，发现俄语应用的范围过于狭窄，只好自学英语，一直处于"瓜菜代"低水平。不过深知，作为世界第一人口大国人口研究走出去、融入世界十分必要，也就增加了几分责任感。经帮助加上本人努力，先后发表 20 多篇英文论文，还有 10 多篇日文、俄文论文，最多语种的是列入《中国基本情况丛书》的《中国人口》一书，笔者为合著第一作者，除中文本外，还译成英、法、俄、德、日、西、阿拉伯 7 种文本。其中的一个机遇，是 1988 年笔者在担任中国社会科学院人口研究所所长和《中国人口科学》杂志主编时，与美国艾勒顿出版公司（Allerton Press, INC）签订了一项 10 年协议，由他们翻译每期《中国人口科学》杂志 1/2 ~ 3/4 文章，出版英文版《中国人口科学》（*Chinese Journal of Population Science*），向各国发行。由于国外翻译水平较高，加上文章较有意义，选入本《文集》13 篇英文文章中，有 6 篇来自该英文杂志。其余 7 篇或为参加国际学术会议论文，或为学术交流演讲稿。13 篇英文论文，主要涉及中国人口问题、人口发展战略、人口城市化、人口老龄化、人口素质、人口政策等内容，力图将有代表性的研究成果推出去，加强国际学术交流，促进人口科学发展。

附录。同《文集》前三集一样，是学术界和相关媒体对笔者研究工作和取得成果的报道和评介。这些报道和评介不一定十分准确，不过还是表达出一种观点，提出一些值得思考的问题。因而选出有代表性的几篇，附录于后，以供参考和指正。

绪论、总论、前言、序

《改革开放中的人口问题研究》绪论[*]

一

　　潮，改革潮。当历史跨入 20 世纪下半叶，伴随着新的技术革命席卷全球而来的，是改革的浪潮。这股浪潮冲击着沉睡的大地，也冲击着因工业化而不断升温的热土，一切力图摆脱困境和寻求新的发展的国家和地区，都在谋求改革，改革成为时代的风尚，也成为人们最热门的话题。

　　中国作为东方古国，正在经受改革的冲击、考验和洗礼。远者且不论，自 1949 年新中国成立后，20 世纪 50 年代前期和中期成功地医治了战争的创伤，提前 1 年完成第一个五年计划，奠定了工业化的初步基础。然而从 50 年代后期开始的 20 年，国民经济大起大落，处于徘徊不前的状态，贻误了宝贵时间。这中间有政治的、经济的、社会的诸多原因，但不容争辩的一点是：当世界新的技术革命及其管理的改革迅速兴起之时，我们却处于封闭或半封闭状态，关起门来搞"以阶级斗争为纲"，既无改革开放意识，更无实际之举，从而拉大了同先进国家之间的差距。1978 年具有历史意义的中共十一届三中全会召开了，纠正了"左"的错误，提出了将工作重心转移到经济建设上来，确定了实行改革开放的方针。经过一段时间的努力，1982年中共十二大以后，改革全面展开，乡村由点到面全面推行联产承包责任制，乡镇企业遍地开花，国有企业从扩大企业自主权到推广经营承包制、股份制，全国城乡形成向社会主义市场经济转变的生动局面。这是一场伟大的革命，是在 960 万平方千米土地上甩掉贫困落后帽子，实现"三步走"发展战略目标的革命。适应经济体制改革和经济发展需要，政治体制改革也已展

---

　　*　本文原载沙吉才主编《改革开放中的人口问题研究》，北京大学出版社，1994。

开；政府转变职能等管理体制和机构改革提到日程上，新的以解放生产力和发展生产力为中心的价值观念正在形成，可以说改革是波及社会生活各个领域的深刻革命。

那么，怎样改革，向着什么方向改革呢？除需要认真总结我们自己的经验外，一个重要的方面是不要忘记我们所处的时代，不要离开我们周围的环境。在当代，任何一个国家或地区成功的改革，都毫无例外地需要汲取外来的经验，争取外援，同开放紧密联系在一起。改革需要开放，开放促进改革，我国10多年来改革开放充分证明了这一点。适应改革发展需要，在深圳、珠海、汕头、厦门和海南省建立经济特区，确立沿海一批开放城市和经济开发区，形成以珠江三角洲、长江三角洲、闽东南三角地带和环渤海为中心，包括2亿人口的沿海开放带，闯出了一条新的改革与开放结合之路。如今在此基础上，扩大沿边、沿江河开放带，加快内陆省、自治区的开放步伐，更有效地利用国外资金、技术和管理经验，使开放同改革结合起来向着多层次、多渠道、全面发展的目标前进，引向深入。

由沿海、沿边、沿江河走向内地，由沿海2亿人口逐渐波及11亿人口的改革开放进程和新的格局告诉我们，改革开放是影响政治生活、经济生活、社会生活各个方面的根本性变革，当然也会对人口再生产，对国家的人口管理和人口目标，对人口变动的主要方面产生重要影响。显然，研究改革开放中新的人口问题的产生及其解决的方略，是实证人口研究的紧迫课题，意义是显而易见的。参加由沙吉才研究员担任主编、鲁景精副教授担任副主编的《改革开放中的人口问题研究》一书撰写的同志，深入实际调查研究，坚持理论同实践相结合，积极探索，反复修改，提出许多有实际价值的新观点和对策性建议，是对改革开放和人口问题解决的一个实际的推动，是脚踏实地的一项具体的努力。

二

改革开放中的人口问题是一个总的题目。关于中国的人口问题，包括本人在内的学术界许多同志认为，主要是人口的数量控制、素质的提高、结构的调节三个方面的问题，应当实行"控制、提高、调节"的方针。不过这三个方面不是平列的，当前和今后相当长时间内人口的数量控制是重点，从解决现存人口问题角度说，数量控制占据主导和支配的地位，数量控制有利于素质的提高,并且是调节人口年龄、性别结构的主要手段,对人口的城乡结构、地区分布结构产生重要影响。但是提高和调节并不是消极的,人口素质特别是文化素质高低直接反映在生育水平上,可以说人口文化素质的提高就是生育率的降低,城市人口生育率远较乡村低,东南沿海人口稠密地区也比西北人烟稀少地区低,人口城乡结构和地区分布结构对人口数量控制也有一定作用。至于人口年龄性别结构属年轻型、成年型还是老年型,对人口数量变动的影响之大,则可以增长型、稳定型、减少型概括,它决定着人口变动的基本态势。因此,研究改革开放中的人口问题,主要是探讨以人口的数量控制为主线,同时涉及人口素质和人口年龄性别结构、城乡结构、地区分布结构等问题。结合我国改革开放进程、目标、模式和表现出来的人口问题,以人口的数量控制为主要链条的关系,可表现如图1所示。

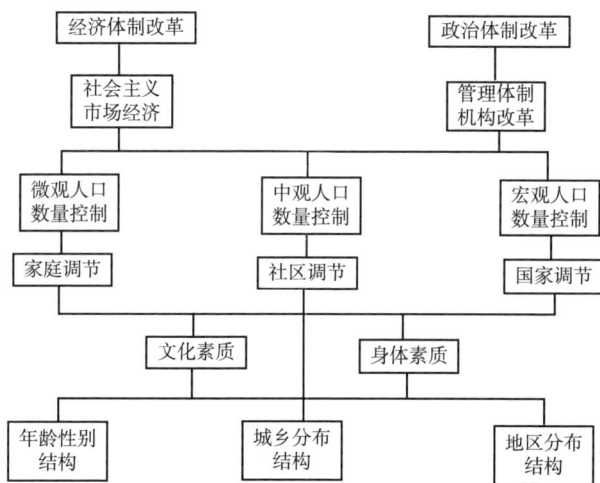

图1 以人口数量控制为主要链条的人口关系

基于上述改革与开放关系的认识和10多年来的实践,改革开放主要是经济体制和政治体制改革及其相应的开放对人口的影响,可以分别加以探讨。经济体制改革及其相应的开放对人口的影响,表现如下。

其一,对人口数量控制的影响。经济体制改革经过10多年的摸索,更早一些可从对三四十年以前的商品生产和价值规律讨论开始,到中共十四大明确提出经济体制改革的目标是建立社会主义市场经济体制。要建立市场经济体制,就要积极发展商品生产,遵守价值法则,其基本的价值观念必然渗透到人口生产中来，给支配人们生育行为的孩子成本—效益学说提供发挥作用的条件。按照西方微观人口经济学中的生育行为理论，个人和家庭对孩子的取舍归根结底取决于生产的边际孩子成本和孩子提供的预期效益：若净成本为正值，该边际孩子父母不需要；若净成本为负值，需要；若净成本为零，取决于随机因素。尽管中国商品经济不发达，但孩子成本—效益的作用仍客观存在；建立市场经济体制无疑加大了孩子成本—效益作用的效应，在实践中产生了比较复杂的情况。在经济体制改革前期或者虽然改革进行时间较长但发展仍较迟缓地区，由于乡村以家庭户为基本单位的联产承包责任制和城镇个体、合营、合资、外资等企业的发展，使丧失已久的家庭生产职能在颇大程度上得到恢复，养老—保险效益刺激了家庭生育特别是生育男孩的欲望，阻碍出生率的下降。众所周知，在中国近40多年的人口变动史上，1953～1957年为一个生育高潮期，人口的年平均增长率达到2.4%；1958～1961年为一个生育低潮期，人口年平均增长率只有0.5%。如以23岁作为妇女生育峰值年龄，则1976～1980年应为高潮期，1981～1984年应为低潮期，然而事实上的上述期间人口出生率和自然增长率的变动，恰好相反，如表1所示。[①]

表1　1976～1984年人口出生率和自然增长率变动

单位：‰

年　份	出生率	死亡率	自然增长率
1976	19.9	7.3	12.6
1977	18.9	6.9	12.0
1978	18.3	6.3	12.0
1979	17.8	6.2	11.6
1980	18.2	6.3	11.9
1981	20.9	6.4	14.5
1982	22.3	6.6	15.7
1983	20.2	6.9	13.3
1984	19.9	6.8	13.1

为什么理应为生育低潮期的1981～1984年的人口出生率、自然增长率明显高出理应为生育高潮期的1976～1980年的水平呢？可能有多方面的原

---

① 《中国统计年鉴1991》，中国统计出版社，1991。

因，但是边际孩子效益上升从而刺激人们多生多育，是本源的原因。与此相对应的是，1986～1997 年的前后因受 1962～1973 年生育高潮形成年龄结构影响而出现了新的一次生育高潮，然而在过去的 6 年中人口出生率维持在 21‰至 23‰之间，自然增长率也均在 16‰以下，仅比 20 世纪 80 年代前期略高一些，并没有形成很高的高潮。这中间除了政府大力加强人口控制，计划生育部门做了许多艰苦工作外，一些地区特别是改革开放较早、经济发展水平较高地区孩子成本—效益发生的某些转变，不能不是重要原因之一。以包括苏州、无锡、常州所辖县、市在内的苏南地区为例，改革开放以来通过兴办乡镇企业等多种形式促进农村商品经济的全面发展，走出了一条经济新发展的"苏南模式"，同时人口数量控制也达到了新的水平。1986～1990 年的人口出生率均控制在 15‰左右，同世界发达地区水平比较接近，创造了低生育率的人口再生产的"苏南模式"。虽然苏南人口模式的产生有着文化的、政治的等多方面的原因，但是经济是基础，由经济发展水平引起的孩子成本—效益的变动是根本的原因。在孩子成本方面，随着人均占有耕地面积的缩小，使得农业劳动力过剩和向乡镇企业转移问题十分突出，转移的重要条件是要具备初中以上文化程度，从而普遍加大了家庭对孩子的智力投资。随着人们生活水平的提高，用于怀孕和分娩期间的费用也在不断上升，因休假和减少工时而减少的收入自然通过影子价格进入孩子成本。这就使边际孩子成本特别是质量成本上升很快，培养一个孩子的周期也大大拉长。另一方面，由于人均收入 1989 年已达到 2470 多元，比全国水平高出 1 倍以上，这就为个人和家庭通过储蓄和寻求保险解决养老创造了条件，也为集体经济壮大后举办养老保险事业提供可能，使得孩子最重要的养老—保险效益显著下降，开始打破"养儿防老"的传统格局。[①] 这样，一端是以孩子质量成本为主要标志的孩子成本的大幅度上升，另一端是以养老—保险效益下降为主要特征的孩子效益的明显下降，导致人们投向孩子的成本由数量成本向质量成本转移，使生育率保持持续下降的趋势，初步展示了，改革开放对人口转变良好影响的蓝图，代表着发展的方向。目前这张蓝图正在改革开放做得卓有成效的地区铺展开来，由沿海向内地伸展；不过对于多数地区尤其是内地大多数地区说来，尚未走出边际孩子主要效益增值的阶段，多子多福、多生多育还有着客观的经济基础。正因为这样，改革开放不仅是解放生产力和发展生产力的必

---

① 参见徐国强等《苏南模式下的妇女生育水平及相关因素》，《人口动态》1992 年第 4 期。

由之路，而且也是实现生育转变和谋求人口与经济协调发展的治本方略。

其二，对人口素质主要是文化素质的影响。这个问题同前面的问题密切相关，在改革开放和经济发展搞得比较好的地区，存在着由投入孩子数量成本向质量成本转移的客观要求，遂使生育率下降。不过这种转移需要一定的条件，如以 Q 代表边际孩子智力投资质量成本，I 代表该成本可能带来的预期效益，则可能有如下三种情况发生。

I Q > I，表明追加的智力质量成本不能带来相应的效益，因而不可能发生转移或者发生了也难以坚持下来。

II Q = I，表明追加的智力质量成本同可能带来的预期效益相当，是可能发生转移的必要条件。

III Q < I，表明追加的智力质量成本能够带来更大的效益，是可能发生转移的充分条件。

那么，改革开放对于 Q 和 I 会产生怎样的影响呢？同样应作具体分析，不可一概而论。从理论上说，在改革开放前期和经济、技术不够发达的情况下，第 I 种 Q > I 的情况是经常发生的，家庭在孩子身上投下的智力文化投资并不能够带来相应的追加效益。相反，由于技术构成比较低，只要将孩子培养到一定年龄，具有一定的体力便可从事一定的劳动，使劳动—经济效益收效早，见效显著，从而阻碍着孩子质量成本的上升。一个时期以来，一些地方出现中、小学生辍学严重，"花钱念书不如挣钱跑运输"，"拿手术刀的不如拿剃头刀的"等现象，Q > I 是根本的原因。随着改革开放的深入，经济、科技、文化事业的迅速发展，一些先进地区将会达到第 II 和第 III 种效应，即 Q ≤ I，从而为增加智力质量成本奠定了基础。在苏南地区，新增人口就业和原农业剩余劳动力转移的主要途径是乡镇企业，主要是工业企业，但几乎都有一项成文或不成文的规定，即乡镇企业招工条件之一，要有初中以上文化程度，某些企业要求还要更高一些。而且这些企业职工的劳动报酬同文化程度、技术熟练程度直接挂钩，体现了复杂劳动是简单劳动倍加的按劳分配原则，反过来激发了人们进行人口智力投资的积极性。从总体观察，打开由投入孩子数量成本向质量成本转移的大门，仅仅是开始，少数先进地区作了示范，少数落后地区对此还很陌生，大部分地区则处在开始转移阶段，还有很长的路要走。

其三，对人口结构的影响。关于人口结构，有所谓自然结构、社会结构、经济结构"三结构"一说，也有一些学者不赞成这种分法。从中国改革开放的实际情况出发，其对人口结构的影响主要表现在对人口年龄性别结构、城乡结构、地区分布结构的影响。由于后两个结构将在本文下一部分有所论述,这里仅说明一下对年龄性别结构的影响。前已述及,家庭生产职能的恢复和强化,增大了边际孩子预期的劳动—经济效益,以及养老—保险效益、继承家业兴衰的风险效益等。显然,不同性别的边际孩子的这些效益有所不同,一般情况下男孩子要比女孩子高得多,使得部分人中固有的性别偏好有所发展。1990 年人口普查表明,总人口性别比为 106.6,尚在基本正常范围之内;但是 0 ~ 4 岁组性别比在 110 以上,5 ~ 9 岁组性别比在 108 以上,已显得偏高;内蒙古、山西、湖南等省、自治区总人口性别比在 108 以上,更显偏高。① 中国人口性别比是一个比较复杂的问题,它有历史的、文化的、社会的、经济的等多种原因因素。当前值得重视的是,在科技进步日新月异的今天,要注意防止人为的性别选择,保持自然生育法则的作用;同时要注意提高妇女在社会和家庭中的地位,提高女性孩子的劳动—经济效益、养老—保险效益,将其纳入改革视野。

中共十四大将建设有中国特色的社会主义民主政治确立为政治体制改革的目标,多年来在精兵简政、机构改革方面作出尝试,不能不对人口再生产产生某些影响。但笔者以为影响甚微,真正值得重视的是政府转变职能,按照政企分开和精简“统一”效能原则对现行管理体制和机构进行改革中可能发生的问题,特别是对下述几个方面的问题予以关注。

其一,加强国家对人口的宏观调控能力问题。改革开放以来中国控制人口增长取得举世瞩目的成绩,而成绩的取得主要是政府制定了明确的政策,贯彻人口目标管理责任制等一整套做法的结果。然而在改革开放走向深入的新形势下,在市场取向和政府转变职能的新的改革开放浪潮中,对原有的国家人口控制管理机构构成新的冲击:一是原有的计划生育管理体制不利于全面解决我国人口问题战略的实施,并最终影响人口数量控制的效果;二是现有的人口管理体制不利于政策上的配套,存在着某些方面的矛盾;三是现有的人口管理体制不利于加强对人口科学研究的领导,影响科研成果效益的发挥;四是现有的人口管理体制不利于对外交往,影响人口管理的对外开放。有鉴于此,在行政管理体制和机构改革中实有建立国家人口委员会作为人口管理综合部门的必要。人口委员会按照国家政治体制改革的要求,可以充分发挥在人口发展战略方面的协调作用,人口政策和措施方面的协调作用,人

---

① 《中国第四次人口普查的主要数据》,中国统计出版社,1991。本文以下引用资料未注明出处者,均属同一来源。

口管理办法方面的协调作用，人口科学研究和宣传方面的协调作用，适应改革开放新形势发展的需要。

其二，人口控制机构的转变问题。成立人口委员会是机构改革，还必须要有机制上的改革与之匹配，才能适应改革开放的要求。方向是随着孩子成本—效益的有利倾斜和个人生育为利益选择的转变，逐步建立和强化相应的利益调节机制，最终完成由以行政手段为主的机制向以利益调节为主的机制过渡。总结一些成功的经验，可以提出：一是统一超生子女费的征收标准，严格管理制度，有效提高超生子女成本；二是在落实独生子女父母奖励费基础上，将奖励费转为子女伤、亡的两全保险，并在 14 年后转为父母的养老保险，有效地增大了独生子女的风险效益和养老—保险效益；三是实行利益导向政策的协调配套及相应的政策法规作保证；四是逐步改变脑力劳动与体力劳动分配不尽合理的状况，加速人们由投入孩子数量成本向质量成本的转移。办法是采取一定的向脑力劳动倾斜的分配政策，诱导人们由追求孩子的数量转变到追求孩子的质量，提高人们进行人口智力投资的积极性。通过这些强化利益调节措施的实施，分步骤地实现谁少生孩子谁付出的成本少，得到的效益却比较高；谁多生孩子谁付出的成本多，得到的利益并不高。建立这种机制的目的，是促使人们从关心自己利益得失上权衡生育子女的数量，自动选择少生、优育、优教的道路。

其三，建立和健全以社区为主要形式的中观人口管理。自 20 世纪 50 年代以来，国际上越来越多的国家和地区积极推进"社区发展计划"，在促进乡村发展和城市更新，包括人口在内的社会问题综合治理中扮演重要角色，提供不少可供借鉴的经验。我国自改革开放以来，随着社会主义市场经济体制的建立和完善，政府转变职能等项改革的加速进行，充任国家人口政策与个人生育行为之间"对接"的中国人口控制的一些做法和管理机制，已很不适应，出现程度不等的削弱，在这种情况下，社区应运而生，开创了新的理论和实践，发挥在全面解决人口各种问题中独具一格的作用。

三

改革开放对人口变动的影响和作用是错综复杂的，然而在作了上面抽象分析之后，在说明生育与开放的关系，将经济体制和政治体制改革分别作了分阶段、分层次考察的基础上，以人口数量控制为主线条的人口变动的图像和发展趋势，也就比较清楚了。最为重要的，是发生了并且还在继续的以下一些趋势。

其一，人口数量继续增长的趋势。1978 年底内地人口为 96259 万人，到 1991 年底增加到 115823 万人，增长 20.3%，年平均增长 1.43%[①]。为什么总体人口继续增长？这是由于人口的年龄结构比较轻决定的。1978 年以来由年轻型向成年型过渡，到 20 世纪 80 年代才完成这种过渡进入成年型初期，因而增长势能还比较强。同时取决于妇女的生育水平，生育水平又受到经济、文化、社会因素的影响。根据联合国经济和社会事务部《世界人口展望 1992》提供的资料，目前世界的总生育率（TFR）为 3.4，发达地区为 1.9，欠发达地区为 3.9；我国 1989 年即已下降到 2.3，应当说我国妇女的总生育率是比较低的。从 1980 至 1990 年，世界人口由 444686 万人增加到 529530 万人，增长 19.1%，年平均增长 1.76%；我国由 98705 万人增加到 114333 万人，增长 15.8%，年平均增长 1.48%，比世界人口增长速度要慢一截。[②] 如前所述，由于改革开放在地区间的发展不平衡和改革开放前期与后期对生育率影响上的差别，人口数量增长也相应反映出来。当前，除个别地区情况特殊外，总体上观察是改革开放成效显著和经济发展迅速地区，人口生育率就比较低，像北京、上海、天津、浙江、江苏、辽宁、山东等省市总生育率已经下降到替换水平以下；改革开放进展较慢和经济发展比较落后地区，生育率就比较高，人口自然增长更快一些。

其二，人口素质不断提高的趋势。关于人口素质，目前尚存在二要素论（身体素质和文化素质）与三要素论（身体、文化和道德素质或身体、文化和心理素质）之争，但对其变动趋势，主要是身体和文化素质不断提高的趋势均是比较肯定的。

身体素质的提高。改革开放、技术进步和管理改革促进了社会生产力的发展，在对劳动者的体力、精力、反应能力提出比以前高得多要求的同时，生活水平、医疗保健、文化生活等的提高，也为年龄别死亡率特别是婴儿死亡率的下降和预期寿命的延长提供了条件。1982 年普查提供的 1981 年年龄别死亡率与 1990 年普查提供的 1989 年年龄别死亡率比较，均有不同程度的降低，不过降低最明显的是两头：0~5 岁组和 55 岁以上年龄组。年龄别死

[①] 《中国统计年鉴 1992》，中国统计出版社，1992，第 77 页。

[②] U. N, World Population Prospects The 1992 Revision p. 284，New York，1993；《中国统计年鉴 1992》，第 77 页。

亡率下降的直接后果，是预期寿命的延长，出生时的人口预期寿命由 1981 年的 67.9 岁提高到 1989 年的 70 岁。

文化素质的提高。改革开放特定阶段尽管在人口文化素质提高方面产生这样那样的一些问题，但是从总体上观察，从发展观点看，则给人口文化素质的提高注入新的生机和活力，大大促进了全民族的科学、技术、文化的发展。以本人提出的假定，以 u 代表具有大学文化程度人口数，H 代表具有高中和中专文化程度人口数，M 代表具有初中文化程度人口数，L 代表具有小学文化程度人口数，I 代表文盲和半文盲人口数，Y_1、Y_2、Y_3、Y_4、Y_5 分别代表具有大学、高中和中专、初中、小学、文盲和半文盲平均接受教育年限，并令 $Y_1 = 16$，$Y_2 = 11$，$Y_3 = 8$，$Y_4 = 4$，$Y_5 = 0.25$，按照公式：

$$c（人口文化素质指数）= \frac{uY_1 + HY_2 + MY_3 + LY_4 + IY_5}{u + H + M + L + I}$$

计算，1982 年普查总体人口文化素质指数为 4.21，1990 年普查上升至 5.18，升高 0.97，它的物理意义，可以近似地看做全国人口平均接受教育的程度增加近 1 年。

在人口的道德或心理素质方面，随着商品经济的发展和对外开放，人、财、物流动数量的增加，客观上为刑事犯罪增加了作案的条件，发案率有所上升，尤其是盗窃案件。国际犯罪活动渗透也明显增加，颇值得关注。根据国际发展经验，当一个国家处于由贫困奔向温饱，由温饱奔向小康的发展过程中时，刑事案件上升是明显的，提高人口的道德素质或心理素质，开展精神文明建设必不可少。

其三，生产年龄人口所占比例上升的趋势。由以往特别是由 1962~1973 年生育高潮期间出生的大量人口形成异常庞大的年龄结构所决定，20 世纪 80 年代、90 年代和 21 世纪前 10 年将有一个生产年龄人口绝对数量迅速上升、所占比例大幅度提高的生产年龄人口激增高潮。改革开放为这一高潮提供了最好的历史机遇，过去的 10 多年已经证明，今后还将继续证明。由于改革开放发展多种所有制经济，开辟人才和劳务市场，大大拓宽了就业渠道，10 多年中在生产年龄人口猛增情况下，实现就业率稳定中有所提高，这是其他国家不大可能做到的。高就业和人力资源的开发利用，又为降低产品成本、吸引外资、发展劳动密集以及劳动密集同资金密集、技术密集相结合的产业创造了条件，反过来加快着改革开放的步伐。这样说并不等于劳动力越多越好，相反，我国劳动力数量过剩和素质不高的矛盾一直就很突出，压力很大。在这方面，改革开放就要去做变压力为活力和动力的文章。需要通过劳动制度的深化改革，建立起新的机制，达到合理就业的所有制结构、产业结构和技术结构要求。

其四，人口老龄化趋势。它是由现有人口年龄构成和国家仍需从严控制人口增长的基本国策所决定，紧随着生产年龄人口激增其后而来的，是人口年龄结构老龄化趋势。在过去改革开放的 10 多年和 20 世纪 90 年代，我国人口年龄结构将完成由成年型向老年型的过渡，预计 20 世纪末基本进入老年型，2030 ~ 2040 年达到严重阶段。改革开放从影响人们的生育行为和延长人们的预期寿命角度，对老龄化有着某种影响，但是这种影响是很有限的，主要是对解决老龄化问题的双重影响：一方面改革开放通过促进经济发展，为开展社会养老和个人储蓄养老打下物质基础，有利于社会养老、家庭养老、个人养老"三位一体"养老保险体系的建立；另一方面改革开放和商品市场经济的发展，对传统的家庭结构和人们的传统观念，对以家庭养老为主要形式的农业型养老又是一个严重的冲击。可见，对于养老这个老龄问题中最重要的问题说来，改革开放有利也有弊。由于我们是在国民经济不够发达的情况下迎来老龄化并走向高潮的，全面估量改革开放的作用和影响，就要量力而行地兴利却弊。

其五，人口城市化趋势。改革开放特别是乡镇企业、集市贸易和城镇人口转移，加速了人口城市化进程。以 1982 与 1990 年两次人口普查比较，市由 236 个增加到 456 个，镇由 2664 个增加到 9322 个，市镇人口占总人口的比例由 20.6% 上升到 26.2%。一般认为这个比例比较接近实际，但本人以为，目前我们在掌握市镇人口标准上对经济方面，尤其是从事职业方面要求过严，从人口集中方面强调不够，加上调查和统计中的一些问题，实际市镇人口比例在此之上。中国人口城市化重点发展小城镇的特点比较明显，而这紧紧同改革开放联系在一起，什么地方改革开放步子迈得大一些，哪里的人口城市化进展就快一些；什么地方改革开放步子迈得小一些，哪里的人口城市化进展就慢一些。

其六，人口迁移新趋势。随着改革开放商品经济的发展，人口迁移的数量增加了。据 1990 年普查，常住户口在外县、市并已离开一年以上及常住户口待定的人数所占比例为 2.61%，即近 3000 万人，比 1982 的普查中 1.13% 翻了一番有余。这种常住地与常住户口登记地不一致所占比例较高的，主要是广东、北京、广西、海南、江苏等省、市，为改革开放活跃地区。从 1985 年 7

月 1 日至 1990 年 6 月 30 日省际迁移情况看，其中净迁入人口占本市、自治区、地辖市人口比例最高为北京、上海、天津、广东，均在 1% 以上；而净迁出人口所占比例最高为广西、四川、黑龙江、浙江 4 个省、自治区。这些省区或者人们为邻省的改革开放所吸引，或者原来迁出者受"推拉理论"支配回老家闹改革，或者发挥人力资源雄厚特长，外出从事工商业和从事劳务。不管怎样，都同改革开放紧密相连，人才涌向改革开放先进地区是新的趋势。

其七，人口流动增强的趋势。改革开放大潮带来市场的活跃，经济的繁荣，商品流通量剧增，同时也带来流动人口的膨胀。据报道，23 个百万以上人口的大城市日均流动人口在 1000 万人左右，北京、上海、广州等特大城市在 100 万人以上，全国超过 5000 万人。[①] 这支流动人口大军绝大多数以务工、经商、办实业为目的，但其中也有一部分人口处在盲目流动状态，需要适当组织疏导。

其八，婚姻和家庭打破传统的趋势。婚姻和家庭作为人口再生产的基本形式和单位，不断变化着。在当今世界，来自各种新闻媒介的信息表明，西方国家离婚率上升方兴未艾，英国独身母亲增多，法国巴黎被誉为"单身之都"，美国独生子女家庭越来越多……中国在几千年的文明进化中，陶冶了富有东方民族色彩的婚姻和家庭，只是改革开放以来这些色彩也发生了变化，有些变化是颇值得关注的。

在婚姻方面最值得引为重视的变化，一是早婚有所抬头，早已在历史舞台基本绝迹的"娃娃亲"在一些地区有卷土重来之势；二是婚姻的不稳定性有所发展，离婚率上升较严重；三是商品观念渗透到婚姻关系中，买卖婚姻甚至拐卖人口也时有发生。

在家庭方面值得重视的，是小型化和微型化趋势。1982 与 1990 年人口普查比较，全国每个家庭平均人口数由 4.41 人下降到 3.96 人，减少 0.45人。西方国家一些人推崇的夫妇不育的"两人世界"，也开始在中国出现；但同时他（她）们又受到无形的社会压力，带来矛盾的心态。其实，改革开放本身就是为解决现存矛盾，为解放生产力，发展生产力，人们的思想也因此进一步获得解放。人口再生产的某些固有格局在这一过程中将被冲破，产生新的矛盾和问题。研究解决这些新的矛盾和问题，不仅是人口治理的当务之急，而且对改革开放全局说来也是必不可少的，有其特殊意义的。

---

① 1988 年 10 月 3 日《中国人口报》。

《中国沿海人口与经济可持续发展》
总论[*]

研究中国沿海人口与经济的可持续发展，本着这样的逻辑思维进行：人口与经济之间关系的理论，可持续发展作为世纪转换之际的最重要命题的提出，中国沿海地区人口与经济可持续发展透视，谋求人口与经济可持续发展目标的战略选择。

一　导论

在 17 世纪下半叶人口学作为一门独立的学科分离出来以后的一二百年里，本原意义上的人口学研究却进展不大，而从经济、社会等角度的人口研究发展比较迅速，尤其是人口经济学方面的研究。英国古典政治经济学优秀代表之一威廉·配第（William Petty，1623～1687 年），在《赋税论》、《政治算术》等著作中，曾将人口因素作为引起经济变动的内在力量加以分析，力图说明二者之间的制约关系。庸俗经济学家托马斯·马尔萨斯（Thomas Robert Malthus，1766～1834 年）于 1789 年发表其轰动一时的《人口原理》，提出人口在食物供给不受妨碍时以几何级数增加，生活资料受土地效益递减规律作用呈算术级数增加，总人口具有一种超乎为其准备的生活资料而不断地、永恒地增长趋势。但他作为牧师反对避孕节育，主张通过饥饿、贫困、战争、瘟疫等"积极抑制"，以及禁欲、无力赡养者推迟结婚等"道德抑制"限制人口增长。波莱士·弗朗西斯（Place Francis，1771～1854 年）等继承了马尔萨斯"人口原理"，但主张用避孕节育限制人口增长，被称之为新马尔萨斯主义；不过在人口与经济之间的关系上，新老马尔萨斯主义并无

*　原载田雪原主编、蔡昉副主编《中国沿海人口与经济可持续发展》，人民出版社，1996。

本质的不同。

马克思和恩格斯在完成唯物史观和剩余价值学说两大革命性过程中，对于人口与经济之间的关系作过许多精辟的阐述。指出：任何人类历史的第一个前提无疑是有生命的个人的存在；历史中的决定性因素，归根结底是直接生活资料的生产和再生产。但是，生产本身又有两种：一方面是生活资料即食物、衣服、住房以及为此所必需的工具的生产；另一方面是人类自身的生产，即种的繁衍。马克思原本计划写一部人口学专著，但未来得及动笔便与世长辞了。然而在《资本论》中，他还是长篇论述了资本主义社会中的人口问题，阐述了相对过剩的人口规律。

当代西方人口经济学说中，影响较大的主要有：现代马尔萨斯主义，即运用系统动力学等方法，将人口与资源、环境、发展放到一起分析，认为经济增长面临"人口爆炸"威胁。主要以埃里兹（P. R. Ehrlich）的《人口爆炸》（1968 年），泰勒（G·Taylor）的《世界末日》（1970 年），麦多斯（D. L. Meadows）等人的《增长极限》（1972 年）著作为代表；适度人口论，主要以英国经济学家坎南（Edwin Cannan，1861 ~ 1935 年）提出的人口增加对工农业收益的影响，法国人口学家索维（Alfred Sauvy）的《人口通论》（1952 年）著作为代表；人口增长经济理论，以英国经济学家凯恩斯（J. M. Kegnes，1883 ~ 1946 年），美国经济学家汉森（A. H. Hansen，1887 ~ 1975 年）等将人口增长与经济增长联系起来，人口增长率下降造成有效需求不足的经济停滞论为代表。西方人口经济学代表人物斯彭格勒（J. J. Spengler），发展经济学开创先驱之一的刘易斯（W. A. Lewis）等人，则从多层次、多角度论述了人口与经济发展之间的关系。

上述学说主要侧重人口与经济关系宏观上的考察，在微观方面则有家庭人口经济理论，尤以孩子成本—效益理论影响为大。这一理论的创始人是美国哈佛大学的莱宾斯坦（H. Leibenstein）教授。他认为，家庭规模的确定由父母对生育子女的数量选择来完成，而父母的选择取决于孩子的成本与效益。孩子成本分为两部分：一部分为直接成本，即从母亲怀孕到抚养成为经济自立所花费的衣、食、住、行、医疗、教育、婚姻等的费用，亦即花费在孩子身上直接的货币支出；另一部分为间接成本，即母亲因怀孕、妊娠和哺乳期间损失的工资，父母因照料孩子而丧失的受教育、获取更好劳动岗位、升迁等而减少的收入，亦即因为抚养损失时间而失去的带来收入的机会，故又称机会成本，表现为间接的货币支出。当然，父母想要生育孩子不是为了付出成本，而是想从孩子那里得到一定的效益。主要是——劳动经济效益：孩子成长为劳动力之后，可为家庭提供劳务，或者从事一定职业的劳动为家庭带来经济收入；养老保险效益：主要是在发展中国家社会保障不发达，老年赡养不得不在相当大程度上依赖子女；消费享乐效益：孩子作为"消费品"，具有满足父母精神情感需要，带来天伦之乐的效应；承担家业兴衰的风险效益：孩子数量多少和质量高低，同未来家庭经济风险相连，影响着家庭经济的继承效益；维系家族延续的效益：孩子作为代际延续的纽带，起着传宗接代的作用；安全扩展效益：生儿育女。人丁兴旺是壮大家庭力量的保证，并且常常同"多子多福"相联系，多数发展中国家孩子对家庭安全具有一种扩展效益。莱宾斯坦指出，边际孩子成本同家庭收入呈正相关关系，而效益除消费享乐效益变动不明朗外，其余呈负相关关系，随着经济的发展，技术的不断进步，社会保障事业的完善，孩子效益呈每况愈下之势。芝加哥大学贝克尔（G. S. Becker）教授发展了莱宾斯坦的理论，提出并论证了孩子的效用最大化，创立了孩子数量与质量可以互相替代的理论，论证了人们由投入孩子数量成本向质量成本转移的客观规律，将其纳入他的人力资本体系，揭示了生育率随着经济发展下降的内在动力。南加州大学伊斯特林（R. A. Easterline）教授，加入因采用控制手段付出的经济成本和克服精神障碍付出的心理成本变量，从孩子的供给与需求两端考察孩子成本与效益的变动，发展了这一理论。澳大利亚国立大学考德维尔（J. C. Caldwell）教授，分析在家庭收入提高、技术进步和社会发展条件下，财富怎样在父母与孩子中间流动，提出财富流理论。毫无疑问，这些理论之间不乏歧意，甚至具有某些根本的不同；学术界对其评论也褒贬不一，有的认为这些理论存在某些非科学成分，对我国更不可能完全适用。但是将人们的生育行为与家庭经济状况、利益得失联系起来，揭示人们生儿育女发动的动机，则有其科学的道理。

中国是一个有着悠久历史且人口最多的国家，关于人口与经济之间关系的论述颇多。从孔夫子到孙中山，将人口视为经济自然力和基本国力的"庶矣哉"，人口经济观一直居统治地位，对上策动着当政者的人口政策，对下左右着家庭的生育行为。尽管其间有自韩非至洪亮吉的人口过剩说教，但立说有限，影响甚微。到 20 世纪初西方人口学说传入中国，二三十年代相继出现了陈长蘅的《中国人口论》，许仕廉的《中国人口问题》，陈达创办的《北平晨报》出版《人口副刊》，发表了不少论著。这些论著受马尔萨斯人口论影响至深，同时不同程度地接受了"适度人口"观点，积极探讨人口与经济发展之间的关系。新中国成立后，1957 年 7 月 5 日《人民日报》全文发表了马寅初的"新人口论"，比较系统地阐述了人口与国民经济发展之间的关系，分析了人口增长过快同加速资金积累之间的矛盾，同提高劳动生产力之间的矛盾，同所需工农业原材料增长之间的矛盾，同提高人民生活之间的矛盾，同发展科学事业之间的矛盾等。可是却遭到批判，使包括人口与经济之间关系在内的人口科学研究长时间中断。粉碎"四人帮"后迎来了人口科学发展的春天，人口与经济关系的研究始有较大突破。

马克思主义政治经济学的创立，科学地确定了人的因素在生产和整个经济活动中的地位和作用，以唯物史观为导线阐明了人口与经济的关系。当代西方人口经济学说，特别是适度人口论和增长极限论，已将人口纳入与粮食、资源、工业化、环境共同发展的视野，只是无法突破其固有的局限性。因此，包括人口与经济在内的可持续发展，事实上早已成为探索的命题，只是没有明确提出罢了。然而随着世界人口激增而来的资源的短缺，某些地区粮食的不足，贫富差距的拉大，陆地、海洋、大气环境的恶化等，越来越引起人们的关注。自 1972 年世界环境大会在斯德哥尔摩召开以来，先后提出了"合乎环境要求的发展"、"无破坏情况下的发展"、"生态发展"、"连续的或持续的发展"等概念，并最终选择了"持续发展"的提法。1987 年世界环境与发展委员会在《我们共同的未来》报告中，将持续发展定义为"既满足当代人需要，又不对后代人满足其需要的能力构成危害的发展"。1992 年 6 月在巴西里约热内卢召开的各国首脑出席的世界环境与发展大会（下简称"里约环发大会"），会议通过的《里约宣言》和《21 世纪议程》，体现了"我们共同的未来"的基本精神，尖锐地指出人口不断增长与资源有限的矛盾，人类赖以生存的生物圈不断恶化的严峻形势。摒弃了传统的大量消耗能源和资源，以环境破坏为代价的发展，选择了与生态系统相协调的经济、社会发展战略。1994 年 9 月在开罗召开了世界人口与发展大会（下简称"开罗人发大会"），有 182 个国家参加，其中有 11 个国家首脑出席。这次大会的突出贡献，是将人口因素放到可持续发展的重要位置。大会通过的《关于国际人口与发展的行动纲领》指出，1998 年世界人口可由目前的56 亿增至 60 亿，各国政府应采取有效措施满足人们自愿实行计划生育的要求。1995 年 3 月还在哥本哈根举行世界社会发展首脑会议，联合国为促进全球经济、社会的可持续发展作出了努力。由此可见，在 20 世纪即将结束和 21 世纪行将到来之际，谋求人口、经济、社会的可持续发展，正成为人类和各个国家合乎理智的选择。

目前国际上各界对"可持续发展"解释不一，有的偏重环境方面，几次世界环境发展大会都围绕着可持续发展主题；有的侧重经济方面，强调消除贫困和缩小发达国家与发展中国家经济差距是关键所在；有的偏重社会方面，注重保证公民参与决策的政治体系和解决不和谐发展的社会体系；有的偏重人口方面，重视人口数量、素质、结构在可持续发展中的重要作用，人力作为一种资源的动力作用。不过随着讨论的深入和实践的发展，渐渐形成较多的共识，也大致赞同《我们共同的未来》报告中关于满足当代人需要，又不对后代人满足需要的能力构成危害的概括。主要包含下述一些内容。

消除贫困和适度的经济增长。在贫困和生产工具落后的条件下。人们为生存奋争的直接手段是向大自然索取，典型的例子是毁林开荒，垦植草原，现今热带雨林大量被采伐，对生态平衡构成新的威胁。怎样才能消除贫困呢？只有发展经济，保持适当的经济增长。可持续发展首先是经济要有一定的长期、稳定的发展，尤其是贫困地区的经济要有发展。

控制人口增长和开发人力资源。在人口、资源、环境、现代化建设等各种问题中，人口为其首，其他各种问题程度不同地同人口数量增长有着直接的关系。随着人口的增长和时间的推移，非更生性资源在减少过程中许多已发出枯竭信号，可更生性资源也面临人口数量增长的巨大压力。虽然近 10 多年来世界人口出生率和增长率稍有下降，但总体上看增长势头仍较强劲，联合国预测 1998 年世界人口可达 60 亿，2015 年可达 75 亿，2050 年可达 98 亿[①]，抑制人口的数量增长仍是一项全球性的紧迫任务。与此同时，一些人口过剩国家的人力资源大量闲置，人口的文化程度、健康水平、妇女和儿童的地位等亟待改善和提高。控制人口数量和提高人口质量是相辅相成的两个方面，也是实现由投入孩子数量成本向质量成本转移，生育率下降和实现人口与经济协调发展的必然途径。

合理开发和利用自然资源。面对非更生性资源的绝对减少和可更生性资源的相对不足，一个科学、合理开发和利用自然资源的问题正提到世人面前，即人类再也不能对资源进行掠夺性索取，而要在满足发展需要的同时，尽量延长资源可供给年限，提高资源使用效益。还要随着科学技术的发展，

---

① United Nations：*World Population 1994.*

不断开辟新的能源和其他资源。

保护环境和维护生态平衡。据科学家估计，地球上生物存在已有二三十亿年的历史，逐渐演化形成相对稳定的生物圈。然而自人类诞生特别是近几百年来人口的迅速增长，却使这个相对稳定的生物圈经受着强烈的震动。1650 与 1994 年比较，世界人口由 5 亿增加到 56 亿，增长 10 倍，而更为重要的是人们不断追求生活质量的提高，物资消耗数量增加，品位也越来越高。致使森林、草场大面积开垦为农田，大大降低了大地植被的保护功能，使沙漠增加，气候变得恶劣；工业化发展的结果，能源消耗激增，排放出大量废气、废渣、废水，形成地球变暖等"温室效应"，臭氧洞已构成对人类自身生存的潜在危害，环境污染已经危及人类自身的生存和发展。因此，可持续发展追求的目标应是保护环境和维护生态平衡的发展，而不应是以牺牲环境质量为代价的发展。将可持续发展解释为"无污染发展"或"无公害发展"固然狭窄了一些，但维护包括人类自身在内的相对稳定的生物圈，切实保护人类赖以生存的环境，则是可持续发展必须遵循的基本原则。

满足就业和生活的基本需求。可持续发展应具备满足社会生产年龄人口就业需要的能力，而不是把大批劳动者排斥在生产和整个经济活动之外。并且能够生产出满足人们基本生活需要的物质资料，使之安居乐业。要达到这样的目标，除适度的经济增长之外，还要求建立起公平的分配原则。

技术进步和危险控制。可持续发展追求技术进步，通过技术进步降低能源和原材料的密集程度，提高劳动生产率，提供更多就业手段，及时将导致破坏可持续发展的信息告诉公众，谋求解决的决策。

可见，实现可持续发展追求的目标，与传统的发展方式相比，要树立明确的增长意识、人口意识、资源意识、环境意识、需求意识和技术意识，并如同《我们共同的未来》报告中提出的那样，建立相应的经济、社会、生产、技术、管理、国际贸易和金融等体系。然而无论哪一项内容、哪一种意识、哪一个体系，都同人口有着不可分割的关系，同经济的发展阶段有着自然的联系，人口与经济的可持续发展构成全部可持续发展的基础。因此，研究人口与经济的可持续发展，实现人口与经济的可持续发展目标，既是可持续发展的基本要求，又是全部可持续发展的基础和关键，是执行里约环发大会《21 世纪议程》和开罗人发大会《行动纲领》的首要之举。

中国是世界上人口最多的国家，又是经济连续高速增长的发展中国家，谋求人口与经济的可持续发展不仅对中国走向 21 世纪有着决定性的意义，而且在很大程度上影响到里约和开罗制定的纲领和目标的实施情况。说到中国人口与经济的可持续发展，则一定要注意人口分布和经济发展不平衡的现实。以人口而论，长期以来瑷（珲）腾（冲）分界线基本未变：此线西北占国土面积52％，人口却仅占5％；此线东南占国土面积48％，人口却占95％。这一人口地理分布既是自然地理条件、经济发展状况的反映，反过来又影响经济的发展和对自然条件的改造。若以沿海12个省、市、自治区与内地、边疆相比较，则分布不平衡情况尤甚，本书后面将有进一步探讨。以经济发展情况而论，沿海、内地、边疆相比较，无论生产能力、发达程度和同国际市场接轨的水平，都形成明显的阶梯，近年来"阶梯"还有增高的趋势。从总体上观察，与沿海地区和包括边疆地区在内的广大内地比较，人口具有密度较高，生育率较低，老年人口所占比例较高，少年人口所占比例较低，城市人口所占比例较高，乡村人口所占比例较低等特征，人口再生产类型完成或接近完成向着低出生、低死亡、低增长的转变。经济发展则走在改革开放前头，经济特区、经济开发区、沿海开放城市等率先引进外资，发展外向型经济，带动着经济起飞，创造了当今世界引人注目的发展速度。足见沿海地区的人口变动和经济发展均超前一步，如何实现人口与经济的可持续发展更具有现实意义。而且，如果研究取得成效，对于内地的人口与经济可持续发展也具有指导意义。改革开放以来15年的实践，沿海某些地区提供了这方面的经验，展现出可持续发展的希望之光。

二 沿海人口与经济可持续发展透视

本书中所说的沿海地区，系指北京、天津、上海3个直辖市，辽宁、河北、山东、江苏、浙江、福建、广东、广西、海南9个省和自治区，即濒临海洋的12个省级行政区划单位，不包括临近辐射的省份。1993年这些沿海地区面积约130万平方千米，占国土面积的13.5％；人口48536万人，占全国118517万人的41.0％；国内生产总值18707.7亿元，占全国31380.3亿元的59.6％（本书中全国除另加说明外，系指祖国内地30个省、自治区、直辖市，未包括台湾、香港和澳门数字，下同）[①]，属于人口相对比较集中和经济比较发达的地区。结合实践，特别是改革开放以来的沿海地区人口控

---

① 《中国统计年鉴1994》，中国统计出版社，1994。

制和经济高速增长的实践，探讨人口与经济的可持续发展，主要是处理好以下几个方面的关系。

（一）总体人口与生活资料的可持续发展

人是生产者和消费者的统一，但是作为生产者是有条件的，一是处在生产年龄段，二是具有一定的劳动能力。作为消费者是无条件的，一个人从生到死均是一个消费者。因此在任何社会形态下，生产满足全部人口生存需要的生活资料，构成该社会存在的前提，总体人口与生活资料之间的关系成为人口与经济可持续发展宏观上最值得重视的关系。可从价值和实物两种形态上加以考察。

价值形态上人口增长与经济增长之间的比例关系。人口增长包括自然增长和机械增长，经济增长则有多种指标，国民生产总值、国内生产总值、国民收入等都可从价值形态上体现出来。按可比价格计算，1953～1992 年全国国民收入年平均增长 7.0%，人口年平均增长 1.8%；1979～1993 年国民收入年平均增长 9.3%，人口年平均增长 1.3%，改革开放以来出现了国民经济要上去，人口增长要下来可持续发展的转变。沿海地区这种转变更明显一些，以 1991 与 1992 年比较，沿海地区人口由 47685 万人增加到 48122 万人，增长 0.9%；按当年价格计算的国民收入，由 8863.8 亿元增加到 11175.2 亿元，按可比价格计算增长 16.7%。[①] 从历史上看，除"二五"（1958～1962 年）特殊时期外，一般情况下国民收入增长速度均高出人口增长速度，能否由此得出总体人口和生活资料之间是协调或可持续增长的呢？本人以为不能简单地得出这一结论。因为国民收入可使用额中用来进行固定资产投资部分要有一定的回收期，称之为固定资产投资系数，目前我国在 3.5～4.0 年之间。如此，这个系数便成为维持原有居民生活水平的经济对于人口增长的自然倍率。按照上例，1991～1992 年沿海地区国民收入增长 16.7% 中的 3.5%～4.0%，被新增的人口消费掉了，所余 12.7%～13.2% 有可能用在提高人民生活上的相当部分。这个"相当部分"有多大，还取决于如下一些因素。

一是人口和消费基金的比例。包括新增部分在内的国民收入使用额分做积累基金与消费基金两部分，要取得社会总体人口与生活资料之间的可持续发

---

① 根据《中国统计年鉴》（1992、1993）提供的数据计算。

展，必须保证消费基金至少不低于人口增长速度增长。就沿海以至全国情况而论，改革开放前除"一五"时期情况较好外，其余时期消费基金增长迟缓，同居民生活水平提高要求不相适应。这中间有在高速度、高指标经济建设指导思想影响下，积累与消费关系处理不当的问题，也有人口增长较快这一客观上的原因。如 1952 与 1978 年比较，全国按可比价格计算，消费额增长 2.1 倍，年平均增长 4.5%；同期人口增长 67.5%，按人口平均的消费额计仅增长 86.9%，年平均增长 2.4%。改革开放以来情况有了很大改变，片面追求高速度、高指标、高积累的发展方针得到纠正，消费基金得到比较快的增长。按可比价格计算，1979～1993 年年平均增长 9.3%，加上人口增长因素作用，人均消费基金年平均增长 7.8%[①]，增长速度可观。不过不同年份增长幅度差别较大，省、市、自治区之间差距也颇大，沿海某些地方曾出现消费超前发展，也有的地方表现出消费相对滞后，需防止不同时期出现的不同偏差。

二是基本建设中生产性与非生产性建设投资的比例。国民收入使用额中积累部分转入再投资，用于生产性和非生产性建设的投资比例，直接关系到生活资料的增长，制约着总体人口与生活资料之间的平衡。包括沿海地区在内，全国总的情况是："一五"时期比较正常，非生产性建设投资（包括住房）占到总投资的 33.0%；"二五"、"三五"、"四五"则大幅度下降，均占 18% 以下；"五五"情况有所好转，改革开放的"六五"、"七五"和"八五"前 3 年从根本上得到了扭转，除"六五"出现带有补偿性的高增长外，基本稳定在 30% 左右的水平上，同"一五"比较接近，使住房和城市基础设施得到加强。实践证明，同我国人口增长态势和生活质量提高趋势相适应，非生产性建设投资比例一般不应低于 30%。

三是实物形态上人口增长与经济增长之间的比例关系。价值形态上的人口与经济之间的增长速度之比固然重要，但由于不同经济发展水平和消费结构的不同，还必须注意到实物形态上消费资料的增长状况。根据《中国统计年鉴》（1994 年）提供的资料，以食品支出占全部消费支出比例计算的恩格尔系数，1993 年城市为 0.501，乡村为 0.581，均在一半以上，乡村所占比例更高一些。这一水平也恰恰表明，目前居民的生活水平处在温饱向小康过渡阶段，基本处在温饱状态。沿海地区情况好一些，北京、江苏、浙江、山东、广东均低于全国平均数，城市和乡村的恩格尔系数分别为：

---

① 根据《中国统计年鉴 1994》数据计算。

北京，城市 0.478，乡村 0.481。

江苏，城市 0.494，乡村 0.502。

浙江，城市 0.494，乡村 0.502。

山东，城市 0.460，乡村 0.574。

广东，城市 0.489，乡村 0.528。

天津、上海二市和辽宁省，城市高于全国平均数，乡村低于全国平均数：

天津，城市 0.546，乡村 0.533。

上海，城市 0.527，乡村 0.463。

辽宁，城市 0.504，乡村 0.551。

福建、广西和海南三省城市和乡村均高于全国平均数：

福建，城市 0.584，乡村 0.606。

广西，城市 0.537，乡村 0.643。

海南，城市 0.618，乡村 0.672。

河北省情况与众不同，城市 0.460 低于全国平均数，乡村 0.584 略高于全国平均数，总水平同全国比较接近。

对于恩格尔系数，国内外学术界有着不同的看法，甚至是截然不同的观点。笔者以为，它从消费结构上反映出居民消费水平，有一定参考价值，但一定要结合具体的经济发展阶段加以分析，并非恩格尔系数越低消费水平越高。如天津、上海和辽宁城市恩格尔系数高于全国平均数，主要原因在于用在包括耐用消费品在内的家庭设备用品及服务支出部分，所占比例较低。1993 年天津占 7.4%，辽宁占 5.7%，上海占 8.7%，远低于广东的 10.5%，江苏的 10.4%，浙江的 9.7%。这说明天津、上海、辽宁城市居民的家庭设备用品满足率已达到一定程度，支出费用上升受到遏制。若再分析一步，这种满足率仍受着现有经济和消费档次的制约，如在主要消费品每百户拥有量中，电视机拥有率均较高，而组合音响拥有率远不及广东和北京。所以，对于恩格尔系数的变动，要作具体的分析。同样的道理，天津、上海、辽宁乡村居民的恩格尔系数则低于全国平均数许多，表明那里农民在解决了温饱之后，用在衣着、住房、家庭设备等项支出的增多，已达到或接近小康水平。就总体而论，恩格尔系数提供的信息大体上表示出：北京、天津、上海 3 市和辽宁、广东、江苏、浙江、山东 5 省生活资料消费水平更高一些，其余 4 省相对低一些。与恩格尔系数相关的沿海城乡居民家庭消费支出构成具体情况，见表 1 和表 2。

表1　1993年沿海地区城镇居民家庭人均生活费支出构成

单位：元

地区	生活消费支出	食品	衣着	家庭设备及服务	交通通信	医疗保健	娱乐教育文化服务	住房	其他商品和服务
全国	2110.8	1058.2	300.6	185.0	80.6	56.9	194.0	140.0	95.5
北京	2939.6	1404.7	471.9	256.2	143.6	66.7	286.5	152.1	158.0
天津	2322.2	1268.3	310.8	171.9	88.6	59.8	209.9	133.9	78.9
河北	1897.9	872.9	301.9	197.5	74.1	43.3	188.1	134.4	85.9
辽宁	1976.6	997.3	394.7	112.5	50.6	55.0	158.4	131.4	76.7
上海	3530.1	1867.9	413.8	307.3	199.3	67.9	301.0	195.8	177.0
江苏	2310.5	1141.4	313.5	240.8	98.2	32.5	206.0	171.9	106.3
浙江	2855.9	1411.7	364.5	277.6	145.0	80.3	248.5	197.4	130.5
福建	2340.6	1366.3	246.3	173.2	93.2	35.5	167.3	163.5	95.4
山东	1946.8	895.8	349.2	194.6	54.2	48.3	195.9	116.3	92.7
广东	3777.4	1847.3	267.9	396.0	298.0	103.7	347.1	350.2	167.2
广西	2303.0	1236.2	237.9	193.0	84.7	48.7	275.7	137.6	89.2
海南	2403.8	1486.5	184.4	158.7	86.0	83.5	185.0	115.8	103.2

表2　1993年沿海地区农村居民家庭人均生活费支出构成

单位：元

地区	生活消费支出	食品	衣着	住房	家庭设备及服务	医疗保健	交通通信	娱乐教育文化服务	其他商品和服务
全国	769.7	446.8	55.3	106.8	44.7	27.2	17.4	58.4	13.1
北京	1255.2	604.5	132.8	141.8	116.2	58.0	38.1	145.8	18.0
天津	938.0	500.1	89.5	149.0	57.2	31.8	23.8	71.2	15.3
河北	696.5	406.7	52.3	96.5	36.0	44.1	11.3	41.1	8.6
辽宁	940.4	518.5	98.5	116.0	45.0	40.5	18.6	83.8	19.4
上海	2200.1	1021.6	157.0	357.3	258.6	50.2	65.6	219.7	70.2
江苏	1058.8	531.6	78.4	189.4	90.9	35.1	29.8	82.2	21.5
浙江	1262.5	633.3	94.2	219.0	96.3	50.2	38.5	86.3	44.6
福建	1069.8	648.3	53.4	143.8	53.9	26.0	31.1	70.8	33.5
山东	724.5	415.6	60.2	98.8	40.6	24.7	14.8	60.3	9.5
广东	1391.0	734.0	51.9	236.2	93.0	44.2	59.5	130.9	41.3
广西	705.0	453.5	30.4	75.4	36.9	19.5	14.2	69.7	5.3
海南	725.6	487.4	33.9	51.2	35.3	18.5	19.3	65.9	14.1

由表 1、表 2 看出，沿海地区城乡居民家庭人均生活消费支出在食品、衣着、娱乐、教育文化服务、住房、家庭设备及服务等八大类别中，均居于较高水平。其中尤为突出的是"家庭设备及服务"一项，沿海城乡均有 8 个省（市、区）高于全国水平，其中城市水平最高的广东省为全国的 2.1 倍；农村水平最高的上海市为全国的 5.8 倍，相差颇为悬殊。仅有 4 个省（市、区）低于全国水平，但大多接近全国水平。随着时间的推移，导致沿海地区居民家庭耐用消费品生活资料拥有量，大大高于全国平均水平，特别是较高档的耐用消费品。如 1993 年全国城镇家庭平均每 100 户拥有彩色电视机 79.5 台，而沿海地区北京达到 107.2 台，天津 94.0 台，上海 93.6 台，广东 91.3 台，河北 88.2 台，浙江 85.0 台，辽宁 83.9 台，山东 82.4 台；录放机全国 12.2 台，北京 45.6 台，上海 38.4 台，广东 27.6 台，天津 23.4 台，浙江 15.7 台，辽宁 15.0 台；照相机全国达到 26.5 架，北京 82.4 架，天津 48.4 架，上海 45.8 架，浙江 29.7 架，广东 29.5 架，辽宁 29.0 架。同年全国农村居民家庭平均每 100 户拥有彩色电视机 10.9 台，沿海地区北京达 53.5 台，天津 40.3 台，上海 35.5 台，广东 23.1 台，辽宁 21.9 台，浙江 19.8 台；照相机全国 1.0 架，北京 12.0 架，上海 4.0 架，天津 3.5 架，福建 2.3 架，浙江 2.0 架，江苏 1.7 架；电冰箱全国 3.1 台，北京 43.3 台，上海 42.3 台，天津 20.0 台，浙江 13.2 台，广东 5.1 台，福建 4.1 台，山东 4.1 台，辽宁 4.0 台。[①] 显然，就实物形态的消费资料消费和拥有情况看，沿海地区总的水平较高，只是也有少数省区尚未达到全国平均水平。

上述情况表明，中国沿海 12 个省市区作为一个总体，人口与生活资料之间的关系解决得比较好，为未来的可持续发展创造了一定的条件。这是由于在人口生产方面，沿海地区率先实现了出生率持久的下降，1993 年全国人口出生率为 18.1‰，沿海地区除广东、广西和海南略高于这一水平外，其余 9 个省市均低于这一水平，上海、北京已降至 10‰ 以内；北京、天津、山东、辽宁、浙江、江苏、河北 7 省市人口自然增长率已降至 1.0% 以内，上海首次降低到零以下。在国民经济发展方面，沿海地区原有工业基础较好，是全国轻重工业的生产基地；改革开放以来获得快速发展，面向市场，满足人民消费资料的生产发展更快，使人均占有的生活资料有了较大幅度的增长。城乡具备较强的购买能力，1992 年全国人均国民收入1726元，沿海

---

① 《中国统计年鉴 1994》。

地区达到 2302 元，高出 576 元。此外，沿海位于改革开放前哨，不仅直接进口大量生活消费用品，而且也引来国外消费意识，"能挣会花"已成为一些人新的消费观念。这样说并不等于已经达到或实现了总体人口与生活资料的可持续发展，某些消费资料不足仍旧是未来可持续发展中必须解决的问题。以粮食为例，1993 年沿海地区共生产 17473.5 万吨，占全国 45648.8 万吨的 38.3%；人均 360 千克，比全国人均 387 千克少 27 千克，除辽宁、山东、江苏 3 省外，其余 9 省（市、区）均低于全国水平①。在沿海总体人口与生活资料可持续发展关系中，目前有的消费资料，如某些机电产品出现过剩征兆，需要适当加以调整；但是基本的方面仍然是短缺经济与过剩人口的矛盾，大力控制人口增长和努力发展国民经济，尤其是满足居民基本生活需求的生活资料的生产，将是长期的历史任务。

（二）生产年龄人口与生产资料的可持续发展

人口学一般将总体人口分成 0～14 岁为少年人口，15～59 岁或 64 岁为成年或生产年龄人口，60 或 65 岁以上为老年人口三个基本的组成部分。一般情况下，由于受年龄组段跨距和特征的影响，成年或生产年龄人口不仅比少年人口多，比老年人口多，而且比老年与少年人口数量之和还要多，是占据数量比例优势的人口。从这部分人口群的作用看，成年或生产年龄人口更为重要。人是生产者和消费者的统一，但确切地说，只有生产年龄人口才是两者的统一。少年人口是消费者，至多是潜在生产者；老年人口则是纯消费者，作为人口群体的质的规定性已退出生产领域。因此，一定时期的生产年龄人口要在生产满足自身需要财富的同时，生产满足少年、老年人口需要的财富，是全社会物质财富生产的担当者，在人口与经济关系中是处于核心和支配地位的人口。

经济学将社会再生产过程分解为生产、交换、分配、消费四个环节，这四个环节是相互制约、紧密联系在一起的，任何一个环节均不可缺少。但是生产不仅决定着可供交换、分配、消费的产品数量和方式，而且决定着进行交换、分配、消费的性质，生产在整个再生产过程中不能不起着决定性的作用，处于支配的地位。

这样，在人口再生产和物质资料再生产过程中，生产年龄人口和生产资

---

① 《中国统计年鉴 1994》。

料之间的关系具有本原的性质，体现了人口与经济关系的核心。生产年龄人口包括适龄的生产活动人口。在校人口和非自立人口，主体是劳动力。从事物质生产的劳动力和生产性固定资产之间最基本的关系，是劳动力就业人数 V 与固定资产 C 的增长成正比，与劳动者技术装备 K 的增长成反比。假设基年的劳动力就业人数为 V_0，则 n 年的劳动力就业人数为：

$$V_0 = V_0 \cdot \left(\frac{I + C}{I + K} \right)^n$$

显然，上式可出现三种不同情况：

（1）$(I + C) > (I + K)$，即固定资产增长速度快于劳动者技术装备增长速度，劳动力就业人数相应增加。

（2）$(I + C) = (I + K)$，即固定资产增长速度等于劳动者技术装备增长速度，劳动力就业人数不增不减。

（3）$(I + C) < (I + K)$，即固定资产增长速度慢于劳动者技术装备增长速度，劳动力就业人数相应减少。

一般地说，在经济发展过程中，物质生产部门固定资产与劳动力就业之间都要经历这样三个发展阶段，直接从事工农业物质生产的劳动力经历由增加、停滞到减少的过程。我国面临的主要问题，可从人口和国民经济两方面进行考察。

从人口方面考察，由于受 1953～1957 年和 1962～1973 年两次生育高潮，特别是后一次长达 12 年之久、出生人数达 3.2 亿人之多的最大的一次生育高潮形成年龄结构的影响，这部分庞大人口群已于 1977～1988 年陆续进入 15 岁，将于 2012～2033 年陆续达到 60 岁以上，2017～2038 年陆续达到 65 岁以上，在相当大的程度上决定着未来生产年龄人口变动趋势。根据各家预测，生产年龄人口绝对数量至少将一直增加到 2020 年，占总人口的比例也将上升至 2010 年左右。20 世纪 50、60 和 70 年代社会劳动者人数年平均增加近 800 万人，80 和 90 年代以来则上升到 1400 万人，"人口压迫生产力"在就业问题上十分突出，实现生产年龄人口与生产资料的协调可持续发展难度很大。同时也要看到，今后 10 多年内生产年龄人口所占比例继续上升，意味着被抚养的老年和少年人口所占比例之和下降，尽管老年人口比例上升和少年人口比例下降同时发生，且二者内涵不尽相同，但是将二者放在被抚养的考虑之中是下降了。这表明在未来的 10 多年内社会负担较轻，对于经济建设说来，是人口年龄结构变动不可多得的"黄金时代"。我们应当利用这一有利的时机，加快经济建设步伐，增加就业手段，为可持续发展打下基础。事实上，日本、泰国、新加坡、马来西亚等亚洲新、旧"四小龙"发展的"秘诀"之一，在于充分利用了本国或本地区的廉价劳动力，发展劳动密集与技术密集、资金密集相结合的产业，有效地降低了成本和提高了在国际市场上的竞争能力。我们要辩证地看待生产年龄人口比例上升的趋势，采取有效措施，用其所长，补其所短。

从经济方面考察，主要是就业手段的增加能否满足生产年龄人口持续增长的需要。由于目前70%左右人口居住在乡村，而乡村现有农业过剩劳动力已达1.2亿人左右，预计20世纪末可增至2亿人，故需首先考察农村生产年龄人口和农业生产资料状况。1993年全国从业人员为60220万人，其中农、林、牧、渔业为33966万人，占56.4%，① 而从事农业栽培业人员又占其中绝大部分。这就碰到农业劳动力过剩和耕地不足的矛盾，这一矛盾在沿海地区表现尤为突出。1993年全国农村居民家庭平均每人经营耕地面积为2.17公顷，沿海地区除辽宁为2.84公顷高于全国水平外，其余11个省市区均低于全国水平，浙江、北京、广东3省市更不足1公顷。② 如果说全国农业剩余劳动力的转移是一个关系到可持续发展的战略问题的话，那么沿海地区这一相关程度则更为强烈，需要寻求根本的方略。

实现城镇生产年龄人口与生产资料的可持续发展，主要的问题，一是原有的工业固定资产基础比较薄弱，经过40多年的建设虽然已大大改观，但是由于人口和劳动力的大幅度增长，就业手段不足的矛盾也相当突出。1993年按当年价格计算的国有企业固定资产原值为20546亿元，按国有企业职工人数10920万人计算，人均占有固定资产18815元，亦即国营企业每增加1名新职工就业，需要追加18815元的固定资产投资。按此标准，目前国有企业固定资产投资仅能满足893万人就业，还不考虑劳动者技术装备提高因素。显然，这同生产年龄人口年增长1400万人以上有较大差距，要实现生产年龄人口与生产资料的可持续发展，也须采取有力措施。

（三）人口文化素质与经济技术进步的可持续发展

人们繁衍子孙后代作为一种再生产，不仅是一定数量而且是一定质量的人口再生产。一般情况下，随着经济的发展和社会的进步，人的身体素质一

① 《中国统计年鉴1994》。
② 《中国统计年鉴1994》。

代比一代增强，最明显的表现是婴儿死亡率和各年龄组人口死亡率降低，预期寿命不断延长。人类在改造自然和社会的长期斗争中发展了自身，积累了大量的经验，发展了智力，人口文化、科学、技术素质的提高最为显著。依据唯物史观，不同历史阶段生产力发展水平不同，对人口数量和质量方面的要求也有所不同。在包括资本主义工场手工业在内的前资本主义诸社会形态，虽然社会生产力发展不断进步，科学和技术有过许多次飞跃，但是一个共同的基本特征是，都以手工劳动为基础，劳动者的手臂就是他们的生产力，劳动者数量对社会生产力的发展起着决定性的作用。18世纪后半叶产业革命发生后，机器大工业逐步取代了手工劳动者，社会生产力的发展由主要依靠劳动者数量变成依靠劳动者的质量，变成依靠提高劳动生产率，劳动者科学、技术、文化素质因素提到了首位。这一趋势到了20世纪更加明显。据估计，20世纪初劳动生产率的提高大约有20%来自技术进步，20世纪中叶提高到30%～40%，目前提高到70%～80%，有的部门提高到100%，科学技术转化为巨大的生产力显示出越来越大的作用。而这一过程，也是家庭追求用在生育子女上面投资效益最大化的结果，发生了由投入孩子数量成本向质量成本的转移，即由追求孩子的数量转向追求孩子的质量，遂使生育率下降，出现由多生多育向少生优教的革命。在当今新的技术革命浪潮中，在中国改革开放加快现代化建设过程中，我们更要十分重视人的科学技术素质，提高全民族的文化水平。一些发展较快国家的成功经验证明，人口文化素质的提高是现代经济发展的强有力杠杆，也是实现经济技术进步的根本保证。

中国作为文明古国之一，曾经是世界上科学、技术、文化高度发达的国家。然而长期受到封建主义的禁锢，到了后来却大为落伍，到了近代则沦为落后的国家。1949年新中国成立后，大力发展科学、教育、文化事业，人口文化素质提高很快。笔者曾经以总体人口平均受教育年限计算人口文化素质指数，其计算公式为：

$$C = \frac{Uy_1 + Yy_2 + My_3 + Ly_4 + Ly_5}{U + H + M + L + I}$$

式中 C 为人口文化素质指数，U、H、M、L、I 分别为具有大学（含大专）、高中（含中专）、初中、小学、文盲和半文盲人口，y_1、y_2、y_3、y_4、y_5 分别为大学（含大专）、高中（含中专）、初中、小学、文盲和半文盲人口平均所受教育年限，本式取 $y_1 = 16$，$y_2 = 11$，$y_3 = 8$，$y_4 = 4$，$y_5 = 0.25$ 年。

计算下来，1964 年全国人口普查人口文化素质指数为 2.41，1982 年普查提高到 4.38，1990 年普查提高到 5.18。不言而喻，全国居民平均接受 5.18 年的教育水平还是比较低的，特别是至今尚有 2 亿左右 15 岁以上文盲和半文盲人口。不过具体到沿海地区，则需要进一步讨论。

1990 年普查沿海 12 个省市区中，有 9 个省市在全国水平以上，分别是：北京 7.65，上海 7.25，天津 6.29，辽宁 6.28，广东 5.54，海南 5.45，江苏 5.39，浙江 5.26，河北 5.20，其中北京、上海高出 2.0 以上，天津、辽宁高出 1.0 以上，居于全国最高水平；有 3 个省区略低于全国水平，分别是：山东 5.13，广西 5.00，福建 4.91。这种情况表明，总体上看沿海人口文化素质较高，为实现与经济技术进步的可持续发展创造较为有利的条件，特别是具备发展技术密集、资金密集高技术产业的条件；同时沿海本身也很不平衡，北京、上海 2 市人口文化素质指数雄居全国之上，高技术带头产业应加快发展，应充分发挥人才优势和科学技术进步的带头作用。

（四）人口年龄结构老龄化与养老保障事业的可持续发展

探讨人口与经济的可持续发展，在人口方面除数量、素质外，结构特别是年龄结构老龄化是颇值得注意的。人口年龄结构老龄化，是指老年人口占总体人口比例不断上升的过程，它的直接原因是人口出生率的下降。1870 年法国 60 岁以上老年人口所占比例达到 12%，成为率先进入老年型年龄结构的国家；20 世纪初瑞典也成为老年型国家，目前发达国家全部进入老年型结构国家，并且达到较高水平。发展中国家人口出生率还比较高，不过从总体上观察人口出生率还是明显下降了，一些国家的人口年龄结构也开始向老年型过渡。这不仅从人力资源供给方面影响国民经济发展，而且从消费需求，满足日益增长的老年人口消费需求方面制约着国民经济发展，如何确立可靠的老年社会保障制度，则是必须认真解决的问题。亦即人口年龄结构老龄化与养老保障事业的可持续发展，是全部人口与经济可持续发展的一个有机组成部分。

中国自 20 世纪 70 年代以来，大力加强计划生育使人口出生率迅速下降，少年人口所占比例不断降低，老年人口所占比例不断上升。1964 年人口普查 0～14 岁少年人口占总人口的 40.4%，1982 年普查下降到占 33.6%，1990 年普查再下降到占 27.7%；65 岁以上老年人口所占比例由 3.5% 依次上升到 4.9% 和 5.6%。未来老年人口所占比例，2040 年以前将加速增长，预计 65 岁以上老年人口比例 2000 年可上升到 6.8%，2020 年可上升到

10.2%，2040 年达到最高峰值时可上升到 16.5%。老龄化速度比较快，达到的水平比较高，且 2040 年以前具有累进增长的性质。[1]

沿海地区人口老龄化，有着同全国大致相似的发展趋势，同时有着某些不同的特点，特别是老龄化来得快和达到程度比较高。1990 年普查全国 60 岁以上老年人口所占比例为 8.6%，沿海地区有北京、天津、河北、辽宁、上海、江苏、浙江、山东、广东 9 个省市在全国水平之上，其中上海最高达 14.0%，浙江、北京、江苏、天津 4 个省市也超过 10%，可视为进入老年型，其余 4 省均达到 9.0% 以上，接近老年型。海南、广西和福建 3 省区比全国水平稍低一些，但相当接近。可以预料，在全国人口走向老龄化年龄结构的过程中，沿海地区将走在最前列：部分省市已跨入老年型，部分省份接近老年型，部分省份稍低于全国平均水平，但仍明显高于西北、西南广大内陆边远地区。因此，建立同人口老龄化相适应的养老保障体系，或者实现人口老龄化与养老保障事业的可持续发展，对沿海地区说来已不是将来而是现实必须解决的问题。

建立同沿海人口老龄化进程相适应的养老保障体系，笔者以为，首先需要积极发展社会供养。发展社会供养，建立日臻完善的社会养老保障制度，是发达国家应付人口老龄化最主要的手段，基本上保证了老年人口的晚年生活。如前所述，中国沿海地区经济比较发达，离退休制度也比较健全，具备发展社会养老保障的有利条件；同时也要看到，沿海某些省市是我国的老工业基地。设备老化、技术老化、职工年龄结构老化的"三老企业"多，社会养老保障压力很大，亟须改革。近年来一些地方已经摸索出一套办法，国家也有相应的政策出台；不过本人以为，还可以结合沿海地区人口和经济发展实际，按照国家、企业、个人三方共同筹集养老基金原则，创造多种办法。其次要继续提倡家庭供养，发挥传统子女养老的作用，避免出现无人赡养老年人的真空。由于沿海处在改革开放前沿，商品和市场经济比较发达，传统观念受到的冲击力比较大，子女赡养父母正经受着历史的震荡，需要大力倡导并寻求行政的、法律的保障。再次是辅之以必要的老年人口自养，组织健康老年人口从事力所能及的劳动。在西方国家，退休意味着从此劳动生涯的结束；在中国、日本等东方国家，相当多数老年人口仍旧愿意从事一定的工作或劳动，把劳动作为生活的一个组成部分。这是观念上的差异，而这

---

[1]　田雪原主编，沙吉才、杨子慧副主编《中国老年人口》，《中国 1990 年人口普查资料》，中国经济出版社，1991。

种差异恰好适合我们的需要。中国社会科学院人口研究所进行的老年人口调查证明，当前老年健康者从事一定的劳作，成为经济来源的重要部分之一，特别是在广大农村。老年再就业在沿海人口和劳动力比较密集的情况下，碰到的一个实际矛盾是同生产年龄人口争夺就业岗位问题。解决的主要办法，是实现老年人口再就业的职业转移。一些职业，如机关、企业的收发、门卫人员，清洁、服务工作人员，仓储、保管人员等，更适合老年人口的体力和心理，老年人口再就业应主要面向这种第三产业部门，由生产型转向服务型。通过上述途径积极发展社会供养、继续提倡子女家庭供养、适当组织老年再就业自养，建立起社养、家养、自养相结合的"三位一体"的养老保障体系，逐步加大社养分量，是实现沿海人口老龄化与养老保障可持续发展的理智选择，实现高度现代化整个历史阶段的合理选择。

（五）人口城市化与产业结构合理化的可持续发展

随着经济、技术、社会的发展，社会形态的变迁，城市的地位、职能、作用也在发展，工业革命后更产生质的飞跃，城市迅速崛起，人口日益向城市集中的趋势加速进行。但是无论怎样发展，一个国家或地区城市化发达程度同产业结构紧紧相联，保持着最初社会分工的基本特征，人口城市化与产业结构合理化的可持续发展，成为研究全部可持续发展中的一个重要问题。

人口城市化作为一大趋势，二次世界大战后发展更为迅速。根据联合国的估计，1994年世界城市人口占总人口比例上升到42%，发达国家高达72%，发展中国家为34%，预计到20世纪末世界城市人口比例可上升到50%，并将继续增高。我国人口城市化也在不断发展着，但是由于中国的特殊国情，划分城市人口几经变动，给研究工作带来一定的困难。国家统计局公布的城市人口，1982年以前市镇人口为辖区内的全部人口，以后则按市所辖区人口，不设区的市按街道人口，镇所辖居民委员会人口计算，1949年以来的人口城市化进程大致可分成三个时期：20世纪50年代为迅速发展时期，城市人口比例由1950年的11.2%提高到1960年的19.8%，10年中间升高8.6个百分点；60和70年代为徘徊时期，城市人口比例先降后升，1980年始回升至19.4%，仅接近1960年的水平；80年代以来为加速发展时期，1993年城市人口比例上升到28.1%，13年间升高8.7个百分点。[①] 尽管

---

① 《中国统计年鉴1994》。

学术界一些同事对这一数据存有异议，多数认为比实际可能低了一点儿，但改革开放以来给人口城市化带来新的生机和活力，大大加快了人口城市化和产业结构调整的进程，则是不容置疑的。这一点对沿海地区说来，尤为突出。1990年普查全国市镇人口占总人口比例为 26.2%，沿海 12 个省市区中有 7 个在这一水平之上：北京 73.1%，天津 68.7%，上海 66.2%，辽宁 50.9%，广东 36.8%，浙江 32.8%，山东 27.3%；5 个省区在这一水平之下：海南 24.1%，福建 21.4%，江苏 21.2%，河北 19.1%，广西 15.1%[①]。从统计材料看，1993 年全国按城乡划分的从业人员中从事城镇各种工商业的占 26.5%，沿海地区有 6 个省市高于这一水平：北京 73.3%，上海 68.3%，天津 63.5%，辽宁 56.3%，海南 38.0%，广东 29.4%；有 6 个省区低于这一水平：福建 25.6%，江苏 25.5%，河北 22.5%，浙江 20.8%，山东 20.2%，广西 16.9%。沿海总体情况怎样呢？根据上述资料计算，沿海 12 个省市区从事城市工商业的人员比例为 29.2%，比全国平均水平高出 2.7 个百分点。需要指出，上述资料尚有需要讨论之处，如浙江城镇从业人员比例较低，有很大一部分外出到其他省、市、区从事工商业，甚至出国经商，统计上很难反映出来，不少沿海省份有这种情况。表现在产业结构上，见表 3。[②]

表 3　1993 年沿海地区三次产业从业人员构成

地　区	合计（万人）	第一产业（%）	第二产业（%）	第三产业（%）
全　国	60220	56.4	22.4	21.2
北　京	659	12.4	43.2	44.4
天　津	478	19.0	50.0	31.0
河　北	3241	57.8	24.0	18.2
辽　宁	1952	33.4	41.6	25.0
上　海	740	9.3	56.0	34.7
江　苏	3743	44.8	33.7	21.5
浙　江	2659	47.9	20.0	22.1
福　建	1521	55.4	23.2	21.4
山　东	4473	59.0	23.3	17.3
广　东	3480	45.0	27.6	27.3
广　西	2277	71.2	11.1	17.7
海　南	320	68.6	11.4	20.0

① 《中国 1990 年人口普查资料》。

② 根据《中国统计年鉴 1994》资料计算。

由表 3 看出，不仅沿海地区有 8 个省市从事第一产业人员的比例低于全国水平，从事第二、第三产业的比例高于全国水平，而且其中 7 个省市从事第一产业人员的比例已下降到 50% 以下，从事第二、第三产业的比例上升到 50% 以上，尤其是从事第三产业人员比例上升显著。不难发现，人口城市化水平同三次产业结构变动息息相关，总的趋势是：人口城市化水平越高，第一产业所占比例越低，第二、第三产业所占比例越高，相反亦然。从这层意义上说，沿海地区人口城市化超前一步，为产业结构的合理化调整创造了一个方面的有利条件。不过由于沿海不同地区原有的国民经济基础不同，产业结构差异很大，通向人口城市化与产业结构合理化可持续发展的道路，也会呈现一定的差异，特别是第二产业与第三产业的调整差异较大。

（六）人口地区分布与生产力布局的可持续发展

人类发展的历史证明，人口过多或过少均不利于经济的发展，人口质量主要是文化素质也要同经济技术水平相适应，不适应也不利于发展。我国人口多，但分布很不平衡，长期以来形成的瑷珲（黑河）——腾冲人口地理分布线未变：在该线西北占国土面积 52% 居住的人口占 5%，在该线东南占国土面积 48% 居住的人口占 95%。而东南部也不平衡，沿海 12 个省市区比其他地区人口密度又胜一筹，长江三角洲、珠江三角洲、山东半岛、辽东半岛、京津地区等不仅为国内人口高度集中区域，在世界上也属于人口高密度区。前已述及，沿海地区丰富的劳动力资源为经济发展准备了条件，同时也有就业等各种问题。就人口分布与生产力布局的可持续发展而言，总体上看不存在劳动力短缺，值得注意的是下面两个问题。

一是沿海地区自身人口分布的不平衡问题。虽然总的说来沿海地区人口过多是矛盾的主要方面，但是一些地区人口密度疏密相差很大，如辽东半岛与辽西，胶东半岛与鲁西，苏南与苏北，珠江三角洲与粤北山区等，前者自然条件较好，劳动力资源雄厚，实现可持续发展基础较好；后者自然条件较差，劳动力资源不同于前者，实现可持续发展，改变生产力布局不够合理状况困难较多。

二是沿海地区人才结构的差异问题。如前所述，从总体上看沿海人口文化素质较高，但同是沿海地区差别也很大，直接影响产业结构的生产力布局。京、沪、津凝集着大量高科技人才。环渤海和上海集中着一大批钢铁、化工、轻纺业等人才，而广东、海南和沪、杭、甬等拥有多方面经贸人才，显示出不同的人才优势，为相应产业的发展创造了有利的条件。

三 沿海人口与经济可持续发展战略选择

以上的分析表明，实现沿海地区人口与经济的可持续发展有着许多有利条件。在人口方面，主要有：人口数量比较集中，劳动力资源丰富，且生育率已经下降到较低水平，人口增长势能减弱；人口素质比较高，具备比较明显的人才优势；人口年龄结构变动超前一步，正以较快速度步入老年型；人口城市化水平也比较高，城乡结构正趋于合理化，等等。在经济发展方面，自然条件比较优越，有着广阔的平原，绵长的海岸线，某些自然资源比较丰富；改革开放以来经济长期、持续、稳定发展，特别是原来不够发达的广东、福建、海南、广西等省区发展很快；经济特区、沿海开放城市和开放地区的经济发展颇具特点，外向型经济占有很大比重，对内辐射作用也很强，等等。同时存在一些不利因素，在人口方面主要是：人口密度高，人口压迫生产力的局面将长期存在；虽然人口文化素质较高，但是同经济、技术发展要求仍不相适应，同外向型经济发展仍不相适应；同是沿海地区，人口文化程度、年龄构成、城市化水平差别很大，某些省区尚落后于全国一般水平，等等。在经济方面主要是：耕地、森林等可更生性资源以及有色金属等非更生性自然资源不足；沿海作为工业基地在工业化过程中发挥了重要作用，相当数量的国营大中型企业主要是重工业，面临固定资产更新和机制转变双重困难；某些地区污染严重，环境恶化令人担忧，等等。因此，实现沿海人口与经济的可持续发展，需要立足现实，着眼未来，扬长避短，在第一步发展的同时为第二步、第三步发展创造有利条件，逐步走上良性循环，作出合理的战略选择。从实际出发并结合可持续发展基本要求，这种选择提出如下4个支撑点。

其一，加快经济发展，推进人口转变。前面的分析已经述及，实现沿海人口与经济可持续发展的基本障碍，在于短缺经济与过剩人口的矛盾，加快经济发展步伐是治本战略的首要之举。这不仅在宏观上可以改善人口生产的条件，为做好计划生育事业提供财力与物力保障，推动政策的进一步落实，而且在微观上可直接导致生育率下降，完成人口再生产类型的转变。尽管学术界对影响生育率变动因素的分析千差万别，但有一个基本的共识：归根结底，是由经济发展水平决定的，人口问题本质上是发展问题。一般说来，生育率与经济发展水平、文化教育水平呈逆相关关系，经济和文化教育发展水平越高，生育率越低，相反越高。考察家庭类型和家庭规模的演变，可以充分说明这个问题。关于家庭的划分，人口学和社会学有多种意见，笔者赞成粗略地划分成以大家庭为标志的传统家庭，由大家庭向小家庭过渡的转型家庭，以小家庭为主的现代家庭三类，因为这样的"三分法"不仅概括了家庭的基本特征，而且比较清楚地区分出家庭同社会演进紧密相联系的不同历史阶段。

以大家庭为标志的传统家庭，家庭中包含几代人，体现世代相传复杂结构的社会基本细胞单位。它的社会经济背景，是以传统农业和小手工业为主的家庭经济，在封建社会表现为自然经济，在封建社会解体和资本主义形成过程中，也残留着自然经济的痕迹。这种家庭在经济上具有独立生产和经营功能，收支和消费功能，老幼和伤残保障功能；在人口生产上则表现为独立的生育单位，抚育单位和安全保障单位。由于生产工具落后，养育孩子成本低廉，而孩子作为劳动力和养老的支柱等效益却一目了然，"财富流"的主流是由孩子流向父母和家庭，联合式的大家庭成为人们追逐的目标。

由大家庭向小家庭过渡的转型家庭，世代相传复杂结构的家族链条已拉开，家庭由多代际向以两代际为主转化。它的社会经济背景，是传统的农业和小手工业向社会化大农业和机器大工业转化，只是这种转化在较大程度上仍没有脱离传统家庭的主要特征。由于工业化的结果使第二产业和第三产业所占比例大幅度上升，农业现代化过程中也释放出大量农业剩余劳动力，妇女大批走出家门到社会上求职，社会劳动生产率迅速提高，抚养孩子成本开始上升。虽然"财富流"的主导方面还是由孩子流向父母和家庭，但是流量大为减弱，因此人们生育孩子的热情大为减低，随着转型经济和转型家庭的发展，生育率开始下降。而在这一过程中，若政府或民间旨在控制人口增长的政策或计划生育服务得到加强，必将产生明显效果。二次世界大战后，包括中国在内的发展中国家生育率奇迹般地下降，充分证明了这一点。

以小家庭为主的现代家庭，则基本上割断了大家庭维系世代相传的复杂结构，形成以两代人核心家庭为主的小家庭。它的社会经济背景是：国民经济现代化达到较高程度，农业所占比例大幅度下降并且实现了现代化，劳动生产率迅速提高，抚养孩子费用特别是用在教育上面的费用急剧上升，而传统家庭具有的生产和经营、收支、消费、老幼和伤残保障等功能，有的已经消失，为相应的社会功能所取代；有的大大下降，为相应的社会组织所填充。如社会保障之取代家庭子女养老，学校之取代家庭成为子女教育的主要场所，丰富多彩的文化、体育生活填充子女"天伦之乐"之不足等，导致人们的生育意愿——包括生育子女的数量、性别和间隔，发生根本性变化。决定这一变化的深层次原因，在于以现代经济为背景的现代家庭，"财富流"已不再是由子女流向父母和家庭，而由父母和家庭流向子女。这是造成现代社会超低生育率的最基本的原因，也是现代小家庭日渐蔓延扩大的基本原因。

我国沿海地区情况怎样呢？1990年普查全国每户平均3.96人，在总体上沿海地区同这一水平相当接近，略低一点儿；分开来看，有8个省市家庭规模小于全国平均数，它们是：上海平均每户3.10人，北京3.20人，天津3.34人，浙江3.46人，辽宁3.59人，江苏3.66人，山东3.75人，河北3.89人。其余4省区家庭规模大于全国平均数：广东4.42人，福建4.43人，海南4.57人，广西4.65人。按照上面的分类，目前处于转型家庭，但3个直辖市已转到以小家庭为主的现代家庭，浙江、辽宁等省也同现代小型家庭接近；而广西、海南两省区则处在转型前期。除广东情况比较特殊外，其余家庭规模生育率的高低，大体上同经济发展、人均收入和消费水平呈逆相关关系。可见，加快经济发展是推进人口转变的基础，也是实现沿海人口与经济可持续发展的基础。

加快沿海经济发展有着不可多得的机遇和良好的条件。当前以微电子技术为先导的新的技术革命迅速在全球铺展开来，发达国家正面临着传统产业转移和某些技术转让，积极寻求国外投资，而在世界性经济不景气中，中国一枝独秀，由于地理位置、自然条件、经济基础、人力资源等因素的影响，"一枝独秀"首先"秀"在沿海地区。关于"天时"和"地利"方面有利于经济发展的条件前面已述及，关于"人和"方面的条件亦不可忽视。沿海地区人力资源丰富，更为重要的是人口文化素质较高，具备加快发展现代技术和产业的优越条件；而且由于沿海经济率先起飞，还吸引着大量内地人才源源流来。站在全国国民经济发展角度观察，这种"孔雀东南飞"现象未必值得赞赏，然而按照人口迁移的"推拉理论"，飞向东南沿海自然有它自身的吸引力。因此，沿海地区的经济发展一定要十分注重人力资源的开发和利用，大力推进技术进步，以劳动生产率的不断提高，支持经济持续、健康地发展。

其二，对外发展外向型经济，对内增强辐射能力。前面的分析表明，中国沿海经济具备加快发展的条件，同时也存在一定的不利因素。这种不利因素之一，是资源有限，人均资源相对更低一些。我国有色金属储量丰富，但金、银、铜、铅、锌、钨等主要有色金属多在内地，沿海地区储量有限；森林、草场等可更生性资源，沿海地区也较贫乏，淡水资源严重不足。这决定了沿海地区除了同内陆地区进行经贸和携手发展外，需要眼睛向外，加强国际贸易与合作。更为重要的是必须适应我们所处的国际经贸合作越来越多的时代。数百年来，我们有两次吃了闭关自守的亏：一次是清朝以"大清帝国"自居，最后被西方资本主义列强的炮舰政策敲开了大门，沦为半封建半殖民地国家；另一次是自中华人民共和国成立后的第二个五年计划始至20世纪70年代末，在国际上受新技术革命驱动加快发展之际，我们却关起门来"闹革命"，结果不仅拉大了同西方发达国家之间的差距，而且造成了同六七十年代某些发展较快的发展中国家的差距。实践证明，当代发展紧紧同开放连在一起，发展国民经济就必须奉行开放方针，亚洲新、旧"四小龙"的经济起飞就是例证。而对外开放就要发展外向型经济，这一任务历史地落到了沿海地区头上。

所谓外向型经济，是以进入国际市场和出口创汇带动经济增长为目标，以发展面向国际市场和具有高附加值的工业替代产品为主的产业结构，以国际通行的自由竞争和市场经济为运行机制的经济。因此，我们发展外向型经济不应是简单的引进和输出，而应是通过合理的引进和输出，向外输出多余的劳动力资源和其他剩余产品，输入先进的技术、设备和短缺资源；促进本国各种生产要素的合理配置，产业和产品结构的合理调整；通过吸收国外资本、先进技术与本国人力资源、自然资源比较优势相结合，提高产品附加值，提高出口竞争力，带动经济全面发展。如前所述，我国沿海12个省、自治区、直辖市，具有人力资源雄厚，人口素质较高的人力资源优势；在原有基础上，经过数十年建设形成比较完整的工业体系，具备较强的开发能力的资源配置优势；绵长的海岸线和众多的良湾深港，便捷的陆、海、空交通，以及濒临海外华人集中的港、澳地区等地理位置优势；背靠内陆广大腹地，在资源配置和产品进出口上可作较大幅度调整和部分替代的风险调剂优势等，这样的优势在世界各国中是绝难找到的。这说明，沿海地区具备发展外向型经济的基本条件，优势十分明显。而不足也是比较明显的，这除了前面提到的人口数量多，人均资源特别是人均耕地、森林、淡水、有色金属等资源水平低以外，生产力发展水平不高和引进配套设施不足，配套资金缺口较大等比较突出。然而立足于人口与经济的可持续发展，这些不足只有依赖改革开放和外向型经济的发展，才有可能从根本上改观。因此，发展沿海外向型经济不仅是发挥优势的需要，也是克服不足，实现可持续发展的需要。

站在全国人口与经济可持续发展战略高度观察，加快沿海外向型经济发展，增强对内辐射能力，逐步实现内地人口与经济可持续发展的需要。外向型经济具有劳动生产率高、技术先进、结构合理、管理比较科学等优点，吸收内地相当数量的原材料和少量劳动力，同时也有部分产品销往内地，技术和管理传向内地，深化改革和扩大开放播向内地，推动整个国民经济跃上新水平。沿海地区这种外向型经济向内地延伸，同交通、信息和整个经济区域的发达程度紧密相联，从而形成粗具规模的沿海、沿江、沿路开放带，产生较强的向内地的辐射功能。北有大连—沈阳高速公路以及延伸至长春、哈尔滨的铁路，塘沽—天津—北京高速公路以及秦皇岛—大同、北京—包头、北京—太原铁路；中有欧亚大陆桥东段连云港—兰州陇海铁路和兰州—乌鲁木齐兰新铁路，上海—武汉—重庆长江黄金水道；南有杭州—株洲浙赣铁路，厦门—鹰潭、广州—武汉、湛江—贵阳铁路及珠江、闽江水道，形成自沿海向内地的网络，将沿海与内地的经济发展连成一片。进一步扩大开放需要发挥沿海经济的这种辐射作用，实现沿海以至全国人口与经济的可持续发展，更需要发挥沿海经济的这种辐射作用，形成以沿海外向型经济为龙头，带动内地经济全面发展的新的格局。

其三，控制人口增长，促进经济发展，这是通向人口与经济可持续发展的道路。对人口方面的基本要求，前已述及，虽然沿海地区人口年龄结构由成年型向老年型转变比全国超前一步，但是总体上说，还具有一定的增长势能，必须继续控制人口的数量增长。1990 年第四次人口普查全国人口密度为每平方千米 118 人，沿海 12 个省、自治区、直辖市均大大高于这一水平，上海高出 17.9 倍，天津高出 5.6 倍，北京高出 4.5 倍，最低的广西和海南也分别高出 0.5 和 0.6 倍。① 从沿海人口、经济、社会发展和深化社会发展和深化改革、扩大开放的实际出发，继续控制人口增长首先需要贯彻好现阶段我国的计划生育政策，运用好以往成功的做法和经验。我国现行的计划生育政策，即提倡晚婚晚育，少生优生；提倡一对夫妇只生育一个孩子，农村中确有实际困难的夫妇，经过批准间隔几年以后可以生育第二个孩子；无论

---

① 国务院人口普查办公室编《中华人民共和国国家统计局关于 1990 年人口普查主要数据公报》。

哪种情况都不能生第三个孩子；少数民族也要实行计划生育。多年来在贯彻这一政策过程中积累了不少的经验，诸如领导重视，实行管理责任制的经验；以宣传、避孕和经常性工作为主的"三为主"经验；提高干部素质，注重队伍建设的经验；推行技术进步，提高服务水平的经验等。对于沿海地区来说，政策和经验同样是重要的，不可因为改革先走了一步，经济、文化等的发展快一些而有所放松。当前有一种倾向，似乎提倡一对夫妇生育一个孩子对于某些生育率较低地区已经失效，可以放宽了，这是一种误解。中国在 20 世纪 80 年代初正式提出一对夫妇只生育一个孩子，既非永久之计，比如五六十年或上百年；也非权宜之计，比如五六年或七八年，而是一定时期的一项特殊政策——控制一代人，大约 25 至 30 年的时间。因为控制住一代人的生育率，独生子女再结婚就可以放宽到生育 2 个孩子，以后的人口控制便可以得到有效的解决。相反，如果不能很好地控制一代人的生育率，过早地抬高生育水平，对未来的人口控制将产生长期不良影响。因此，着眼中国控制人口增长全局，沿海地区即使生育率低一些，控制一代人生育率的任务也需要到位地完成，只是这种完成除运用以往行之有效的行政手段外，需要结合改革开放特别是社会主义市场经济体制改革实际，面对人口控制和计划生育管理行政调节弱化和利益调节增强的现实，研究市场经济对人口控制的有利和不利影响，寻求改革的思路。

市场经济对人口控制和降低生育率的有利影响，从本质和长期发展上看，主要表现在以下几个方面。

一是市场经济体制的建立和不断完善，实现生产经营自主化、经济活动市场化、宏观调控中介化、经营管理规范化，摆脱过去高度集中统一计划经济"一统就死、一放就乱"的困境，有利于人、财、物各种资源的合理配置，必然大大解放生产力、发展生产力，为生育率的进一步降低打下新的物质基础，沿海地区经济一步步向市场经济体制过渡的实践已经说明了这一点。

二是劳动力市场的形成，人才竞争加剧，从发展上看，正诱使家庭由投入孩子的数量成本向质量成本转移。现在，沿海一些经济发展水平和市场化程度较高的地方，人们的生育偏好已经发生由追求孩子的数量向追求孩子的质量转移，由投入孩子的数量成本向投入孩子的质量成本、尤其是用在孩子教育上面的质量成本的转移。1992 年包括沿海 6 个省市在内的 10 省市家庭经济与生育抽样调查表明，全国加权汇总家庭愿将子女培养到小学、初中、高中、中专、大专、大学、研究生和没有要求 8 个层次，所占比例依次为 3.6%、18.8%、16.8%、9.6%、6.5%、29.2%、3.1% 和 12.3%，比例最高为培养到大学毕业，其次为初中毕业，再次为高中毕业。这说明在市场经济条件下，已有相当一部分人认识到市场的竞争归根结底是人才的竞争，舍得进行家庭人口智力投资，"望子成龙"很自然地同市场经济联系起来。劳动力市场是市场经济的一个组成部分，随着整个市场经济体制的建立和完善，人才的竞争更显得突出，人口质量成本增加到一定阶段会有一个质的飞跃，促使人们由多生多育型转向少生优育优教型。

三是商品和市场经济的发展，使孩子养老—保险效益下降。这有如下三方面的情况。

一为市场经济体制的建立和国民经济的高速成长，劳动生产率的提高和社会积累的增加，为国家、企业和不同社会组织举办老年社会保障事业奠定基础，养老社会化趋势增强。尤其是富裕起来的乡村，大都程度不同地兴办起养老保障事业，削弱了子女养老的地位和作用。

二为按现行离退休政策规定不享有老年退休金的个体、集体企业职工，乡村广大劳动者，在富裕起来以后，有能力为养老储备一笔资金，投保养老保险。据统计，养老金保险费 1991 年达到 331378 万元，为 1985 年的 18.8 倍，足见增长之迅猛。[①] 数以千万计的劳动者的未来养老将脱离子女供养的传统轨道，孩子的养老—保险效益相对下降。

三为"养儿防老"传统观念淡化。商品和市场经济发展之后，对人们的思想是一种潜移默化的巨大腐蚀剂，它改变着人们的价值观念，使感情色彩的东西贬值，传统的赡养父母老人观念在一部分人的头脑中淡薄下来，拒不赡养的案件增多，使人们对子女的养老—保险效益期望值下降。

四是人们为了在激烈的市场竞争中获得胜利，不得不投入更多的精力，使闲暇时间减少，自然逗孩子取乐的时间也随着减少。同时，由于市场经济的紧张性和多样性、多变性，把孩子作为主要精神慰藉的小农乐趣也开始更张改弦，为更富有刺激性、科学性的现代娱乐方式所取代，孩子作为"天伦之乐"的精神效益下降的势头，在市场经济高度发达的地区亦较明显。

五是市场经济诱使人们将更多的财力用于市场竞争，用于提高竞争本领的自我发展，而不愿更多地用来养育子女。人口学中有一种称为社会"毛细

---

① 《中国统计年鉴 1992》。

管理论"认为：在家庭收入一定的条件下，用在父母生存、发展和享乐需要部分越少，用在生育子女上面部分就越多，好比一个 U 型管连通器，此消彼长，在此种情况下必然是多生多育；相反，用在父母需要部分增多，用在生养孩子部分就要减少，此种情况必然导至少生少育。市场经济体制的建立将强化社会"毛细管效应"，从根本上动摇"多子多福"的传统生育观，有利于控制人口的数量增长。

六是市场经济因推进产业结构合理化和加速人口城市化进程，为人口控制和生育率下降创造有利条件。市场经济促使农业由过去单一型经营向多种经营方式转变，由自给半自给向商品经济转变，广大农民直接进入市场，进入城镇，成为实际上的城镇人口；而城镇工商业活跃起来之后，特别是城乡之间交流的扩大和第三产业发展的需要，吸引着大批农业剩余劳动力转移过来，乡镇企业异军突起，人口城市化的加速进行终将人口控制引入一个新的阶段。

上述市场经济对人口生产作用的几个方面——人口生产赖以进行的物质基础、边际孩子成本与效益、人口城市化进程——是紧密相连和互相促进的。市场经济发展越完备，越能促进社会生产力的发展和改变人口生产的物质基础，越是有利于边际孩子效益的下降和质量成本的上升，越能有效地加快人口城市化的步伐。某一方面取得进展固然有益，但成效可能不一定显著；只有当这几个方面都取得进展，市场经济对人口控制和整个人口问题解决的威力才能真正释放出来。因此要用发展的观点、历史的观点看待市场经济为人口问题的解决提供的机遇，将其视为较长时间的发展过程，不可能取得同步式的立竿见影效果。一般说来在市场经济发展初期，上述积极作用和有利影响不易充分发挥出来，而某些方面的消极作用和不利影响反倒比较突出，更应引起关注。

当前，市场经济建立初期，对人口控制和生育率降低带来的消极作用和不利影响，主要表现在以下几个方面。

首先，是同市场取向相关联的孩子成本—效益作用的不利倾斜。主要在于：

一是边际孩子劳动—经济效益升值。改革开放和走向市场经济，乡村以联产承包责任制为主要形式的建立，使丧失已久的家庭的生产职能得以恢复。城镇个体、合营一类工商业的兴起，也使相当一部分家庭具有不同程度的生产和经营的职能。这类生产和经营职能得到恢复和扩张的家庭，对劳动力尤其是男性劳动力的需求变得比较迫切，孩子劳动—经济效益增值是这类家庭超生的重要原因。虽然孩子生下来要经过十几年后才有可能成长为劳动力，似乎远水解不了近渴；但是在他们从劳动力市场上取得劳动力来源后，如果同时生产出归自己家庭所有的指日可待的劳动力，在小生产者看来是最可靠、最廉价、最划得来的，对那些缺少男性劳动力家庭说来更是如此。

二是孩子养老—保险效益的反向变动。前面曾经论及，从根本上讲市场经济的建立会使孩子养老—保险效益下降已相当明显。然而在经济发展水平和市场化程度不高的地区，传统的子女养老仍占据主导地位，把生儿子作为将来养老的主要手段。在乡村特别在经济比较落后的乡村，相对过去人民公社时期落后的社会生产力说来，"敬老院"、"老年之家"一类养老保障事业超前发展，免除了相当多数无子女的老年人的后顾之忧。改革开放和转向市场经济之后，不乏还有某些养老保障事业办得好的典型，但很多地方大大削弱了，农民从切身感受中体验到还是生个儿子最可靠，重又提高了"养儿防老"效应。

三是在城乡富裕起来的个体经济家庭中，孩子继承家业的效益显著上升。尽人皆知，我们的社会主义市场经济体制是在这样的历史背景下建立起来的，即封建社会有长达数千年的历史，商品经济发展很不完善，1949年以来又长期把商品经济和市场经济当做资本主义进行批判。因此，目前在市场经济中发展起来的个体户，很容易将产业视为家业，为家业后继有人，不惜一切代价生了几个女孩之后还要再生，大有"不生儿子不罢休"之势。

四是在孩子成本方面，如前所述，从根本和发展战略上考察，市场经济为提高孩子质量成本主要是用在教育上面的质量成本创造了条件，将在诱导人们由投入孩子数量成本向质量成本转移中发挥关键作用。不过这种转移的发生也要有一个前提，即追加的孩子质量成本能带来相应的效益。如果说这一前提在沿海一些经济和市场相当发达地区已经具备了的话，还有相当一部分地区尚不具备，而在经济不够发达和市场影响又已波及的地区，率先映入小生产者眼帘的是孩子市场效应，把孩子推到市场中去赚钱。一些调查表明，这种"学生卖鸡蛋"的现象是中小学生流失的主要原因。

其次，发生了生育观念和生育行为市场化的偏向，即以金钱标准衡量和婚育金钱交易的倾向。

本来旧社会遗留下来的买卖婚姻、卖淫嫖娼、拐卖妇女等已经绝迹，然而近年来随着改革开放和市场经济发展，某些人变成货币拜物教者并影响到婚姻和家庭，旧社会的一些丑恶现象死灰复燃，并且出现了新的离婚率升高，婚外恋增多，未婚先孕上升等新问题。这种新旧现象交织在一起，兼具"传统"和"现代"双重特色，解决起来难度颇大。由拐卖妇女，婚外恋，离婚后再生等意外生育引起的超生问题，近年来上升较快，某些地区表现尤为突出。

再次，管理跟不上市场经济和人口变动的新情况。

市场经济对人口生产的制约和影响，许多在量上难以作出准确的估计，形成一时间管理跟不上客观变化形势的矛盾。主要有：

一是流动人口激增同管理跟不上客观变化形势的矛盾。随着改革开放和市场经济的发展，流动人口大量增加，目前估计在 8000 万 ~ 10000 万人之间，其中北京、上海、广州等大城市日流动人口量超过 200 万人，出现空前规模的流动人口大军，给人口控制带来新的难题。主管部门对此已制定出一定的管理办法，并且取得不少成效，但由于流动人口流动性大的基本特点，管理起来仍旧十分困难。对于同一流出地且流入相对比较集中的地方，如浙江省温州市流动人口流向北京、广西、云南等，流出地派人到各地的"温州村"进行管理，有的还成立了专门的计生管理组织和计生协会，收到不少效果。然而，这样的遥控和长途跋涉开支甚大，而且流出地和流入地如此集中的流动人口群毕竟所占比例很小，多数地方无法效法，只好依靠流入地。流入地管理起来确有不少困难而且又要增加人力、物力、财力支出，形成额外负担。这样从总体上看，存在着流出地和流入地都在管，但都很难管好，投入很大和效益不够高的矛盾。

二是客观上要求强化管理同管理自身弱化的矛盾。面对市场经济条件下的人口问题，客观上需要强化人口管理，尤其是计划生育管理。然而市场经济的发展却有使管理弱化的可能：各级领导的精力更多地转向经济，转向市场，抓人口生产相对减弱；主管部门的人力，包括机构改革中的稳定和工作人员的某种市场取向，都产生了新的情况和问题；财力和物力也更多流向市场经济，希望带来价值增值倾向，不同程度地影响到管理"硬件"的现代化，削弱了管理的手段和力量。

三是出现了新的特殊的问题和矛盾。如 B 超胎儿性别鉴定屡禁不止，一个重要原因是罚款失效：接受 B 超鉴定者自动分担罚款，使 B 超技术与生育交易市场化。又如城市高级公寓日渐增多，某些经理、"大款"雇有保镖长期居住，给计生管理增加很大难度。随着市场经济和价值观念的改变，这类特殊问题还会不断增加，给市场经济条件下的人口控制提出了新的课题和任务。

市场经济对生育的作用和影响是错综复杂的，从沿海地区的实际情况出发，人口控制和计划生育改革的基本思路如下。

微观上，加大利益调节分量。方向是增大独生子女和其他计划内生育子女的效益，如适当提高独生子女奖励标准，开展独生子女和其父母的人身和养老保险。在入托、入学、医疗、住房分配等方面，同等条件下给予独生子女和其他计划内生育子女优惠等。适当增加超生子女成本，如变一次性罚款为全部未成年期罚款，同独生子女奖励时间一样长，改变超生子女父母"痛苦一时（一次性罚款），享福（子女提供效益）一世"的心态。最为重要的，是在分配上逐步走上向脑力劳动倾斜的轨道，从根本上改变"拿手术刀不如拿剃头刀"、"教授笔杆不如小贩秤杆"的脑力劳动和体力劳动分配不合理状态，实现复杂劳动是简单劳动倍加的按劳分配原则，确保人口智力投资得到相应的效益，实现人们由投入孩子数量成本向质量成本的转移。

中观上，发挥社区调节功能。社区（Community）是在共同经济利益基础上，并在政治、文化、社会生活方面有着某种共同属性的地理区域。就目前沿海地区情况而论，大致可分成三种类型：一类为现代产业结构型社区，即三次产业结构基本过渡到现代型，生产的专业化和商品化程度较高，经济收入较高，已实现小康并由小康向富裕过渡阶段，人口与经济发展开始进入低生育率—高劳动生产率—低生育率循环模式；二类为传统农业型社区，即社区成员以从事农业传统产业为主，生产力不发达，收入水平低，处于由饥馑向温饱过渡或温饱初级状态，边际孩子成本—效益利于较多生育，基本上停留在高生育率—低劳动生产率—高生育率循环模式；三类为过渡型产业结构社区，即由单一的传统农业型向现代产业结构型过渡，生产手段由以手工为主向半机械化、机械化为主过渡，经济收入由低水平向高水平过渡，人口与经济发展由高生育率—低劳动生产率—高生育率向低生育率—高劳动生产率—低生育率模式过渡的社区。就沿海总体上观察，一类社区已占有相当的比例，二类社区正迅速减少，多数处于三类过渡型社区。我们控制人口增长，就要结合社区发展，对少生、优生、优育、优教实行必要的倾斜，帮助独生子女户和计划内生育子女户脱贫致富达小康，走向市场奔富裕。在这方面，各地创造的将发展生产、提高生活、控制生育结合起来的各种"三结合"典型经验，如沿海地区辽宁的计划生育中心户，苏北的少生快富合作社，海南的人口与社区综合发展等典型很有意义，值得总结和推广，展现出地区性人口与经济可持续发展的曙光。

宏观上，增强综合调控能力。影响因素多元化和经济因素作用的明显增强，是市场经济条件下人口控制的突出特点，需要增强国家和各级政府对人口的综合调控能力。首先是认真落实各项人口政策的调控能力，使政策贯彻到底，奖罚分明，真正纳入法制化管理轨道；其次是协调有关部门的综合调控能力，将有关政策协调起来，全面贯彻落实控制人口数量、提高人口质量、调节人口结构基本方针，保证改革沿着正确的方向进行。

其四，保护耕地，改善环境。我国耕地不足，沿海地区表现尤为突出。1993 年沿海人均耕地和耕地减少情况，如表 4 所示。[①]

表 4 1993 年沿海人均耕地与年内耕地减少情况

地 区	耕地（公顷/100 人）	年内减少（千公顷）
全 国	8.0	732.4
北 京	3.7	3.0
天 津	4.6	1.1
河 北	10.3	8.7
辽 宁	8.5	25.3
上 海	2.2	16.0
江 苏	6.5	28.8
浙 江	3.9	33.3
福 建	3.9	11.2
山 东	7.8	47.0
广 东	3.6	102.3
广 西	5.9	34.6
海 南	6.2	7.9

由表 4 看出，沿海人均耕地面积除河北、辽宁稍高于全国平均水平外，其余 10 个省市区均低于全国平均水平，且多数低得很多。京、津、沪 3 个直辖市自不消说，就是广东、浙江、福建也不足全国平均水平的一半，广

---

① 《中国统计年鉴 1994》。

西、海南、江苏为全国平均水平的 0.8 左右，山东接近全国平均水平。令人担忧的是，尽管人均耕地面积如此之低，却在年复一年地减少，1993 年沿海 12 个省市区共减少耕地 319.2 千公顷，占全国减少 732.4 千公顷的 43.6%，比内地减少幅度大许多。随着经济建设的发展和人民生活水平的提高，建造住房，发展乡镇企业，修筑铁路和公路等占用耕地还会有所增加，对于沿海地区说来，保护耕地是一项关系到当前和未来发展的一个十分尖锐的问题，是实现人口与经济可持续发展战略的根本立足点之一。

探讨人口与经济可持续发展，从本原意义上说，是为了给人类的生存和发展创造一个更为适合的环境。然而随着人口增长和人们对提高生活质量的追求，无限制地向周围环境索取，致使环境的破坏危及人类自身。同对人口控制一样，我国在环境保护方面也取得世人瞩目的成绩；但是存在的问题是严峻的，不容忽视的。根据国家统计局提供的数据资料，以工业"三废"治理为例，情况如表 5、表 6 和表 7 所示。①

表5 1993 年沿海地区工业废水排放及处理

地　区	工业废水（万吨）	排放达标量（万吨）	达标占全部废水（%）
全　国	2194919	1204858	54.9
北　京	39173	24260	61.9
天　津	21290	13844	65.0
河　北	87052	58815	67.6
辽　宁	149081	99495	66.7
上　海	128083	90721	70.8
江　苏	211643	141583	66.9
浙　江	105734	71569	67.7
福　建	57316	23316	40.7
山　东	86350	41607	48.2
广　东	139762	71252	50.9
广　西	93158	45062	48.4
海　南	9950	3145	31.6

① 《中国统计年鉴 1994》。

表6　1993年沿海地区工业废气排放及处理

单位：亿标立方米

地　区	工业废气排放量	经过消烟除尘量	经过净化处理量
全　国	93423	51782	23411
北　京	2595	1288	909
天　津	1202	837	181
河　北	6282	3409	2029
辽　宁	8591	3853	2809
上　海	3859	2017	1152
江　苏	5202	3726	913
浙　江	2878	1579	704
福　建	1593	768	525
山　东	6275	4002	1256
广　东	5839	2841	2013
广　西	1792	950	528
海　南	181	127	33

表7　1993年沿海地区工业固体废物排放及处理

单位：万吨

地　区	工业固体废物产　生　量	工业固体废物综合利用量	工业固体废物处　置　量
全　国	61708	24826	15720
北　京	868	620	4
天　津	420	305	114
河　北	6216	2650	2190
辽　宁	7591	2238	1234
上　海	1198	1045	187
江　苏	2323	1872	86
浙　江	949	468	244
福　建	701	352	119
山　东	4021	23539	997
广　东	1611	841	547
广　西	1705	609	161
海　南	132	41	1

沿海是我国工业基地，对工业"三废"治理程度颇能说明环境质量。表5、表6、表7显示，目前工业废水排放达标量较低，占70%的仅上海一家，有6个省市在60%～70%之间，有5个省区低于全国平均水平，其中4个省区不足50%，可见情况之严重。工业废气经过消烟除尘所占比例较低，经过净化处理所占比例也不高，包括占用耕地在内的占地面积很大。除工业"三废"外，还有噪音的污染，超采地下水带来的海水入侵和地面沉降，以及大量施用化肥和农药造成的水、土、空气污染，使包括鱼类在内的近海资源衰竭，环境质量下降，沿海自然环境向我们亮出"黄牌"警告。

改善沿海地区的环境，在控制人口增长和合理开发资源前提下，关键在于摆正和处理好环境与建设的关系。是先建设、后治理，边建设、边治理，还是先治理、后建设？吸取各国的成功经验和付出沉重代价换来的教训，我们理智地选择了后者，保护环境被列为另一项必须长期坚持的基本国策。然而或者由于客观上过去条件差，资金不足，技术手段跟不上难以改变；或者由于主观上认识不足，重视不够，没有下决心去改变；或者由于客观和主观两方面兼而有之，使得这项基本国策的贯彻落实在许多情况下被打了折扣。在沿海人口还要继续增长，资源相对不足，而经济又要快速发展，从国外引进项目中又有一些污染比较严重的项目的情况下，必须把保护环境和维护生态平衡摆到重要议程，作为实现人口与经济可持续发展战略目标的一个重要前提和支撑点。

《中国家庭经济与生育研究》绪论[*]

世界各地迅速的人口和社会经济变动过程
已影响到家庭形成的方式和家庭生活
——联合国《国际人口与发展会议行动纲领》
1994. 开罗

在 20 世纪即将结束和 21 世纪行将来临之际，谋求人口、资源、环境、经济、社会的可持续发展，成为全人类共同关注的最重要命题。中国政府履行里约环发大会《21 世纪议程》的承诺，率先制定了《中国 21 世纪议程——中国 21 世纪人口、环境与发展白皮书》，将经济的发展、人口问题的解决、环境的保护等作为可持续发展战略的基本立足点提了出来。人们发现，当今任何一项问题的解决都不是孤立的，而是互相联系和彼此互动的。中国自 20 世纪 70 年代以来控制人口增长取得举世瞩目的成就，无疑首先归功于认真贯彻落实计划生育基本国策的结果；同时也不可否认，在根本动因上得益于发展，尤其得益于改革开放以来经济超高速增长，以及科学、文化的发展和包括生育观念在内的传统观念转变的结果。然而在论及人口与经济的相互作用和影响时，还要同时借助望远镜和显微镜：既重视宏观上的考察，如人口出生、死亡、迁移等变动与国民生产总值、国民收入增长等经济发展的关系，又要注重微观方面的研究，特别是作为人口再生产基本单位的家庭生育与家庭经济方面的研究。

在中国，这后一个方面的研究是比较薄弱的，但在深化改革和扩大开放的新形势下，却是异常重要的。

---

[*] 原载田雪原主编、胡伟略副主编《中国家庭经济与生育研究》，中国经济出版社，1997。

一 中国的改革开放与微观人口经济发展

中国家庭经济与生育研究，特别是将二者之间的关系理论清楚，除了借助于国内外已有研究成果进行一般的静态分析外，则必须结合中国实际，尤其是结合改革开放实际作出动态研究。因此，本书以农村和城市的经济改革作为切入点，这对于全书的分析和论证都是重要的。

（一）由农村开始的改革

1978 年 12 月，具有重要历史意义的中共十一届三中全会在北京召开。这次会议重新确立实事求是的思想路线，批驳了"两个凡是"的错误，进行了理论上的拨乱反正，明确作出将工作重心转移到现代化建设上来，深入讨论了农业问题，将《中共中央关于加快农业发展若干问题的决定（草案）》和《农村人民公社工作条例（试行草案）》发到各省、自治区、直辖市试行。农业问题的两个文件强调在经济上要充分关心广大农民群众的利益，在政治上保障他们的民主权利，尊重公社和生产队的自主权，按劳分配，以及不得干涉社员从事自留地、家庭副业和集市贸易等活动。显然，这同以往文件精神大有不同，过去下发文件着重强调的是坚持社会主义道路和"割资本主义尾巴"，因而在全国农村引起很大震动，率先引起震动的是安徽省凤阳县小岗村。

凤阳县是出了名的贫困县，有这样几句民谣：

说凤阳，道凤阳，

十年倒有九年荒。

自从出了个朱皇帝，

百姓从此更遭殃。

1949 年新中国成立后，经过土地改革和农业合作化运动，广大农民生活比过去有所改善；但在追求"一大二公"、"穷过渡"极左思想指导下，直到 20 世纪 70 年代仍十分落后，一些人逃荒在外。党的十一届三中全会有如春风化雨传来，春节刚过，小岗村除 2 户人家外出未归，18 户人家召开"秘密会议"，商定了实行"大包干到户"，"瞒上不瞒下"，万一走漏风声支部书记进班房，其余 17 户将其孩子抚养到 18 岁协议，摁上 18 户人家的手印。第二天清晨，小岗人来到属于自己"包干"的土地上开始了 20 多年来全新意义上的劳作，那种与土地休戚与共、精耕细作的传统又重新降临，当年小岗村人均收入超过 400 元，为当时全国农民人均收入的 2.5 倍，一下子由贫困进到温饱水平。改革取得立竿见影的效果，中国农村改革迅速由此推广开来，几年内完成了以户为单位的联产承包责任制。到 1983 年底，全国实行联产承包制的已占总农户和生产队数的 95% 以上，标志着农村经济体制改革第一个任务的基本完成。新体制的建立和不断完善，为农村商品经济的发展和走向市场经济创造了条件，表现如下。

第一，农民获得生产和经营自主权。在人民公社"三级所有，队为基础"的经济体制下，公社一级拥有的财产归公社范围内集体所有，生产大队一级拥有的财产归生产大队范围内集体所有，生产队则拥有农业生产经营的基本财产，对土地、山林、水利设施、农具、耕畜等有权支配和使用，并有权调配本队内劳动力的使用，为独立核算、自负盈亏的经营自主单位，农民个人处于被支配的地位。实行联产承包责任制后，一般将土地、山场、林木、池塘等生产资料按产量产值包给社员户，超产超额归己或分成奖励，未完成产量产值的要受罚。这是一种"一揽子"的承包办法。虽然这一办法未改变土地等的生产资料所有权，但是承包一经确定，且一般承包时间较长，刺激了农民对土地改良、山地修整、林木更新的优选、池塘整治、水利维修等的积极性，投入增加。农村家庭联产承包责任制表现出所有权与使用权既相分离又相结合的情况。就所有权来讲，同改革前没有什么区别；就使用权来讲，则有天壤之别，农民事实上成为土地的占有者，不仅是使用的全权支配者，而且可以进行投资、转包、联合经营等举动，唯独不得进行土地买卖。市场经济要求产权明晰化，农村联产承包责任制在实践上解决了生产和经营权归农民的问题，为农民走向市场经济打开通道。

第二，农村专业户和新经济联合体的出现并获得发展。实行家庭联产承包责任制，激发了广大农民的劳动热情，农业劳动生产率提高很快，在资本和劳动力两方面为发展专业化生产作了必要准备。随着生产力和分工的进一步发展，不仅出现猪、牛、马、羊、鸡、鸭、鹅、兔等饲养专业户，而且出现规模较大的粮食、棉花、油料、林场、果园等种植专业户，将农村的商品生产迅速提高到一个新的水平，推动了走向市场经济体制改革的深入。"菜篮子工程"作为城乡结合天然的市场工程，对促进城乡市场经济的融合起到了纽带的作用，提高了农产品的商品率。在专业化生产基础上发展起来的新的经济联合体，有别于人民公社的合作经济，它没有任何行政组织色彩，而纯然是适应生产力发展和市场经济需要，真正出于自愿互利、提高经济效益的经济组织。这种新的经济联合体从诞生的第一天起，就将窥测方向瞄准市场，将农村经济发展带进市场经济体制改革大潮中去。

第三，乡镇企业和农村私营企业的发展。实行家庭联产承包责任制后，一些原有社办、队办企业财产一时不好分配，镇、乡、村政府自己或委托别人承包下来，成为早期的乡镇企业。这种乡镇企业有原有的固定资产作基础，当地有较充裕的劳动力和原材料，又有当地行政部门的扶植，在体制转换之机借助市场作依托而发展起来。一些没有原来社办、队办企业的地方，更主要的是在承包后迅速发展起来的家庭，瞧出"无工难富"门道儿，纷纷如法炮制，出现乡镇企业空前发展的局面。据统计，1978 到 1992 年，全国乡镇企业由 152.4 万个增加到 2079.2 万个，增长 12.6 倍；从业人数由 2826.6 万人增加到 10581.1 万人，增长 2.7 倍；总产值由 493.1 亿元增加到 17975.4 亿元，增长 35.5 倍；纯利润由 88.1 亿元增加到 477.6 亿元，增长 4.4 倍。[①] 与此同时，农村私营企业迅速增长，其中大部分私营企业主为农民，农村各级干部、个体户和社会闲散人员所占比例不足 3%。乡镇企业和农村私营企业的崛起，以市场为生存和发展之本，不仅促进了农村商品和市场经济的发展，而且对整个社会主义市场经济体制的建立是强有力的推动。

第四，人口流动和劳动力市场的形成。我国农村原本存在大量过剩人口，对剩余劳动力的估计在 1 亿~2 亿人之间不等，但在旧体制下被束缚在土地上，只能以潜在过剩形式表现出来。实行家庭联产承包责任制后，农民有了生产和经营自主权，没有必要自己对自己潜在过剩；而封闭、半封闭状态被打破的商品流通量与日俱增，人口流动随着增长，过剩人口和劳动力以绝对过剩形式表现出来。一些调查表明，目前全国流动人口总数超过 8000 万人，主要是农村过剩劳动力涌向城市，尤其是涌向东南沿海开放城市的"民工潮"大军。随着市场经济体制的进行和对劳动力管理的加强，劳动力市场逐步形成，填补了市场形式中的一个重要方面。而流动人口中的相当一部分人在城市中找到相应的职业，成为事实上迁移居住在城市的人口，加速着人口城市化的步伐。

除此之外，国家在政策上减少以至取消对粮、棉、油等农副产品征购的数量和品种，提高收购价格等促进了农村商品经济的发展，引导农民走向市

---

① 《中国统计年鉴1993》，中国统计出版社，1993。

场。通过全面地看待农村经济改革对市场经济体制形成的作用和影响，在肯定有利的主导方面的同时，也要注意到广大农民真正进入市场经济，农村经济全面纳入市场经济体制获得健康发展，仍有其艰巨性的一面。小农经济存在上千年，传统的经营方式、思想观念、习惯势力根深蒂固，农民进入陌生的市场经济难免步履艰难。前面提到的农村改革第一村的小岗人在改革之初就立即见效，然而在10多年中却进展不大。缺少资金、缺乏人才、条件较差是客观原因，而传统观念，包括"传宗接代"旧生育观念在内的影响，缺少市场经济新观念，满足于种好地、吃饱饭才是最主要的原因。当小岗人意识到这一点以后，通过到经济特区开阔眼界和向先进村典型学习经验，转变观念，便又走出招商引资、走向市场经济发展的新路子。不仅如此，前面提到的农村联产承包责任制改革有利于市场经济的诸多方面，同时也存在着一定的局限性或不利因素。如乡镇企业的发展拓宽了市场经济视野，然而乡镇企业多存在政企不分、产权不明问题，多数为高消耗、低产出、低效益企业，加剧着能源、原材料的紧张和环境恶化。又如人口流动和劳动力市场的形成，人口流动和城市化步伐的加快，在使生产力中人的要素活跃起来的同时，造成某些农村责任田荒芜，流动人口使城市基础设施无法承受，就业压力增大等新问题。所有这一切，即首先开始于农村的经济改革的积极的和某些一时难以除却的消极方面，必将深刻影响到农村家庭经济变革，是一次革命性变革。毫无疑问，这样的经济变革必将对人口生产产生深远影响，尤其是家庭的生育行为。

（二）城市改革的深入

继农村经济改革之后，城市经济改革也接着展开。城市经济改革紧密结合开放，改革与开放相互促进不断深入。1979年设置深圳、珠海两个"出口特区"后扩展为经济特区，并增加汕头、厦门二市，以及海南省。1984年批准大连、秦皇岛、天津、烟台、青岛、连云港、南通、上海、宁波、温州、福州、广州、湛江、北海14个市为对外开放城市，并在其中一些城市兴办经济技术开发区。同时国务院相继通过批准《中华人民共和国中外合资经营企业所得税法实施细则》、《关于进一步办好中外合资企业的报告》等文件，大胆吸引外资，扩大出口贸易，加快了沿海地区的经济起飞，改变着人们的观念。外资独资和中外合资企业的发展和新的经营管理方式的出现，使人们耳目一新，了解到现代企业经营管理为何物，平等竞争、人才流动为何物，市场经济为何物，为何必须进行以企业改革为核心的城市经济体制改革。企业改革起源于四川省扩大企业自主权试点，围绕放权让利展开。先是打破由国家统收统支将企业包下来的办法，试行利润分成。利润分成起到一定的作用，调动了一部分企业的积极性，但由于管理体制、价格体制等未根本触动，造成企业之间不具备平等竞争的条件，经营好的企业得利不多，经营差的企业得利不少的现象未真正改变。针对这一现象，企业按统一税率上缴所得税，获利高的企业税后再上缴一定调节税。"利改税"同样起到了一定的作用，但双重纳税标准又引起"鞭打快牛"的不良后果，不利于企业追求利润最大化。20 世纪 80 年代后期至 90 年代初兴起"承包热"，企业在承包规定期间内实行超收多留、欠收自补原则，对克服"利改税"带来的弊病起了一定作用，但是面对大批国有企业效益差、亏损比较严重的现实，承包也不能彻底解决问题。究其原因，上述改革均围绕着国家与企业在利润分配上兜圈子，限于分配领域，没有触动旧体制要害处，因而在改革之初收到一定效果后便很快不再灵验了。1991 年下半年提出转换企业经营机制，并且出台转换机制条例，提出将企业推向市场，才有所前进。1993 年 11 月中央《关于建立社会主义市场经济体制若干问题的决定》提出建立现代企业制度，将改革推向新的阶段。按照《决定》的阐述，现代企业制度，一要产权关系明晰，国有企业产权属于国家，企业拥有法人财产权，成为承担责任的法人实体；二是企业依法自主经营，自负盈亏，实行政企分开，对出资者承担资产保值增值责任；三是出资者按照投入企业资本额享受所有者权益，包括资产受益、决策和选择管理者权利等。企业破产时，出资者以投入企业的资本额对企业债务负有限责任；四是企业依照市场需求组织经营，政府不直接干预企业的生产经营活动；五要建立科学的企业领导体制和管理制度，调节所有者、经营者、职工之间的关系，形成激励与约束相结合的经营机制。一年多来的实践表明，已有一些企业在改革中取得成效，建立起具有新型经营机制的公司；但是按照现代企业制度进行改革，其经营机制不仅是转换问题，而且在一定意义上是重新再造问题，因而改革起来相当艰难。

城市经济改革中还应提到价格改革，建立主要通过市场形成价格的机制；在发展商品市场的同时，发展劳动力、金融、房地产、技术、信息等市场，构成完整的市场体系；建立适合企事业单位和机会时点的工资及其增长制度，包括社会保险、社会救济、社会福利、优抚安置、社会互助、个人储蓄等在内的社会保险制度，尤其是失业和养老社会保险体系，是城市经济体制改革中不可缺少的配套改革。

虽然城市经济体制改革远比农村复杂得多，也困难得多，收效也不及农村那样迅速，但仍比较明显地看出改革的市场取向。以国有企业为重点的城市经济改革，无论是早期以扩大企业自主权、放权让利的改革，还是后来建立产权明晰、政企分开、责任明确、管理科学的转换经营机制和建立现代企业制度的改革，都向传统的高度集中统一、政企不分、效益不高的旧的企业体制提出挑战，取向于平等竞争、自负盈亏、自我约束、自我发展的适合市场经济的企业。至于价格、工资、失业、养老等配套改革的市场取向更为明显，正一步步向着市场经济体制逼近。无需更多赘述，过去发生、现正进行、将来更加明确的市场取向的城市经济改革，对于城市家庭经济的来源、结构和变化趋向产生了很大影响，并且影响着包括生育在内的人口变动。

（三）市场经济与微观人口变动

中国大力控制人口增长和加强计划生育工作，始于 20 世纪 70 年代早期。当时正处于史无前例的"文化大革命"中，政治思想领域形而上学教条主义泛滥，人们的思维方式是自上而下，由国及家，而不是由下而上，由家及国。更为重要的是，正当各国竞相加快步伐发展，实现二次世界大战后加快经济起飞时，我们自己关起门来打内战，使本来十分落后的社会生产力更加落伍，国民经济长期停滞不前。而这种低下的生产力，在当时农村以手工和半手工劳动为主的情况下，孩子的抚养费用较为低廉，但确能给家庭带来明显经济效益。这在城乡公有制经济一统天下，城市主要为国有经济，乡村主要为人民公社集体经济，以及"大锅饭"一套分配制度下，家庭添人增口没有后顾之忧，劳动者的数量就是他们的质量，知识不能在生产中体现其价值和应得的报酬，加上计划经济在粮食、布匹等生活必需品和住房等的按人头分配，多生多育有着明显好处。在这种情况下如采取国外那种单纯服务型的"家庭计划"，则很难取得效果。此外，20 世纪 60 年代末中国人口总数即超过 8 亿，人口年龄结构异常年轻化，增长势能强劲，控制人口增长任务十分急迫。同时中国有着自己的具体国情，除人口多、生产力不够发达外，是一个有着严密组织的高度集中统一的国家，或者如同某些西方人士所说是一个"有组织社会"，可以发挥政治组织优势。正是在诸多情况交汇综合下，中国政府大力控制人口增长把重点放在了宏观上。首先将控制人口增长纳入国民经济发展计划，提出人口增长控制目标；其次制定为实现这一目标的政策和措施，并在实施过程中从上至下建立起计划生育机构；再次在实践中摸索出一套行之有效的做法，不断将以宏观人口控制为重点的工作推向前进。现在看来，在当时人口控制要"急刹车"的条件下，是一种必然的选择，实践证明也是成功的选择。然而在 20 多年后的今天，特别是在改革开放和向社会主义市场经济体制目标过渡的新的历史条件下，人口控制的重点是否继续放在宏观上不动，有无必要转向中观和微观？我们认为回答是肯定的，有必要明确提出逐步实现人口控制由宏观向中观，尤其主要向微观的转移。理由如下。

其一，宏观人口控制相对稳定。从实践上看，中国的宏观人口控制主要着眼于人口控制目标、生育政策和控制手段，当前这三个支撑点都处于相对稳定状态。

人口控制目标的相对稳定。目前，第一步，20 世纪末全国人口控制在 13 亿的目标已经确定下来，且是比较有把握的目标。第二步，长远人口发展战略目标的确定，实现人口的零增长也为各界所认同，并且国内外的多种预测大同小异，预计 21 世纪中叶全国人口达到 16 亿左右时可以实现零增长。第三步零增长后人口控制目标的选定，有两种意见：一种是保持替换水平生育率，总人口保持在略低于 16 亿水平；另一种是从我国自然资源、环境、经济和社会发展实际出发，确定适度人口目标，而具体目标的选定从七八亿至 10 多亿不等。我们以为，适度人口的研究是有益的，但不要忘记那是五六十年以后的事情，在此期间内的人口控制目标是不会有更大变动的，而且最终理想人口目标的实现也必须建立在达到零增长目标基础上。

生育政策的相对稳定。1980 年中共中央在正式出台提倡一对夫妇生育一个孩子之前，曾经召开多次由有关部门负责同志和部分专家学者参加的座谈会，对独生子女各种问题进行过多层次、多角度的讨论。这些问题，如人口老龄化、劳动力供给、社会赡养等在随即发表的中共中央致全体共产党员、共青团员的《公开信》中作了阐述，但关于一对夫妇生育一个孩子维持多长时间等，是关键的问题，需要明确。笔者在参与起草给中央的《关于座谈会情况的报告》文件中，本着认真负责的精神，以个人名义附上《目前我国存在的人口问题》、《关于一对夫妇只生一个孩子方案的建议》两个附件。后一个附件论证了提倡一对夫妇只生育一个孩子既非权宜之计，很短几年难以奏效，也非永久之计，时间过长就会造成诸多人口堆积问题，而是一定时期的一种特殊政策，这个"一定时期"定义为一代人，即 25 年左右。这样，一是可有效控制住人口的猛烈增长，控制住一代人的生育率，减少了下一代做父母的人口，自然再下一代及以后的生育可以受到有效控制。二是可使生育一个孩子带来的人口问题不至于过于严重，如人口老龄化可控制在一定限度，社会负担可以承受等。个别家庭可能出现老年、中年、少年"四二一结构"，整个社会则不会出现。15 年来的实践比较好地坚持了这一生育政策，既大力提倡一对夫妇只生育一个孩子，各地计划生育条例又都明文规定，双方均为独生子女结婚者可以生育两个孩子。近年来中央多次强调政策的稳定性，因为任何变动，无论是收紧还是放松的变动，都会在实践上导致生育率的升高。

人口控制基本方法的相对稳定。中国大力加强人口控制 20 多年来，积累了一套成功的做法和经验，诸如：领导重视，实行人口目标管理责任制；坚持宣传教育、经常性工作、避孕为主的"三为主"做法；提高干部素质，注重队伍建设；加强基层建设，提高服务水平；应用先进技术，开发生产高效、安全、便捷的药具等。在当前向市场经济体制过渡过程中，要随着情况的改变，最终过渡到以利益调节为主的管理机制目标；但在相当一段时间内，这些行政管理方法的有效性不容置疑，处于相对稳定状态。有一种观点认为，实行市场经济体制改革就应将人口生产和计划生育推向市场，实行同国外一样的"家庭计划"。这是值得商榷的。不说从计划经济体制向市场经济体制过渡需要较长时间，不具备可以接受人口生产的完全的市场，就所要建立的社会主义市场经济体制本质特征说来，也是不切实际的。前已述及，市场主体法人化是市场经济的首要特征，我们能否将其推演到人口生产，将生育子女数量多少，何时生育，生男生女都变成个人家庭的市场行为，完全由家庭自己决策，政府不能干预呢？显然不能。中国控制人口增长的顺利进行，固然有经济、文化、社会的发展进步作基础，但它既不同于西方发达国家由发展决定的生育率的自然而然的下降，也有别于某些发展中国家的"家庭计划"，而是由中国特殊国情决定，主要依靠行政手段实现的。如果我们放弃以行政手段为主的一套做法，由生产率下降与经济发展程度之间"时间差"造成的"反弹力"就会释放出来，重使生育率上升。要素流动市场化、宏观调控间接化等市场经济特征，也不能原封不动地搬到人口生产中来。除劳动力市场应当充分发展，并使之规范化外；人口生产尤其是影响生育控制的各种要素，如生育控制指标、使用 B 超进行胎儿性别鉴定等则不能搞市场化，还需要政府的直接宏观调控。

其二，微观人口控制的增强。在宏观人口控制目标、政策、方法处于相对稳定的情况下，微观人口控制至关重要，作用得到增强。

一般情况下，任何社会的宏观人口目标、政策的实施总要落实到人口再生产的基本单位微观家庭上来。迄今为止，家庭总是与社会生产力发展的一定阶段相联系，原始社会低下的生产力形成血缘家庭、普那路亚家庭，后期又产生对偶家庭；随着生产力的发展和私有制的出现，财产继承变得重要，一夫一妻制家庭才得以确立。家庭始终具有生育的功能；生儿育女是家庭的天职；具有经济的功能，是一个消费的单位，在一定条件下也是生产的单位；具有社会的功能，组织家庭成员履行公民的义务与权利。特殊地说，在中国走向市场经济和宏观人口控制处于相对稳定的条件下，家庭的功能、规模都发生了某些变动，在人口控制中的地位和作用显得更为重要。过去在自给自足的自然经济条件下，家庭生儿育女和生育子女数量无须耗神，接受自然生物规律支配，一切听其自然。在商品竞争和市场经济条件下，市场主体追逐的目标是效益最大化或利润最大化，因而才有建立在这一基础之上的孩子成本—效益理论。我们进行旨在建立市场经济体制的改革，随着劳动力市场的建立和完善，人们越来越意识到家庭对劳动力生产的投入和产出效应，将人口生产纳入市场经济视野。即人们在生育子女数量、生育间隔、性别构成、智力投资等进行估量，做出符合效益最大化的选择。而生命科学、医药科学的发展和技术手段的提高，为进行这种选择提供了可能。适应这种变化了的情况，人口控制重点向微观转移，体现在以下几个方面。

一是立足点的转移。20多年前中国大力控制人口增长主要立足于宏观，立足于宏观人口战略目标和政策的制定，然后层层贯彻下去，收到实效，是符合现实的。现在在市场经济条件下，宏观人口控制目标和政策的落实，从根本和最终意义上说来，还必须解决家庭微观方面存在的问题，完成生育观的转变。亦即将立足点转移到家庭微观和未来上。这里"立足点"是指人口控制工作建立在什么基点上，而不是指站在哪一点上观察人口问题。因此，提出人口控制立足点转移并不是不要站在宏观重微观，不要站在国家立场要求家庭实行计划生育，而是强调家庭微观作用的增强，将微观家庭作为工作的重点，通过微观保证宏观。

二是机制的转变。宏观人口控制建立的是以行政手段为主的调控机制，如前所述，现阶段还必须基本依靠这种机制。其中也有经济利益调节因素，如发给独生子女奖励费，征收一定的父母计划外生育费，以及在入托、入学、就业、住房等的倾斜政策。当前在走向市场经济改革中，受价值观念变动影响的人们生育观念的改变，利益取向明显增强，人口生育开始走向同物质生产一样的经济核算，尽管永远不能走到同样的核算上。适应这种变动的，是人口控制行政手段弱化的趋势和经济手段增强的趋势。适应这种趋势，人口控制机制要求增大利益调节分量，并且最终转移到以利益调节为主的轨道上来。

三是工作方式的转换。与立足点转移相适应，人口工作主要是计划生育工作方式也有一个转换问题，即以过去"灌输型"为主向以"服务型"为主的转换。过去在很大程度上是要求人们做什么和怎样做，无疑这种要求是必要的和合理的，现在要逐渐转换到主要是帮助人们做什么和怎样做，使之自觉自愿地达到规范化的要求目标。这种"服务型"工作方式内容很多，包括继续做好宣传教育服务，强调软件教育的科学性和针对性，结合《中国21世纪议程》宣传人口、资源、环境、经济、社会的可持续发展，紧密联系本地区、本部门进行宣传教育；包括开展避孕节育科学技术服务，研制高效、安全、简便避孕药具，普及避孕节育、优生优育、母婴保健知识，做好孕情检查、母婴保健工作，加强计划生育站（所、室）建设，使"面向基层，深入乡村，服务上门，方便群众"的方针得到更好的贯彻落实，包括推进生产、生活、生育三者结合起来，帮助群众勤劳致富的服务。"三结合"是群众的一大创造，它体现了将生育纳入以经济建设为中心的战略，实现向以利益调节为主的机制转变和实现可持续发展的深刻内涵，是改革的方向。它发源于吉林，辽宁、江苏、北京、四川、浙江、湖南等省市，也都创造了自己发展"三结合"的具体形式。其基本点在于在坚持自愿原则下，将独生子女和计划内生育子女户首先组织起来，通过提供信息、贷款、技术咨询、帮助开拓市场等办法，发展经济实体，促使计划内生育户走向富裕。由于"三结合"将生育同发展市场经济联姻，与走向勤劳致富结缘，显示了旺盛的生命力，着眼于这样的服务是根本性的服务。

二 西方微观人口经济学说

上述情况表明，中国改革开放以来人口增长的有效控制和经济的超高速增长，正将人口与经济的发展推向新的阶段，面临历史转变的阶段。即一方面完成高生育率向低生育率转变的人口革命，另一方面使国民经济保持持续、快速、健康发展，实现"三步走"战略目标，实现人口、经济、社会的可持续发展。这就需要对人口与经济、社会发展之间的关系作出深入的研究，特别是微观人口经济方面的研究。

（一）人口与经济关系研究概说

自 1662 年伦敦人约翰·格兰特（John Grant）依据当时教会结婚、洗礼、死亡等登记发表的《关于死亡的自然的和政治的观察》一书，首次通过死亡表对死亡现象作出有规律性分析，使人口学成为一门独立的学科以来，其后一二百年内原本意义上的人口学却进展不大，而从经济学、社会学角度对人口学进行的研究，尤其是人口经济学研究却取得了突破性进展。英国古典政治经济学优秀代表之一威廉·配第（William Petty，1623～1687）在《赋税论》、《政治算术》等著作中，曾将人口因素作为引起经济变动的内在变量加以分析，企图说明二者之间的关系。庸俗经济学家托马斯·马尔萨斯（Thomas Robert Malthus，1766～1834）于 1798 年发表轰动一时的《人口原理》，提出人口在食物供给不受妨碍时以几何级数增加，生活资料受土地效益递减规律作用呈算术级数增加，总人口具有一种超乎为其准备的生活资料而不断地、永恒增长的趋势。但他作为牧师反对避孕节育，主张通过饥饿、贫困、战争、瘟疫等"积极抑制"，禁欲、无力赡养者推迟结婚等"道德抑制"限制人口增长。《人口原理》接连出了 6 版，可见当时反响之大。波莱士·弗朗西斯（Place Francis，1771～1854）等继承马尔萨斯人口论基本观点，但主张用避孕节育限制人口增长，被称为新马尔萨斯主义。不过，在人口与经济关系基本方面，新老马尔萨斯主义之间并无本质的不同。

马克思和恩格斯在完成唯物史观和剩余价值学说两大革命过程中，对人口与经济之间的关系作许多精彩的论述。指出："任何人类历史的第一个前提无疑是有生命的个人的存在"；[1]"历史中的决定性因素，归根结底是直接生活资料的生产和再生产。但是生产本身又有两种。一方面是生活资料即食物、衣服、住房以及为此所必需的工具的生产；另一方面是人类自身的生产，即种的繁衍"[2] 马克思原本计划写一部人口学专著，但未来得及动笔便与世长辞了。然而在《资本论》中，他还是长篇论述了资本主义社会中的人口问题，阐述了资本主义相对人口过剩的规律。

当代西方人口经济学说中，影响较大的主要有：现代马尔萨斯主义。即

---

① 《马克思恩格斯文选》第 1 卷，人民出版社，1972，第 24 页。

② 《马克思恩格斯文选》第 4 卷，人民出版社，1972，第 2 页。

运用系统动力学等方法,将人口与资源、环境、发展放到一起分析,认为经济增长面临"人口爆炸"的威胁。以埃里兹(P. R. Ehrlich)的《人口爆炸》(1968),泰勒(G. Taylor)的《世界末日》(1970),麦多斯(D. L. Meadows)等人的《增长极限》(1972)为代表。由于这些论著将人口过剩后果描绘得相当恐怖,前途渺茫,又称为人口悲观派理论。

适度人口理论。这一理论最早由瑞典经济学家威克塞尔(J. G. Wicksell,1851~1926)提出,而由英国经济学家坎南(Edwin Cannan)在《财富论》(1914)一书中作了明确阐述。他论证了使工农业生产获得最大收益点的人口,即为理想的适度人口。20世纪二三十年代适度人口研究曾经风靡西方,如法国人口学家索维(Aldred Sauvy)发表的《人口通论》(1952),将适度人口概念推演到包括财富的增加、个人福利程度、就业、健康、寿命、文化等多个领域,提出不同的适度人口分析模型。西蒙(J. L. Simon)、柯尔(A. J. come)等人关于适度人口理论模型的创立,使研究大大地推进了一步。

人口转变理论。法国的兰德里(A. Landry,1874~1956)研究人口与经济发展之间的关系,提出人口变动经历原始、中期和现代三个阶段,并将这种转变称之为"人口革命"。美国的汤普森(Warren Thompson,1887~1973)将世界分成经济和人口发展的三种不同类型,阐述人口转变的内在原因。不过对人口转变作出比较全面论述的,还是诺特斯坦(F. W. Notestein,1902~1983),他在《人口变动的经济问题》等论著中,创立了人口转变的理论模型,成为比较完整的学说。

人口增长经济理论。英国经济学家凯恩斯(J. M. Kegnes,1883~1946)分析资本需求取决于人口、生活水平和资本技术三因素,人口增长率下降会导致资本有效需求不足和经济危机。美国经济学家汉森(A. H. Hansen,1887~1975)等人,将经济的停滞归为人口增长的停滞,人口和劳动力的变动成为决定经济增长的直接因素。

此外,发展经济学家刘易斯(W. A. Lewis)等人,以及库兹涅茨(S. Kuznets)、舒尔兹(T. W. Schuty)等,都十分重视人口变动对经济成长的影响,然而上述研究中,人口与经济发展的宏观研究居多,微观相对不足。有的研究,如马尔萨斯人口论、适度人口论,主要限于宏观;有的研究,主要立足宏观,如人口转变理论和人口增长理论;有的同时涉及宏观和微观,如库兹涅茨、舒尔兹等的研究。可以这样划分,20世纪50年代以前关于人口与经济发展之间关系的研究，主要在宏观方面，微观方面有限，而在 50 年代以后，人口与经济发展微观方面的研究，才得到突破性进展。

（二）当代西方微观人口经济理论

人口转变理论已将生育率变动同社会经济发展联系起来，这对后来生育率的微观分析产生了重要影响，不过对生育率微观分析成为体系并提出孩子成本—效益学说的，当首推莱宾斯坦（H. Leibensten，1922～）教授。他在 20 世纪 50 年代发表的《经济——人口发展理论》、《经济落后与经济增长》，70 年代发表的《超经济人》、《超经济人：经济学、政治学和人口问题》等论著，奠定了其基本的理论框架。可表述如下。

家庭规模的确定由父母对生育子女的选择完成，而对子女生育与否的选择取决于孩子的预期成本与效益。孩子成本可分成两部分：直接成本，即从母亲怀孕到抚养成长到生活自立所花费的衣、食、住、行、医疗、教育、婚姻等的费用，亦即花费在孩子身上的直接的货币支出；间接成本，即母亲因怀孕、妊娠和哺乳期间损失的工资，父母因照看孩子耗时而丧失受教育、获取更有利工作岗位、升迁而减少的收入，亦即因抚养时间而失去的带来收入的机会，因而又称机会成本，是一种间接的货币支出。

显然，家庭和父母想要生育某个孩子付出一定成本必不可免，但这绝不能构成生育动机，生育的动机在于取得预期的效益。莱宾斯坦从以下 6 个方面说明孩子提供的效益。

一为劳动—经济效益。孩子成长为劳动力之后，可为家庭提供劳动，或者从事一定的职业劳动为家庭直接提供经济收入。

二为养老—保险效益。在经济不够发达的国家，由于社会保险事业不发达，老年经济保险和生活服务不得不在颇大程度上依赖子女，子女天然具有老年保险潜在功能。

三为消费—享乐效益。孩子作为"消费品"，具有满足父母感情和精神上需要的作用，可以带来"天伦之乐"。

四为承担家业兴衰的风险效益。孩子不仅一般地具有劳动—经济效益，而且该预期效益大小同未来家庭经济风险相连，预期效益越大承担风险能力也越大，反之亦然。

五为维系家庭地位的效益。包括继承父母遗产，长期将家庭地位维持下去，也包括承担家庭和社会的义务，使家庭在这类活动中占有应有的地位。

六为壮大家庭作贡献的效益。大多数发展中国家父母希望家庭的繁荣昌盛，生儿育女"多子多福"，而且人丁兴旺家庭安全有保障，孩子对家庭有一种扩展效应。

莱宾斯坦指出，孩子的成本同收入呈正相关关系，直接成本随着收入增加而上升十分明显，间接或机会成本也因时间的价值增值而上升。孩子的效益呢？除消费—享乐效益变动不明朗外，随着经济的发展和家庭收入的增加，技术的不断进步，孩子质量特别是受教育程度的提高远比数量的增多会带来更多的追加收入，孩子的劳动—经济效益减弱下来。同时由于经济的发展和收入的增加，社会和家庭储蓄的增大，社会能够举办包括老年保险在内的更多的福利事业，建立起比较完备的老年社会保险体系；劳动者也有条件在进入老龄之间积蓄一笔资金进行老年保险；在实践中这种社会的和家庭的保险往往结合起来，形成强有力的老年保险制度，使孩子的养老—保险效益呈江河日下之势。其他继承家业兴衰的风险效益，维系家庭地位的效益和为壮大家庭作出贡献的效益等，也都程度不同地呈下降的趋势。

莱宾斯坦还考察了家庭类型中核心家庭的比例上升、人口城市化、死亡率下降、妇女受教育程度的提高、父母对男孩子性别偏好的减退、传统观念的淡化、各种避孕药具的推广使用等社会因素在生育率下降中的作用，但他认为主要的还是经济因素的作用。他依据每户的平均收入划成不同层次的社会经济群体，从总体上观察，发展中国家正由农业型向工业型转变，孩子的直接成本和间接成本随着这种转变而上升，除孩子消费—享乐效益外，其他效益随这种转变而下降，尤其是养老—保险效益和劳动—经济效益。

贝克尔（Gary S. Becker）发展了孩子的成本—效益理论，建立起孩子数量与孩子质量的相互替代理论。贝克尔就读于美国普林斯顿大学，后在芝加哥大学获经济学博士学位，并长期任教，与著名经济学家弗里德曼、舒尔茨等一起构成颇有影响的芝加哥学派。他应用经济学理论和方法研究人口问题，成为独具一格的人力资本专家。20世纪60年代初发表《生育率的经济分析》、《人力资本》等著作，80年代以来又发表了《家庭论》等论著，阐述了他对生育率经济分析的系统理论。他将家庭劳动力置于市场之中，运用消费需求理论阐述家庭生育决策，作出创造性研究。

贝克尔的孩子数量与孩子质量替代理论和替代模型，建立在消费需求理论基础之上。为此，他将消费需求中的无差异曲线论、商品互补和替代理论、消费者均衡理论等分析方法引入，探讨了家庭对孩子的需求，提出孩子净成本概念，论证了孩子效用的最大化，创立了孩子数量与质量替代的理论。他认为，孩子净成本等于家庭为某孩子预期支付的直接成本加上父母时间的间接成本（通过影子价格），减去孩子提供的预期收入现值和劳务的现值。贝克尔以18岁作为抚养和孩子走向社会的分界年龄，在此期间为支付孩子成本期，以后则为孩子提供效益期。当然，这个年龄的确不是绝对的，因不同国度和同一国度的不同时期、地域有所不同，贝克尔指出，若孩子的净成本为正值，说明孩子对家庭父母提供的效益不足以补偿付出的成本，这样的孩子对父母说来只相当于一般的耐用消费品，父母从孩子那里取得的是心理上的效益。若孩子的净成本为负值，说明孩子对家庭父母能够提供追加的大于成本的效益，这样的孩子对父母说来相当于耐用生产品，能够带来价值增值。

论证孩子效用最大化和孩子数量与质量替代的理论，是贝克尔的一大贡献。莱宾斯坦侧重考察了孩子特别是边际孩子的效用，贝克尔则进一步研究了孩子效用最大化问题。他阐述孩子的价格效应：孩子相对价格上升，对孩子数量需求减少；孩子相对价格下降，则对孩子数量需求增加。随着经济的发展和人均收入的增加，劳动力特别是女性劳动力的市场工资率明显上升了，而非市场活动时间的影子价格可近似地等同于市场工资率，因而使得孩子相对价格上升，而随着农业现代化的推进，乡村儿童就学时间延长，一方面增加了孩子成本，另一方面减少了孩子提供效益的时间，也直接导致孩子相对价格的上升。尽管孩子作为耐用消费品在家庭收入增加时，用在孩子身上的数量成本和质量成本都有可能增加，但是由于数量弹性小于质量弹性，人们的选择偏好更倾向于孩子质量，发生以高质量取代多数量的替代关系。而使这种替代成为现实的决定性因素，是避孕技术的引入，人们按照自己的志愿进行生育成为可能。不仅如此，在家庭收入一定的条件下，孩子数量与质量还是一种负相关关系。家庭为了追逐效用最大化，自然选择以增加孩子质量成本替代数量成本的道路，因而才有随着经济发展和收入增加而来的生育率的大幅度下降。

莱宾斯坦和贝克尔等主要从家庭对孩子的需求角度，运用成本—效益理论，阐述人们的生育行为和生育子女的数量。美国南加州大学伊斯特林（R. A. Easterline）教授在这样的分析基础上，加进孩子的供给变量，发展成为生育率的供给—需求理论。伊斯特林关于孩子需求量的定义没有什么特殊之处，即不考虑其他变量的影响及父母期望的存活子女数。关于孩子的供给变量，是指不受外来因素影响条件下生育子女数决定于父母的自然生育率和子女的存活率。关于生育控制的成本变量，包括因采用控制手段而付出的经济成本，同时包括因采取节育措施克服精神障碍而付出的心理成本。在不考虑生育控制成本的情况下，若孩子的供给小于对孩子的需求，如农业社会那样，不发生生育控制的要求，若孩子的供给大于对孩子的需求，便发生生育控制的要求。有了控制生育的要求，伊斯特林指出生育控制成本的影响是一个值得重视的变量。他认为，发达国家生育控制成本已趋于零，而婴儿和儿童死亡率大大下降后，亦即由于子女存活率的提高而加大了孩子的供给，使节育普及，生育率保持相当低的水平。相反，发展中国家生育控制成本一般相对较高，婴儿和儿童死亡率也较高，亦即由于子女存活率相对较低而减少了孩子的供给，节育的普及程度要差一些，生育率常常居高不下，尤其是经济和文化发展水平很低的国家和地区。

澳大利亚人口学家考德威尔（J. C. Caldwell）教授在吸取上述孩子成本—效益学说基础上，通过考察不同类型社会父母与子女间财富的流向和流量，提出"代际财富流"理论。考德威尔所说的财富不仅包括货币和财产，而且包括提供劳动和服务，这在代际之间是不可忽视的。为了说明问题的实质，考德威尔提出净财富流概念，即父母与子女之间财富净流向和流量。分析表明，在工业化以前的传统社会，净财富流主要是由子女流向父母；在工业化以来的现代社会，由于父母选择增加对子女教育投资作为增加子女向父母财富流的手段，选择偏好由追求孩子的数量转向追求孩子的质量导致生育率下降。

伊斯特林和考德威尔向前发展了莱宾斯坦和贝克尔的孩子成本—效益理论。有人认为伊斯特林否定了贝克尔的观点，其实并不然，无论伊斯特林还是考德威尔，尽管他们说明问题所站角度不同，纳入视野范畴宽窄有别，得出的结论自然呈现某种差异，但其基本的理论框架都离不开生产某边际孩子所花费的成本，孩子对家庭父母提供的各种效益，以及这种孩子的成本—效益如何随着家庭收入的提高，技术进步和社会发展而变动，即家庭规模和生育率如何受到收入效应、价格效应、替代效应的制约。所以，可以将我们的生育率理论归结到孩子成本—效益这一中心点上，从这一点出发寻求可借鉴之处。

三　中国家庭经济、孩子成本效益与生育研究

（一）理论的借鉴与局限

自从人类诞生以来，人们的生育行为和生育子女数量多少由什么因素决

定，一直困扰着许多为此付出辛勤探索的志士仁人。中国是一个有着悠久历史传统和人口众多的国家，从孔夫子到孙中山孜孜不倦的探求者自然不乏其人，但将人口视为经济的自然力和基本国力的传统观点，对上策动着历代当政者的人口观和有关政策行为，对下则影响着民众的生育意愿。一个 15 ~ 49 岁育龄妇女共 408 个月，如果包括怀孕和哺乳期在内生育两个孩子间隔 37 个月，一生可生育 11 个孩子；如果间隔 45 个月，可生育 9 个孩子，等等。这种情况今天似乎已不存在，但中国 1987 年 60 岁以上老年人口抽样调查表明，女性老年人口中终生只生育 1 个孩子的占 5.4%，2 个孩子的占 6.9%……7 个孩子的占 11.3%，8 个孩子以上的占 25.8%，8 个孩子以上所占比例最高，足见数十年前自然生物规律是如何支配人们的生育行为和生育子女的数量的。然而由于经济的发展，科学和技术的进步，人们生育观念的改变，人类终于挣脱了生育行为完全由生物规律支配的羁绊，进入自己可以调节生育数量的时代。这时并且只有在这时，探讨影响家庭生育子女数量的决定性因素才有现实意义。中国尽管从孔子开始的众民主义一直居统治地位，但同时也存在从韩非至清朝洪亮吉的人口节制主义。以洪亮吉（1746 ~ 1809）而论，大体处于同马尔萨斯同一时代且早生 20 年，在他所著的《意言》中"治平"和"生计"两篇，提出"为农者十倍于前而田不加增，为商贾者十倍于前而货不加增"的观点，与马尔萨斯人口超过生活资料增长规律不谋而合，有异曲同工之妙。近代以来的人口思想，特别是 20 世纪二三十年代陈长蘅、陈达、潘光旦等人的一批人口论著的发表，将马尔萨斯人口论、适度人口论等西方观点介绍进来，推动了人口学的发展。1949 年新中国成立后，50 年代中后期曾有一段人口研究活跃时期，特别是 1957 年马寅初先生《新人口论》发表前后，然而那时关于中国人口问题的论著也主要侧重人口与国民经济发展、社会进步、生活水平提高、教育事业的发展方面的分析，即主要是人口与发展的宏观方面的分析。而且即使是这样的分析，也为 20 世纪 50 年代末的"大批判"所扼杀，直至 70 年代特别是粉碎"四人帮"后才真正冲出"禁区"。应当说，20 多年来中国的人口科学有了突飞猛进的发展，在人口的规模、分布、结构、特征、发展等取得全面进步，理论与实践相结合研究取得突出成绩。不过除人口理论方面的研究外，在实证研究中，宏观的研究占据绝对优势，微观的研究特别是家庭经济与生育的研究很少。而在走向社会主义市场经济体制改革过程中，在强调要继续控制人口增长和人口控制机制转变过程中，显然这种微观研究占据突出的重要位置。因此，尽管上述西方微观人口经济和孩子成本—效益理论有不少缺陷，这在下面将有点评，但是这些理论的一个共同点，是将人们的生育同家庭经济联系起来，阐述了生育率怎样随着家庭经济的变动而改变，二者之间的相互作用和影响，可用量化指标表示的相关关系，则是一种带有普遍性规律的总结，无论对于正在形成的人口经济学学科建设还是现实人口控制的实证研究，有着带根本性的可借鉴意义。并且，上述诸人口经济研究的分析方法，包括研究微观家庭经济与生育、孩子成本与效益的各种相关因素的确定，相关程度的计量，理论假说和理论模型的构造，静态与动态研究的关系等方法论，也是值得研究和借鉴的。

当然，微观家庭经济与生育理论，尤其是孩子成本效益理论也有缺陷。一是这方面的理论不同程度地忽视了经济和人口状况不同国家和地区之间的差异，使其不能"放之四海而皆准"。不同国家间的一些调查表明，就某个国家或地区说来，调查结果可以由该理论得到说明，颇为得当，若将不同情况的国家或地区合并到一起，往往很难得出较清晰的概念，不能完全套上这一理论。二是这一理论没有或很少涉及社会干预，特别是各国政府奉行的人口和生育政策的影响。这在当今世界人口激增和许多国家加大人口生育政策调节力度的情况下，大有乏力之感，需要加以补充和发展。正是由于这两点，西方孩子成本—效益理论既有可供我们借鉴之处，也不能照抄照搬，而要结合我国实际，作出创造性的研究。

（二）开展调查与研究

为了探索改革开放新形势下对人口生产的影响，主要是家庭经济变动对生育的影响，给人口控制开辟新思路；同时也为了在通过研究和吸收西方孩子成本—效益理论合理成分的基础上，建立和发展具有我们自己特点的微观人口经济理论，根据中国政府和联合国人口活动基金达成的 CPR/90/P06 协议，选择了"中国家庭经济与生育研究"课题，并列入中国社会科学院"八五"重点项目。该项目由中国社会科学院人口研究所牵头组织，协调河北省社会科学院人口研究中心、辽宁省计划生育委员会、上海市社会科学院人口发展研究所、杭州大学人口研究所、山东省社会科学院人口研究所、江西省社会科学院人口研究室、广东省社会科学院人口研究所和省统计局城市抽样调查队、陕西省社会科学院人口研究所、四川省社会科学院人口研究室、贵州省社会科学院经济研究所 10 个单位共同完成。本次抽样调查总体排除内蒙古、新疆、西藏、青海、海南 5 个省和自治区，因为它们对于推论全国缺少代表性。其余 25 个省、自治区、直辖市按照人均国民收入、农业人均收入、城市人均收入、农村人均消费、城市人口比例、总生育率（TFR）、妇女识字率 7 项指标聚合成五类，并按随机抽样原则每一类抽选 2 个省或市，抽中发达类上海、辽宁，次发达类广东、浙江，一般发达类山东、吉林，较不发达类四川、陕西，不发达类江西、贵州。由于吉林不能参加调查，改为同类中水平接近的河北。然后在 10 个样本省市内用 πPS 方法各抽取 2 市、2 发达县、2 不发达县，并按随机抽样原则在 4 个县政府所在地抽取 2 个镇。样本分配：每个省市 1400 户，其中市 500 户，镇 300 户，发达县 300 户，不发达县 300 户。并设计了二相调查补充调查户，既保证随机抽样原则，又保证了调查问卷回收率。在培训调查员等方面也高度重视，尽量减少非抽样误差。最后验证精确度较高，推论全国的精确度为 98%，省市一级在 92% 左右（详见本书第六部分：抽样调查方案及评估）。

抽样调查完成后，对数据资料进行了录入和电子计算机汇总，出版《中国 1992 年家庭经济与生育 10 省市抽样调查资料》。本课题与美国南加州大学人口研究室开展合作研究，举办多期讲习研讨班，1993 年召开有中、美、瑞、波等国 50 多名学者参加的"中国家庭经济与生育国际学术研讨会"。在此基础上，由课题主持人牵头，课题组骨干承担写作，出版本专著。其结构框架如下。

绪论，通过对中国城乡经济体制改革的概述，说明在走向市场经济过程中，家庭经济的地位和作用突出出来，必然对人们的生育行为产生比较强烈的影响。在这方面，西方微观人口经济研究已取得相当成果，孩子成本—效益理论为我们提供借鉴的合理成分，同时也有其一定的局限性，亦不能照搬过来。需要结合中国实际，尤其是对改革开放深入发展实际进行调查研究，在理论与实践相结合中，探索解决中国人口控制的新的思路，发展具有我们自己特点的微观人口经济理论。

第一部分，孩子成本。在合理吸收西方理论的基础上，划分孩子的直接与间接、数量与质量等成本，依据 10 省市抽样调查资料，对孩子成本构成作出多层次分析。通过对孩子期望成本不同的家庭收入，不同年龄和性别的分析，看出发展趋势；对孩子数量成本与质量成本的理论与实证模型分析，揭示目前在完成由投入孩子数量成本向质量成本转移的情况、条件、问题，并提出改革建议。

第二部分，孩子效益。通过对中国 1992 年家庭经济与生育 10 省市抽样调查资料分析，说明当前中国孩子提供家庭的效益状况，经济、养老、精神等效益的构成，探讨孩子总效益，以及不同性别、年龄、职业、文化等孩子效益的差别。同时借鉴西方"财富流"理论，说明家庭父母与子女经济关系的实质、生育的动机，寻求改革的途径。

第三部分，孩子的价值。这部分力图在评介国内外关于孩子价值研究成果基础上，依据 10 省市抽样调查资料的比较分析，运用市场分析方法，作者探讨了期望孩子交易价格的形成及其形式，提出人口控制机制转变的利益导向思路。

第四部分，生育意愿。这一部分从生育意愿概念的内涵和外延，到影响生育意愿的人口经济、社会条件的分析，意在找出影响人们生育意愿的本质的原因，提出转变人们生育观念的重要性及加快转变的建议。

第五部分，中国家庭经济与生育研究抽样调查方案及其评估。本书应用的主要数据资料，来自 1992 年 10 省市的抽样调查，因而有必要对该抽样调查的方案设计、抽样原则和方法、代表性与精确度等作出阐述和论证。本书将这些单列出来，也便于有志于这项研究的同志一起讨论，求得研究的深化。

参考文献

[1] 《坚持改革、开放、搞活——十一届三中全会以来有关重要文献摘编》，人民出版社，1987。

[2] 《邓小平文选》第 3 卷，人民出版社，1993。

[3] 卢希悦、刘能坚主编《社会主义市场经济理论》，中国财政经济出版社，1994。

[4] 宋健主编《现代科学技术基础知识》，科学出版社、中共中央党校出版社，1994。

[5] 刘国光、汝信主编《有中国特色的社会主义》，中国社会科学出版社，1993。

[6] 《田雪原文集》，中国经济出版社，1991；《田雪原文集》（二），中国经济出版社，1995。

[7] 李竟能主编《当代西方人口学论》，山西人民出版社，1992。

[8] 彭松建编著《西方人口经济学概论》，北京大学出版社，1987。

[9] H. Leibenstein, *A Theory of Economic Demographic Development*, Princeton University Press, 1954, U. S. A.

[10] G. S. Becker, *An Economic Analysis of Fertility*, Princeton University Press, 1960, U. S. A.

《人口革命论》序[*]

对于世界人口变动和发展来说，20 世纪末 21 世纪初是一段引人注目的历史时期。1999 年联合国宣布了两项信息和决定：10 月 12 日世界人口达到 60 亿，还象征性地认定第 60 亿个婴儿的诞生；同时确定这一年为国际老年人年，提出"建立不分年龄人人共享的社会"主题。这两件人口大事似乎有一些矛盾，然而又不容置疑地联系到一起，表明一个人口革命时代的来临。这一年 10 月初，新闻媒体就世界 60 亿人口日采访了本人。为了便于理解和记忆，本人将中国的属相与世界人口增长联系起来说明：60 亿人口的 1999 年是兔年，50 亿人口的 1987 年也是兔年，40 亿人口的 1975 年还是兔年，表明最近增加两个 10 亿人口的时间均间隔 12 年；30 亿人口日是 1960 年，为鼠年，间隔 15 年；20 亿人口日是 1930 年，当为马年，间隔 30 年；而世界人口首次达到 10 亿的时间，大致为 1830 年，间隔 100 年。呈加速度运动高速开来的"人口列车"的轨迹清晰可见。不过"1999 国际老年人年"信号的发出并将持续闪亮，标志着这列"人口列车"在达到最高时速后开始减速，人口正在经历开天辟地以来的最深刻的革命。

"人口革命"在联合国编著的人口学词典中名不见经传，该词典有"人口转变"（Population Transition 或 Demographic Transition）和"生命革命"（Vital Revolution）二词。前者指人口再生产由高出生、高死亡、低增长向着高出生、低死亡、高增长，再向着低出生、低死亡、低增长的转变；后者进一步将人口转变与工业化、城市化联系起来，同社会经济进步结合起来分析。该词典 1982 年在比利时列日市奥迪纳出版社出版（Ordina editions, Liege，Belgium），当时生育率、人口增长率都比现在高，人口列车正处于全速行驶当中。如今，虽然这列满载 60 多亿的人口列车还在高速前进，但是

———————————
* 本文发表于 2002 年。

速度已经减慢下来，情况有所不同。更为重要的是，一个时期以来特别是20世纪80年代末90年代初以来，一系列可持续发展战略会议宣言、报告、公约、行动计划、行动纲领等的颁布，传统的以国内生产总值GDP为唯一目标的发展观被扬弃，以人为本的可持续发展观被普遍认同，全方位适度人口论、稀缺资源论、生态系统论、总体经济效益论、社会协调发展论的提出，理论体系比较完整的论证和阐发，使人们进一步认识和摆正了人类在自然界的位置，可持续发展作为各国承诺的一项国际协议确定下来。就中国而论，自20世纪70年代国家大力提倡计划生育，切实控制人口增长以来，生育率长期持续下降，人口再生产开始由高、低、高转变到低、低、低类型，进入低生育水平国家行列。尽管对于中国的生育率下降极少数人还有异议，但是世界上绝大多数人越来越看清楚，中国生育率的下降和出生人数的减少，在世界生育率和生育水平的降低中起到了莫大的作用，得到越来越多人的理解和称赞。仅将近30年中国出生率的下降和出生人数的减少，便将世界50亿人口日向后推迟了2年，60亿人口日向后推迟了3年。而在可持续发展方面，中国更是第一个履行1992年巴西里约热内卢国际环发大会承诺，制定《中国21世纪议程——中国21世纪人口、环境与发展白皮书》的国家，起到了率先垂范的作用。我们惊奇地看到，进入20世纪90年代以来，世界人口出生率逐步走低，出生人数也有所减少，更多的国家选择了旨在降低生育水平的家庭计划，特别是发展中国家。可持续发展战略在全球强有力地推出并且越来越深入人心，人口问题的解决最终纳入了可持续发展视野，标志着从根本上解决人口问题的"人口革命"时代的来临。

正是在这种背景下，周广庆博士的《人口革命》一书的推出使人们耳目一新。他写道："一场革命，一场静悄悄的、没有刀光剑影、没有隆隆炮声，只是减少了婴儿坠地呱呱哭声的人口革命，正在全世界以各种形式展开。"该书是作者积7年艰难探索之成果，尤其是从中国传统的分家制度特殊视角潜心探索的成果。该书从自定义"人口革命"内涵出发，分析了分家制度的人口、经济影响，如何使古代农民家庭生产规模最小化、生产效率最低化，土地买卖和兼并在"怪圈"中循环；从人与自然、人与人之间关系分析中，得出"工业革命使人类异化为自然之敌，人口革命使人类归化为自然之友"；从养老保障考察中，提出"养老革命"新概念，主张建立集子女养老、自我养老、集体养老于一体的"老人公社"等，无不闪烁着作者创造性的独立思维，具有难能可贵的创新精神。正是这种精神，使我乐于为之作序。我这样说并不意味着该书观点完全正确，我们也不能要求一本书所有观点都那么正确，尤其对青年学者，而是要倡导一种精神，一种认真积累资料、潜心研究，经过长期思考认认真真做学问的一种精神。中国是当今世界人口最多的国家，具有研究人口以及与人口相关问题的生动舞台，难道我们的年轻学者不应该作出富有创造性的研究吗？！

《中国民族人口》绪论[*]

中国是当今世界人口最多的国家，也是民族最多的国家之一。在历史走到 20 世纪即将结束和 21 世纪行将来临之际，全国社科基金设立民族人口研究项目，意在对 56 个民族人口的来龙去脉、现状特点、未来走势等分别作出研究，留下历史民族人口的记录，无疑是一件十分有意义的事情。同时也是一件十分艰巨的事情：一想到世居在青藏高原的藏族、门巴族、珞巴族，接受这项任务就犹如举步维艰地在攀登喜马拉雅山；一想到世居在福建省和台湾省的高山族、海南岛的黎族，又仿佛置身于无垠大海的一只船，在同风流搏击中艰难地行进。好在中国有句古训，叫做"知难而进"，正是因为困难，搏击和奋斗才有意义。更重要的是有领导和众多同行的支持，完成也是有希望的。如今《中国民族人口》（一），包括满族、蒙古族、朝鲜族、锡伯族、达斡尔族、鄂温克族、鄂伦春族、赫哲族人口即将付印，第一缕希望之光即将变成现实，随之而来的全部完成的希望之光也依稀可见，因而也就有了更大的希望。

"民族"一般指不同历史发展阶段形成的，各种人的共同体；特指具有共同地域、共同语言、共同文化并以相近经济生活方式为基础的人的群体。"民族"由"民"与"族"合成。"民"即人民、大众之意；"族"则有一个历史的演进过程。据考证，"族"字早在殷商的甲骨文中就曾出现过，古代通"镞"，即箭头。后在"矢"、"丛集"之意上推演引申，赋予聚众、群众、聚集意义，表达有某种血缘关系的人的群体，形成亲族、家庭、氏族、王族、宗族等概念。显然，这里的"族"不是民族的概念，古代的民族直称羌、狄、夏、番、匈奴、女真等，均不加"族"；如加则加"人"或"民"。直到 19 世纪晚些时候，"民族"一词才开始出现，但意义并不确切，

---

* 本文发表于 2003 年。

常同"种族"、"人种"等概念交织在一起。进入 20 世纪后，"民族"含义逐渐清晰起来，应用也多了起来；不过仍与"民"、"人"混用，既称某某族，也称某某民、某某人。后来由于"民族"一词的高频率使用和广泛地应用，意义的进一步明确，一提"族"很自然地想到"民族"。但是作为具有某种相同属性的事物一大类总体的"族"，有着更为宽泛的含义，如"水族"、"芳香族"，"上班族"、"追星族"……"族"只有同具有共同语言、共同文化并以相近生活方式为基础的人口和人种联系起来形成的人群，才称得上我们所说的民族。中国 56 个民族作为一个整体，从历史的长河中走来，与世界其他民族比较，在数量、素质、结构变动中具有自己的某些特点，制约着经济、文化、社会的发展。因而研究民族人口，对于推进民族经济和社会的发展，实现"三步走"发展战略目标，有着现实的重要意义。

一 "提前起飞"与提前进入低生育水平

中国是世界文明古国之一，现在发现的人类化石可追溯到距今 210 万年以前。在漫长的历史长河中，中国人口同世界人口相似，长期处于高出生、高死亡、低增长状态。没有文字记载的时代无从考证，有文字记载以来，有关历史文献表明：夏朝（约公元前 2100 ~ 前 1600 年），全国人口约 1355 万人；西周（约公元前 1100 ~ 前 771 年）增至 1372 万人；春秋（约公元前 770 ~ 前 476 年）减至 1185 万人；秦统一中国期间（公元前 221 ~ 前 207 年），人口在 2000 万人左右。其后，随着朝代的更替，人口呈现波浪起伏式增减变动，一般是一个封建王朝初期，往往实行休养生息政策，人口明显增加；到了后期土地兼并严重，农民与地主阶级矛盾加剧，战乱和饥荒不断，人口又有所减少。到了明代，农业、手工业和商业得到较快发展，人口开始稳步攀增，不过增长最快的是清代。清乾隆六年（公元 1741 年），人口总数达到 14341 万人，揭开了中国人口史上新的一页。乾隆二十七年（公元 1762 年）增加到 20047 万人，乾隆五十五年（公元 1790 年）增加到 30148 万人，而到道光二十年（公元 1840 年），已增加到 41281 万人①。中国人口在 18 世纪 30 年代增加到 1 亿人，在其后的 100 多年里接连翻了两番，于 19 世纪 30 年代末 40 年代初超过 4 亿人，形成"乾隆盛世"前后空前巨大的人口

---

① 参见赵文琳、谢淑君《中国人口史》，人民出版社，1988；刘洪康主编、吴忠观副主编《人口手册》，西南财经大学出版社，1988。

增长，人口的平均增长速度达到 1.00% 左右。而在大致相同的时期，世界人口由 1750 年的 77000 万人增加到 1850 年的 124000 万人，年平均增长速度仅为 0.48%；1850～1950 年增长速度有所提高，达到 0.70%；只有 1950～1960 年的世界人口增长速度始提高到 1.03%[①]，同上述中国人口增长速度相仿。就是说，中国在 18 世纪下半叶和 19 世纪上半叶，创造了世界 20 世纪前 60 年的人口增长速度，比世界人口"提前起飞"一个半世纪，从而奠定了中国人口众多的基础。

对于中国人口在清朝"提前起飞"现象，可从封建王朝有关政策的改变和社会经济基础的改变两个方面加以说明。在有关政策方面，历史上自征收人丁税役起，人们为了逃避赋税和徭役，每每少报人丁，致使长期无法获得真实的人口数字，文字记载的数据距实际要偏低许多。清朝统一中国后，康熙于 1712 年（康熙五十一年）下令免除了按人头征赋税制度[②]，户口人数统计彻底摆脱缠绕，使人口统计数字大大接近了；同时"摊丁入亩"税制的实施，增人不增税也刺激了人口的增长。在社会经济基础方面，经过明末清初的战乱，国家进入相对平稳发展时期，居民安居乐业，有利于人口增加；水稻种植的大面积推广和产量的增加，满足了人口增长对食物扩大的需求；医学主要是中医获得很大发展，虽然尚不能有效防治严重传染疾病的发生和蔓延，但是治疗水平有较大提高，降低了人口死亡率。显然，这一时期中国人口"提前起飞"的原因同欧美工业革命后的人口增长有着天壤之别，中国的人口增长不是伴随工业化和城市化而起，相反是在自然经济占统治地位情况下发生的，是有别于工业化国家人口增长的一种东方特例。

1840 年鸦片战争以后，中国一步步沦为半殖民地半封建社会，民族压迫、阶级压迫双重袭来，军阀混战不断，人口数量变动陷入徘徊状态，至 1949 年人口年平均增长率仅为 0.25%。但是由于人口基数已经相当庞大，致使全国人口在中华人民共和国成立时高达 54167 万人，较 1840 年净增 12886 万人。

新中国成立后，随着经济的恢复和发展、医疗卫生事业的加强和人民生活的改善，人口死亡率出现了大幅度的下降，人口出生率却一直维持在较高水平，导致人口增长率的上升，人口再生产迅速步入了高出生、低死亡、高增长类型，形成了 1953～1957 年的第一次生育高潮。人口年平均增长率上

---

① United Nations, *Demographic Yearbook*, 1994.
② 参见吴希庸《人口思想史》第 1 册，北平大学出版社，1936。

升到 2.4%，其间人口净增加 5857 万人。1958～1961 年为一次生育低潮，主要受到国民经济三年困难时期死亡率升高的影响，人口年平均增长率下降到 0.46%。1962 年国民经济开始好转，随即出现持续达 11 年之久，年平均增长率高达 2.6% 的第二次生育高潮。1962～1973 年全国共出生 3 亿多人口，人口总数由 65859 万人增加到 89211 万人，净增 23352 万人，成为人口年龄结构中异常庞大的部分，也是人口压力最为严重的部分。这一部分人随年龄增长移动到哪里，中国人口问题的难点就在哪里出现。尽管人口变动如此复杂，但在总体上处在高增长之中，1949～1973 年人口年平均增长率达到 2.10%。人口增长对经济、科技、社会发展的制约和负担的加重日益积累起来，终于使政府定下大力控制人口增长、切实加强计划生育的决策。1972 年 12 月 10 日中共中央转发《国务院关于粮食问题的报告》，该报告明确提出"在城乡人民中，要大力宣传和提倡计划生育"。1974 年在转发上海市和河北省两份计划生育报告批语中指出："实行计划生育，是一场破旧立新、移风易俗的深刻的革命"，"要充分发动群众……把计划生育落实到人"，要求各级党委"切实加强领导，经常抓、抓得紧"。由于加大了计划生育工作力度，1975 年以来又将其列入每年的国民经济计划；1978 年改革开放后，经济持续快速增长，为马寅初先生《新人口论》平反带动了人口理论的拨乱反正，使人口控制的社会基础和外部环境不断获得改善，创造了中国人口变动的"奇迹"。人口出生率由 1973 年的 27.93‰ 下降到 1999 年的 15.23‰，下降 12.7 个千分点；自然增长率由 2.10% 下降到 0.88%，下降 1.22 个百分点。中国实施计划生育有效地将世界 50 亿人口日的到来向后推迟 2 年，60 亿人口日向后推迟 3 年，取得了举世公认的成绩。与此同时，总（和）生育率（TFR）也由 20 世纪 70 年代初的 5.8，下降到 1999 年的 1.9 左右，在 2.1 更替水平以下，母亲的净再生产率（NRR）下降到 1.0 更替水平以下，表明我国已经提前进入低生育水平国家行列。所谓"提前进入"，是指按照社会经济发展而论，我国处在发展中国家一般水平；而人口生产，则接近发达国家水平，二者之间存在一个明显的"时间差"。

不过就全国 56 个民族而论，"提前起飞"和"提前降低"情形很不一样。两个"提前"主要是对汉族以及少数民族中人口较多、同汉族经济发展水平比较接近的民族而言，多数特别是居住在边远地区人数较少的少数民族，既谈不上第一个"提前"，也同第二个"提前"无缘。但是同样重要的一点在于，近年来许多少数民族的生育率也下降了，缩短了与生育率更替水平之间的差距，创造了有利于经济、社会发展的条件。

二　较低的素质与跨越式的提升

人口素质有身体素质、文化教育素质"二要素"论与"二要素"之外加上思想或道德素质"三要素"论之争，我们这里仅考察"二要素"的变动。

在古代社会，中国在科技、文化、经济和社会发展上长期居于领先水平，人口素质水平也相对较高。18 世纪中叶产业革命发生后，中国仍沉浸在往日的农业文明中，经过 1840 年鸦片战争及其后列强瓜分的一系列震撼，中国一步步跌落到半殖民地半封建主义的泥潭，广大民众的身体素质和文化教育素质不能不受到摧残。到 1949 年新中国成立前夜，一般估计婴儿死亡率在 200‰左右，出生时的人口预期寿命城市不到 40 岁，乡村在 35 岁左右。人口文化教育素质低下，经过新中国 15 年的大力发展教育事业和扫除文盲半文盲，1964 年第二次全国人口普查时，具有大学文化程度人口仅为 288 万人，占 12 岁以上人口的 0.42%；具有高中文化程度人口 912 万人，占 1.32%；具有初中文化程度人口 3235 万人，占 4.68%；具有小学文化程度人口 19582 万人，占 28.33%；文盲半文盲（初识字不识字）人口 26340 万人，占 38.10%[1]。但是由于国家大力发展医药、卫生事业，开展全民健身和体育运动，大力发展教育、科学事业，扫除文盲和半文盲，使得人口身体素质和文化教育素质随着经济的发展和社会的进步不断提高，尤以改革开放以来提高十分显著。在身体素质方面，1990 年第四次全国人口普查表明，婴儿死亡率已下降到 32.9‰，出生时男女合预期寿命目前已超过 70 岁。尽管国际上对中国的这两项指标的估计有些出入，如联合国估计 1990～1995 年间在 46‰左右，1995～2000 年间在 41‰左右，联合国人口基金主席 N. 兹迪克估计 1999 年为 38‰[2]，均比中国的人口普查高一些；然而即使按照这些估计进行比较和衡量，中国婴儿死亡率的下降也是异常迅速的。1950～2000 年发展中国家婴儿死亡率从 178‰降至 63‰，50 年中下降了 115 个千分点；同期中国下降在 150 个千分点以上，由原来高出发展中国家变动到现

① 《中华人民共和国第二次人口普查统计数字汇编》，国家统计局人口统计司翻印，1986 年 9 月。

② United Nations，*World Population Prospects*，*The 1998 Revision*，New York，1998.

在低于发展中国家许多，正向发达国家的低婴儿死亡率靠近。与此同时，1950～2000 年发展中国家人口出生时预期寿命从 40.9 岁提高到 63.3 岁，50 年间提高 22.4 岁，同期中国至少提高了 30 岁以上，同样高出发展中国家许多，并以比较快的速度接近发达国家水平。

在文化教育素质方面，一是文盲半文盲人口所占比例大幅度下降。2000 年第五次全国人口普查，中国内地 31 个省、自治区、直辖市的文盲半文盲人口为 8507 万人，文盲率下降到 6.72%，较 1982 年第三次人口普查降低 16.78 个百分点。二是具有中等教育水平人口所占比例急剧上升。2000 年与 1982 年两次人口普查比较，具有高中（含中专）文化程度人口上升到 14109 万人，所占比例上升到 11.15%，升高 4.88 个百分点；县有初中文化程度人口上升到 42989 万人，所占比例上升到 33.96%，升高 16.2 个百分点。三是具有大学文化程度人口所占比例上升很快，2000 年达到 4571 万人，所占比例上升到 3.6%，升高 3.01 个百分点[①]。

需要指出，人口身体素质、文化教育素质比较快的提高，是在少数民族人口增长相对较快的情况下取得的，少数民族人口素质的提高更为显著一些。1953 年第一次全国人口普查汉族人口 54728 万人，占 93.94%；其余 41 个少数民族人口 3532 万人，占 6.06%。经 1977 年民族人口识别和认定，正式定为 56 个民族，到 2000 年第五次全国人口普查汉族人口 115940 万人，占总人口 91.59%；其余 55 个少数民族人口 10643 万人，占总人口的比例上升到 8.41%，升高 2.35 个百分点[②]。当然，由于过去少数民族人口素质总体水平相对低一些，因此虽然提高更快一些，但是目前同汉族人口总体素质比较仍有一定差距。不仅如此，少数民族之间也存在某些差距，归根结底受民族居住地区经济、科技、文化、社会发展水平制约，是社会发达程度的反映。

三　失衡的结构与谋求发展的平衡

人口结构包括人口年龄、性别自然结构，人口就业、城乡、地区分布等经济结构，人口婚姻、家庭、文化、宗教等社会结构，从一个重要的方面反

---

① 《中国 1982 年人口普查资料》，中国统计出版社，1985；《2000 年第五次全国人口普查主要数据公报》，中华人民共和国国家统计局，2000。
② 《中华人民共和国 1953 年人口普查统计汇编》；《2000 年第五次全国人口普查主要数据公报》。

映着人口的特征。结合我国民族人口实际，主要分析一下人口年龄、城乡和地区分布结构。

其一，人口年龄结构。2000 年全国第五次人口普查表明，0～14 岁少年人口下降到占总人口的 22.89%，较 1990 年降低 4.80 个百分点；15～64 岁成年人口上升到 70.15%，较 1990 年升高 3.41 个百分点；65 岁以上老年人口上升到占 6.96%，升高 1.39 个百分点[1]。这次人口普查标准时间为 2000 年 11 月 1 日零时，到年底 65 岁以上老年人口比例应达到 7.0% 的水平。据此，老年人口比例、年龄中位数、老少比等衡量人口年龄结构变动的基本指标，均已达到或接近老年型年龄结构标准，2000 年底中国人口年龄结构已跨进老年型门槛。然而这是对全国 31 个省区市和现役军人总体说的，分开来看则差别很大。据国家统计局 1999 年所作的抽样比为 0.976‰ 的人口抽样调查显示，1999 年 65 岁以上老年人口比例为 7.63%——尽管这一数值比 2000 年人口普查高出 0.67 个百分点显得偏高，但是作为省区市之间比较还是可用的——不过，地区间的差别是明白无误的。最高的上海市达到 13.84%，其次北京市为 10.27%，再次江苏省为 9.83%，浙江省为 9.54%，天津市为 9.36%，其余在全国水平之上的依次为重庆市 8.84%、山东省 8.61%、四川省 8.33%、福建省 8.04%、湖南省 7.98%、广西壮族自治区 7.96%、广东省 7.89%、辽宁省 7.81%。在老年人口比例高于全国水平的 13 个省区市中，除重庆、四川、湖南三省市为中西部地区外，其余 10 省区市均为东部沿海地区。相反，老年人口比例低于全国水平排列，依次为西藏自治区 4.08%，宁夏回族自治区 4.47%，新疆维吾尔自治区 4.69%，黑龙江省 5.42%，青海省 5.46%，甘肃省 5.60%，内蒙古自治区 5.85%，贵州省 6.05%，山西省 6.41%，河北省 6.60%，海南省 6.63%，江西省 6.71%，吉林省 6.78%，云南省 6.83%，河南省 7.08%，陕西省 7.14%，湖北省 7.15%，安徽省 7.43%[2]。可见，老年人口比例较低的省区市主要集中在西部，中部次之，沿海地区仅有两个省低于全国水平。总体上东部已进入老年型年龄结构，上海、北京、江苏、浙江、天津等省市已达到中期较高阶段；中部是过渡地带，一些省份进入老年型，另一些省份正向老年型过渡；西部除重庆、四川两省市外，处在由成年型向老年型过渡阶段，基本上属于成年型。西藏、新疆两个自治区属于由年轻型刚刚过渡到成年型。人口

① 《2000 年第五次全国人口普查主要数据公报》。
② 《中国统计年鉴 2000》，中国统计出版社，2000。

年龄结构尚具有年轻型的一些特征。据此，可将目前中国人口年龄结构变动划分成"三大平台"：西部以成年型为主，总体上还具有较强增长势能；中部呈老年型与成年型"二元结构"交叉型，成年型结构省份将很快步入老年型；东部以老年型为主，一些省市老龄化水平已达到较高阶段，个别成年型省份也将很快步入老年型。这种情况表明，汉族人口则基本达到老年型，少数民族人口则基本处在成年型。不过不能笼统而论，以世居在东南沿海为主的某些少数民族，其年龄结构也已步入或接近老年型；而世居在西部地区的少数民族，年龄结构相对要年轻一些，增长的势能强一些。

其二，人口城市结构。2000年人口普查全国市镇人口所占比例达到36.09%，比1999年国家统计局公布数据30.90%升高5.09个百分点，有人对此抱有疑虑。本人以为，这是一个比较接近实际的数字，因为此次人口普查将长期居住生活和工作在城镇的人口列入市镇常住人口，反映了客观存在的人口现实。过去始终受户籍管理束缚，主要以非农业人口和农业人口划分城乡人口，而农业与非农业人口又以是否享受国家按定量标准供应商品粮为转移，造成城乡人口与实际情况不符。加上设置市镇标准的多次调整，形成1949～1960年城市化发展较快，20世纪六七十年代的徘徊，改革开放以来的快速发展几个不同的历史时期。从总体上看，以往计划经济和行政色彩浓厚了一些，公布的市镇人口数据偏低了一些。对此世界银行1984年在中国经济考察报告中称：对于数千人口的集中区，许多人从事的是非农业劳动，然而却将他们定为农业人口很不理解，当时即估计中国市镇人口已占总人口的34%左右。本人赞同以人口学、经济学、社会学、管理学等多学科角度综合考察，包括行政管理区域、人口集中程度、非农业人口所占比例、基础设施条件、文化生活方式等划分市镇人口，不过人口集中的程度具有基础的性质，据此全国人口普查公布的36.09%的市镇人口比例并不为高。不过这是全国的比例数据，分地域观察则存在很大差异，这是研究民族人口结构应当注意的问题。

目前总的情况是：经济比较发达和工业化程度较高的地区，人口城市化水平就高一些；经济不够发达和工业化程度差一些的地区，人口城市化水平就低一些，发展就滞后一些。大致上自西向东，形成人口城市阶梯式公布格局，逐步走高。这有几方面的表现：一是市镇人口所占比例自西向东逐步升高，东部沿海某些省市城市人口已超过50%，西部某些地区还在20%以下。二是在大中小城市结构上也有所表现：西部较小城市（含镇）所占比例更高一些，大城市和较大城市所占比例低一些；东部则倒了过来，较小市镇所占比例低一些，大城市和较大城市所占比例要高一些。这种城市化结构状况反映到民族人口结构上，汉族市镇人口比例相对更高一些，市镇人口中大城市和中等城市人口比例也相对高一些；少数民族市镇人口比例相对低一些，城镇人口比例相对高一些。因此，谋求民族人口平衡发展，适当加快中西部特别是少数民族地区人口城市化进程，是一种带有战略性的举措。

其三，人口地区分布结构。人口地区分布结构与民族人口分布有着密切的关系，许多少数民族世居在地广人稀的高山、高寒地带，从而形成我国人口地区分布的"三大平台"：1999 年西南、西北 10 个省区市人口 28771 万人，占全国 22.85%，人口密度（人/平方千米）52.7；中部 9 个省区人口 46031 万人，占全国 36.56%，人口密度 162.2；东部 12 个省区市 51107 万人，占全国 40.59%，人口密度 393.1[①]。需要指出，"三大平台"式人口地区分布由来已久，其成因主要如下。

第一，自然环境的制约。自然环境是人类进行繁衍生息的场所，是人口再生产得以进行的空间条件。不过人类发展的历史越往前追溯，依赖自然环境因素越大，甚至人类本身便是自然环境变动的产物。历史越往后推移，自然环境因素对人口再生产的影响便越小，但是仍不失为影响人口生产的重要因素，甚至是决定因素。表现如下。

一是地质构造和地形因素的影响。由适宜耕作土地构成的平原，石英砂组成的荒漠，岩石结构的土地显然承载人口的数量大不相同。冰雪覆盖的高山不适合人类居住，山地雪线以下一般方可生存，但生存数量与等高线成反比。1950 年世界的情况是：海拔 350 米以下地区的人口密度为每平方千米 28 人，350~750 米为 11.5 人，750~1250 米为 5.3 人。在我国 960 万平方千米土地中，山地占 33.3%，高原占 26.0%，两项相加占 59.3%。而西北、西南大部分为高原和山地，最高的几座山脉喜马拉雅山、昆仑山、天山等都雄踞西部，并有横断山、祁连山、秦岭、大巴山等连续向东南延伸，形成以青藏高原为依托的"世界屋脊"。北部则有阿尔泰山、阴山、大小兴安岭等山脉，虽然高度远不能同青藏高原相比，但是架起了内蒙古高原，构成了北高南低的走向。按照人口"等高线分布"理论，是造成西北部人烟稀少的主要原因。

---

① 《中国统计年鉴 2000》。

二是气候因素的影响。光照和年积温差别很大，华北平原年平均积温在
4000℃～5000℃之间，长江流域以南地区在5800℃～8000℃，而青藏高原
和黑龙江北部只有2000℃～2500℃。年积温过低、光照不足、无霜期短不利
于农作物生长和人类生产活动，一般人口密集较低，降水量差别很大。西北
内陆年平均降水量只有100～200毫米，按人口分布"等高线"划分，本来
可以居住和生存更多人口的塔里木盆地、柴达木盆地等，因年降水量在25
毫米以下，主要靠积雪灌溉，严重限制了居住人口的数量。全国干旱和半干
旱地区占全部国土面积的53%，主要分布在西北地区，成为那里人口密度
低的主要原因。

第二，自然资源因素的影响。土地特别是耕地，被称为人类生存的命
脉。西部地区平原少，耕地多为丘陵和山地，或处于高山高寒地带，或者水
资源缺乏，土地的人口承载力很低。东部有东北、华北两大平原，以及淮河
流域、长江流域、闽江流域、珠江流域等长期形成的冲积平原，雨水充沛，
光照充足，利于农作物生长，人口十分集中，形成高人口密度区。介于西部
和东部之间的中部地区，具有明显的过渡性质：平原和山川河谷地带人口相
当集中，丘陵和山地人口则比较稀疏，土地的决定性作用更为突出。

此外，西部地区森林、草场资源不少，但是由于缺少雨水，草原畜载量
不高。我国江、河、湖、海面积广阔，沿水域周围为人口集中区，特别是较
大城市多位于河流要道和沿海口岸。西北部地区金属和非金属矿产资源比较
丰富，但由于受到经济发展程度和开发利用的条件限制，除少数地区矿山、
冶金比较发达外，并没有形成众多工矿区吸纳大量人口的现象，不足以改变
人口地区分布的格局。

第三，经济、社会发展的作用。人口的地区分布是漫长历史发展中形成
和积淀下来的结果；同时这种积淀又反过来影响经济、社会的发展，形成特
定地域人口—经济—社会的互动组合。由于中国长期处于封建社会，近代又
沦为半殖民地半封建社会，农业一直是国民经济的主体，农业资源首先受到
开发和利用，人口地区分布首先表现为农业经济发展的积淀。新中国成立
后，1953年第一个五年计划工业化开始启动，出于对各种矿产资源的需求，
西北部一些地区开发石油、钢铁、煤炭、有色金属等矿产，有的发展成为新
兴工业城市，吸纳了部分外来人口，不过总量有限。

进入20世纪70年代后期，随着对内搞活和对外开放的扩大，随着市场
经济的发展，80年代中期以来中西部农村过剩人口受经济利益的驱动，在

"推—拉"理论作用下，大举"孔雀东南飞"。这点比较一下沿海和中西部农民家庭纯收入的差距便可一目了然，1978～1999年东部沿海农民家庭纯收入增长20.4倍，同期全国增长16.5倍，中西部增长13.4倍。

除经济发展水平直接关系人口的集中程度外，社会发展的影响，主要指政治、军事、国家行政中心及其辐射力的影响也不可低估。盛唐建都长安，开辟丝绸之路，这不仅是贸易之路，也是文化之路、交往之路，带来了西部地区的一度繁荣，人口增加很多。但随着后来朝代重心的东移，宋朝迁都开封、临安（杭州），元朝以后定都北京，占据华北平原，人口也随着转移，一步步形成现在的格局。从发展上看，科学和技术的发展及其在实践中的应用对人口分布的影响有加大的趋势，但在科技进步没有达到对自己环境改造产生革命性变革之前，比如能使沙漠变良田，从根本上解决干旱，那么改变人口分布失衡的梦想就无法变成现实。因此，中国西部、中部、东中部人口分布格局的形成是自然条件和社会经济条件综合作用的结果。自然条件是基础，它制约着人类的产生和生存环境；社会经济条件是调节器，在自然条件和人口生产之间起着协调的作用，通过改变自然环境，创造适合人口居住和生存的环境；人口密度则是这种协调能力的指示器，提示调节的方向，调整人口分布的格局。不过迄今为止，其调节的能力是相对有限的，百年依旧的分布格局难以改变。了解到这些，也就了解了中国人口地区分布和世居少数民族人口分布格局之间的关系，对未来的变动趋势作出合理的判断。

四 西部开发与可持续发展

中央在世纪之交提出西部大开发，为21世纪中国经济和社会发展奠定了新的格局，也为人口相对集中在西部的少数民族人口发展带来新的机遇，引向可持续发展之路。为此就必须弄清西部的资源配置状况，从实际出发发挥比较优势，加强薄弱环节，沿着人口、资源、环境、经济、社会协调发展方向走下去。

1. 资本结构现状

当今国际社会，流行用自然资本、产出资本、人力资本、社会资本评价财富理论方法。目前西部10省、区、市"四大资本"状况，概述如下。

自然资本。土地面积546.2万平方千米，占全陆地面积960万平方千米的56.9%；人均耕地20世纪90年代中期全国平均1.7亩，西部仅四川、贵州两省略低于这一水平，其余则高出这一水平许多；人均水资源西南除重庆市外，均大大高出全国人均 2221.2 立方米水平，最高的西藏高出全国人均水平 80 倍。居全国之冠；人均生物量仅重庆、宁夏、贵州三市、自治区、省低于全国水平，其余高于全国水平，尤以西藏、青海、新疆、云南等省区为高；45 种矿产资源潜在价值达 22723 亿元，占全国 57288.9 亿元的 39.7%，四川、云南、贵州三省名列前茅。从总体上看，西部自然资本积聚较多，蓄势较强，开发潜力较大。不过也要作具体分析。如耕地中质量较好的一、二等耕地所占比例较低。目前只有云南、新疆两省区高于全国占 76% 的水平，其余均低于这一水平，甘肃、青海、宁夏、陕西和重庆等省市区仅占 50% 或 50% 以下，高山、高寒和干旱、半干旱耕地居多，耕地的利用率和效率不够高；人均水资源西南与西北一多一少严重"苦乐不均"，宁夏、甘肃、陕西等省区成为我国严重缺水地区[①]（参见附表 1：1998 年西部地区自然资本状况）。

产出资本。1998 年西部 10 省区市国内生产总值 11552.1 亿元，占全国国内生产总值 79395.7 亿元的 14.6%；人均 GDP 4051.9 元，占全国人均 GDP 6361.3 元的 63.7%。资本形成总额 5153.9 亿元，占全国资本形成总额 30396.0 亿元的 17.0%；人均资本形成额 1807.8 元，占全国人均资本形成额 2435.4 元的 74.2%。非农产值占国内生产总值比例为 75.7%，比全国占 81.6% 低 5.9 个百分点[②]。西部除新疆维尔族自治区人均资本形成总额、人均国内生产总值高于全国水平外，其余均低于全国水平，有 1/3 省区仅及全国水平的一半左右。总体水平低、蓄势较弱、与东部地区比较差距拉大是西部产出资本的显著特点。

人力资本。所谓人力资本是指相对于物化资本而存在，表现为人所具有的知识、技能、经济、健康等人口质量素质总和，是具有经济价值的资本。1998 年西部地区人口 28510 万人，占全国人口 124810 万人的 22.8%。6 岁以上人口中不识字或识字很少的占 18.0%，比全国占 13.7% 高出 4.3 个百分点；小学文化程度占 44.5%，比全国占 39.8% 高出 4.7 个百分点；初中文化程度占 26.7%，比全国 33.0% 低 6.3 个百分点；高中文化程度占 8.6%，比全国 10.7% 低 2.1

---

① 《中国统计年鉴 1999》，中国统计出版社，1999；《2000 年中国可持续发展战略报告》，科学出版社，2000。

② 《中国统计年鉴 1999》；《2000 年中国可持续发展战略报告》。

个百分点;大专以上文化程度占 2.2%,比全国 2.8% 低 0.6 个百分点①。以平均所受教育年限计算的人口文化教育指数,西部地区为 5.66,比全国 6.29 低 0.63。总起来看,如以 E 代表人力资本积聚量,T 代表人口数量,Q 代表人口质量(Q 可分解为:i 人口的知识,t 人口的技能,e 人口的经验,h 人口的健康水平),则:

$$E = T \cdot Q = T \cdot (i + t + e + h)$$

若暂不考虑 h 健康因素,i、t、e 集中反映在人口所受教育程度上。将上面人口文化教育指数代入 1998 年西部 10 省区市人力资本积聚量为 161181 万人年,占全国人力资本积聚量 785055 万人年的 20.6%。这一比例比人口数量所占比例低 2.2 个百分点,原因在于平均所受教育年限较低。将上述主要数据汇成一简表,西部地区的资本结构便可以比较清晰地显现出来(见表 1)。

表 1　1998 年西部地区资本结构

	土地 (万 km²)	人口 (亿)	45 种矿产资源(亿元)	资本形成额(亿元)	GDP (亿元)	文化教育 指　　数	人力资本积聚 (万人年)
西部	546.2	2.85	22723	5154	11552	5.66	161181
全国	960.0	12.48	57289	30396	79396	6.29	785055
西部占 全国(%)	56.9	22.8	39.7	17.0	14.6	90.0	20.6

表 1 表明,从总体上观察,西部地区自然资本蓄势较强,不过不要忘记,一是较强只能是相对而言,而且强中有弱;二是自然资本在西部各省区市之间,分布也很不平衡。产出资本和人力资本较弱,同自然资本不相匹配,阻碍着西部的发展。至于市场化程度、管理水平、改革开放力度等社会资本相对滞后,已是人们公认的不争事实。本人以为,弄清西部地区资本结构现状非常必要,它是开发的客观基础和如何开发的基本立足点。

2. 人力资本"瓶颈"

出于经济、政治、军事等的需要,国家组织区域性经济开发,古今中外早已有之。从中国古代的戍边屯田,到近代美国的西部开发,苏联的远东开发就是例证。新中国成立以来的西部开发也已有过两次,"一五"时期和后

① 《中国统计年鉴 1999》;《2000 年中国可持续发展战略报告》。

来的"三线"建设。这些区域性经济开发有成功的经验，也有失败的教训，根本在于能否形成融资金、人才、物资、技术、信息于一体的"能量流"。所谓开发，开垦发展之谓也，即通过外界注入"能量流"启动当地资源而造成持续发展的态势。就当前我国的西部开发而言，就是要通过产出资本、人力资本、社会资本的积聚，启动蓄势较强的自然资本，形成一个强有力的发展态势。毫无疑问，任何一种资本的注入积聚都是必要的。以产出资本价值形态出现的货币资本的注入和积聚是必要的，市场经济条件下舍此则自然资本难以启动；深化改革、扩大开放和提高市场化程度，实行必要的政策倾斜等社会资本的注入和积聚是必需的，无此也不能创造有利于开发的社会环境；但是这两种资本都不能同人力资本并驾齐驱，人力资本是西部开发战略"能量流"中的主流资本，制约开发"瓶颈"的资本。

要认识这一点，需对当前西部开发所处的背景和环境，尤其是同"一五"和"三线"建设时的不同情况，作出比较分析。首先，当前的西部开发同前两次开发社会经济环境有很大不同，人力资本的作用进一步增强了。前两次开发，是在高度集中统一的计划经济体制下进行的，从建设项目的确立到投产后的生产、交换、分配、消费各个环节均纳入严格的计划，加上当时又处于短缺经济状态，生产多少国家收购多少，没有销售不了的后顾之忧。在这种情况下，能否争来项目和投资，成为能否开发和开发力度大小的标志。现在的情况则有原则上的不同：一是经过 20 多年的经济体制改革，原来高度集中统一的计划经济体制已经不复存在，让位于以市场主体法人化、要素流动市场化、宏观调控间接化、经济运行法制化为基本特征的市场经济；二是经过二三十年、三四十年的建设和发展，特别是改革开放以来国民经济长期持续的快速发展，经济运行有了明显改观，短缺经济也已不复存在，如今主要消费品已经形成买方市场。经济大环境这样两点带有根本性的改变，决定了当前的西部开发不能走"一五"和"三线"建设的老路，不能把开发视为就是争来项目和投资。应当承认，开发离不开一定的建设项目和投资；但是建设项目和投资不仅要立足于当地的自然资本优势，还必须立足于市场经济、立足于建设项目投产后有无充足的市场销路。而且还要考虑开发建设项目的成本与效益以及在同类产品中的市场竞争能力。如果在上马开发建设项目生产的产品市场上没有多少销路，或者虽有销路但生产成本很高或质量较差，因而缺乏市场竞争力，这样的项目上马后短期内可能显现"开发效益"（实施开发的"政绩"）；时间一长因经济效益不济或亏损日益严重而被市场淘汰,弄得不好还要破产,反倒成了继续开发建设的包袱,转化成"负开发效益"。如何避免这种负效益并提高开发的正效益呢?除了在选择开发项目上要做好市场调查和科学论证外,必须明确,提高开发项目建设和投产后的效益,关键在人力资本的积聚。只有具备项目建设和生产所需要的专门人才和熟练劳动者,才能提高劳动生产率,才能有效降低成本,才能不断提高市场竞争能力。这一点甚至在计划经济下的"一五"和"三线"建设西部开发中,也有所体现。这两次开发投资建设不少项目,有些项目已经发挥良好作用;但是确有不少项目上马不久即成为"下马工程"、"胡子工程"和人去厂空的"留守工程",造成严重浪费。究其原因,除立项本身缺乏科学论证和存在交通不便、保障不力、后续资金投入不足等客观原因外,没有相应的机制引进和留住人才,更缺乏培养当地人才人力资本积聚的战略举措,造成人力资本积聚始终不能同自然资本、产出资本相匹配是根本原因。我们应当汲取这一经验教训,今天人力资本的作用更为重要。

其次,当前的西部开发与前两次开发技术背景有很大不同,人力资本积聚紧密同技术进步结合在一起。前两次的西部开发发生在 20 世纪 50 年代和六七十年代,可视为我国工业化起始阶段,经济技术基础相当落后。当今世界已进入以微电子技术为前导的新技术革命高潮期,并开始向以生命科学为主导学科的更新的技术革命过渡,基因工程、克隆技术叩响了 21 世纪大门,知识经济正向我们走来。在这种情况下,包括西部开发在内的任何较大规模的经济建设,都要选择相应的经济技术结构。所谓"相适应",一是同本地区的实际经济技术水平相适应,以我国西部而论,不能盲目追高,各地都要大量发展高新技术产业,二是同新技术革命潮流相适应,不可视新技术革命、知识经济于不顾,固守陈旧落后的技术。发展高新技术产业靠什么?人才是关键成为共识,而人才只能从人力资本不断积聚中来。然而实事求是的估量,高新技术产业西部除少数地区可成长为主导产业外,多数则难以做到,只能发展以中间技术为主体的传统产业,或传统产业与现代产业相结合的较先进的技术产业。无论发展哪种产业,有一个基本的观点是必须明确的,科学技术的贡献率在不断提高。据估计,科学技术在经济成长中的贡献率,已从 20 世纪初的 20% 左右上升到中期的 40% 左右,目前已上升到 80% 左右。西部开发建设要想在激烈的市场竞争中站住脚和不断发展壮大,必须提高科技的含量和贡献率。这就不能不求助于人口所受教育水平的提高,求助于人力资本的积聚。一个有胆识的领导者和决策者,应当在西部开发中树起优先发展科学和教育的旗帜。这样做表面上暂时发展慢一些，经济建设项目上得不够多；实际上通过不断增加人力资本积聚而增强发展后劲儿，从长期观察将持续推动开发不断深入，发展反而要更快一些。在这方面改革开放总设计师邓小平同志为我们树立了榜样。1976 年在粉碎"四人帮"反革命集团后，在国家百废待兴、百业待兴严峻形势下，邓小平同志毅然决然地首先抓恢复高考，召开全国科学大会和教育大会，将人才培养和人力资本积聚放在首位。实践证明，这一战略决策保证了改革开放 20 多年来经济高速成长对人力资本追加的需要，如今将科教兴国作为一项基本的发展战略确定下来，"西部大开发，人才是关键"。谁能从本质上真正认识到这点并能在实践中卓有成效地解决，确保人力资本积聚的不断增长，谁就能在未来的开发建设中赢得主动权，不断将开发引向深入。仅仅将其视为一句时髦的口号，实践中只是抓住项目和投资不放，谁就会在未来的开发建设中暴露出后劲儿不足，甚至受某种效益不佳项目的拖累而举步维艰，难以赢得继续发展的主动权。

3. 人口决策选择

人力资本在西部开发中有着举足轻重的作用，如何加速人力资本积聚也就成了西部开发战略中的关键。如前所述，总体人力资本积聚量等于人口数量与质量的乘积，由此提出西部开发要不要伴随大量的人口增长，包括当地人口自然增长和外来流动人口的机械增长？数量和质量的矛盾如何处理？等等。故本文从人口变动角度，探讨西部加快人力资本积聚的人口学思路。这一思路的基本点是：西部开发不需要伴随人口数量的大幅度增长，相反还要有效地控制人口增长；同时要大力提高人口素质和调整人口的结构，实行"控制"、"提高"、"调整"相结合；当前实行以数量控制为重点的方略。

控制人口数量增长是西部开发的必要前提和推进器，开发与控制是相辅相成的两个方面。从人口与资源、环境关系角度观察，控制人口增长是维护和发挥西部人均自然资本优势的需要。西部地区作为一个总体自然资源比较丰富，环境破坏相对较轻，同"地广人稀"密切相关。1998 年全国人口密度（人/每平方千米）为 130，西部地区为 52，其中新疆为 10，青海为 7，西藏为 2[①]，使耕地、淡水、生物量、矿产资源等的人均占有量保持在较高水平。土壤、河湖、空气质量较高，没有或较少受人工破坏的自然环境所占

①　《中国统计年鉴 1999》。

的比例较高。要保持西部地区自然资本的这种优势，控制人口的数量增长无疑是必要的前提条件。尤应值得指出的是，我国地势西高东低，西部位于长江、黄河等主要河流源头，环境怎样不仅关系到西部开发和居民的生存与发展，而且关系到中部和东部的生存与发展，甚至对全球大气质量也将产生很大影响，应予特别关注。尽管西部环境受破坏的程度轻一些，但是自然植被的损坏，高山积雪退却和消失，沙漠化、石漠化等的加剧也已向我们发出警告，环境的破坏有认识不高、重视不够、抓得不力等社会方面的原因，有"二元经济"下建设与治理矛盾客观方面的原因，毋庸置疑也有人口增长方面的原因。西部地区自 1949 年以来人口增长 1.4 倍有余，即使出于"土里刨食"需要而毁林开荒、变牧为农、围湖造田也要同倍增长，更不要说工业化的推进使资源"加权"消耗带来的环境效应，遂使西部地区的环境也日益变得脆弱起来。

从人口自身再生产角度观察，控制人口增长有利于素质的提高和结构的调整，有利于人力资本积聚的增进。如果生育率受到有效控制，社会则可因出生率的下降和出生人数的减少，每年节约相当一笔未成年人口抚养费用而增加积累，支持经济建设和科教事业的发展。个人和家庭也因少生子女而减轻负担，供养已有子女上学深造，父母也赢得相对多一些的学习进修时间，双重地有利于人口文化教育素质的提高。西部新生儿出生缺陷率和地方病发病率较高，控制人口增长和加强计划生育工作，开展少生优生服务等有助于人口健康素质的提高，有效地增加了人力资本和积聚。控制人口增长有助于人口结构的调整。人口年龄结构的调整，主要取决于出生率。目前全国人口年龄结构开始进入老年型，西部仅重庆、四川老年人口比例稍高于全国水平，其余均低于全国水平，多数处在由成年型向老年型过渡阶段，有的自治区还处在年轻型后期，有着较强的人口增长势能。西部人口要完成向老年型的转变并最终消除人口增长的势能，只有求助于出生率的持续下降，少年人口比例的逐步减少和老年人口比例的缓慢增大来完成。人口城乡结构和地区分布结构的调整，主要依靠迁移人口机械变动实现，似同控制人口增长没有多少直接的关系，但是由于西部的某些特殊情况，对居住在高山、高寒或严重干旱地带不适合人类生存和发展的居民组织并村移民，在新的移民居住区开展计划生育和优生优育服务，腾出原来的荒山荒漠植树种草，实为控制人口增长、保护生态环境与开发相结合的一项综合治理措施，增进人力资本积聚的一条途径。

控制人口数量增长有利于人口素质的提高和结构的调整，但是不能代替素质的提高和结构的调整，增强人力资本积聚在这两个方面要另辟蹊径。前已述及，西部高山、高寒地带占据很大比例，少数民族人口多，全国 55 个少数民族世居西部的有 42 个，大都居住生活在地势较高地区。交通不便，医疗保健事业不发达，地方病发病率较高，通婚圈较小等造成新生儿伤残和死亡率较高，造成总体人口健康素质不够高。因此要大力发展医疗卫生保健事业，开展优生优育教育，扩大通婚圈和禁止近亲结婚，努力提高居民的健康素质。教育事业的发展也要适合人口的分布和居住状况，合理的并村移民不仅是保护生态环境的需要，也是发展教育和提高教育层次的需要。针对西部地区的教育现状，要认真普及九年义务教育，扫除文盲半文盲的工作要加快步伐。同时也要加快中等和高等教育的发展，特别是民族高等和中等专业学校的发展。发展西部教育，国家和地方政府义不容辞，要着眼于人力资本投资——比产出资本投资更具潜力、更有效益的战略投资高度来认识。提倡"少盖一栋办公楼，多修一所小学校"。义务教育部分政府投资必须保证兑现，也要提倡运用市场机制办学，鼓励个人、合资办学，以优惠条件鼓励国外和东部地区投资西部办学，把义务教育外的教育事业的发展纳入产业经营轨道，有力促进西部人力资本积聚的增强。

必要的高山高寒地带居民点的并村移民，有限度的人口分布结构调整利于人口控制和发展教育已如前述。人口结构调整的另一重要方面是城乡结构，西部地区应因地制宜地适当加快城市化进程。人口城市化是世界也是中国人口发展的一大趋势，1998 年世界城市人口比例为 46.5%，预计 2025 年可达 58.9%。我国人口城市化水平落后许多，1998 年为 30.4%，预计 2025年可超过 60%，赶上并略高于世界总体水平①。西部地区人口城市化水平相对更低一些，1995 年为 24.1%，比全国低 4.8 个百分点，近年来差距有拉大的趋势，即使按照原来的差距不变计算，1998 年西部的人口城市化水平也只有 25.6%②。适当加快西部地区人口城市化进程，不仅是发挥大城市中心、辐射、调控功能，中小城市城乡结合功能加大开发步伐的需要，城市多吸纳一些农村人口利于环境保护的需要，而且也是提高人口素质特别是提高

① United Nations, *World Urbanization Prospects*, *The 1996 Revision*, New York, 1998. 中国部分参见田雪原《大国之难》，今日中国出版社，1999，第 162 页。
② 根据国家统计局 1995 年全国 1% 人口抽样调查数据计算。参见国家计生委计财司和中国人口信息中心编《人口与计划生育常用数据手册》第 33、43 页。

人口文化教育素质的关键之举，人口城市化的推进就是人力资本积聚的增进。经过编委会和全体作者的努力，《中国民族人口》终于和大家见面了。作为主编，我由衷地向彭珮云副委员长和国家计生委、民委、国家社科基金、各省区市计生委等有关领导的指导和支持表示感谢，向编委、作者表示敬意和感谢！是的，这一成果来之不易，有关领导多次过问，国家计生委办公厅特意发文要求各地计生委予以支持；有的省区市领导和有关部门领导亲自出马，当做一项基本省情、市情、区情来抓；有的教授骑着毛驴、骆驼奔走于崇山峻岭、戈壁沙漠；有的作者自带干粮，一口山泉一口饼干地搜集资料，潜心写作……正所谓"宝剑锋从磨砺出，梅花香自苦寒来"，《中国民族人口》的出版就是最大的慰藉了。不过时代在发展，历史在前进，当我们完成第一部书稿时，跟不上时代发展已在潜意识中萌生。或许理论与实践的关系就是这样，本书盼望得到专家和读者的指正，帮助我们更快地跟上时代前进的步伐。

《中国人口管理现代化研究》绪论[*]

世纪之交，国家社科基金将"人口信息化管理研究"列为资助课题，对于推动人口管理现代化以及整个信息化管理事业的发展，有着重要的意义。

一

历史推进到 21 世纪，未来学家和各方面的专家对于新世纪的发展趋势，作出种种推断，提出全球化、国际化、成熟化、市场化、多极化、知识化、数字化、网络化、老龄化、城市化等一系列"化"的概念。不过，"化"提出越多，就越是感到要将"化"区分成不同的层次，否则什么东西都有可能被"化"所瓜分掉。笔者以为，在这诸多"化"中，信息化和经济全球化是最高层次的"化"，是最值得关注的影响发展全局大趋势的"化"。

信息化是 21 世纪发展的大趋势，现在已经没有人再怀疑。第二次世界大战结束后，以微电子技术为前导包括新材料技术、宇航技术、激光技术、海洋技术、生物技术等新的技术革命的兴起，当前以生命科学为主导学科包括基因技术、克隆技术、纳米技术等更将这一新的技术革命推进到一个新的阶段，信息对经济和社会发展的作用被提到前所未有的高度，受到越来越多的重视，发挥出越来越大的作用。主要表现是：在产业构成中，信息产业扶摇直上，所占比重日益增大，成为增长最快的产业；信息技术一方面促进了现代信息产业高速发展，另一方面又进入生产、劳务、管理等经济活动领域，改变着整个国民经济技术基础；信息资源受到广泛重视，传统物质资源的作用相对降低，信息市场发展迅速；从事信息劳动、服务的劳动者人数越

* 本文发表于 2003 年。

来越多，在劳动力就业结构中所占比例越来越大；信息产业投资增长十分迅猛，传统物质产业投资相对减少，经济增长正向着知识密集型转化。

信息化首先同计算机技术的迅猛发展相关，计算机技术的发展带动通信现代化、网络现代化、消费现代化，即所谓的4P。目前，关于信息化的定义有多种，笔者以为，信息化的基本内涵和外延，应当以信息技术和信息产业的高度发展为核心，以发达的信息产业、技术、咨询、服务为外部环境，是一个完整的信息现代化体系。据此，可将信息化概括为：信息化是建立在现代电子技术基础上，通过不断开发利用信息资源推动经济、科技、社会现代化的过程。这一定义既包含计算机技术和产业的主要内涵，强调建立在计算机技术基础上，又涵盖信息环境主要外延，要有一个不断开发利用信息资源并在推动经济、科技、社会现代化过程中广泛应用信息技术的环境，概括了信息化的主要之点。信息化是21世纪最重要的发展趋势之一，影响所及，不仅在经济、科技、社会发展宏观领域，而且渗透到社会生活诸多微观方面，渗透到个人生活的方方面面。人口信息化管理，是信息化发展的必然结果，是宏观与微观相结合的信息化发展的必然结果。

二

人口信息化管理，无论国内还是国外，都是一个新课题。不过由于中国是世界上人口最多的国家，又是20多年来经济发展最快、满怀信心奔向现代化的国家，对于中国来说这一课题就更有意义。

中国是世界文明古国之一，长期以来积累了丰富的人口管理经验。中国又是世界最早进行人口普查的国家，很早便懂得应用人口数据资料登记造册，进行人口户籍管理。中国封建社会长达几千年，农业社会以农为本，人口管理常常同土地制度结合在一起，成为征集赋税和徭役的凭证。因此中国的户口制度异常发达，从中央到地方形成一套严密的网。1949年新中国成立后，推翻了旧有的土地制度，广大农民成为土地的主人，因而也打破了原来的将人口与土地或紧或松地联系在一起的管理制度。同时，废除了旧有的户口管理办法，启用了新的户口簿，成为居民身份和居住的法定证明发放到每个居民户，构成国家治安保卫的基本依据。后来又在户口簿基础上，于1984年核发了居民身份证，成为随身携带的个人法定证件，使户口管理向前大大推进了一步。身份证不仅方便了居民个人，随时可以证明自己的身份；而且提升了国家人口管理的水平，它对于国家及时掌握全国的人口变动，加强社会治安保卫，以及从业、教育等一切需要人口信息的地方，都是不可缺少的重要凭证。至此，形成了一套自上而下的相当完整的人口管理体系，在经济和社会管理中发挥了莫大的作用。在高度集中统一的计划经济下，居民被区分为农业人口与非农业人口两大类，依据这两类人口，确定是否享受计划供应商品粮，棉布以及其他消费品供应数量；同样依据这两类人口，决定城镇招工对象以及其他相关事项。中国的这一套人口管理办法相当完整和独特，可以说是其他国家所不具有的，在长期的经济建设实践中发挥了重要的作用。这种高度集中统一的人口管理体系，是高度集中统一的计划经济体制的产物；反过来，人口的高度集中统一管理，又巩固和加深着计划经济的高度集中统一。如此，人、财、物高度集中统一的调度，显示出计划经济完整运转的配套体系，这是任何其他经济体制所不可能做到的。

然而，随着党的十一届三中全会改革开放方针的确立，商品和市场经济特别是社会主义市场经济体制改革的深入，高度集中统一的计划经济让位于市场经济，高度集中统一的人口管理办法也出现了危机。主要表现如下。

其一，"二元经济"及其人口管理体制同商品经济发展和人口流动的增长不相适应。长期以来，我国实行的是城乡分割的"二元经济"，即城市以现代工业为主导产业、农村以传统农业为主导产业的经济，形成城乡分割式的经济结构。与这种城乡分割"二元经济"相对应的，是城乡分割的"二元人口"结构：城市居民属非农业人口，乡村居民属农业人口，形成不能随意改动的两种人口，尤其是农业人口不得随意改动为非农业人口。然而，市场经济体制的逐步建立和商品经济的迅速发展，物流和财流的大量增加，人口和劳动力的流动随之大量增多起来，20多年来形成多次"民工潮"，对原有的高度集中统一的、城乡分割的人口管理体制是一个很大的冲击。据估计，20多年来，全国流动人口较少年份在五六千万，较多年份超过1亿，城乡分割的人口管理壁垒实际上已经被冲破。

其二，城乡分割的人口管理同城市化的加速进行不相适应。由于旧中国是一个落后的农业国，城市工商业不发达，人口城市化水平很低。新中国成立后半个多世纪以来，人口城市化又经历了几起几落的曲折发展过程，其中改革开放以来的20多年是人口城市化发展最快的时期，也是稳步发展的历史时期。但是，人口城市化受到原有的"农业"与"非农业"人口的限制，"农转非"十分困难。针对这种情况，国家先是放宽小城镇

"农转非"的限制,一直发展到像广东省等在全省范围内取消"农转非"限制,城乡分割的户口管理制度已同人口城市化的加速发展不相适应,改革势在必行。

其三,旧有的管理办法同现代化发展不相适应。长期形成的一套人口管理办法,可以归纳为:一查,即通过人口普查和各项调查,取得相应的人口数据资料;二册,即将调查得来的数据资料加以汇总、列表并登记造册;三簿,即依据表册资料发放户口簿,1984 年以后又发放个人身份证;四管,即依据户口簿和身份证对居民进行人口管理,掌握相应的人口信息。这样的管理办法很规范,曾经起到过重要的作用,当年就是依靠这一套办法做到有效的人口管理的。但是在改革开放和商品经济迅速发展的新形势下,这种管理办法显得过于落后了。一是这种手工作坊式管理办法形式呆板,只能靠人工办法取得信息,效率太低;二是表册一类信息载体容量太小,只能有效地记录数量十分有限的人口信息资源。显然,人口管理的这种落后状况同经济、社会的发展不相称,不能适应现代化发展的需要。

其四,本册一类载体同资源的有效性不相适应。在流动人口与日俱增和劳动力市场需求不断增长的情况下,本册一类人口信息载体容易被伪造的现象泛滥起来,给劳动力市场管理带来很大困难。在有些地方,身份证造假、文凭造假很是猖獗,真实的人口资源传递成了问题。这一方面说明社会风气需要改进,另一方面也说明传统的本册一类信息载体本身的防伪性能很差,同样需要改进。

如何改进?实行人口信息化管理是当前最好的方法。按照上面关于信息化的定义,人口信息化管理,就是以信息技术和信息产业为依托,以良好的信息技术、咨询和服务为外部环境的规范化的现代化人口管理及其管理体系。人口信息化管理的主要优点是:可以储存大量的人口信息,既可以包括现在户口簿、身份证等各种证件的个人信息;也可以包括更多的这些载体所不能包括的信息,可以将信息量提高千百倍。可以有效地解决防伪问题,以最简单的 IC 卡为例,不仅能够放入人像以及相应的文字;而且可以存入指纹、基因、瞳孔等防伪性极强的辨认信息,几乎可以达到无法伪造的地步。可以将公共资源和个人信息资源区分开来,对个人资源加密,既能够满足上学、求职、迁移等公共资源的需求;又可以保证属于个人的资源不被泄露,有效地做到个人隐私的保密。正因为人口信息化管理有这一系列优点,目前已有一些地方开始试点,并取得良好效果。

三

人口信息化管理是 21 世纪发展的必然趋势，构建人口信息化管理体系也就成了紧迫的课题。首先，需要构建人口信息化管理的理论体系。如前所述，信息化主要是指以计算机技术为核心带动通信、网络、消费的现代化，推动整个社会经济发展的现代化。人口信息化管理即广泛应用计算机技术，实现包括人口信息资料的搜集、整理、储存、检索、应用等在内的人口管理的计算机化、网络化和现代化。这是一套全新的管理体系、机制和方法，要在实践中加以总结和提高，逐步形成人口信息化管理的理念，形成新的管理理论。需要看到，实行人口信息化管理是一场革命，是一场打破传统思维、传统管理办法、传统技术的革命，在进行资源再分配中也会牵涉利益的再分配和得失，因而不可能一帆风顺。2000 年日本启动新的身份证，全国 1.26 亿人口的姓名、地址、年龄、性别等资料，连同身份证号码一起被输入计算机联网的个人资料数据库中，以后个人的学业、医疗等资料也将被输入该库中。这是日本首次进行居民身份证信息化改革，本是一件大好的事情，但是也有的居民担心黑客，也有的担心个人隐私被泄露，因而在正式启用当天便引来一些抗议之声。有 5 个城市公然拒绝执行，最主要的一个理由，是"我们不想在政府的监视之下"，不愿将个人资料提供出来。因此，实施人口信息化管理不是一蹴而就的事情，需要理论的阐释和必要的宣传教育，进行信息化的宣传教育。

其次，要创建一套相应的管理机制。我国的人口管理以往主要在公安部门，目前也不可能脱离这个部门。但是应当看到，人口管理绝不仅仅是公安部门一家的事情，它还牵涉计生、卫生、民政、统计以及诸多经济和社会发展部门，需要一个综合的部门来管理。这个综合部门最好是建立国家人口委员会，在国家人口委员会没有建立的情况下，可由国家发展和改革委员会来承担，便于协调政府各相关部门工作。

再次，要进行技术创新。应用信息技术于人口管理，并不是一件很难的事情。但是，一要考虑实际的应用价值，即能够从根本上改变过去本、表、册一类管理办法，做到真正的管理现代化。二是要适应目前的发展水平，即适应居民对信息技术掌握的能力，不能超越居民的驾驭能力；适应居民的经济承受能力，信息化管理不能过多地增加居民的负担。三要考虑政府的实际支付能力，即考虑政府投入的成本，不应成本过高。从现代化水平、居民承受能力、政府成本投入三个方面定位人口信息化管理技术应用，就要从实际出发，选择技术先进、经济实用的技术，就要进行技术创新。目前，人口信息化管理尚无固定的技术模式，从我国实际出发，第一步，可选取 IC 卡智能化管理。即将必要的个人信息储存到卡中，同时将人像指纹等也储存到卡中，需用时由读卡机读出和打印出相应资料；第二步，可考虑进行计算机联网，实行网络化管理。

《人口经济社会可持续发展》绪论[*]

　　迄今为止，一般是将可持续发展作为一种发展战略或行动纲领提出和阐述的。那么，这种发展战略或行动纲领以什么样的理论作指导，或者可持续发展构不构成某种理论，具不具备一定的理论体系，现在到了应当深入研究和作出回答的时候了。无疑，这样的深入研究和作出回答要建立在以往实践和已有研究成果基础上，然而一俟作出比较科学的论证和理论的升华，则会推动理论和全部可持续发展事业的发展。因此本书以理论的探讨作为开篇，力求从理论与实践的结合上切入和展开。

一　可持续发展的前期理论

　　人口与经济、社会发展之间的关系，早为历代思想家、政治家、军事家所重视，甚至可追溯到古代社会。古希腊大思想家柏拉图（Plato，公元前427～前347）在《理想国》一书中，就曾阐述过这样的思想：不可使人口过多而国家过大，也不可使人口过少而国家过小。另一位大思想家亚里士多德（Aristotle，公元前384～前322）在《政治学》中宣称：最完美的国家是维持人口不超过一定的数量。他们都把一定的人口数量视为"理想国"的一个组成部分，在这个意义上说，有了理想适度人口的思想萌芽。1662年被誉为"人口学之父"的约翰·格兰特（John Grant）发表了《关于死亡的自然的和政治的观察》一书，将人口学作为一门独立的学科提了出来，人口与发展研究取得长足进展。1798年马尔萨斯（Thomas Robert Malthus）的《人口原理》（*An Essay On the Principle of Population*）发表，28年内连续出了6版，产生很大影响。马尔萨斯的观点正确与否另当别论，但由此引起的

---

　　* 本文发表于2003年。

论争大大推动了人口与经济发展等的研究，则是毋庸置疑的。到了 19 世纪中叶，英国经济学家坎南（Edwin Cannan）提出"适度人口"（Opti-mum: Population）论，其后经道尔顿（H. Dalton）等人的解释和公式化，给"适度"以多重定义。道尔顿提出一个计算公式：

$$M = \frac{A - O}{O}$$

式中 A 代表实际人口，O 代表适度人口，M 代表人口失调程度。若 M 为正值是人口过剩，M 为负值是人口不足，$M = 0$ 为适度人口。法国人口学家索维（A. Sawvy）在《人口通论》中多角度考察了适度人口，区分成经济适度人口，即获得最大经济受益或经济福利的人口；实力适度人口，即国家取得最大实力的人口。他认为，国家取得最大实力的人口应高于经济受益最大人口，因而才有国家为了扩大实力要求人口增加。他将人口数量、预期寿命、文化程度、健康状况、就业、个人福利、社会财富、国家实力等项指标引入适度人口，建立起适度人口理论模型，从静态与动态两方面展开分析。适度人口一般以稳定人口或静止人口作为出发点和归宿，发生适度人口增长和零增长、静止人口关系的争论。第二次世界大战后形成的"婴儿高潮"，以及其后发展中国家人口增长率长期居高不下，促使人口零增长研究活跃起来，产生人口爆炸论、人口零增长理论。1968 年埃里奇（P. R. Ehrlich）《人口爆炸》一书发表，提出由于人口增长造成了"环境危机"；20 世纪 70 年代斯彭格勒（J. J. Spengler）考察人口零增长与国民收入、人均产量的关系，具体阐述了人口零增长对发达国家和发展中国家的不同影响；1972 年由麦多斯（D. L. Meadows）等人撰著的罗马俱乐部报告《增长的极限》发表，认为如果世界人口、工业化、污染、粮食生产、资源消耗的增长保持目前水平不变的话，100 年内即达到地球的极限，因而必须实现零增长。也就是在这一年，"可持续发展"首次在国际会议上提了出来。

中国作为世界文明古国之一，早在公元前 500 多年的春秋战国时代的诸子百家争鸣中，便有了人口多一些好还是少一些好的不同观点，即众民与寡民之争。其后，虽然历代封建王朝众民主义占据统治地位，但也不无反对者，不断有思想家提出人口数量要适中，清人洪亮吉甚至在马尔萨斯之前就已提出生活资料落后人口的增长。到 20 世纪二三十年代，社会学派节制主义将西方人口学说引入中国，著书立说阐述的一个核心问题是"适中人口"。20 世纪 50 年代后期马寅初的《新人口论》，论述的中心也是人口增长过快拖了经济增长的后腿。20 世纪 70 年代后期开展的 "两种生产" 的讨论，一些学者从不同角度对中国适度人口数量作出的研究，其中包含着一定的可持续发展的思想，探求的是人口与资源、经济等的协调发展。

二 当代可持续发展理论

（一） 可持续发展的提出与实践

经过上述理论准备和工业革命以来，特别是第二次世界大战结束以来 "后工业化" 的实践，可持续发展作为人们普遍关注的问题在一系列国际会议上提了出来，并经过激烈争论写入有关文件，成为各国相约遵守的行动纲领和发展战略。

1972 年 6 月联合国人类环境会议在瑞典首都斯德哥尔摩召开，会议通过了《联合国人类环境会议宣言》，强调人既是环境的产物，又是环境的塑造者，人类在计划行动时必须审视造成的环境影响，提出 "合乎环境要求的发展"，"无破坏的发展"，"连续的和可持续的发展" 等概念。这是各国政府讨论当今环境问题并寻求全球环境保护的第一次会议，将可持续发展提到世人面前。

1987 年由当时挪威首相布伦特兰夫人（Gro Htarlem Brundland）主持的联合国世界环境与发展委员会在《我们共同的未来》报告中，从发展的公平性、持续性、共同性 "三原则" 出发，对可持续发展作出带有定义性的解释：既满足当代人的需求，又不对后代人满足其需求的能力构成危害的发展。这一定义性解释得到广泛认同，对后来的发展产生很大影响。

1992 年 6 月有 183 个国家和地区代表参加的联合国环境与发展大会在巴西的里约热内卢召开，其中有 102 个国家元首或政府首脑出席，通过了《里约热内卢环境与发展宣言》、《21 世纪议程》、《联合国气候变化框架公约》、《生物多样性公约》、《关于森林问题的原则声明》重要文件，否定了工业革命以来高投入、高生产、高消费、高污染的传统发展模式，提出为建立保持环境发展的全球新 "伙伴关系"，可持续发展以与会者宣言的形式承诺下来。

1994 年 9 月在埃及开罗召开的国际人口与发展会议将可持续发展列为中心议题，182 个国家参加，规模空前巨大。会议通过的《关于国际人口与发展的行动纲领》，提出"可持续发展问题的中心是人"的观点，是对《里约宣言》和《21世纪议程》的重要补正。针对世界人口继续有较大幅度增长的态势，强调了人口因素在可持续发展中的地位和作用。

1995年3月在丹麦哥本哈根举行的国际社会发展首脑会议，从社会发展角度讨论可持续发展，强调社会公平，强调建立国际的伙伴关系，将可持续发展由环境、资源、人口、经济发展领域扩展到社会领域，成为整个社会的系统工程。

在上述以及近年来一系列国际会议推动下，目前已有100多个国家和地区建立了本国、本地的可持续发展委员会一类机构，制定了本国的《21世纪议程》。中国政府履行里约热内卢国际环发会议承诺，经1994年3月25日国务院第16次常务会议讨论通过，率先推出《中国21世纪议程——中国21世纪人口、环境与发展白皮书》。《议程》共20章，可归纳为总体可持续发展、人口和社会可持续发展、经济可持续发展、资源合理利用、环境保护5个组成部分，70多个行动方案领域。同年7月，来自20多个国家、13个联合国机构、20多个外国有影响企业的170多位代表在北京聚会，制定了"中国21世纪议程优先项目计划"，用实际行动推进可持续发展战略的实施。这说明，中国在实施可持续发展战略方面走在了世界前列。

（二）以人为本可持续发展理论与理论体系

可持续发展自从提出以来，主要是作为国际的一种行动纲领，国内的一种发展战略取得共识并展开实施的。那么何谓可持续发展，可持续发展是一种什么样的发展观，是否存在可持续发展的理论，对此不同学科的回答不尽相同，许多学科都不同程度地强调了本学科范畴在可持续发展中的分量，各种定义不下几十种。我们原则上赞同布伦特兰夫人的定义，即可持续发展是"既满足当代人需求，又不对后代人满足其需求的能力构成危害的发展"；但原定义对这一概念内涵和外延的解释颇不足，需要加以补充和发展，特别是要有相应的理论作支撑。

我们认为，以人为本发展观及其理论构成可持续发展的理论基础。不过研究发展观和发展理论，应首先弄清发展的含义。就词语解释，发展指事物由小到大、由简单到复杂、由低级到高级的变化过程，但这样的解释偏重于外在形态变动的描述，没有揭示发展的内在变动，研究可持续发展更需要后一个方面的挖掘。为此提出：一切发展都可归纳为资源（包括自然资源和社会资源）的物质变换。如人们采掘铁矿石炼成钢铁，制成各种有用器具，推动冶金、制造业的发展；进行经济体制改革，实现人、财、物资源合理配置的国民经济和社会的发展等，都可归结为一定资源的物质变换。从这样的定义出发，以人为本的可持续发展观及其理论，当有如下五重含义。

第一，可持续发展宗旨是为了满足人的全面发展需要。发展是为了满足人的需要本属天经地义，然而随着社会生产力的发展，特别是工业革命后竞争日趋激烈，空前积聚起来的资本强烈地表现出自我增值的本性，国家、企业无不追求发展速度和规模，很难保证不脱离满足人的需要轨道，甚至走上为发展而发展的道路。这种传统的经济增长＝发展的模式，即使不偏离满足人的需要轨道，它所满足的也仅是某些方面的需要，没有或很少顾及其他方面的需要。如为了满足人的粮食需求，毁林开荒、变牧为农造成水土流失，气候变得干燥恶劣；加快化肥、农药的生产，造成水、土污染。这样的谷物生产和化学工业的发展，从一个方面看满足了人们的食品需求，维系了人口再生产的正常进行；从另一方面看则破坏了人们赖以生存的环境，妨碍了人的全面需求和人口再生产的健康进行。可持续发展着眼于人的全面发展，包括人的生理、心理、交往、文化等的全面发展，也包括有利于人的全面发展的自然环境和社会环境，摒弃有利于一个方面而损害其他方面的发展。以本例而论，就不能毁林开荒和变牧为农，发展化肥和农药也要清洁化生产，不能危及环境。1994 年开罗人口发展会议提出的"可持续发展问题的中心是人"，通观会议通过的《行动纲领》，本人以为这里的人指的就是人的全面发展。可持续发展的出发点和基本立足点，在于人的全面发展。

第二，可持续发展应将满足当代人的需要放在首位。众所周知，可持续发展率先由发达国家一些领导人和少数学者倡导，其中确有少数人想借可持续发展约束和限制发展中国家的发展。不过事与愿违，经过多次会议讨论和交锋，妨碍可持续发展的全球环境的破坏主要是发达国家不顾一切地推行工业化的结果，以至于工业化国家不得不在 1992 年的国际发展会议上作出承诺：每年从国内生产总值中拿出 0.7% 作为海外援助资金（ODA），支援发展中国家尽快摆脱贫困和改善环境。虽然仅有北欧等少数国家兑现了诺言而多数国家没有兑现，但有一点是明白无误的：可持续发展不是不要发展，相反发展中国家应加快发展以满足当代人的需要和脱离贫困。按照传统的需要划分，人的需要可分成生存需要、享乐需要和发展需要三个层次，最基本的是生存需要。满足当代人以生存需要为基础的需要，既为世界实现和平与发展两大主题所必需，也为一个国家或地区谋求在社会稳定中发展所必需。如若不能满足当代人对生活资料的需要，就难免"饥寒起盗心"，社会秩序混乱；不能满足当代生产年龄人口在就业上对生产资料、产业结构的需要，存在大量"无事生非"失业人口，社会就难以安定，正常的发展就会受到影响，更谈不上可持续发展。所以，可持续发展的前提是发展，首先是满足当代人需要的发展。尤其是发展中国家要牢牢把握住以经济建设为中心的发展，不要陷入可持续发展减慢或不发展的误区。结合中国实际，自1949年新中国成立50多年来，20世纪50年代坚持以经济建设为中心总体上比较好，50年代末至70年代后期则离开经济建设中心轨道，改革开放以来重新回到这一中心轨道上来，脱离和坚持以经济建设为中心的时间之比大致是"四六开"，有许多值得认真总结的经验和教训。始终不渝地坚持经济建设为中心，坚持首先满足当代人需要的发展，不仅证明对增强综合国力和提高人民生活水平来说是"硬道理"，而且为今后的可持续发展打下一个坚实的基础，也是可持续发展的"硬道理"。

第三，可持续发展不能损害后代人满足其需要的能力。可持续发展强调发展的连续性，这种连续性主要的不是取决于某一项或几项经济指标，而是取决于人口与经济、社会发展的代际公平，充分体现出人本主义的发展观，也是布氏《我们共同的未来》报告对可持续发展阐述的一个基本点。传统的发展＝经济增长发展观，拼命追求高经济增长，结果导致环境污染加剧，资源浪费严重和有些临近枯竭，给满足后代人需求能力的发展设置了障碍。包括大气在内的地球资源本属于全人类，不仅包括当代人也包括陆续涌来的后代人，全体人类可持续发展立足于此特别注重代际公平，是一条最基本的原则。如果当代人的发展建立在牺牲后代人利益的基础上，给后代人的发展留下障碍，便破坏了代际公平原则，也就无可持续发展可言。

以人为本发展观涉及的一个理论问题，是哲学中的人本主义学说。按照罗森塔尔、尤金编的《哲学辞典》的观点，人本主义是一种"离开具体的历史的社会关系而把人主要看做生物学上的生物的哲学原则"，但他们同时承认人本主义属于唯物主义。如果说可持续发展以人为本的发展观是一种人本理论的话，无疑包含原人本主义唯物主义成分，但不是脱离社会生产活动等的抽象的"一般人"，相反是处在具体时代，具体经济和社会发展阶段的人。人本理论的核心，是以人的全面发展为宗旨，谋求人口、资源、环境、经济、社会的协调发展，将发展可能产生的负面影响减少到最低限度。

第四，发展的根本驱动力在于人力资本。纵观人类社会发展的不同时代，自然资本、产出资本或生产资本、人力资本、社会资本的作用不断转移。大体上说来，农业及农业以前诸社会形态，经济和社会发展以自然资本为主。考察世界文明古国和农牧业发达较早的国家，大都平原广阔，土质肥沃，灌溉便利，天然的自然资本丰厚。18 世纪中叶产业革命发生后，产出资本或生产资本地位提升，首先是资本的原始积累成为工业化的条件，传统工业化借助产出资本的不断积累而推广开来。以自然资本、产出资本为主的经济和社会的发展，大都伴有对资源的掠夺性开发和利用，造成资源的严重破坏和环境的污染，尤其是传统工业化最为严重。第二次世界大战结束后，发生了以微电子技术为前导，包括新材料、新能源、宇航、激光、海洋、生物工程等在内的新的技术革命，使传统工业化升级，并且为过渡到更新现代技术革命奠定了基础。当前以基因技术、生命科学、纳米技术为标志的现代技术革命已经拉开序幕，人类基因组图的提前绘制完成，将揭开生命的奥秘；基因技术、克隆技术的新发展，生命科学的带头作用将开辟一个科学和技术发展的新时代。在这种情况下，人的知识、技能、经验和健康具有的价值，即人力资本以及同人力资本相关联的组织、管理、市场化程度等社会资本的作用，将充分展现，构成发展的决定性要素。人所共知，当今世界财富日益向知识集中，据《福布斯》公布的全球最富有人排行榜，首富为盖茨（Gates，William H. 111），2001 年个人资产达到 587 亿美元，比第二富有者巴菲特（Buffett，Warren Edward）323 亿美元多出 264 亿美元，即相当于第二富有者财富的 181.7%。微软的另一位创始人艾伦（Allen，Pawl Gardner），也以 304 亿美元位居第三。传统工业化时期的钢铁大王、煤炭大王等从最富有者中消失，知识就是财富的时代已经来临。从可持续发展角度观察，只有实现以自然资本、产出资本向人力资本以及同人力资本紧密相关的社会资本的转变，才能充分利用自然资源，提高资源利用率，有效地节约资源和保护环境。发展以人力资本为主要推动力，是具有原动力性质的发展观的一大转变。

第五，以人为本的可持续发展理论体系。建立在以人的全面发展需要为宗旨和以人力资本为发展基本驱动力基础上的以人为本可持续发展观，其理论体系应由如下五部分构成。

其一，全方位的适度人口论。前已说明，以往关于"适度人口"的理论主要限于人口的数量方面，从人口的数量变动考察与资源、发展之间的关系，说明人口是多了还是少了，找到一个合适的度。可持续发展不仅对人口数量，依据资源、环境承载量和经济、社会发展提出人口数量变动要求，寻求适合的度，而且对人口身体素质、文化教育素质、人口质量方面提出要求，对人口年龄和性别结构、城乡结构和地域分布结构提出要求，寻求人口数量、质量、结构的最佳结合，即全方位适度人口论的人口可持续发展。

其二，稀缺资源论。按照发展是资源的物质变换定义，包括可持续发展在内的任何发展，都需要有一个科学的资源发展观。所谓资源发展观，是对资源在发展中的地位和作用的基本观点，其前提建立在资源主要是自然资源有限的认识上。这个问题如同绝对真理和相对真理一样，既是绝对的、无限的，又是相对的、有限的。绝对和无限的，指随着科学和技术的不断进步，人类认识、开发和利用资源的潜力无限，能力不断增强，资源的范围也不断扩大，原本未列入资源范畴的成为新的资源，甚至是价值更高的资源。如60年前才发现核裂变，然而从第一颗原子弹爆炸到当今大规模核电站的兴建，谁都公认核能是一种最重要的能源，开创新的动力时代的能源。另一方面，在一定经济技术发展水平条件下，任何资源的数量均有一定限度，人类认识、开发和利用程度受到一定的限制，因而资源又具有相对性和有限性，并非永远取之不尽和用之不竭。正确的资源观应建立在这种绝对与相对、无限与有限相统一的基础上，对于可持续发展来说，最主要的是要树立稀缺资源发展观。即对于处于一定发展阶段的人类社会来说，资源特别是自然资源总是稀缺的，要在节约资源和合理开发利用资源中求发展。前面提及的麦多斯等罗马俱乐部的《增长的极限》报告，结论过于悲观，有些在后来自己也作了某些修正，但该报告提出的人口不断增长和人们追求高质量生活促使经济增长，经济增长加速资源的开发和利用，导致资源消耗超过人口增长速度，引起了很大关注。可持续发展必须面对资源的加剧消耗，树立稀缺资源发展观及其理论。

其三，生态系统论。可持续发展最早由国际环境会议提出，近二三十年来可持续发展讨论不断升温，同人们对环境问题的关注密切相关。发达国家惊呼，世界环境破坏已经到了十分严重的地步，传统工业化发展方式再也不能继续下去了；发展中国家虽然更强调经济发展，但是也对环境的破坏颇为担心，因而能在保护环境问题上形成较多共识。一系列关于可持续发展的国际会议通过的宣言、公约、声明，环境问题是关注的焦点。一些国际组织的环境学家多从环境和生态平衡角度阐述可持续发展，将可持续发展定义为保护和加强环境系统生产和更新能力（国际生态学联合会 INTECOOL、国际生物科学联合会 IUBS，1991）。可持续发展是一种最佳生态系统，用以支持生态的完整性和人类全体生存生活愿望的实现，使人类赖以生存的环境得以持续（弗曼，R. T. T. Forman，1991）。维护良好环境和保持生态平衡是可持续发展的前提，从这一前提出发看待人口、资源、经济和社会发展，树立相应的发展观。

环境人口观，就是要在一定生产力发展水平条件下，寻求适度人口数量以及相应的人口质量和结构。以往适度人口研究，更多侧重于经济发展和资源总量，运用不同量化分析方法计算出适宜的人口当量，自然有它的科学价值。从可持续发展要求出发，还应考虑适度人口的环境效应，有无对生态系统造成破坏，有利还是不利于已有的生态平衡。

环境资源观。就是将资源纳入生态系统考察，使资源的开发和利用有利于维持生态平衡。自然界生物之间、生物与环境之间相互依存，通过一定的信息传导、能量交换、物质循环形成特定生态系统，构成相对稳定的生物圈。从资源在生物中的作用划分，可分成由无机物质和有机物质组成的非生物环境资源，主要由绿色植物组成的生产者资源，主要由多种动物组成的消费者资源，以及主要由多种菌类和原生动物组成的分解者或还原者资源。这四类资源在生物圈运动中扮演着不同的角色，彼此间存在着一定的比例关系，形成不可分割的生物链。环境资源观就是保持这种正常的比例关系，不使生物链中断。为此就要对资源进行合理的开放和使用，注意保护那些濒临危境的资源。

生态经济观。近年来随着可持续发展研究热持续升温，一门新的生态经济学正在形成。如果说 1968 年新制度经济学家爱布尔丁（K. E. Bou-Ldting）发表"一门科学——生态经济学"一文揭开生态经济学序幕的话，其研究已由最初批评传统经济增长给环境造成的危害，提出新的价值判断和目标设想；发展到探求经济增长与环境保护的协调发展，即在维护生态平衡条件下协调经济增长与环境保护的关系，当代经济增长与满足后代人需求能力的关系；进而发展到生态经济优先发展论，环境的改变和生态的发展对经济发展目标、模式的制约呈加强的态势，人类正经历由"征服自然"、破坏生态到维护环境和生态平衡条件下的经济，任何经济的发展都不应损害环境的质量。工业要求清洁生产，农业要求生态农业，生态经济观是生态平衡发展观的中心。

其四，总体效益经济效益论。传统经济发展观追求的是产量最大化和产值最大化，通过产量和产值的最大化实现利润最大化，企业获得明显效果和利益。自从 20 世纪 30 年代凯恩斯（John Maynard Keynes）主义盛行，各国纷纷将国民生产总值（GNP）作为衡量经济发展最主要甚至是唯一的指标以来，这种工业化规模经济模式成为发展的必然选择。可持续发展针对这一发展模式提出质疑，即发展不能仅顾及企业的效益，还应顾及整个社会的效益；不能仅顾及当代的效益，还要顾及子孙后代的效益，树立总体效益经济发展观。如果说利润最大化是指导以往经济运行的基本准则和基本理论，那么总体效益最大化就是可持续发展经济追求的目标，是指导经济发展的新的发展观和理论。这一新的经济发展观和理论，有如下三重意义。

一是质量效益发展观。传统经济发展单纯追求产量、产值、利润的增长，将发展等同于经济增长，经济增长等同于数量的增加，走的是外延式扩大再生产道路。如今这样的工业化已临近尽头，经济的发展不仅取决于产品的数量，还在越来越大程度上取决于产品的质量。举一个简单的例子：$1+1=2$，1 辆可载客 4 人的小轿车，再增加 1 辆便可载客 8 人。若情况稍复杂一点儿：从 A 地送客人至 300 公里的 B 地，假定原轿车平均时速 60 公里，则每 10 小时往返一次运客 4 人，增加 1 辆运客 8 人；现增加的 1 辆是平均时速可达 120 公里的轿车，5 小时即可往返一次，10 小时送客 8 人，从送客效益说变成 $1+1=3$。即使从单纯的增长量观点观察，也是增长和发展。结合工业化颇进到现在出现的种种"工业病"，在经济增长数量和质量问题上，可持续的经济发展观看重的是效益，更强调发展的质量，以质量求发展。

二是广义空间效益发展观。上例增加的时速提高 1 倍的轿车，其质量的提高可能在用料的节省、密封和稳定性能更好、燃油更充分和减少废气排放等方面同时表现出来，如此不仅体现出 $1+1=3$ 的经济增长效益，还体现出广义空间的 $1+1>3$ 的效益。总体效益经济发展观，就是要跳出仅就本企业、本地区的经济效益狭隘眼界，把包括资源、环境、社会发展在内的外部效应收入评价视野，从经济增长和发展造成的内外部结合上看待效益，对待发展。由此产生两种投入产出：一为狭义经济意义的投入产出，即生产或经营投入成本与产出效益之比；一为广义空间意义的投入产出，即计算全社会对生产或经营投入成本与产出效益之比。传统经济发展观只注重前一种投入产出，可持续发展在注意前一种投入产出的同时，更注重后一种投入产出。

在设定发展指标体系上，也要跳出国民生产总值 GNP 或国内生产总值 GDP 单一指标束缚，选择更能表现广义空间意义的指标。美国在 20 世纪 60 年代以来开始采用包括经济、社会、环境、文化、生活质量等在内的发展指标，世界银行多年来选取人均 GNP、年平均通货膨胀率、人口出生时预期寿命、成人文盲率等指标，联合国开发计划署选用"人文发展指数"、"生活质量指数"指标，中国社会科学院社会学课题组按照人均 GNP、非农业产值比重、第三次产业产值比重、城市人口比例、非农业人口比例、大学生占 20～24 岁人口比例、人口增长率、平均预期寿命、每 1 名医生负担人口数、成人识字率 10 项指标，对中国 1993 年打分，结果在 120 个国家中排在第 73 位（朱庆芳，1995）。采用这些综合指标评价发展，更有利于说明可持续发展的能力和达到的水平，比人均 GNP 或人均 GDP 单项指标要好得多。单一的人均 GNP 或人均 GDP 指标不仅难以反映发展的程度，而且受国际外汇比价不合理因素影响，比较发展更是一个难题。如按照 1993 年外汇比例计算中国人均 GNP 不足 400 美元，而世界银行依据购买力平价法（PPP）对人均 GNF 的测算为 2330 美元，相差甚远。

三是长远时间效益发展观。发展经济注重当前的经济效益自不待言，因为任何经济发展的目标都是具体的，近期的经济效益是明显的。可持续发展总体效益经济发展观，要求在重视近期经济效益的同时，重视长远时间效益，不能以牺牲长远效益为代价获得近期效益。布伦特兰夫人定义"不对后代人满足其需求的能力构成危害"的发展，既有人口生产的代际问题，又有近期和长远时间效益的关系问题，可持续发展更注重长远时间效益是区别于传统工业化发展的一个根本性标志。由于更注重长远时间效益，发展不仅要看经济增长成果的积累，还要看这种增长对自身能力的影响，是有利于增强自身的发展能力，还是不断削弱自身的发展能力，后者是不可持续的。总体效益经济发展观着重点放在可持续发展能力的培育上，保证具有不断涌现的发展潜力，保持发展的连续性。

其五，社会协调发展论。什么是社会？社会是指由一定经济基础和上层建筑组成的总体，反映的是由共同物质条件联系起来的人群之间的关系。由此社会一是由人口生产、自然资源、劳动就业、社会保障、科学教育、卫生保健、基础建设等社会事业组成的经济基础部分组成；二是由一定的政治、法律、宗教、艺术、哲学观点等的意识形态，以及维护占统治地位意识形态政治的、法律的、军事的等国家机器所组成。社会可持续发展的基本理论，就是要随着社会生产力的发展和生产关系的改变，发展相应的社会事业，建立起促进人的全面发展的经济基础；上层建筑也应随着改变，进步的意识形态和政府管理机构、组织应运而生，推动着社会向前发展。由此可见，社会的协调发展带有整合性质，是人口、经济、资源、环境能否协调发展的整合体，强调解决人口、失业、教育、环境、贫困、安全等"热点"问题。中国政府从第六个五年计划起（1981），将原来的国民经济计划更改为国民经济和社会发展计划，社会发展被纳入总体规划。按照社会协调发展观及其理论，尤应注意解决好以下一些基本的发展关系。

第一，经济与社会发展的关系。发达国家和某些发展中国家发展的历史表明，先发展经济，待到经济发展以后再来解决社会发展的路子是不可取的。因为经济发展造成的人口问题，失业、污染、资源浪费严重、贫富差距拉大等社会问题不仅与人的全面发展背道而驰，而且这些问题达到一定程度也会妨碍经济的发展。可持续发展主张在发展经济的同时，及时公平地解决由发展造成的新的社会问题，使经济和社会同步或协调发展。这不仅有利于创造一个和谐、进步的社会，而且即使对于经济发展来说，也是必要的和必需的。

第二，经济和社会发展的合理产业结构。第一、第二、第三次产业结构怎样，既表明总体的国民经济结构，也表明社会发展的程度。医疗、卫生、保险、环保、商业、饮食、服务等产业与社会发展关系密切，第三次产业占国内生产总值GDP的比例反映出社会事业的发展状况，与经济的发展是否相协调。理论上，处在不同发展阶段上的国家，第三次产业应占一个恰当的比例，过高可能陷入福利国家泥潭，妨碍经济的发展；过低则可能拖经济发展或改革的后腿，同样有碍于经济的发展。

第三，经济和社会发展的外部形象。随着经济的发展和科学技术的进步，国家、地区之间的距离拉近了，联系增多了，一个国家的经济发展状况怎样，会对周边乃至更远的国家和地区发展产生影响。如一个国家、地区生产排放的二氧化碳、二氧化硫的数量，可能影响相邻国家、地区的大气质量，近海污染严重可能波及公海，酸雨传播由于其危害性大更受到不同国家和地区的关注。当前，在可持续发展深入人心和一系列国际公约公布于众的情况下，一个国家的经济发展及其大气、河流、海洋等环境质量怎样，受到各个国家、地区和有关国际组织的密切注视。与可持续发展密不可分的社会问题，如消除贫困、知识产权、环保立法等解决得怎样，同样受到各国和国际组织的重视。由于对人权本质认识存在分歧，除少数人利用人权做文章想达到某种政治目的外，在维护人的生存权、发展权等基本权利方面形成越来越多的共识，真实的人权状况为国际所关注。可持续发展推进到今天，各国都在塑造自己的总体形象，也就是集经济发展、环境状况、社会进步于一体的总体形象。人们依据这样的形象，判断不同国家、地区在通向可持续发展道路上的位置，估量其发展的进程。

三　可持续发展战略结构

（一）可持续发展战略总体框架结构

自可持续发展战略提出以来，迄今为止，主要涉及人口、资源、环境、经济发展和社会发展五个领域。不过这五者在可持续发展中各自处于什么样的位置，彼此之间关系怎样，立足于环境主张"生态核心论"者有之；强调人口因素的作用，主张"人口中心论"者有之；认为经济是包括可持续发展在内的一切发展的基础，主张"经济决定论"者有之，等等。我们以为，这五个方面在可持续发展中的基本关系如图1所示。

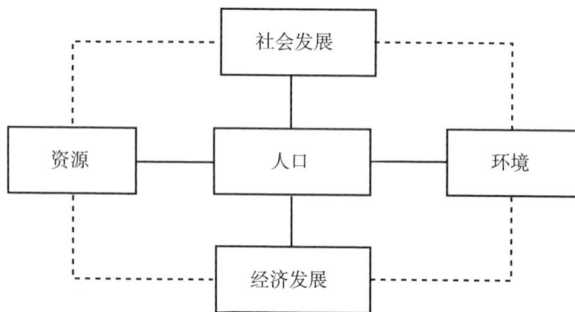

图1　人口、资源、环境、经济发展、社会发展在
可持续发展中的位置和关系

图1中，实线"——"表示要素之间直接作用关系，虚线"……"表示要素之间间接作用关系。宏观上可概括为：资源是可持续发展的起点和条件，人口是总体可持续发展的关键，环境是可持续发展的终点和目标，经济和社会发展则是宏观可持续发展的途径和调节器。

资源——可持续发展的起点和条件。从资源角度审视发展，包括可持续发展在内的一切发展，都可归结为资源的物质变换：自然资源的物质变换，社会资源的物质变换，更多的是自然资源与社会资源相结合的物质变换。因而没有资源的物质变更便谈不上发展，资源是可持续发展的起点和条件。

人口——总体可持续发展的关键。没有人类参与的自然资源进行的物质变换，是自然进化；只有人类参与并且按照人的目的进行的物质变换，才称得上发展和可持续发展。按照联合国环境与发展委员会1987年《我们共同的未来》报告中的解释，可持续发展是"既满足当代人的需要，又不对后代人满足其需要的能力构成危害的发展"，从代际关系上定义可持续发展取得较多共识，确立了以人为本的可持续发展宗旨。发展是可持续还是不可持续，紧紧同人口变动，包括人口数量、质量（含发展意识）、结构联系在一起。通过人口的生产活动和社会活动，即经济发展和社会发展改变着资源和环境，形成一定历史时期的发展模式。

环境——可持续发展的终点和目标。随着人口的迅速膨胀和人们进行物质变换手段的增强，尤其是第二次世界大战后工业化突飞猛进发展造成的环境破坏，使人们不得不反省自己的传统发展方式。如此发展下去后果怎样，发展的目的和目标是什么？于是自20世纪70年代以来率先在一系列国际环境会议上，提出和讨论环境与可持续发展，可持续发展最早由环境问题引起。环境是不同发展方式结果的警示器，可持续发展归根结底是为了创造有利于人的全面发展的环境。

经济发展和社会发展——可持续发展的途径和调节器。可持续发展要求人口、资源、环境三者相协调，依靠什么协调呢？依靠经济和社会的发展。一方面，现有资源物质变换的能力和环境的状况，是以往经济和社会发展的结果；另一方面也可以通过经济和社会发展方式、结构等的调整，改变资源变换方式和环境质量，使之向着有利于可持续发展的方向发展。

（二）人口、资源、环境可持续发展——可持续发展基本问题

由上述可持续发展总体框架结构看出，可持续发展所要解决的基本问题，就是立足于以人为本处理人类自身与外界的关系，在人类自身不断发展中，得到资源的永续利用和环境的和谐。当今表现在由人口膨胀、资源短缺、环境变坏引起的不和谐。可持续发展首先要认识这种不和谐，调整三者之间的关系使之向着和谐的方向发展，并最终实现和谐。

1. 人口——总体可持续发展的关键

目标是实现全方位的适度人口。从当今世界和中国人口现状和发展趋势出发，全方位适度人口的基本要求是控制人口的数量增长，提高人口的质量，调整人口的结构，实行"控制"、"提高"、"调整"相结合，当前则实行以数量控制为重点的方略。

继续控制人口的数量增长。世界人口变动的历史表明，第二次世界大战后迎来的"婴儿高潮"，创下20世纪60年代人口年平均增长率2.0%的记录；70年代略有下降，80和90年代继续下降，人口增长速度有所减慢。但是依据联合国的中位预测，世界人口可由2000年的60.57亿人，增加到2025年的79.37亿人，2050年的93.22亿人，2100年的94.59亿人，2150年的97.46亿人。即未来半个世纪增加32.65亿人，增长速度仍较快；2050年以后增长速度变得缓慢，但仍在不断增长，5种增长趋势如图2所示。[①]

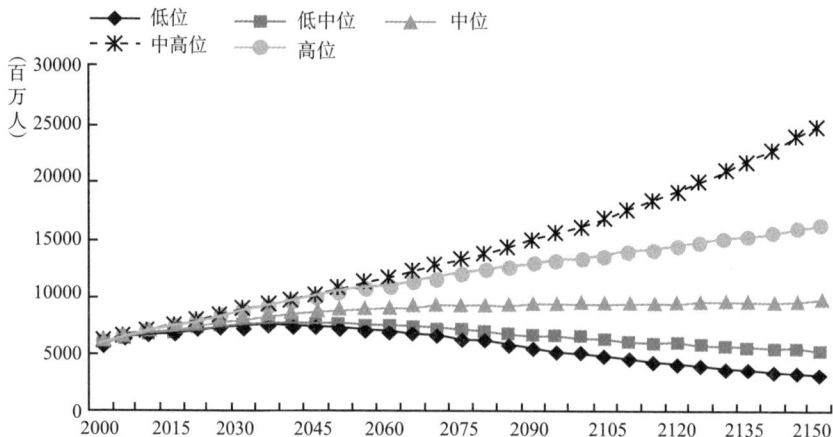

图2　2000～2150年世界人口增长预测

中国自20世纪70年代大力控制人口增长、切实加强计划生育以来，取得了举世瞩目的成绩。30年减少出生人口3亿以上，总（和）生育率（TFR）下降到2.1更替水平以下，净再生产率（NRR）下降到1.0以下，步入低生育水平国家行列。

---

① United Nations, *World Population Prospects*, *The 2000 Revision*, New York, 2001; *Long-range World Population Projections*, New York, 2000.

不过超载的"人口列车"并未停下来，联合国中位预测中国人口可由
2000 年的 12.78 亿增加到 2020 年的 14.54 亿人，2040 年的 15.04 亿人，
2050 年的 14.78 亿人，2100 年的 13.40 亿人，2150 年的 13.61 亿人。未来
50 年低、中、高 3 种预测，如图 3 所示①。

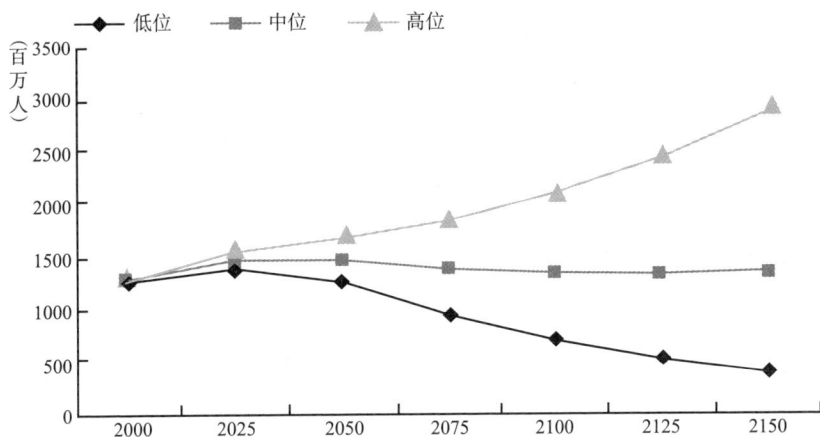

图 3　2000～2150 年中国人口变动预测

比较图 2 与图 3 可以看出：尽管中国人口增长趋势弱于世界，21 世纪
40 年代人口总数达到 15 亿～16 亿时即可实现零增长，但届时仍将再增加 2
亿多，这对于已经属于人口过剩的国家说来，数量控制仍是长期的任务。不
仅如此，控制人口的数量增长和减少未来人口消费，有助于增加积累和发展
医药卫生、文化教育事业，家庭个人和子女也可获得更多深造机会，双重有
利于人口身体、文化教育素质的提高。通过控制出生率和每年出生人口数
量，年复一年地逐渐改变年龄结构，是调整生产年龄人口、老年人口比例等
年龄结构的基本手段。城乡、地区分布受制于不同的生育率和出生率，不过
这两种结构的调整还受到人口迁移和流动机械变动的影响，而机械变动也直
接或间接同城乡、地区间的生育控制程度相关。因此，人口的数量控制牵动
"控制"、"提高"、"调整"人口全局，是目前中国乃至世界总体人口实施可
持续发展战略的首要立足点和重点。

---

① United Nations, *World Population Prospects*, *The 2000 Revision*, New York, 2001；*Long-range World Population Projections*, New York, 2000.

提高人口的质量。人口作为居住在一定地域内的居民总体而言，是数量和质量的统一。一般认为人口质量包括人口的身体素质和文化教育素质，也有的主张应包括人口的思想道德素质。前已述及，在人口过剩国度控制人口数量增长有助于人口素质的提高，而人口素质尤其是文化教育素质的提高，也有利于人口的数量控制，生育率与人口文化教育程度高低呈反向变动趋势。结合 21 世纪初中国实际，人口身体素质的提高，2005 年婴儿死亡率下降到 31‰左右，2010 年可下降到 30‰以内，预期寿命按国际一般规律年平均升高 0.2 岁，2005 年可上升到 72 岁，2010 年可上升到 73 岁。人口文化教育素质的提高，重点是加强贫困地区和少数民族地区普及九年义务教育，城市和有条件的农村地区基本普及高中教育，初中毛入学率达到 90% 以上，高等教育毛入学率大幅度提高。

调整人口的结构。主要是人口年龄结构、城乡结构和地区分布结构的调整，使之适应可持续发展要求。

人口年龄结构的调整。人口学依据总体人口的年龄结构状况，区分为年轻型、成年型、老年型三种基本类型。目前中国人口年龄结构开始步入老年型，前已述及，这是实现人口零增长和可持续发展的必经阶段。根据预测，中国 60 岁以上老年人口比例和年龄中位数，可由 2000 年的 10.1%、30 岁上升到 2010 年的 12.2%、34.5 岁，2020 年的 16.6%、37.3 岁，2050 年的 29.7%、43.7 岁，21 世纪上半叶将持续升高。实现上述年龄结构老龄化进程调整，关键在于生育率控制的水平，总（和）生育率 2000~2010 年控制在 1.86 左右，2010 年以后保持在 1.90 左右即可达到。

人口城乡结构的调整。2000 年全国人口普查城镇人口占 36.22%，乡村人口占 63.78%；第一、二、三次产业就业结构为 1.00∶0.45∶0.55，按产值计算的产业结构为 1.00∶3.20∶2.09，同塞尔奎因—钱纳里（Syrquin M. and H. Chenery）国际标准模式，人均 GDP 达到 800 美元时城市人口比例占 60%，三次产业就业结构在 1.0∶0.3∶0.4，三次产业结构为 1.0∶1.1∶1.1 左右比较，我国城市化水平严重滞后，三次产业就业结构二、三次产业偏高，而按产值计算的产业结构二、三次产业则成倍超标。为什么会出现这种情况？一是统计口径上的原因，尽管大量流动人口长期居住生活在城市，统计上仍计为"乡村人口"；尽管长期从事城市工商业，统计上仍计为"农业人口"。二是长期以来限制乡村人口进城务工经商，使人口城市化水平滞后。有鉴于此，我们从 2000 年市镇人口占 36% 作为基期，以过去 50 年市镇人口年平均增长 3.85% 为中值外推，则 2005 年市镇人口可达 5.48 亿，占 41.3%，2010 年可达 6.62 亿，占 48.2%，即略高于届时的发展中国家一般水平。

人口地区分布结构的调整。按人口密度划分，自西向东逐步加大，呈"三大平台"分布：2000 年西南、西北 10 省区市人口 28666 万，人口密度（人/平方公里）52.4，中部 9 省区人口 43940 万，人口密度 155.2，东部沿海 12 省区市人口 53622 万，人口密度 412.5，东部为中部的 2.66 倍，为西部的 7.88 倍。不过这种"三大平台"式分布，是地理、环境、自然资源和经济社会长期发展作用的结果，可持续发展不要求作出大的改变。正在实施的西部大开发战略，西部缺少的不是人口的数量，而是人口的质量，特别是现代化建设要求的高素质人才。改革开放以来，西部人才"孔雀东南飞"严重，这给本来人口文化教育素质较低的西部带来新的人力资本短缺。如将西部地区自然资本、产出资本、人力资本、社会资本加以比较发现，自然资本蓄势较强，如土地占全国 56.9%，45 种矿产资源占 39.7%；其余 3 种资本相对不足，但是最贫乏的是人力资本，仅占全国 20.6%，是制约西部开发的"瓶颈"。因此，西部开发不需要大量增加人口的数量，需要的是提高人口的质量，重在人力资本的积聚。创造留住和吸引人才相应机制，发展科学和教育事业是西部开发的基础和重心所在，也是人口地区分布可持续发展的核心所在。

2. 资源——总体可持续发展的前提

关于资源，联合国环境规划署（UNEP）定义为：所谓资源特别是自然资源，是指在一定时间、地点条件下能够产生经济价值，以提高人类当前和未来福利的自然环境因素和条件。我们基本赞同这一观点，在此基础上将资源定义为：自然界和人类社会一切有价值的物质，即为资源。它包括三层含义：一是资源不仅存在于自然界，如土地、淡水、矿产等自然资源；而且存在于人类社会，主要是人力、科技、管理、信息等社会资源。二是资源的价值属性，任何资源均有其可开发、利用的价值。三是资源的物质属性，虽然科学家正在探索是否存在非物质和反物质，但是现存世界的统一性仍在于它的物质性；有的社会资源，像管理一类被称为"看不见的资源"，然而这种"看不见"或储存在人的大脑中，或储存在大脑的物化形态计算机、书刊资料中，以看得见的物质载体存在为条件。据此可将资源分成两大类：自然资源和社会资源。自然资源可分成再生性资源、非再生性资源和恒定性资源三种。太阳能、风能、潮汐能源基本是恒定性的，不过这种恒定性也是带有某种相对性质。土地、森林等再生性资源，可以重复使用，可以通过人工修整、营造使之复得和再生；但若再生的速度赶不上人口增长和经济增长的需要，便产生资源短缺。至于各种金属和非金属矿产非再生性资源用掉一点儿少一点儿，一般均不能复得和再生，则处于绝对短缺状态。因此在总体上，资源是稀缺的，而且稀缺的程度同人口的数量变动和消费水平的提高密切相关。如上所述，世界人口在工业革命后神话般地增长起来，21世纪仍旧方兴未艾，1650～2050年的400年间由5亿人增加到近90亿人，增长17倍，即使以简单的算术倍加，对资源消耗的增加也十分可观。而事实上远非如此，人口对资源消耗的增加不仅来自人口绝对数量的增加，而且来自每个人消耗量的增长，在人均资源减少过程中表现为很强的"加权效应"。在农业社会，由于社会生产力不发达，生产扩张受到限制，消费资源的生产规模和结构受到限制。进入工业化社会冲破许多限制，在人们追求高生活质量驱动下，消费资料尤其是多种耐用消费品的巨大增长迅速更新换代，使人均消耗资源大增，人口作为分母对资源消耗表现出强有力的"加权效应"。联合国的一项统计表明，1960～1985年世界人口由30亿增加到48亿，增长60%；同期世界能源消耗增长130%，倍加于人口增长最主要的原因，是由于人均能源实际人口作为分母对资源消耗产生的"加权效应"所致。随着经济的发展，人们追求高生活质量欲望的增强，21世纪人口作为分母对资源消耗产生的"加权效应"呈增强态势。尤其是人口城市化的加速推进，使这种"加权效应"不断升级，资源短缺加剧，许多国家和地区已亮出"黄牌警告"。

中国素以"地大物博"著称于世，自然资源比较丰富且品种比较齐全，是少数可以基本上依靠本国资源建立起比较完整的国民经济体系的国家之一，同时也是"人口众多"且增长较快的发展中国家，人口增长对资源消耗的"加权效应"也相当明显。所以常常是某些重要资源绝对数量在世界名列前茅，而人均占有量却名落孙山。如具有潜在价值的矿产资源总量排在世界第3位，人均占有量却仅相当于世界平均水平的1/2，草场、耕地、森林资源的人均占有量，也只有世界平均水平的1/2、1/3、1/6，由总量"资源大国"变成人均"资源小国"。随着人口增长和资源消耗量的增大，总体资源稀缺性加剧，耕地、淡水等资源短缺严重，制约着可持续发展。因此，对于中国来说，控制人口的数量增长是一项拯救资源短缺带有根本性的战略举措，是治本方略之一。只是不要忘记，这是减少资源短缺的外部效应，解决资源短缺还必须从资源的开发利用本身具有的内部效应去寻找。

改革开放总设计师邓小平讲过一句名言："发展是硬道理"。中国要发展，就不能接受某些西方人士关于"低增长"、"零增长"的说教，中国已将"十五"计划经济增长率选定在 7% 左右。那么面对人口增长、经济快速增长对环境压力增大的客观形势，如何走出资源可持续发展的路子？综合已有研究成果，不外乎三剂"药方"：一曰保护资源。即对现有的资源主要是自然资源加以保护，不得随意滥垦滥伐、胡挖乱采破坏资源。二曰提高再生能力。对再生资源加强维护、扩大再生规模和提高质量，尤其是耕地、林木、草场的再生。三曰提高资源利用率。包括节约资源，发展替代资源，减少单位产值的自然资本消耗。毫无疑问，三剂"药方"均不可缺少，但是笔者以为三者不是并列的，必须面对 21 世纪首先是 21 世纪初中国将加快社会经济发展实际，而发展又是资源的物质变换，面对资源消耗增加选择战略重点——提高资源利用率，走节约资源型发展道路。主要是：建立节约和集约化资源的产业结构，包括节约和集约化使用水、土地、生物资源的农业产业结构，节约和综合利用水、能源、矿产资源等的工业结构，节约和集约化经营使用再生和非再生资源的国民经济三次产业结构、消费结构、技术结构、城乡结构、外贸结构和社会结构，将最大限度地提高资源利用率与社会经济发展结合起来。

3. 环境——总体可持续发展的目标

地球 15 公里以下大气层和 11 公里厚度以内地壳，是人类和其他动植物生存和活动的基本领域，也是我们讲环境的基本范畴，定义为生物圈。生物圈内绿色植物生产者、消费者、分解还原者的数量保持着一定的比例，形成一定的生物链，维持着生态的平衡。人类诞生以前，生物圈保持着良好的循环，人类诞生直到农业社会，生态平衡也基本保持在良好状态。工业革命发生后，随着人口的迅速增长和社会生产力的发展，人类"征服自然"手段的无比增强，城市化的迅速推进，对生物圈内的生产、消费、分解还原实行全面干预的结果，从人类角度说取得了无与伦比的巨大胜利，从自然界角度说受到越来越严重的破坏，对人类干预的一种报复性破坏。谋求环境的可持续发展，就是根除这种"战胜自然"的破坏，保持生物链不受损害，摆正人类和人类活动在自然界的位置，维护生态系统的平衡。

中国作为人口最多的发展中国家，随着人口的增长和工业化的加速推进，不可避免地带来诸多环境问题。值得称道的是，继控制人口增长列为基本国策后环境保护列为第二项基本国策，一面加强宣传教育，增强人们的环境意识；一面增加投入，加大环境治理力度，在国民经济高速增长的同时控制住环境污染恶化趋势，环境保护取得显著成绩。与此同时，近年来环境问题也出现了一些新的变化和特点：一是工业污染有所减轻，农业污染和城市生活污染加重。如全国县以上工业企业工业废水排放量由 1995 年的 2218943 万吨，减少到 1999 年的 1607678 万吨，2000 年的 1530558 万吨；工业二氧化硫排放量由 1405 万吨，减少到 1078 万吨和 1149 万吨；工业粉尘排放量由 639 万吨，减少到 458 万吨和 404 万吨；工业固体废物产生量有升有降，变动不大①。总体上工业"三废"有所减少。农业化肥和某些农药的施用量却不断上升，污染加重；城市生活垃圾清运量和污水排放量也上升较快，一多半的城市被"垃圾山"和污水"护城河"包围。二是污染由工业点源式，逐步扩大到面源式。20 世纪 90 年代以前工业污染源主要以工矿企业为主，星罗棋布分散各地；现在随着工业化的推进和乡镇企业的发展，各种杀虫剂在农业生产、园林绿化、家庭生活中的广泛应用，汽车尾气和塑料白色污染的加剧等，面源污染呈扩张之势。三是随着环境破坏面的扩大，发展到危及生态平衡。主要指毁林开荒、变牧为农、围湖造田造成水土流失，水旱灾害严重，尤其是黄河、长江两大"母亲河"令人担忧，使广大流域面积生态均遭到不同程度的破坏。

面对上述严峻形势，寻求中国环境的可持续发展，需要将保护环境、改善环境、人口与环境和谐发展结合起来，实行融"保护"、"改善"、"和谐"于一体，当前实行以保护环境为主的方略。这几个方面是相互促进的，而且由于中国人口众多、幅员辽阔和发展不平衡，能够做到人口与环境和谐发展，即人口呈稳定态势，环境质量良好，如某些生态模范试验区所做的那样，毕竟是少数；目前总体人口在增长，环境不同程度受到损害，"和谐"尚待时日。改善环境正在全国普遍展开，长江中上游实行退耕还林、还草、还湖，国家在政策上予以补贴；黄河小流域治理、城市污染治理等也以不同的规模展开，许多已取得明显成效，都需要继续坚持并扩大已经取得的成果。但是不要忘记，一是 21 世纪中国仍将继续进行大规模的经济建设，特别在相对落后的中西部实施西部大开发战略，通过注入资金、技术、人才等社会资本启动西部的自然资本，保护西部的环境是大开发首先必须解决的问

---

① 《中国统计年鉴 2000》，中国统计出版社，2001。

题。西部生态系统脆弱，西北干旱少雨，沙漠化严重；西南青藏高原、云贵高原土地贫瘠，石漠化严重，必须严加保护。东部地区固然要加大治理和改善环境力度，但是首先还是要保护现存环境不再遭到大的破坏，不让工业化、城市化的推进造成新的更大的破坏。二是人口仍在继续增长，在人口压力不断增强的条件下控制环境质量下降趋势，是一件相当困难的事情。面对这一现实，当务之急就是要使环境不再恶化，守住现有环境质量水平线。其次是根据经济社会发展水平和提供的能力，有计划、有重点地进行治理，改善和提高环境质量，并逐步实现人口与环境的和谐发展。

依据上述环境可持续发展战略，相应的决策选择，一是要扩大宣传，加强全民的环境意识。使更多的人认识到环境直接关系到人类的生存和发展，认识到只有一个地球、一种选择——保护环境。唤起近 13 亿民众关心环境、爱护环境、改善环境。二是要严格执法，贯彻落实《环境保护法》。中国政府已将环境保护列为基本国策之一，并且颁布了《环境保护法》，就要依法行事，违法必究。目前"上有政策、下有对策"，执法不严比较普遍，要严格执法检查和查处力度。三是要加大环境治理投入，包括中央财政、地方财政都要增加必要的资金投入。四是实施环保市场取向的改革。主要是两方面：其一，发展环境保护产业。企业排放的废水、废气、固体废物大都含有可利用物质，为相应产业的发展提供了原材料，应当大力发展环保产业，变废为宝。实践已经证明，在这方面是大有作为的。其二，推动环保市场取向的改革。按照美国经济学家科斯（Coase）的理论，将社会效益转化成企业内部的效益，企业的存亡取决于社会效益的最大化，而不是单纯的个别企业行为。如一个种植小麦的农场和一个饲养奶牛的牧场比邻，如果因为奶牛常常去吃农场的小麦而关掉牧场，社会效益仅是农场一家，减少许多；相反，如果通过契约形式在农场与牧场之间建立一种于双方均有利的赔偿规定，农场主不再担心小麦被奶牛吃掉，双方照常经营，则社会效益是农场与牧场两家之和，达到最大化。目前中国处在加快发展又要大力整治环境"二律背反"境地，因而要实行兼顾原则。即在国家允许的排污限度内，通过污染生产者和消费者之间达成某种协议，实行补偿制，达到社会效益最大化。现在的问题是，要么污染生产过于严重，下令停产整顿或干脆关掉；要么不闻不问，受污染者得不到补偿。简单的取缔和不予补偿均不符合市场经济原则，也不符合社会效益最大化的最高准则，必须进行改革。改革的方向就是在允许排污限度内，污染生产者（排放者）与消费者（受害者）之间建立一定的补偿制度，符合市场经济通行原则的一种补偿制度，使加快发展与保护环境兼顾起来。

（三）经济和社会可持续发展

以上的分析表明，衡量一个国家或地区可持续发展水平，主要标志是人口、资源、环境状况以及彼此之间的关系。这种状况和关系既是静态的，在一定时点上有着具体的指标，因而三者之间的关系得到明显的体现；也是动态的，不断变化和发展着的。这种变化和发展有着人口、资源、环境自身方面的原因，人口变动有着一定的规律，非再生性资源逐步减少的趋势，生态系统演变的规律等，受到社会政策因素影响颇大，而社会政策也是社会经济发展到一定阶段的产物。更为重要的是，人口、资源、环境直接受经济发展和社会发展制约，经济和社会发展是可持续发展主要的调控杠杆。

1. 对人口可持续发展的作用与调控

考察世界特别是发达国家人口由高出生、低死亡、高增长向低出生、低死亡、低增长的转变，虽然某些国家也曾有过某些生育政策，发挥过一定的作用，但是一致的认识是：人口转变的完成主要是经济发展和社会进步的结果，是"自然而然"完成的转变。中国自20世纪70年代大力加强计划生育完成的人口转变，较多的共识是控制人口增长生育政策的实施居首位，同时也承认经济发展和社会进步的作用，尤其是改革开放以来社会经济发展的基础作用。今后这种作用还会进一步增强，成为生育观念转变的基础。为什么呢？依据经济学家、人口学家莱宾斯坦（Harrey Leibenstein）、贝克尔（Gary S. Becker）、伊斯特林（R. A. Easterline）等的孩子成本—效益理论，可以作出这样的阐述：家庭规模的确定由父母对生育子女的选择完成，而是否生育子女的选择取决于孩子预期的成本与可能提供的效益。孩子成本可分做两部分：直接成本，即从母亲怀孕时起至将子女抚养成为成年人止所花费的衣、食、住、行、医疗、教育、婚姻、交往等的费用，亦即直接花费在孩子身上的货币支出；间接成本，即指父母亲因为生育子女耗费时间损失，主要是母亲因怀孕、妊娠和哺乳期间损失的工资收入，父母因为照料子女耗时而丧失的获取更有利工作岗位、升迁以及接受教育时减少的收入。亦即因为抚育子女占用时间而减少可能收入的机会，故又称为机会成本，是一种间接形式的货币支出。

家庭生育子女付出一定的直接成本、间接成本不可避免，不过这绝非父母想生育的目的，父母生育的动机在于孩子对父母可能提供的效益。莱宾斯坦学说大致从以下 6 个方面说明孩子提供的效益。

一为劳动—经济效益。孩子成长为劳动力以后，可以为家庭提供劳动或服务，给家庭创造经济收入。

二为养老—保险效益。主要是在经济不够发达的社会保障比较薄弱国家，老年经济生活保障和生活服务不得不在较大程度上依赖子女，表现出代际交换的子女供养功能。

三为消费—享乐效益。孩子作为"消费品"，具有满足父母情感和精神需要的功能。这是其他消费品所不具备的，可以带来"天伦之乐"的特殊的精神效益。

四为继承家业效益。子女为父母财产的天然继承人，无论在发展中国家还是发达国家，除特殊情况外普遍存在。

五为安全保卫效益。子女同样为家庭安全的天然卫士，子女多少、强弱关系到家庭安全系数，在不发达社会家庭或家族势力显然尤为重要。

六为维系家庭地位的效益。孩子不仅一般地具有上述功能，其数量多寡，智商和智能高低，性别结构怎样，对家庭现实和未来地位有重要影响，关系到后继有人问题。

莱宾斯坦指出，孩子的成本同收入呈正相关关系，直接成本随着收入的增加而上升，间接成本或机会成本随着时间价值的增值也呈上升趋势。孩子的效益除消费—享乐效益变动不明显外，随着经济的发展和家庭收入的增加，技术的进步，教育水平的提高，呈下降趋势。孩子质量成本上升，这是因为在经济、技术进步条件下，家庭投入教育等方面的成本可以带来更多的效益。而随着收入增加和储蓄的扩大，家庭老年自身保障能力的增强，社会养老保障事业的发展，孩子的养老—保障效益大为削弱。其他继承家业的效益、安全保卫的效益、维系家庭地位的效益等，也都程度不同地随着经济、技术、社会的发展表现出下降之势。莱宾斯坦还考察了家庭中核心家庭比例上升、人口城市化、死亡率下降、妇女受教育程度提高、父母对男性孩子性别偏好的减退、传统观念的淡化、各种避孕药具的推广使用等诸多社会因素在生育率下降中的作用，但他认为归根结底还是经济因素的作用。他按照每户平均收入水平划分成不同层次的社会经济群体，从总体上观察，发展中国家正由农业型向工业型转变，孩子的直接成本和间接成本随着这种转变而上升，除孩子消费—享乐效益外，其他效益则随着这种转变而下降，尤以养老—保险效益、劳动—经济效益下降为最快。发达国家孩子成本大幅度上升，效益却明显下降，许多为社会所取代因而导致出生率一降再降。

贝克尔将家庭劳动力置于市场之中，运用消费需求理论阐述家庭生育决策，创立了孩子数量与质量替代理论和替代模型。他运用无差异曲线论、消费均衡论等方法论分析孩子效用的最大化，决定家庭对孩子的需求。

如果以孩子作为一类耐用消费品，其他商品作为另一类耐用消费品，令 πn 代表孩子数量价格，πz 代表单位商品价格，N 代表孩子数，Z 代表商品单位，Y 代表家庭总收入，则家庭预算限制线表示如下关系：

$$Y = \pi n N + \pi z Z$$

不过这里 N 代表孩子数量，抽象掉了用于孩子医疗、健康、教育等孩子质量成本上的差别。如考虑到这种差别，u 代表家庭取得的效益，N 仍代表孩子数量，Q 代表孩子质量，Z 代表其他商品，那么家庭效益函数可表示为：

$$U = u(N, Q, Z_1 \cdots\cdots Z_n)$$

将以上二式联系起来，首先可以看出孩子的相对价格效应：孩子相对价格上升，对孩子的数量需求减少；孩子相对价格下降，对孩子的数量需求增加。其次可以看出，随着经济的发展和人均收入的增加，劳动力特别是女性劳动力市场工资率上升，而非市场活动时间的影子价格近似地等同市场的工资率，使得孩子相对价格上升。随着农业现代化的推进，乡村儿童就学时间的延长，直接导致孩子相对价格的上升。尽管当孩子作为耐用消费品，当家庭收入增加时用在孩子身上的数量成本和质量成本都可以增加，但是由于孩子数量成本弹性小，质量成本弹性相当大，人们的选择偏好便自然投向后者，发生由孩子质量成本替代孩子数量成本现象。这种替代之所以成为可能，是避孕药具的发明和避孕节育手段的发展，人们可以自己选择生育子女的数量。而且，在家庭收入一定的条件下，孩子数量与孩子质量还是一种负相关的关系。家庭父母为了追求效用最大化，自然而然地选择了以发展和家庭收入增加带来的生育率的下降。

伊斯特林提出并论证了孩子供给与需求对生育的影响，即不考虑其他变量的影响，父母期望的存活孩子数，决定于父母的自然生育率和子女存活率。关于生育控制的成本变量，包括因采用控制手段付出的经济成本，因采取节育措施、克服心理障碍而付出的心理成本——在不考虑这些成本情况下，若孩子的供给小于对孩子的需求，如农业社会那样，不发生生育控制的要求；若孩子的供给大于对孩子的需求，便发生对生育控制的要求。有了控制生育的要求，伊斯特林指出生育控制成本就会影响这个值得注意的变量。他认为，发达国家生育控制成本已经趋近于零，在婴儿和儿童死亡率大大降低后，亦即由于子女存活率的提高大大加大了孩子的供给，使节育的普及有着较好的社会经济基础，故生育率可以保持在比较低的水平。相反，发展中国家无论是在控制生育率手段上付出的经济成本，还是在消除节育障碍上付出的心理成本均比较高，在婴儿死亡率和儿童死亡率较高的情况下，亦即由于子女存活率比较低减少孩子供给，节育的普及程度往往就差一些，生育率便不容易降下来，尤其在经济、文化、社会发展水平很低的地区。

上述西方孩子成本—效益理论，给予生育率变动以经济学解释，从微观经济学角度科学地解析了家庭生育决策选择。然而它忽略了其他因素，特别是社会政策因素的影响。中国以及许多发展中国家由于奉行节制生育政策而导致出生率下降的事实，证明社会发展的政策作用不可低估。据此，提出孩子社会附加成本—效益理论（田雪原，1995）。伊斯特林曾经提出过生育控制的经济成本和心理成本，前者指的是用在节育措施上而支付的费用成本，后者指的是因不愿采取某种节育措施而付出的心理上的一种损失，即个人在接受节育实施中付出的有形和无形的成本。它不涉及社会干预，特别不涉及政府的或民间的生育政策的干预的影响，因而没有突破西方微观人口经济学中孩子成本—效益基本理论框架的约束。本人的孩子社会附加成本—效益与伊斯特林的阐述是不同的概念，它所阐述的是，如何将政府的生育政策等社会因素纳入孩子成本—效益视野，科学地说明社会因素在生育率变动中的作用，由社会外在因素决定，在原家庭孩子成本—效益之外增加或减少的成本—效益之上，故称为孩子社会附加成本—效益，包括下面三层含义。

一层含义，由社会外在因素决定。本来孩子成本—效益是用来解释家庭生育子女数量选择，说明家庭规模变动的一种理论，属微观人口经济学范畴，不受社会变动左右。然而随着人口的增加，经济和社会的发展，不同类型的人口问题突出出来，政府直接或间接的干预变得重要起来，而政府干预人口生产的手段之一，便是通过经济的办法影响孩子的成本—效益。故在这个意义上，可分成直接孩子社会附加成本—效益和间接孩子社会附加成本—效益两种。所谓直接孩子社会附加成本—效益，是指政府通过具有法律效力的规定条款，特别是关于鼓励或限制生育的规定条款，通过直接的经济的办法影响孩子的成本—效益。如目前中国普遍实施的独生子女奖励费，就是动用社会外在力量，在孩子远未达到可为家庭提供经济效益之前，父母从领取独生子女证起便可按年度领取奖励费，实为提前实现孩子的经济效益。而所谓间接孩子社会附加成本—效益，是指社会通过非直接的经济干预，特别是关于鼓励或限制生育的非直接经济干预，影响原家庭的孩子成本—效益。非直接的经济干预，主要指政府和社会各界运用行政的、舆论的手段，影响家庭生育边际孩子的精神或心理上的成本—效益。如中国目前大力提倡一对夫妇生育一个孩子，开展这方面的宣传，给独生子女家庭发"光荣证"，父母所在单位也对其进行表彰，这无异于增加了该独生子女父母的精神或心理效益。同样，对计划外生育子女父母进行批评教育和必要的行政处分，这在事实上形成了父母的精神或心理成本，影响父母生育子女数量的选择。

二层含义，总体孩子成本—效益由家庭和社会两部分构成，但家庭的孩子成本—效益是基础，没有家庭的孩子成本—效益，便谈不上社会附加的成本—效益。不过在一定历史条件下，一旦孩子社会附加成本—效益形成严格规范，具有相对独立的性质，其对家庭生育决策的作用便不可低估，中国等一些国家推行计划生育成功的经验就是例证。家庭的孩子成本—效益更接近市场经济，其理论模型和估算方法多借鉴市场经济学说。孩子社会附加成本—效益似乎主要体现政府的意志，偏离市场经济较远，实则科学地确定这种社会附加的孩子成本—效益非但不排斥市场经济，相反同样要借助市场经济，运用市场经济分析方法，找出社会附加成本—效益的适当量值。不言而喻，量值过高或过低不是对家庭就是对社会不利，最终影响孩子附加成本—效益作用的发挥。

三层含义，增加或减少孩子成本—效益的意义。包括用社会附加手段增加孩子成本，减少孩子成本，增加孩子效益，减少孩子效益4项单因素调整，也包括成本与效益相结合的4项调整：增加孩子成本与增加孩子效益，增加孩子成本与减少孩子效益，减少孩子成本与减少孩子效益，减少孩子成本与增加孩子效益。单项调整与结构式调整合计达8项之多，从而为孩子社会附加成本—效益政策和措施的出台，提供了广阔的思路。它同时告诉我们，孩子社会附加成本—效益的调节影响是比较复杂的，一般来说，即使是单项措施的调整，其影响也会波及另一方面。如我国实行的独生子女奖励费属提高孩子社会附加效益范畴，也会对某些经济条件困难家庭起到一定的作用。但独生子女地位在现代家庭中的确立，大大提高了家庭支付的成本，提高的幅度一般远非很少一点儿的奖励费所能抵上。我们运用孩子社会附加成本—效益理论实施某种调节时，一定要注意它的直接效果和影响，也要注意它的间接效果和影响。

孩子社会附加成本—效益同样是可以计量的。直接的经济成本—效益可以计量，间接的心理的和精神的成本—效益，则可以通过"影子价格"计算出"影子成本"和"影子效益"。如此，将社会调控同市场经济结合起来，给经济发展和社会发展调整人口的生产以新的思路。不仅有理论创新意义，而且有助于对人口变动作出实事求是的估量，把握人口变动的"脉搏"。

需要指出，经济和社会发展在通过孩子成本—效益调整生育率变动的同时，也改变着人口的年龄、城乡、地域分布结构，改变着人口身体和文化教育素质。生育率和出生率在人口转变中的变动，由高出生、高死亡、低增长向高出生、低死亡、高增长转变，发生人口年龄结构年轻化趋向；而由高出生、低死亡、高增长向低出生、低死亡、低增长转变，发生人口老龄化趋向，人口年龄结构变动是生育率和出生率，也是经济发展和社会发展的人口学表象。人口城市化历来伴随经济和社会发展而发展，现代意义上的人口城市化则是工业化的产物。人口城市分布是生产力布局的反映，而人口地域分布又影响生产力布局则是不争的事实。在人口数量与质量关系中，出生率的下降和出生子女数量的减少有利于出生人口素质的提高，有利于优生优育也是不争的事实；而生育率与经济发展水平、人口文化教育素质高低成反比，也是人口转变中带有普遍意义的现象。这一现象的含义同孩子成本—效益变动相关联，体现经济发展和社会的基础作用。因此，从长远和战略上观察，人口可持续发展要建立在经济和社会不断发展的基础上，基础的不断改善是人口可持续发展的保证。

2. 对资源可持续发展的作用与调控

经济和社会发展对资源的影响和调控，可从三个层面上把握。

其一，经济和社会发展表现为量的扩张的影响和调整。从实践上看，发展首先表现为量的扩张，由量变到质变是普遍的规律，经济发展和社会发展也不例外。在发展史上，这种表现为量的扩张的经济和社会的发展，往往伴随着人口的量的扩张，人口消费的扩张。消费扩张要求生产需求扩张，从而形成资源消耗的扩张。因此，经济发展和社会发展在表现为量的扩张时，是资源消耗的增加，资源短缺的加剧。

其二，经济和社会发展表现为质的提高的影响和调控。经济和社会发展表现为质的提高，贯穿于人类发展史全部，只是这种提高具有阶段的性质，对资源的消耗也有阶段性的特点。在人类诞生的早期阶段，对资源的消耗以自然界直接提供的用品为主，如淡水、鱼、虾类水产品，果实、野菜类天然食品，木材、药材类天然资源。随着经济的发展和技术进步，农业、手工业、商业三次社会大分工的完成，社会进展到农业社会，经济和社会发展由以消耗天然生活资料为主进入耕作和驯养为主，土地、森林、草场等自然资源成为人类消耗即人口生产的生活资料的主要对象，总体上对资源的消耗大大增加了。18 世纪中叶产业革命发生后，随着工业化的逐步展开，机器大工业取代工场手工业，大批农民流进城市变成产业工人，使自然资源的消耗产生了一个飞跃。一是煤炭、石油等化石能源大量开采和使用，带动矿山、冶金、机器制造业等迅速发展，金属和非金属矿产资源得到空前的开发利用；二是化学工业的蓬勃发展，带动了化工、塑料、材料工业等的崛起，开辟了利用自然资源的新领域。三是第二次世界大战后以微电子技术为前导和当前以生命科学为带头学科的新技术革命的兴起，新能源、新材料、新技术不断涌现，使人类对资源的消耗进入了一个新的阶段。一方面资源消耗量与日俱增，包括不断扩大的资源种类，尤应提及的是人们追求高生活质量欲望无止境，人口增长表现出很强的"加权效应"，加剧着资源短缺态势；另一方面以质的提高为主的社会经济发展，必然以科技进步为杠杆，而科技进步又必然带来资源的新的发现和新的应用。以能源为例，农业及农业以前社会以薪柴为主，伴有少量煤炭的开采；工业社会由煤炭为主逐步转向石油、天然气、电力、核动力为主，发生传统工业化向现代工业化能源结构的改变，大大扩展了能源资源。化学工业发展引发材料革命，各种合成材料的出现拓展了材料资源。总的趋势是，以质的提高为主导的社会经济发展，正经历由消耗资源型为主向以扩张资源型为主的转变，转变的关键在于技术进步和经济的发达程度，呈倒"U"形运动轨迹。目前发达国家已越过这一转折点，发展中国家总体上尚未到达这一转折点。

其三，经济增长方式转变的影响和调控。传统经济增长方式以增加投资外延式扩大再生产为主，资源消耗随之增加；现代经济增长方式以技术进步、科学管理提高劳动生产率为主，内涵式扩大再生产降低了单位产品的资源消耗。在这方面存在的差距是很大的。无论是钢铁、化工，还是粮食、蔬菜，我们消耗的铁矿石、焦炭、酸、碱、盐、电能、淡水、化肥等，都比世界先进水平高出一大截，资源的利用率不够高。虽然改革开放以来屡屡强调经济增长方式"两个转变",即由过去高度集中统一的计划经济向市场经济转变,由粗放式经营向集约化经营转变。但是后一个转变则始终不甚理想,外延式扩大再生产占据一定的优势,资源利用率不高和浪费比较严重。要谋求资源的可持续发展,经济增长方式的转变是重要的环节。发达国家发展的历史也提供了这方面的经验。

3. 对环境可持续发展的作用与调控

经济和社会发展对环境的影响,同人口增长、迁移和资源消耗联系在一起,对可持续发展来说更为重要,具有本源的性质。

其一,农业社会和农村经济发展的影响与调控。迄今为止,除原始社会外,农业社会占据历史长河中的很长一段时间,人类从事农耕的历史可追溯到一万年以前。即使在当代,农业和农村经济在国民经济发展中的地位和作用仍不可忽视,许多发展中国家还处在农业社会或由农业社会向工业社会过渡阶段。那么农业社会和农村经济发展在环境变动中扮演了什么样的角色呢?需要作一点历史的考察。

最初的农业生产是刀耕火种式的粗放经营,通过焚烧森林、草地、清除天然植被开垦为农田和驯养场。清除天然植被还有另一个作用,将野兽驱逐出来进行捕猎,发展畜牧业。然而由于生产工具落后和缺乏有效的增肥方法,只能利用土壤表层的肥力,肥力耗竭即行转移,造成大面积荒漠化和沙漠化。工业革命发生后不仅为工业化开辟了道路,而且也为农业的发展提供了手段。特别是农业机械和化肥、农药等的发展,为农业"起飞"插上了翅膀。工业革命带来的巨大人口增长,提出了扩大耕地面积和增加食物等农产品供给的需求,于是发生了更大规模的毁林开荒、变牧为农浪潮。据《世界环境数据手册》提供的资料,19世纪以来全球耕地面积增长2倍,一半左右的森林被改造成农地、牧场和其他用途。1981~1985年世界封闭式森林每年以750万公顷的速度被采伐,疏林地以389万公顷的速度被采伐,而每年新营造的森林面积仅相当于毁林面积的1/10,世界森林"赤字"越来越严重。

森林、草场除具有自身的生产价值外,还具有环境保护的多种价值和功能:缓冲、吸收、疏导、散发降水、辐射、风力的作用,保护水土,保护包括人类在内的动植物良好生存空间的价值和功能;通过吸收、储存二氧化碳、空气悬浮物净化空气,释放氧气改善和调节空气的价值和功能。全世界每年失去大片森林和草场,意味着对土壤水分,空气温度、湿度、透明度、清洁度调节功能的巨大丧失，年复一年下来，使很多地区气候变得干燥恶劣，水、旱等自然灾害频频发生且大大加重，加剧着土壤的退化和沙化，大气条件的恶化。据统计，全球每年600万公顷土地变成沙漠，另有2100万公顷肥沃土地丧失经济价值。而在过去的150年中，大气积聚的1/3的二氧化碳是毁林造成的，也是导致物种减少的重要原因。大批动植物在森林、草场破坏中死亡，有的已经灭种。令人关注的热带雨林生活着全世界一半左右的物种，目前的乱砍滥伐令人颇感忧虑，大片雨林消失后带来的严重后果，专家们预料要大大超过人们现在的估计。①

在农业社会，由于生产工具落后，劳动生产率低下，人们为了满足食物等基本生活资料的需求，只有直接"向自然开战"，用"土里刨金"办法向大自然索取。这种办法中国农民沿用了几千年，一些地区竟直接开荒到山顶，将森林和草木保存水土、调节气候、净化空气等功能砍掉和刨掉，使有些地区变成沙漠，有些地区水土大量流失变成不毛之地，而气候变得干旱和恶劣则是共同的现象。如今这类直接破坏资源的环境问题大大减少，但在边远地区、经济落后的贫困地区还时有发生。不计后果地开荒种田，以林木和牧草作烧柴，都使大地植被遭到破坏。传统农业型环境问题根源来自贫困，消除贫困，是解决传统农业型环境问题的根本所在。同时科学的普及，弄明白了不计后果地向大自然索取的危害，使资源的开发利用建立在科学基础上，显然是有益和必要的。

现代农业型环境问题。主要指农业生产中应用现代科学成果和技术带来的环境质量下降，对人的健康和全面发展造成的危害问题。当前主要是化肥、农药和地膜等大量使用，造成污染加剧问题。众所周知，氮、磷、钾等化学肥料的发明，由于含量纯度高，作物吸收快，比起传统农家有机肥来增产效果大大提高，化肥的大量施用成为农作物产量迅速提高最重要的办法。发展化肥需要投资，而高投入的结果，一是提高了农产品的成本，使得粮价等一直上涨，直至高出国际市场价格；二是高投入中很大部分用在增加化肥施用上，施用化肥的负面作用凸显出来，致使土壤造成板结，土壤质量下降，造成水质污染，大量施用化肥的农田用水特别是稻田用水排入河湖，使鱼、虾、蟹等水生动物减少直到灭绝，因而现代型农业对环境的破坏更值得重视。

---

① United Nations, *Population*, *Environment and Development*, *The Concise Report*, New York, 2001.

一是从现实上看，传统型的破坏主要发生在贫困地区，目前这类地区所占份额不多，而这些地区人民的环境意识在加强；现代型破坏无论是化肥还是农药，都已达到相当严重的程度，危害甚大。这里还要提到地膜覆盖和各种暖房生产问题。无疑这是现代农业发展的一大进步，它有效地提高了蔬菜、水果的单位面积产量，冲破季节性、地区性生产限制给居民带来莫大实惠。然而同其他种种好事一样，弄得不好也会带来负面影响。据科学家考证，现在使用这类塑料薄膜，埋在土壤中200年也不会腐烂，塑料大棚之类的迅速发展和不规范的废旧处理，已构成新的"白色污染"，成为农田建设和社会的一大公害。

二是从发展上看，传统农业型破坏随着20世纪末消除贫困问题的解决，居民环境意识的不断增强，破坏程度继续下降，乐观一点儿估计，有望从根本上解决。现代农业型破坏形势严峻，缺乏切实可行的监控办法和机制，且有继续发展的趋势。因此，解决农业型环境破坏问题，应将重点转向现代农业发展中带来的负面影响，特别是化肥的生产和施用，农药生产和科学使用，塑料薄膜等的"白色污染"问题；同时也要建立健全立法监督机制，加强管理，在产出和进入市场的"出口"上把关。

其二，工业社会和工业经济发展的影响与调控。产业革命发生后，适应工业化发展对劳动力的需求，人口城市化进程加快，出现工业化与人口城市化相互促进、共同成长的局面。其结果，对环境造成前所未有的巨大破坏：工业化产生大量废气、废水、固体废物，人口城市化形成高度集中人口群，人的生理活动对环境的影响亦产生集中效应，更为重要的是有别于农业社会人口在能源消耗、生活资料消耗中的"分母的加权效应"。如今除少数"绿色城市"环境质量保持较好外，一般"三废一噪"普遍严重，城市空气、水质、地表、地下污染相当普遍，成为遍布地表的一个个不同程度的污染点、污染源，产污排垢之地，造成严重后果。像二氧化碳等气体具有截留太阳辐射到地球岩石反射回来的长波辐射的能力，其大量增多和加厚，产生"温室效应"，使地球变暖，继续下去可能使两极冰雪融化，导致海平面上升，气候发生重大变异；氯氟烃大量增加不仅对"温室效应"有煽风点火作用，而且因损耗同温层中的臭氧，逐渐形成臭氧洞，太阳紫外线没了遮挡而长驱直射地球，改变人们生存的条件，造成皮肤癌等发病率升高，更多的影响还有待观察，目前在南极这样的臭氧洞已发展到两个美洲的面积；二氧化硫等硫化物、一氧化氮氧化物的增加，在大气环境复杂的作用情况下，形成酸沉降和干酸沉降。而工业化产生的大量废渣、废液，或直接污染表土，或流入江、河、湖、海造成污染，致使鱼类、鸟类、水生动植物死亡。某些有毒液体渗入地下，污染水源直接威胁人类的健康和生存。

世界环境破坏尤其是工业型环境的破坏，发达国家应负主要责任。目前发达国家人口仅占世界人口20%多一些，而消耗的各种能源总和占到近80%，人均GDP为欠发达国家的十几倍，自然成为工业污染的大户。但是当前值得注意的是，一些国家在饱尝了污染之苦以后，在经济和社会发展中普遍加强了环境治理的力度，有些国家取得明显成效，开辟了融经济社会发展与环境保护于一体的发展道路。而在总体上，发展中国家在这方面取得的进展还相当有限，需要付出不懈的努力。

中国作为当今世界人口最多和社会经济发展最快的发展中国家，发展带来的工业型环境问题表现在以下几个方面。

一是传统工业型环境问题。传统工业包括采矿、钢铁冶炼、机械、食品、纺织品、纸张、烟草、木材加工等工业，以煤炭为主要能源，环境问题也同煤炭关系密切。中国煤炭储量和产量早已跃居世界首位，并且在各种能源消耗中占70%以上，成为考察工业污染首先关注的焦点。我国煤炭分布不平衡，多在华北和西北，要经过长途运输才能抵达东南部，煤炭生产地的土地复垦率、原煤入洗率、矿井水利用率均较低，一般情况不超过20%；加上利用率低、粉尘多、矿井塌陷严重、堆放占地面积过大等，造成的污杂十分突出。此外由于传统工业总体技术水平较低，有些设备老化陈旧，加上过去没有或很少有污染处理设施，使得传统工业污染成为工业型污染的"重灾区"。

二是新兴工业型环境问题。新兴工业为后来兴起，特别是在第二次世界大战后迅速发展起来的工业，如新兴机器制造业、新兴化工业、家电工业、核工业、宇航业、海洋工业等。这些新兴工业在一般情况下能源消耗不像传统工业那样巨大，但质量要求比较高；原材料也如此，新材料本身即属于新兴工业之一；技术要求高，对废物的排放做过不同程度的处理，因而"三废一噪"污染大大降低。但是新兴工业也有新兴工业的环境问题，如汽车、飞机、精密仪器制造要求高，工艺复杂，抛光、电镀、烤漆等产生新的污染；新兴化学工业技术大为改进，然而再有效的净化也不可能百分之百地解决碳、硫、氮氧化合物等的排放；核动力的开发和应用避免了煤炭、石油一类燃料的污染，但是却增加了放射性污染的可能性。消除新兴工业可能带来的较大污染的危险，是一项长期的战略任务。

三是乡镇企业型环境问题。改革开放首先在农村开始并获得成功后，世世代代"脸朝黄土背朝天"的农民思想解放了，他们考虑要"换个活法"，从生产到生活都要变一变。而原有的人民公社的部分公共财产还没有处理，包括部分房屋、设备等资产。城市的改革 20 世纪 80 年代前期没有大规模推开，原有的以国有企业为主的一套计划体制还束缚着发展的手脚，一部分农民包括原公社时期一些社队干部，看到某些工商业特别是某些经济发展和人民生活需要的短线产品大有市场，于是试探着办起了乡镇企业。这在我国"二元经济"和城乡差别客观存在的条件下，由于乡镇企业产品适销对路，设备因陋就简，原材料充足，劳动力廉价，一般都收到投资少、见效快、利润高的效果，为农村广大农民勤劳致富奔小康找到一条捷径。又可以有效解决或部分解决农业劳动力过剩问题，为农业劳动生产率的提高创造了条件。于是以经济比较发达的东南沿海农村为龙头，乡镇企业迅猛崛起，很快成为工业生产的一支生力军。不过从环境角度考察，一个不容回避的问题是污染严重。乡镇企业主体是工业，一般投资较少，设备较陈旧，技术较落后，对于生产中产生的有害气体、液体和固体废物，则很难进行处理，甚至酿成河流污染事故。在加强法制建设的今天，乡镇企业发展必须面对污染挑战，通过环保这一关。

四是城市型环境问题。这同工业型环境问题有着一定的联系，因为工业一般多集中在城市。但是也有所区别：一是城市不全是工业集中地，也有一些商业型、文化型、民族型城市；有的工业也不一定集中在城市，特别是新兴工业。二是城市污染对环境的影响不限于工业生产，还有居民生活、交通等多方面因素，作为城市有其特殊的环境问题。结合中国经济发展和人口城市化，城市环境问题会更为突出。除工业污染外，生活消费型污染全面表现出来。空气污染：人口集中的城市生活性能源，包括做饭、洗澡、取暖以及餐饮服务等多以煤作为燃料，空气煤烟粉尘、二氧化碳、一氧化碳等有害气体大量增加。城市中众多煤场的堆放，煤球、蜂窝煤等加工所建煤厂的生产，更使附近居民平添几层黑色。汽车尾气污染：尽管人们对于要不要发展私人小汽车争论不休，但是包括私车在内的汽车猛增已成事实，北京市的汽车日流量已超过 160 万辆，尾气已构成城市空气污染的主要因素之一。水质污染：由于城市人口密集，生活用水耗费量大，洗浴、粪便冲刷等脏水处理很难。特别是各种洗涤剂、洗衣粉、浴液、洗发液等的大量增加，使城市废水中各种化学成分有毒物质比例直线上升，给水源清洁造成威胁。垃圾污染：随着城市规模的扩大，居民的增多和集中，居民生活水平的不断提高，垃圾造成的污染也随着成为城市环境的一大问题。许多城市垃圾运往郊区露天堆放，不仅占用了大面积土地，而且"垃圾山"成为新的污染源。噪音污染：这是一个容易被忽视但却危害很大的污染。医学已证明，经常处在噪声超标环境下工作和生活的人，发病率上升，影响预期寿命，而且容易引起烦躁，工作效率降低。中国人口城市化和城市建设方兴未艾，城市水泥板块式建筑迭起，使噪声回荡和产生共振。大片绿地、林地被建筑物挤占，丧失了原有对声音的吸纳、缓冲作用，使城市噪音污染严重起来。现在，有关环境保护的法律相继出台，居民对噪音污染的危害认识还跟不上，不善于用法律手段保护自己。而且技术手段落后，缺少必要的仪器设备监测噪音的侵扰，也限制了居民维护自身不受侵害的权益和行动。

五是区域型环境问题。中国幅员辽阔，自然条件复杂，差别很大，因而环境问题带有一定的区域性。地势西高东低，长江、黄河等主要河流大都由西向东流向。气温和降水量南高北低，形成具有明显差别的不同气候带。经济发达程度和人口密度，西部和北部低，东部和南部高，人口经济发展差距有拉大的趋势。气候、地质、水资源以及经济、人口、社会发展的这种不同情况，受自然条件影响灾害的分布和不同地区抗御自然灾害的能力，形成某些地域性环境问题。主要环境问题如下。

西部干旱、寒冷型环境问题。西北甘肃、宁夏、青海、新疆4省区，省会（首府）的年平均气温均在10℃以下，银川、乌鲁木齐年平均降水量在240毫米以下，兰州、西宁也在380毫米以下，以寒冷和干旱为特征。森林覆盖率低，水土保持差，沙漠多，风沙大，气候恶劣，环境质量差。值得提出的是，在干旱和半干旱地区有些地方生态退化还在扩展，荒漠面积在扩大，水土流失在加剧。这种情况最容易发生的灾害是沙暴，沙丘淹没良田和村庄则时有发生。

东部和中部水患型环境问题。中国处在东亚季风区，雨水比较集中，又受地形等因素影响，造成夏秋之交中东部水灾严重。水灾不仅给人民生命财产造成很大损失，而且造成大量水土流失，加速土壤沙化；河流改道淤塞，排污能力减弱；冲毁水利设施，土壤盐碱化加剧等。如果城市在洪水中被淹，即使不被吞没，造成的水源污染、环境的破坏也是严重的，恢复起来比较困难。

沿海污染环境问题。海洋作为陆地水、土污染的最后接纳者，四大洋均露出疲态。据报道，20 世纪 70 年代以来由于油船沉没和海上油井泄漏等大量原油流入海洋，每年有 300 万～400 万吨之多，形成海洋"黑潮"。发达国家对海洋污染的这类事例，在我国已经发生，而有些发达国家已经基本停止的事情，我国却仍在发生。我国有将近 300 万平方千米的管辖海域，相当于陆地面积的 1/3，蕴藏着丰富的资源，在现实经济活动中创造出可观价值，对未来可持续发展而言，则是很有希望的补给线。然而日益严重的污染着实令人担心。如具有内海之称的渤海，是辽东工业区、京津塘工业区污染的最后接纳地，专家们考证后说污染程度已达到临界点。由于是内海，水浅且通向黄海的出口狭窄，自身水体交换能力差，继续污染将难以挽救。黄海胶州湾一带、东海长江口一带、南海珠江口一带的污染也相当严重，已到了必须采取坚决措施的时候。

六是国际公害型环境问题。中国是一系列国际环境保护公约的发起国和签字国。中国不但签署了 1992 年在巴西里约热内卢通过的《21 世纪议程》和《里约热内卢环境与发展宣言》，而且忠实履行会议承诺，率先推出《中国 21 世纪议程——中国 21 世纪人口、环境与发展白皮书》。此外，也是国际《气候变化框架公约》、《保护臭氧层维也纳公约》、《濒危野生动植物国际贸易公约》等的签字国，在保护世界环境方面作出积极努力。中国是《控制危险废物越界转移巴塞尔公约》的签约国，然而却遭到违反该项公约的个别国家"洋垃圾侵略"的危害，国际公害型污染问题应引起关注。进入 20 世纪 90 年代以后，陆续发现的发达国家将它们的垃圾装入集装箱运到我国，到 1995 年这类事件发展到顶峰，一年达到数十起，多达几千吨，北京、上海、青岛等城市相继发现大宗"洋垃圾"，对水、土、空气构成严重危害。这是近年来新出现的一种来自国际的、侵略性的污染，其性质是严重的。必须采取果断措施，制止国际公害型环境侵害。

《全国生育文化理论与实践研讨会论文集》序[*]

在人类长达 400 多万年的历史发展长河中，生育过程以及同生育有关的文化现象的研究，由来已久。从原始人的自然生育、生殖崇拜，农业社会追求多生多育、多子多福，到现代社会人们崇尚优生优育、发生生育观念的改变，折射出在生育问题上人们价值观念的不断升华，本质上反映的是文化的变动。这种生育文化的变动，在中外文化发展史上早已引起注意：文化学注意到生育这一范畴表现出的文化的内涵；人口学研究中，也注意到文化因素的作用与影响。1662 年被誉为"人口学之父"的格兰特《关于死亡的自然的和政治的观察》一书发表，揭开人口学成为一门独立学科的序幕。其后人口学沿着具有统计意义和边缘交叉学科两个方向发展下来，而无论哪个方向，都涉及文化，涉及人口与文化变动、发展的研究。不过从发展的角度观察，历史越往近追溯，文化研究对生育关注的程度有所减弱；而人口研究则相反，对文化关注的程度则不断加强。西方关于生育率的理论中，不乏关于文化的论述，尤其是从社会学角度的研究。布莱托曾将"社会和文化因素"与"夫妇和家庭户特征"、"认知能力"并列为决定生育的"三大基本因素"，给文化以很高的定位。联合国 1983 年发表的《生育率与家庭》综合了这方面的研究成果，认为中国、斯里兰卡和印度的克罗拉邦生育率的下降同经济、教育的发展关系不很大，主要表现出包括文化在内的非经济因素的影响。但是从总体上观察，国外关于生育的文化研究还不很多，没有形成比较系统的理论和方法；较有影响的，当属宗教文化方面的研究，不同宗教信仰对生育率变动的影响受到青睐。中国的情况也相类似，虽然早已注意到文化在生育中的作用，形成比较系统的一套传统的生育理念，但是并没有提到生育文化高度认识和作出总结，没有上升到理论和建立相应的理论体系。

---

[*] 本文发表于 2003 年。

20 世纪 70 年代以来，国家大力加强计划生育，切实控制人口增长，出现 30 年来生育率长期持续下降，实践为科学研究开辟了一片广阔的天地。在这种背景下，生育文化被提了出来，并以"婚育新风进万家"活动的广泛开展为契机，获得迅速的发展。同时，随着近年来文化研究的深入，文化研究中涉及生育方面研究的增多，生育文化研究中出了一些较有分量的研究成果。值得提出的是潘贵玉主编、陈胜利等副主编的《中华生育文化导论》，以及 2003 年 4 月在浙江省杭州市召开的全国生育文化科学讨论会提交的一批论文。这些成果对生育文化的定义、基本范畴、涉及的主要领域、研究的意义、研究的方法等进行了不同层面的探讨，对如何发挥文化因素在计划生育基本国策中的作用作了实证分析，提出了许多有益的见解和建议，代表了目前的研究水平。会议主办单位将这次会议提交的论文搜集起来，进行了编辑和筛选出版本《论文集》，无疑是对以往研究成果的一次检阅，是对未来研究的一个实际的推动。

应当看到，尽管生育文化研究取得令人欣慰的成果，但是无论研究的深度还是研究的广度都是很不够的，亟须作出深入一步的研究。要跟上时代前进的步伐，立足于学科前沿，合理吸纳国内外研究成果中的科学成分，对生育文化作出反映其本质的科学的抽象，建立起比较完整的理论体系，可谓任重而道远。我们要紧密联系实际，体现生育文化源于实践、高于实践、服务于实践的原则，在理论与实践相结合的研究中，谋求创新和发展。从这个意义上说，本《论文集》的出版不仅是以往研究成果的汇集，表明我们已经走过的路程，而且是一个新的起点，是集众学人研究之所长，向着未来新型生育文化理论的创立而进军的一个新的起点。

《国土资源、环境、生态与人口可持续发展战略》序[*]

　　1972 年对于可持续发展来说，是一个开局之年。这一年，由麦多斯（D. L. Meadows）等人撰著的罗马俱乐部报告《增长的极限》发表，提出若世界人口、工业化、污染、粮食生产、资源消耗保持过去增长水平不变，则100 年内将达到地球的极限，因而必须实现零增长。也在同一年，联合国人类环境会议在瑞典首都斯德哥尔摩召开，会议通过的《联合国人类环境会议宣言》，在强调人是环境产物的同时，指出人也是环境的塑造者，人类在计划自己的行动方案时应当考虑到环境造成的影响，首次提出"合乎环境要求的发展""无破坏的发展""连续的和可持续的发展"等概念，将可持续发展提到世人面前。1987 年由挪威前首相布伦特兰夫人（Gro Harlem Brundland）主持的联合国环境与发展委员会在《我们共同的未来》报告中，对可持续发展作出带有定义性的解释：既满足当代人的需求，又不对后代人满足其需求的能力构成危害的发展，取得较多共识。1992 年 183 个国家和地区代表在巴西里约热内卢聚会，其中有 102 个国家元首或政府首脑出席，讨论并通过了《里约热内卢环境与发展宣言》、《21 世纪议程》、《联合国气候变化框架公约》、《生物多样性公约》、《关于森林问题的原则声明》等一系列文件，否定了以 GDP 为主要目标、不顾环境后果的发展模式，各国相约会后分别制定本国的《21 世纪议程》。1994 年在埃及开罗召开的国际人口与发展会议，《关于国际人口与发展的行动纲领》提出"可持续发展问题的中心是人"的重要命题，是对《21 世纪议程》的重要补正。

　　中国政府履行国际会议承诺，于 1994 年 3 月颁发《中国 21 世纪议程——中国 21 世纪人口、环境与发展白皮书》。从总体可持续发展战略、人口与社会可持续发展、经济可持续发展，资源合理利用、环境保护等方面，

---

　　*　本文发表于 2003 年。

阐明可持续发展的战略、方针、目标和行动方案，可谓率先垂范。同年 7 月，来自 20 多个国家、13 个联合国机构、20 多个外国有影响企业的 170 多位代表在北京聚会，制定了《中国 21 世纪议程优先项目计划》，有力地推动了可持续发展战略的实施。

以上情况表明，至 20 世纪 90 年代中期，可持续发展主要是作为一种发展战略、行动纲领提出和加以阐发的。那么可持续发展有没有理论作支撑或者有没有可持续发展的理论呢？笔者以为，是有理论支撑或者存在一种可持续发展理论的。它的理论基础或曰基本理论，就是以人为本或者说是人本理论。不过这里的以人为本或人本理论，与罗森塔尔、尤金在哲学词典阐述的不尽相同。这里的人不是脱离社会的抽象的"一般人"，而是处于具体时代、具体经济和社会发展阶段的人，不同代际的人。以人为本，就是要以人的全面发展为宗旨，满足人的生理、心理、交往的生存、享受和发展的需要；当代发展的主要驱动力来自人力资本，人力资本以及与之相联系的社会资本比自然资本、产出（生产）资本具有更大价值；以人为本的可持续发展理论体系，包括全方位的适度人口论、资源稀缺论、生态系统论、总体经济效益论、社会协调发展论。即人口是可持续发展的关键，资源是可持续发展的前提，环境是可持续发展的最终目的，人口、资源、环境构成可持续发展的基本问题；经济发展和社会发展，则是实现可持续发展的途径和手段。

鉴于上面的分析，近年来，可持续发展研究对人口、资源、环境给予更多关注。不久前，在一次聚会中与国土资源部赵超英先生谈起，他新近完成一部书稿《国土资源、环境、生态与人口可持续发展战略》，邀我写一篇"序"。我们虽然素昧平生，但是谈论起来共识很多，于是便欣然应诺。赵先生积多年实际工作经验，收集大量典型事例和数据，写成了书，实是难能可贵。该书在合理吸纳国内外已有研究成果基础上，从中国实际出发，力求在可持续发展难点上有新的突破；特别是在实证研究方面，运用大量翔实资料展开分析，提出可供政府决策选择的建议，具有参考价值。不言而喻，目前关于可持续发展方面的研究还有待深入，期望有更多的精品力作问世。

《军事人口学概论》序[*]

1981 年秋，中国社会科学院人口科学考察团考察欧美人口科学发展状况，最后一站到达洛杉矶位于太平洋西海岸的兰德公司座谈。出乎意料的是，竟有十五六位专家出来同我们交流，包括几位资深专家，会议室里几乎座无虚席。他们研究人口吗？我的头脑中不仅闪过这样的问号。然而交谈之后，我得到一个答案：他们不是专门研究人口的专家，但是他们研究的内容都同人口有着某种联系，或者对人口很感兴趣。他们把军队战斗力同人口文化教育素质、人的智商和智能，甚至同居住地、迁移、种族、性格等联系起来，把第二次世界大战后军事上的新技术革命同人力资本的积聚联系起来，将现代化战争指挥同人的信息化能力联系起来，使我们看到人口学在军事科学中的地位和作用。自此，萌发出应当研究军事人口科学的念头，只是由于时间、精力和能力的限制，未能真正进入。偶有触及，也仅是蜻蜓点水而已，不能算做真正意义上的研究。

人口学（demography）是研究人口变动和发展规律的科学，研究的客体是总体人口（universe）。这个"总体人口"，可分做不同层次：在横断面上，依据一定的地理界限，可分成某个国家的"总体人口"，指这个国家的全部人口；一个地区的"总体人口"，指该地区的人口总数；在纵断面上，依据居住、劳动、生活等特征，可分成少年人口、成年人口、老年人口、男性人口、女性人口、农业人口、工业人口、在校人口、军事人口等不同类型的人口。中国 2000 年第五次人口普查，全国总体人口为 129533 万人，其中内地 31 个省、自治区、直辖市和现役军人为 126583 万人，现役军人为 249.9 万人，占 0.197%。尽管军事人口所占比例不足 0.2%，但是由于这部分人口在社会分工和从事的职业性质的不同，人口年龄、性别、文化、教育

等的不同，在国家总体人口中的地位和作用也有所不同，一般都受到格外重视。这个重视没有因为第二次世界大战后以微电子为前导，当前又发展到以生命科学为主导学科的新技术革命而削弱，相反还有所加强。两次海湾战争打的是科技战、信息战，而再强大的科技信息战争，也离不开人口素质的提高，离不开人对信息和高科技的掌握和运用。至于军事人口中数量和质量、年龄和性别结构、兵源的城乡和地域结构、官兵的文化和教育结构、军事人口的婚姻和家庭等，更需要借助人口学的理论和方法，是人口学以外的其他研究所难以取代的。在这样的意义上说，军事人口学研究具有不可替代的作用，应当加强。

令人高兴的是，改革开放以来军事人口科学研究取得很大进展，20世纪八九十年代已有一些科研成果面世。进入21世纪后，由李顺发教授主编的《军事人口学概论》出版，标志着这门分支学科由初创走向正式确立，迈出分支学科建设的重要一步。《概论》集多名专家4年辛勤劳动结晶于一体，创建了体系比较完整，分析有理有据，资料丰富翔实，具有理论联系实际、讲史与现实相结合、立足当前与放眼未来相统一的鲜明特点，是研究军事人口理论，分析当代中国军事人口状况和制定军事人口发展战略，颇有实际参考意义的佳作。作为交叉研究的一位同行，期望以此为契机，与时俱进地将军事人口科学研究不断推向前进。

《中国京族、毛南族人口研究》序[*]

　　1993 年本人作为审稿人之一，参加了宋健主编的《现代科学技术基础知识》一书的书稿讨论。当时科学家们取得较多共识，认定银河系中最老恒星的年龄为 100 亿～150 亿年，地球的球龄约 47 亿年，地球上最早的生物出现在距今 23 亿年前，人类诞生的历史当在 200 多万年。后来非洲、中国等的考古发现，将人类出现的历史推进到 400 多万年前，给原始人的出现、进化和发展，留出了更大的空间，也大大拓展了人口学、人类学、种族学、民族学等的研究空间。中国是一个多民族、多种族的国家，虽然以往这方面的研究取得很大成绩，但是就总体而言仍同民族人口大国不相称，特别是民族人口研究。为了填补这方面研究的某些空缺，"中国民族人口研究"被列入"九五"国家社会科学重点课题。按照原定计划，分别出版几套合订本，将 55 个少数民族人口分列其中，每个民族独立成卷，包括京族、毛南族。为了推动这两个民族人口的进一步研究，对广西民族人口研究和自治区社会经济发展发挥应有的作用，除列入《中国民族人口》统一出版外，现由中国人口出版社另出版单行本《中国京族、毛南族人口研究》。应两书主编之邀，作一序，发表一些意见。

　　京族、毛南族以世居在广西壮族自治区为主，以其居住地理位置和自然条件，称这两个民族为我国南方的海洋民族和山地民族。2000 年全国人口普查，京族人口有 22517 人，毛南族人口有 107166 人，分别占全国少数民族人口的 0.002% 和 0.102%，属于人口数量较少的少数民族。正因为人口数量较少，加上过去民族地区经济、科技、文化发展比较落后，造成对这两个民族尤其是民族人口方面的研究甚少，这次两个民族专著的出版，填补了这方面的空白。课题同志在组长广西壮族自治区委党校副校长、

＊　本文发表于 2004 年。

广西壮族自治区人口研究所所长央吉教授带领下，克服重重困难，多方查找资料，开展调查研究，积极汲取国内外已有研究成果，进行了创造性研究，作出了应有的贡献。

纵观全书，这本专著站在新世纪起点上，力求学术创新是最大的特点和贡献。首先，课题组在组长带领下，查阅了能够得到的所有关于京族、毛南族的文献，在认真分析基础上，加以去粗取精、去伪存真，提供了可以经得起推敲的数据资料，填补了以往研究中的某些空白点。其次，课题组深入京族世居的"京族三岛"和毛南族世居的毛南山乡调查研究，取得第一手资料及富有活性的现实资料。客观地说，这种调查十分艰苦，是非常难能可贵的，因而取得调查材料价值更大。再次，严格进行规范化研究。课题组遵照《中国民族人口》总编委会要求，按照人口学规范开展研究，从京族、毛南族的起源与变迁、人口规模与分布，到人口身体素质与文化素质、人口自然与非自然结构，再到生育、死亡、婚姻、家庭、人口预测与人口发展，分析研究体现了较强的人口学规范性，这在少数民族人口研究中也是可贵的。又次，进行了预测和交叉研究。本专著对未来京族、毛南族的人口变动，分别作了预测，描绘了21世纪特别是21世纪初全面建设小康社会期间，两个少数民族变动和发展的趋势、图像，提出了相应的决策选择。对两个民族生存和发展的自然环境和社会环境，作了考察和分析，阐发了可持续发展的战略思想，并结合资源、环境、经济发展和社会发展，提出和阐述了实施可持续发展战略的思路和方略。可贵的一点是，所有这些分析研究，都尽可能地站在时代前沿，尽可能吸收国内和国际社会已有研究成果，尽可能做到理论与实践相结合，积极提出改革建议，具有很强的实证研究价值。

读了《中国京族、毛南族人口研究》一书，颇有感慨，觉得作者们是"用心"写作的。这里的"用心"有两重含义：一是用"心思"，即有思想、有理论、分析研究方法上力求创新；二是"用心"中的"用"非同一般的"用"，是一种严肃、认真、科学的应用和使用，不是草率的"拿来主义"随便地使用。那么，还有"不用心"写书的吗？恐怕也是有的。就社会科学特别是人口学界而言，"不用心"写作而出书者也不能说没有。这也难怪，在一定意义上，市场经济支配下学术炒作的出现有着某种可理解性，但是仅仅是"理解性"而已，却绝不是"正宗"，不是方向，不是学术繁荣和发展之路，应当立上一枚挡箭牌：此路不通。包括民族人口在内的中国人口科学的发展和繁荣，只能靠那些脚踏实地、深入实践、认真进行调查研究，同时又能站在时代前沿、广泛吸收国内外研究之所长、勇于探索和创新的人。随着21世纪全面建设小康社会的启动，我们相信，这样的研究队伍会不断壮大起来。民族人口学和整个人口科学应当也一定会有新的发展和新的作为，在"后小康"建设中发挥更大的作用。

《流动性发展》序*

中国改革开放 20 多年来的实践表明，一个国家在不同的历史阶段可以有自己的发展特点，并且可以创造出令世人惊奇的业绩。但是，像市场经济的充分发展等大的历史发展阶段是不大可能超越的，弄不好，由于人为设定的发展轨迹长期严重地偏离甚至背离历史规定的自然必然性道路，因违规"超越"而带来的负面效应将会越来越严重，发展的成本和代价日益累积，有悖于社会公众的理性预期，最后还得回过头来重新按规范走路。20 世纪五六十年代，我们曾经批判过商品生产和价值规律，将其说成是资本主义特有的经济范畴，建立起高度集中统一的计划经济体制。然而 20 多年后，这种计划经济走到历史的尽头，终于让位于社会主义市场经济。社会主义市场经济中的"社会主义"，不能理解为定语，绝不是独立于一般市场经济之外的"社会主义的市场经济"，而是状语，是社会主义条件下的市场经济，因而是通行一般市场规则的市场经济，即以市场主体法人化、要素流动市场化、宏观调控间接化、经济运行法制化为基本特征的市场经济。市场主体法人化主要是指在市场上大家都以平等的法人身份出现，可谓"市场无上级"；要素流动市场化（包括资金、产品、技术、劳动力等各种要素）主要是指在生产、交换、分配、消费等各个再生产环节中资源配置的实现，都要靠市场来完成；宏观调控间接化主要是指不能把市场经济理解为毫无计划的经济体系，只是这种计划不同于以往计划经济依靠行政手段调拨来实现，而主要是通过市场供求、竞争、价格、税收、必要的补贴来调节；经济运行法制化主要是指市场经济是法制化经济，彼此都要按照法定的游戏规则办事，经济运行在法律监督下有条不紊地进行。基于这样的认识，计划经济可形象地比做依靠人们搬动的被动经济，市场经济则是依靠自身内在动力流动的主

---

* 本文发表于 2004 年。

动经济，人、财、物按照一定的规律流动是市场经济主要而显著的外在表征。

联系我国实际，在由计划经济向市场经济的转变过程中，市场经济的形成始终同流动人口的增强分不开，二者是相互促进的。不过在不同阶段有所不同，开始人们对于物的流动即物流比较看重，生产需要的原材料供给，产品销售链接，贸易物流状况等，都是政府和厂商所首先关注的对象；而对于包括劳动力在内的人口流动即人流，则不大重视，这同我国人口和劳动力过剩不无关系。后来人们的观念逐渐改变，发现人才、劳动力的流动在市场经济中发挥着越来越大的作用，市场竞争最终归结到人才的竞争。中国的改革开放发生在20世纪70年代末80年代初，尽管这时中国的生产力和科学技术发展水平还比较低，但是从一开始经济的发展就是多层次的：既有传统的工业化，又有广泛吸纳"后工业化"先进科技成果的现代化，是立体推进的。站在全球高度看，20世纪80年代以来对人类发展最有影响的事件，是地球的"财政赤字"：在此之前，人类消耗的是地球资源的"利息"，非再生资源供给无忧，再生资源基本维持在供求平衡状态；在此之后，人类消耗的是地球资源的"利息"＋"本金"，发展走到必须转变发展理念和发展模式的历史转折关口。1971年的诺贝尔经济学奖得主美国哈佛大学教授西蒙·库兹涅茨（Simon Kuznets，1901～1985）认为："经济增长的同时必定伴随着流行价值观念的迅速变化。这种变化既是经济增长的结果，又是推动经济进一步增长的动因。"① 在这种大背景下，特别是中国经过20年的发展在世纪之交步入一般意义上的小康社会（前小康）以后，经济增长越来越在更大程度上依赖人力资本②，1992年的诺贝尔经济学奖得主美国芝加哥大学教授加利·S.贝克（Gary S. Becker，1930）认为："人力资本包括个人的技能、知识、健康……我们不能把一个人与他的知识、他的健康和他通过受培训所掌握的技能分割开来，这些就是我们所指的人力资本。人力资本对现代经济增长至关重要，因为现代世界的进步依赖于技术进步和知识的力量，但不是依赖于人的数量，而是依赖于人的知识水平，依赖高度专业化的人才。在当代世界，你必须努力开发人力资本，不掌握大量的知识，没有一个国家会成功。"因此而看出转变发展理念，建构以人口发展为主导的发展模

① 西蒙·库兹涅茨：《现代经济的增长：发现和反映》，商务印书馆，1981，第23页。
② 经济学消息报社编《追踪诺贝尔——经济学奖得主专访录》，中国计划出版社，1998，第176页。

式的极端重要性。

市场经济与流动人口的结合也在原有的基础上升级，成为新世纪完善市场经济体制、转变发展理念的重要因素。市场经济是流动性经济，首先是人口的流动性，但是，人口流动性又必须和只有通过市场机制的有效调节和市场体系的有效运行才得以完成。因此，建构统一开放和竞争有序的现代市场体系，尤其是建构统一开放和竞争有序的有利于劳动力按照自己的意愿偏好而自由流动的现代市场体系，从而拆除不利于劳动力自由流动的各种制度壁垒如户籍制度等，就变得极其重要。以人为本的科学发展观，首先是以民为本的科学发展观，首先强调的是人口发展和人口现代化，这是其他一切发展的根本解释变量。但人口发展过程首先是人口按照自己的意愿偏好而自由流动的社会过程，人口现代化是其他一切现代化的强力引擎。

中国是当今世界上人口规模最大的国家，也是当今世界上流动人口最多的国家。改革开放初期，全国有流动人口二三百万。2000 年人口普查，现住地与户口登记地不一致的流动人口为 14439 万人，扣除 2707 万人本市区内人户分离的其他街道人口，其余 11732 万人可视为跨省和省内的流动人口。其中流入市镇的流动人口占 78.6%，流入农村的占 21.4%，农村人口流入城镇扮演着流动人口主力军的角色。预计在 21 世纪全面建设小康社会前 20 年这一中国社会发展和社会转型的重要战略机遇期间，中国人口的行业分布和就业分布，或称之为中国在新世纪的人力资源配置格局，必定会发生重大的社会变化和历史变迁，流动人口在持续增长的基础上将保持相当庞大的数量。其对经济、科技、社会发展的动能不可低估，对市场化率的提升不可低估，市场经济与流动人口研究仍将是中国社会发展所需要的一个重大历史课题。强化、深化、广化和续化市场经济与流动人口研究，就不仅具有重大的理论创新意义，而且更具有对策性的巨大调控运作价值。

俞宪忠教授的《流动性发展》一书，是研究市场经济与流动人口关系的一部力作。该书紧密联系中国改革开放实际，沿着市场经济建立健全发展的历史变迁轨迹，从现代市场经济健康发展和高效率运行的视角切入，考察流动人口增强的态势；同时从流动人口、劳动力流向流量，探讨人口流动和流动人口与市场经济发展的内在必然联系，从理论与实践的结合上，提出自己的新见解。尤其难能可贵的是俞宪忠教授的研究视野较为开阔，他在吸纳西方发展经济学、制度经济学等理论成果的基础上，始终把人口流动和流动人口视为最富有市场经济特征的人口现象，并将其作为优化人力资源配置和其他一切资源配置效率，从而实现帕累托改进和达到帕累托最优分布的根本解释变量。尤其是俞宪忠教授立足于发展就是硬道理的科学思想，从全面建设小康社会和实现中华民族伟大复兴的历史需要出发，紧密结合中国实际，在人力资本市场、市场经济所特有的人口规律、人口流动与资源配置、人口现代化和人口流动化发展路径、适度流动人口及其人口流动规律、新型人口城市化框架、就业与救助、政府职能创新、制度现代化和人口学科创新等领域所作的创新研究，提出了许多发人深省的重要问题，很值得人口学界、经济学界和社会学界等理论界、关心中国社会发展命运的有志之士们给予高度重视。自然，这些问题的研究和解决，还必须着眼于21世纪人口、资源、环境的可持续发展，人口、经济、社会的协调发展，沿着生产发展、生活富裕、生态良好的文明发展道路进行。

《人力资本开发研究》序[*]

当人类跨入 21 世纪时,在信息化、经济全球化大背景下,区域之间、国家之间合作与竞争的广度与深度日趋加强,货币资本获取与投资的单一竞争形式已经向人力资本、货币资本获取向投资的多元化竞争形式转变,劳动力资本化已经成为知识经济时代资本变动的一种重要趋势。强化人力资本,提高人力资本利用效率显得越来越迫切,各国政府无不把人力资本的提高摆到重要位置。

人力资本研究伴随着古典经济学的建立而发展起来,英国古典经济学家亚当·斯密(Adam Smith,1723~1790)、德国学者弗里德里希·李斯特(Friedrich List)等从不同角度对人的知识、技术在生产中的作用进行了探讨。1935 年美国哈佛大学教授沃尔什(S. R. Walsh)发表《人力资本观》,从个人教育经费和个人收益相比较中,计算教育的经济收益,阐述了初期的人力资本观。比较完整的人力资本理论形成于 20 世纪中期,其代表人物当推被称为"人力资本之父"的舒尔茨(T. W. Schutz)和加里·贝克尔(Gary Becker)。舒尔茨认为,人力资本是对人的投资而形成的并体现在人身上的知识、技能、经历、经验和熟练程度,在货币形态上表现为提高人口质量、提高劳动者时间价值的各项开支,并将人力资本分为医疗保健、在职培训、正规教育、成人学习项目、就业迁移等五大类。贝克尔以人力资本收入确定劳动收入分配关系,使人力资本研究数学化、精细化,为人力资本提供了坚实的微观经济分析基础。20 世纪 80 年代以来,随着以知识经济(knowledge-based economy)为背景的"新经济增长理论"在西方国家的出现,将人力资本纳入经济增长模型之中,人力资本进入发展与完善阶段。1986 年美国经济学家 P. M. 罗默(P. M. Romer)将生产要素分为资本、非熟

---

* 本文发表于 2004 年。

练劳动、人力资本（以受教育年限来衡量）、新思想（以专利数量衡量）四个方面，1990 年又建立了包括最终产品、中间产品和研究与开发（R&D）三部门在内的增长模型，把技术进步作为总生产函数的一个变量。1988 年卢卡斯（R. E. Lucas）建立了"两时期模型"（Two Periods Model）与"两商品模型"（Two Goods Model），将人力资本作为独立的因素纳入经济增长模型，认为具有"专业化的人力资本"（specific human-capital）是经济增长的原始动力。

自 20 世纪 80 年代末开始，我国学术界对人力资本也进行了研究，出现了一批重要成果。除对国外人力资本理论进行介绍、阐释外，许多人口学、经济学、社会学等领域的学者从不同角度对人力资本的作用与功能、人力资本的知识效应和外部效应、人力资本投资与收益问题等进行了研究，取得了一批有价值的成果。

新一届中央领导集体提出的坚持以人为本，全面、协调、可持续的科学发展观，是对发展内涵、发展要义、发展本质的深化和创新。我国是世界人口最多的发展中国家，政治、经济、文化等各方面均表现出巨大的非均衡性。提高国民素质、调整人口结构、缩小区域差距、消除贫困、保护生态环境、合理利用资源，是全面建设小康社会的根本任务，而实现由人口大国向人力资本强国的转变，则是把我国建设成富强、民主、文明的社会主义国家的关键。同自然、社会、经济现象存在区域差异一样，人力资本也存在投资方式、投入数量、现有存量、利用方式、产出效益等诸多方面的区域差异。因此，在全面建设小康社会实践中，必须对这个支撑动力——区域人力资本进行准确的判断；在理论上，必须深入探索区域人力资本的运行规律和形成机制，科学评估区域人力资本对一个拥有 13 亿人口并且发展很不平衡的对发展的支撑能力。

山东师范大学人口·资源与环境学院李玉江博士主持 2001 年国家自然科学基金课题《人力资本时空结构及对区域可持续发展支撑能力研究》，同年又获得了教育部人文社会科学研究"十五"规划第一批立项课题《人力资本对区域产业结构调整影响效应及支撑能力》，以及"十五"规划山东省社科重点课题《山东省人力资本区域评估及调控系统研究》三项课题。这三个项目有一定交叉，相互促进，课题组在研究中对理论和方法不断进行探索，取得可喜成果，写成了书，完成了《人力资本区域研究》专著。

在研究方法上，运用区域人口学、区域经济学原理，以山东省为个例，在进行大量专题调查与典型调查的基础上，宏观与微观相结合，在进行定性分析的同时，对人力资本的空间结构、区域差异变动规律、动力机制分析采用了定量研究方法，在建立指标体系、聚类分析、定量评估、相关系数计算、需求函数等方面，体现了量化研究的特点，使研究建立在可靠的基础之上。

在研究内容上，该成果有诸多创新之处。首先，对区域人力资本从经济发展水平、居住区域、地域尺度、经济单元、自然因素等进行了分类，总结了人力资本空间分布的非均衡性、地域结构的层次性、投资类型与主体的多元性、区域投资的相对均质性、人力资本存量与受益的地域集中性、功能上的结节性、区域管理的可调控性等；第二，分别从基础消费、投资角度对人力资本定量计算方法进行了有益的探讨，建立了人力资本计算模型；第三，从需求与供给角度探讨了人力资本对区域产业结构调整的作用，并在人力资本区域差异及其形成机制研究上，从人力资本总量、质量、积累能力方面进行了区域人力资本定性分析，并运用人力资本丰裕系数法对区域人力资本进行了定量分析；第四，在人力资本对区域可持续发展支撑能力方面进行了系统的探索，根据人力资本在经济增长中的外部性作用，建立了有效劳动模型生产函数和人力资本外部性模型生产函数，根据模型计算得出资本、人力资本存量、人力资本水平及其各要素在经济增长中份额和贡献率，测定了区域人力资本供给量以及经济增长对人力资本增长的需求量；第五，成果运用地理信息系统手段，通过人力资本重心模型的建立，发现了人力资本重心变动的规律，构建了人力资本决策支持系统。

该成果突出了实践性，分析了人力资本区域协调的主要障碍约束、发展趋势及区域协调发展对策。认为 21 世纪初，我国区域人力资本发展的基本趋势是人力资本投资实力东西部仍将保持较大差距；西部地区人力资本投资增长幅度将高于东部地区；北方地区人力资本投资能力与存量增长速度将快于南方地区；人力资本投资效益区域差距将继续扩大；人力资本"极化效应"仍将十分明显；人力资本流动的制度性障碍将逐步减少；人力资本存量区际差距将出现倒"U"形转变的特征；人力资本对区域可持续发展支撑能力将出现逆向变动等。这些创新和突破，使该书具有较大的应用价值，这是课题组同志所作的一个实际的贡献。

《嵊州市全面建设小康社会人口与可持续发展报告》绪论[*]

　　从杭州出发，驱车向东沿着杭甬、上三高速公路行驶 120 公里，便来到四面环山、中间由剡溪及其支流冲积平原形成的一片盆地嵊州市了。嵊州市辖区面积 1784.43 平方千米，2003 年户籍人口 735395 人，人口密度 412 人/平方千米，为全国的 3 倍，是一个"七山一水二分田"以山地为主的县级市。提到剡溪，人们会联想到历史上诸多文人墨客，依山傍水吟诗作赋的情景；说到嵊州，一个个动人的故事造就了一批又一批越剧名家，成为耳熟能详的越剧之乡。改革开放以来，嵊州在浙江经济飞速发展中拔地而起，使领带等龙头产业走出国门，一举成为世界市场占有率很高的名城。这里还是著名经济学家、人口学家、教育学家马寅初的故乡，对于像我这样聆听过马老教诲、从北大走出的学人来说，则又多了一层情结。因此，浙江省马寅初研究会一成立，我便动议为马老家乡做点儿事情——思来想去，定下"嵊州市全面建设小康社会人口与经济可持续发展研究"课题，将马老生前最关心、研究最多的两个方面的问题放到一起，并赋予可持续发展当今时代前沿问题作研究，得到研究会和市委市政府领导的重视和支持。现在，经过课题组全体同志的辛勤努力，花了近一年的时间完成课题研究，算是众学人对马老家乡的一种回报吧！

　　可持续发展（Sustainable Development）自 1972 年联合国斯德哥尔摩社会发展会议首次提出以来，逐渐引起各界关注，研究也不断深入。1992 年里约热内卢国际环发大会后，我国忠实履行国际承诺，于 1994 年颁布《中国 21 世纪议程——中国 21 世纪人口、环境与发展白皮书》，起到了率先垂范的作用。其后随着全面、协调、可持续科学发展观和全面建设小康社会、构建和谐社会的相继提出，推动着理论研究的深化和可持续发展战略的实

---

　　*　本文发表于 2005 年。

施。改革开放以来浙江省经济发展很快，民营经济扮演着主力军角色，那么对于可持续发展来说，情形又是怎样，能否有效地推进可持续发展战略的实施呢？我想，研究一下嵊州市走过的路子，不难从中找到某种答案。因为嵊州市在浙江省经济和社会发展中处于中等水平，具有一定的代表性；更为重要的是，从嵊州市党政领导到广大民众，对可持续发展尤其是人口与经济的可持续发展有着较为深刻的认识，他们的做法和经验值得总结，也需要结合当今世界发展趋势不断加以充实和提高。

《嵊州市全面建设小康社会人口与经济可持续发展报告2005》（以下简称《报告》），就是出于这样的目的而写的。《报告》由六个部分组成，这六个部分阐发的主题及其创新之处，分述如下。

一　发展观的转变——人口与经济可持续发展

这是整个《报告》的灵魂，《报告》始终坚持以全面、协调、可持续的科学发展观为指导，寻求走出一条生产发展、生活富裕、生态良好的"三生"文明发展道路。这一部分在概括地回顾了可持续发展战略从提出到形成的历史进程之后，重点阐释什么是以人为本的科学发展观和可持续发展战略。最主要的，一是要明确发展的目的性：传统发展观以追求产值（GDP）的增长为主要目标，陷入"发展＝GDP增长"误区；科学发展观首先阐明的是，发展的目的是为了满足人的生理、心理、交往、文化等的全面发展的需要。二是要认识发展动力的转移：发展的主要驱动力由过去以产出（生产）资本为主转移到现在以人力资本为主上来，今后的竞争将主要表现为人才和人力资本的竞争；三是要清楚可持续发展观追求的终极目的：人与自然的和谐，实现人口、资源、环境的可持续发展；人与人之间关系的和谐，逐步构建起和谐型社会。

以这样的科学发展观为指导，立足于信息化和经济全球化趋势并结合嵊州市实际，提出嵊州市人口与经济可持续发展战略思路选择。人口发展战略选择，实施控制人口数量、提高人口质量、调整人口结构相结合，融控制、提高、调整于一体的人口可持续发展战略。目前嵊州市人口数量变动已接近零增长，提前达到中国人口发展战略的第二个目标。人口身体素质、文体教育素质同全国水平不相上下，提高人口素质尤其是终身教育素质任务比较艰巨。人口年龄结构大约还有近20年的年龄结构变动的"黄金时代"或"人口盈利"期，于经济的发展十分有利，应当加快发展。但是不要忘记，"人口盈利"期过后，便是"人口亏损"的老龄化严重阶段的到来，需要未雨绸缪地科学估量老龄化的影响和建立可靠的养老保障体系。嵊州市人口城乡结构稍高于全国水平，但是总的状况同全国相近：人口的城乡结构落后于三次产业就业结构，三次产业就业结构落后于按产值计算的三次产业结构，需要适当加快人口城市化步伐，使之与城市规模、农村劳动力向城镇转移、三次产业结构和经济技术结构的变动相适应。但是需要走统筹城乡发展的新路，即城市化不仅要立足于城市的发展，还要兼顾到乡村发展，避免重蹈"拉美陷阱"式城市化覆辙。

人口与经济可持续发展战略选择，重点阐发人口数量变动与消费资料、劳动年龄人口与生产资料、人口老龄化与养老保障、人口素质提高与科技进步、人口流动与城市化、人口地域分布与生产力布局的基本比例关系。经济可持续发展战略的立足点，应放在总体经济效益论上。如前所述，传统经济发展观追求的是产量和产值的最大化，通过产量和产值的最大化实现利润最大化。可持续发展针对这一发展模式提出质疑，即发展不能仅仅顾及企业的效益，还应顾及整个社会的效益；不能仅仅顾及当代的效益，还要顾及子孙后代的效益，树立总体效益经济发展观。主要体现在：一为质量效益发展观。打破将发展等同于经济增长、经济增长等同于数量和产值增加的传统经济发展观，转变到经济发展不仅取决于产品的数量，还在越来越大的程度上取决于产品的质量，在经济增长数量和质量问题上更看中质量和效益，更强调以质量求发展、求效益的可持续发展。二为广义空间效益发展观。要跳出仅就本部门、本企业、本地区的经济效益狭隘眼界，把包括人口、资源、环境、社会发展在内的外部效应收入评价视野，从经济增长和发展造成的内外部结合效益上审视发展。由此产生两种投入产出比：一为狭义的投入产出，即生产或经营投入成本与产出之比；一为广义空间意义的投入产出，即计算全社会对生产或经营投入成本与产出之比。传统经济发展观只注重前一种投入产出，可持续发展观在注重前一种投入产出的同时，还要注意到后一种投入产出。在设定发展指标体系上，也要跳出 GDP 单一指标束缚，选择更能表现广义空间意义包括某些人文因素在内的发展指标。三为长远时间效益发展观。发展经济注重当前的经济效益自不待言，因为任何经济发展的目标都是具体的，近期的经济效益是明显的。可持续发展总体经济效益发展观，要求在重视近期经济效益的同时，还要重视长远时间效益，不能以牺牲长远效益为代价获取近期效益，这是区别于传统工业化发展观的一个根本性标志。总体经济效益发展观着重点放在可持续发展能力的培育上，使之不断涌现出新的发展潜力，保持发展的连续性。

二 小康社会发展目标——人口与经济发展预测

《报告》第二部分利用 2000 年人口普查资料和近年来调查取得的最新数据，作出全面建设小康社会 20 年多种方案的人口变动预测和经济发展预测，展现出嵊州市 21 世纪前 20 年人口与经济发展的趋势、图像与目标。

（一）人口变动与发展预测

包括：（1）总体人口变动趋势。基于目前人口增长的势能已经大为减弱，2006 年可实现零增长；同时基于迁出人口略多于迁入人口的事实，自然变动与机械变动两种变动产生的合力作用，中位预测方案显示：全市常住人口可从 2000 年的 67.12 万人，减少到 2010 年的 63.26 万人、2015 年的 61.89 万人、2020 年的 61.11 万人；其后减少的速度进一步放慢，大致可稳定在 60 万左右的水平。（2）劳动年龄人口变动趋势。劳动年龄人口伴随总体人口数量的减少而减少，中位预测显示：15~64 岁劳动年龄人口可从 2000 年的 47.98 万人，减少到 2010 年的 46.60 万人、2015 年的 43.62 万人、2020 年的 40.16 万人。但是占总人口的比例却呈现出先升后降的变动，可从 2000 年占 71.49% 上升到 2008 年峰值时占 73.86%，其后转向回落走势，2015 年可回落到占 70.47%，2020 年可回落到占 65.73%。这表明，未来 15 年尤其是未来 10 年，嵊州市一直处于劳动年龄人口所占比例较高、老年和少年被抚养人口之和所占比例较低的人口年龄结构变动的"黄金时代"或"人口盈利"期。老少被抚养人口比（从属年龄比）2000 年为 0.399，2008 年下降到最低点 0.354；2015 年微升到 0.419，2020 年则上升到 0.521。从属年龄比超过 0.5，表明"黄金时代"或"人口盈利"期的结束，步入"人口亏损"期。（3）人口老龄化趋势。由于自 20 世纪 70 年代以来出生率长期持续地下降和人口预期寿命的不断延长，到 90 年代人口年龄结构老龄化现象显现出来，2000 年全市 65 岁及以上人口达到 7.08 万人，占总人口比例达到 10.55%。中位预测 2010 年可达到 7.88 万人，占 12.47%，2015 年达到 10.02 万人，占 16.19%，2020 年达到 12.98 万人，占 21.24%。其后由于出生率的继续下降，老龄化加深的速度也有所加快，21 世纪 40 年代将进入老龄化高潮期。（4）人口城市化趋势。20 世纪 90 年代以来嵊州城市化步伐开始加快，市镇人口比例由 1990 年的 16.84% 迅速上升到 2000 年的 44.14%，虽然落后于绍兴市和浙江省平均水平，但已高出全国平均水平 7 个百分点。按照改革开放以来嵊州市并参照全国和浙江省的城市化速度外推，21 世纪前 20 年市镇人口比例每年提高一个百分点是可能的，如此，嵊州市城市化水平 2010 年可达 54% 左右，2020 年可达 64% 左右，略高于全国平均水平。

（二）经济发展预测

按照上述人口变动和近二三十年嵊州市经济发展速度外推预测，全市人均 GDP 可由 2003 年的 1.40 万元，提高到 2010 年的 3.23 万元，2020 年的 9.50 万元；第一产业占 GDP 比重可由 2003 年的 13.50%，下降到 2010 年的 11.58%，2020 年的 7.45%；农民纯收入可由 2003 年的 0.53 万元，提高到 2010 年的 0.87 万元，2020 年的 1.69 万元；城镇居民人均可支配收入可由 2003 年的 1.27 万元，提高到 2010 年的 2.38 万元，2020 年的 5.47 万元。对照国家全面建设小康社会指标体系和 2020 年发展目标[①]，嵊州市人均 GDP 在 2008 年、城镇居民人均可支配收入在 2010 年、农村居民人均纯收入在 2007 年可分别达到全面小康目标，即嵊州市可在 2010 年前后达到全面小康社会主要目标，提前 10 年左右进入全面小康社会。不过值得重视的一点是，按照预测城乡收入差距仍在扩大，2003 年农民纯收入与城镇居民可支配收入之比为 1∶2.4，到 2010 年扩大到 1∶2.7，2020 年扩大到 1∶3.2，如何缩小城乡差距，是嵊州市提前跨进全面小康社会需要着力解决的一大问题。

三　就业发展战略——基于劳动力供给的思考

从嵊州市劳动年龄人口变动趋势和开放型经济发展对劳动力需求实际出发，如何利用好人口年龄结构变动的"黄金时代"或"人口盈利"期，实现合理和比较充分的就业，对嵊州的经济和社会发展具有决定性意义。如前所述，在全面建设小康社会的 20 年中，劳动年龄人口绝对数量随着总体人口的减少而减少，但是减少的数量不很多，其占总人口的比例在 2010 年之

---

① 参见田雪原、王国强主编《全面建设小康社会中的人口与发展 2003》，中国人口出版社，2004。

前还是上升的，即社会劳动力供给比较充裕，可以保持劳动力成本廉价优势。同时，每个劳动年龄人口从而劳动力负担的老少之和人口，即从属年龄比2010年以前保持下降势头；2010年以后转而上升，但上升的速度不快，直至接近2020年才上升到0.5，即2个劳动力养活一个老年或少年人口，社会负担较轻，为经济发展提供了来自人口方面的有利条件，是可以利用和提取的来自人口方面的"盈利"。机不可失，时不再来。过了这一"黄金时代"，2020年以后老年人口比例持续升高拉动社会总抚养比不断上升，"人口亏损"就会接踵而至，对社会经济发展将产生不利影响。针对人口年龄结构变动的这一趋势，全面建设小康社会的20年，应当尽可能地实现比较充分的劳动就业，在推进技术进步的同时，多发展一些劳动密集型产业，以及劳动密集与技术密集、资金密集相结合型产业。嵊州市具备这方面的有利条件：对于第一产业而言，中国加入WTO后，使主要依赖劳动密集型的农产品增强了在国际市场上的竞争力，农业劳动力是可以有所作为的；对于第二产业而言，打造国际领带服饰制造中心、全国电机制造基地、小家电制造基地、电声配件制造基地和珠茶出口生产加工基地等，嵊州优势传统劳动密集型产业的发展，为吸纳更多的劳动力就业创造了条件；对第三产业而言，可以吸纳更多的劳动力就业，则是共有的规律。要充分利用产业结构调整的有利时机，实施积极的就业政策，实现人力资本与自然资本、产出资本、社会资本的合理有效配置，实现比较充分的就业。为此，一要大力发展教育，提高全市人民的受教育水平；还要有计划、有组织地进行包括农民工在内的职业培训，提高适应产业结构变动的就业能力。二要建立和完善劳动力市场机制，包括国有、集体企业等的劳动力存量调整机制；城乡劳动力市场一体化，为城乡劳动力流动提供准确信息、指导和服务的机制等。三要适当加快人口城市化进程，顺利实现农村剩余劳动力向城镇工商业的转移。四要完善社会保障制度，建议先按照"低水平、全覆盖"原则，将社会保障覆盖面逐步扩大到每一个劳动者；建立与劳动者与所在单位脱钩的社会保障个人账户，确保失业保障等的按时足额发放。

四 加快城市化进程——三次产业结构变动调整

观察世界各国的城市化进程和社会经济特征，不难发现，尽管城市化进程处于不同发展阶段，与之对应的社会经济也显现出不同特点，但当经济越过人均 GDP 1000 美元进入快速增长期，城市化也驶入快车道的情况下，城市化成为带动人口与经济发展的强有力的引擎：城市化快一些，经济发展和人口结构变动就快一些；城市化慢一些，经济发展和人口结构变动就慢一些。自 20 世纪 90 年代以来嵊州城市化提速，强有力地推动着全市社会经济发展和人口的转变。然而进一步分析发现，在市镇人口比例超过 40% 的情况下，有相当一部分人口仍居住在农村，有些人口还从事着农业生产性劳动，城市中街道人口所占比例偏小，表现为已经纳入城镇常住人口的市民化程度不够高，以及三次产业就业结构与产业结构的错位。按照一般规律，城市化率处于低于 20% 的初级阶段，第一、二、三次产业就业比重分别在大于 50%、20% 左右、20% 左右；城市化率处于 20%～50% 的中级阶段，第一、二、三次产业就业比重各占 30% 左右；城市化率超过 50% 的高级阶段，第一、二、三次产业就业比重分别为小于 10%、30% 左右、大于 50%。2000 年嵊州市城市化率达到 44.14%，第一、二、三次产业产值占 GDP 的比例分别为 17.4%、52.4%、30.2%；而第一、二、三次产业就业结构，却分别为 57.2%、28.0%、14.8%，二者很不相称。解决的途径，主要是适当加快城市化的进程，进行合理的产业结构调整。一是加快工业化步伐，发展有自己特色的优势工业，以工业化带动城市化；二是促进农业产业化经营，提高农业劳动生产率，加速农村剩余劳动力向城镇工商业的转移；三是大力发展旅游、服务等第三次产业，提高第三次产业增加值和所占比例。这里讲"适当加快"城市化步伐，是针对盲目推进城市化而言的，强调城市化的速度和规模都要"适当"。要防止城市化过程中的"圈地"运动，确保失地农民能够及时地转为城镇市民，防止贫民窟的出现；保护好资源和环境，沿着统筹城乡发展的城市化道路推进；在融入长三角和杭州湾产业带过程中，注意发挥嵊州优势，特别是用领带服饰、小家电、文化等支柱产业的发展带动城市化。

五 提前基本实现现代化——人口素质与人力资本

嵊州市要在 2010 年前后率先建成全面小康社会和提前基本实现现代化，科技是关键，基础在教育，归根结底在于人口文化教育素质的提高和人力资本积聚能力的增强。改革开放以来嵊州市人口文化素质有了很大提高，人才建设也得到较快发展，有力地促进了全市经济社会的发展。但是必须看到，现在的人口素质无论是身体素质还是文化教育素质都还不够高，同经济持续、快速、健康发展和提前基本实现现代化很不相适应。特别是具有较高文化教育水平人口所占比例较低，目前全市 6 岁以上人口平均受教育年限仅 6.7 年，距全国的平均 7.5 年尚差 0.8 年；人才总量不足，人才结构和分布不尽合理，某些企业尤其是私营、外商和港、澳、台商投资企业的专业技术人员严重不足，阻碍着这些企业的健康发展；人口文化教育素质的性别差异和城乡差异明显，女性和农民的文化教育素质相对更低一些等。面对全面建设小康社会 20 年和更长远一些时间的全市人口与经济发展，需要充分利用人口年龄结构变动的"盈利"期加快发展，最有效的途径就是大力提高人口素质和增强人力资本积聚的能力。为此，一要充分认识人才的重要性，树立投资于人的理念，加大用于科学、教育、文化、卫生等的财政投入，确保人口素质的不断提高。二要加强基础教育和劳动技能的培训，解决一般教育与职业教育结构失衡、城市与乡村教育失衡问题。三要建立富有竞争力的吸引人才机制和管理机制，除了需要建立符合市场经济的人才激励机制外，还要培育一批有吸引力的大中型企业，按照企业的规模大小、技术含量高低以及产品的性质，实行按层次分别选用人才制度；建立专业人才继续学习、考核奖励的机制，对做出过重大贡献的科技人员予以重奖；鼓励各种形式的成人教育和终身教育，推进学习型社会和服务型政府建设。四要采取得力措施缩小男女之间、城乡之间文化教育上的差距，实行教育、卫生等的资源共享，对妇女、农民等人口素质相对处于不利地位的"弱势群体"，实行必要的政策倾斜，保证国民总体素质的不断提高。

六　人口、资源、环境——生态市建设基本问题

谋求人口与经济的可持续发展，还必须立足于嵊州市"七山一水二分田"的自然地理条件，从实际出发将经济、社会的发展同人口、资源、环境状况结合起来，这是生态市建设的基本问题。当前的形势和面临的主要问题如下。

（一）人口消费增长和资源、环境压力增大问题

根据预测，嵊州市在 2006 年达到人口零增长以后，人口规模将呈一定程度的缩减趋势，来自人口数量增长方面的压力减弱。但是人们追求高生活

质量的愿望无限，正是这种愿望才使经济的发展具有需求的动力，这是 400 多万年人类发展的历史所证明了的；然而也正是这种无限制地追求高生活质量愿望，使人均资源消耗"加权效应"升级，导致资源的匮乏和环境的恶化，这是嵊州市未来人口与经济可持续发展中非常突出的矛盾。按照嵊州市全面建设小康社会人均收入和消费增长目标推算，能源和资源的消耗要随着增长几倍，废水、废气、固体废物的排放也要增长几倍，这不能不是严峻的挑战。

（二）工业化提速与资源匮乏、环境污染加剧问题

在由传统工业化走向现代化过程中，以加工业为主的第二次产业呈现先升后降的走势，即现代化从起步到完成，工业产值占 GDP 的比重呈倒 U 型曲线变化。目前，嵊州市的工业化正处在倒 U 形曲线前部，在相当长时间内第二次产业将扮演拉动 GDP 增长的主要角色，一些传统意义上污染较重的行业仍然具有较大的发展空间。特别是要打造"一大中心、四大基地、六大主产区"的工业化格局，与之相联系的印染、电镀、化工等高污染企业的发展，必然在造成资源匮乏加剧的同时，带来"三废"排放的进一步增长和环境的恶化。

（三）农业产业化和农村面源式污染扩散问题

据嵊州市 2001 年农业面源污染调查，随着农业产业化的推进，化肥、农药、畜禽养殖、水产养殖、塑料农膜、生活垃圾、生活污水、人类尿粪等构成农村面源式污染的主要污染源。"十一五"规划把"八大特色产业"列为嵊州实现农业强市的重点项目，这在生产方式、技术水平、生产效率不能得到明显改善和提高的情况下，农业面源式污染有进一步扩大的趋势。

（四）农产品商品化和粮食生产问题

嵊州地处浙东平原与丘陵交会地带，是农业比较发达的地区之一，如果农业生产能有更快的发展并且农产品商品率能有较大幅度的提高，农业对嵊州人口与经济的可持续发展会作出更大的贡献。然而最近几年全市耕地面积和农作物播种面积连续缩小，粮食产量减少，整个粮食生产有萎缩的趋势。这不仅不利于城乡差距的缩小，而且不利于统筹城乡经济和社会发展。就粮食生产而论，固然嵊州市不一定建立在粮食自给基础上，可以通过发展城镇

工商业和市场交换搞到居民需要的口粮；但是不要忘记，如果作为农业和产粮较多的大县（市）之一粮食也要依靠外供，于情、于理、于利都是说不过去的，也没有尽到对国家粮食安全应尽的责任。

要实现全面建设小康社会人口与经济的可持续发展，创建国家级生态示范城市，就要认真对待和解决上述几个突出的问题。首先要转变观念，牢固地树立起全面、协调、可持续的科学发展观和求真务实的政绩观。倡导"既要产量产值，更要发展实际价值"新理念，实现发展观和政绩观的根本转变。其次，政府在运用"看得见的手"进行干预和政策调节时，要特别注意发挥市场"看不见的手"的作用。解决资源和环境问题，政府要运用行政的、法律的、舆论的等手段，采取法律、法规、制度、政策、规划、技术等办法解决。但是仅凭这一只"看得见的手"是不行的，还必须通过市场"看不见的手"即运用利益调节手段去解决，二者是相互补充、相辅相成的。既对资源实行有偿定价、有偿开发、有偿使用，又对污染生产者征收相应的排污费，对污染消费者给予必要的经济补偿，使企业从关心成本—效益的变动上，关心资源的节约和环境的保护。再次，要坚定不移地依靠科技进步，建设学习型社会和节约型社会。实现人口、资源、环境的可持续发展，关键在人口素质的提高。只有不断提高人口的科学、文化、教育素质，才能使全市人口和劳动力多的优势，转化为人才和人力资本的优势。一旦人才和人力资本的优势树立起来，也为采用先进技术保护资源和环境创造了条件。为此不仅要大力发展国民教育，而且要提倡终身教育，包括节约资源和保护环境在内的公民意识教育，建立起学习型城市和学习型社会。同时，要牢固地树立起资源稀缺的观念，从政府到社区，从生产到生活，都要尽可能地保护资源、节约资源和提高资源的利用率，建立节约型城市和节约型社会。走生产发展、生活富裕、生态良好的"三生"文明发展道路，是嵊州市人口与经济可持续发展的必由之路。

由于受水平和嵊州市情况了解的限制，本《报告》不当之处，请有关领导和广大读者批评指正。

《老龄化：从"人口盈利"到"人口亏损"》绪论[*]

　　站在全球高度观察，在人类长达400多万年的历史长河中，人口的生产和再生产绝大部分时间处于高出生、高死亡、低增长状态。18 世纪中叶产业革命发生后逐渐转入高、低、高阶段，20 世纪开始后发达国家总体开始了向低、低、低阶段的过渡，并在后半叶完成了这一过渡，步入老年型社会。随着出生率的下降，一些发展中国家也开始了这种过渡，中国作为当今世界第一人口大国，于世纪之交率先完成这种过渡，对世界人口转变和老龄化时代的到来产生着举足轻重的影响。纵观过去 100 年和未来 100 年的人口变动，可以说 20 世纪是全球人口暴涨的世纪，21 世纪则是人口年龄结构走向老龄化的世纪。

　　问题与解决问题的手段总是同时发生的。发达国家对老龄化研究较早，我国也在 20 世纪 70 年代末 80 年代初提倡一对夫妇生育一个孩子时，便注意并开始了老龄化问题的研究。然而以往的研究更多侧重于老龄问题的解决上，即如何妥善解决众多老年人口的有所养、有所医、有所教、有所学、有所为、有所乐，满足与日俱增的众多老年人口的生理、心理、文化、交往、发展等的需要问题；忽视或很少注意到老龄化可能给经济和社会发展带来的影响的研究。为此，中国社会科学院将"人口老龄化对经济、社会发展的影响研究"列为院重大课题，经过三年潜心研究，完成本专著最终研究成果。

　　本成果共分三部分：第一部分老龄化与人口发展，为全书的基础部分。通过对全球人口老龄化进程的回顾和展望，为中国人口老龄化对比分析提供了背景材料。重点分析自 20 世纪 70 年代以来的中国的人口转变，世纪之交步入老年型；以 2000 年第五次全国人口普查资料作基础并对其中的某些数据作出必要的调整，特别是将漏报的 1.81% 人口按性别和年龄别回填后，

---

* 本文发表于 2005 年。

得到 2000 年全国总和生育率为 1.72，城镇为 1.31，农村为 2.06 的基础数据，作出 21 世纪人口变动低、中、高三种方案的预测①，揭示出 21 世纪上半叶中国人口老龄化的趋势和主要特点：一是人口老龄化的速度比较快。65 岁以上老年人口比例从 7% 上升到 17%，西方发达国家一般要经历 80 到 100 年，我国仅 32 年时间；二是达到的水平比较高。到 2050 年达到最高峰值时 65 岁以上老年人口比例可达 23.07%，比届时发达国家 25.9% 仅低 2.83 个百分点，在发展中国家居最高水平；三是老龄化增长速度呈先扬后抑走势。21 世纪 40 年代以前具有加速增长的态势，2000 至 2020 年 65 岁以上老年人口比例可从 6.92% 上升到 12.04%，年平均升高 0.25 个百分点；2020 至 2040 年可由 12.04% 上升到 21.96%，年平均升高 0.45 个百分点，增速提高近 1 倍；2040 至 2050 年增速趋缓，仅由 21.96% 上升到 23.01%，年平均升高 0.11 个百分点。四是地理分布不平衡的特点。（1）21 世纪三四十年代特别是 2020 年以前人口城市化加速推进期间，由于农村人口向城镇流动和迁移以成年人口为主，相当多数的农村老年人口在原籍滞留下来，造成农村老龄化程度要比城镇为高的"逆转"态势；待到 21 世纪三四十年代城镇人口比例上升到 70% 以上、改革开放以来进城务工经商的大批农民过渡到老年以后，城乡老龄化的"逆转"态势才能从根本上纠正，城乡 65 岁以上老年人口比例可由 2030 年的 1.0∶1.4，变动到 2050 年的 1.0∶0.87。（2）在老龄化地域分布上，西部和中部的老龄化程度趋于接近，东部与中西部之间的差距拉大，东部老龄化要更严重一些。老龄化是出生率下降和预期寿命延长的结果，因而老龄化对人口的数量变动有着不容忽视的作用和影响。尤其应当明确：一为一定程度的老龄化不仅是不可避免的，而且是必需的，是实现人口零增长必须经过的一个阶段。我国人口问题属人口和劳动力过剩性质，控制人口数量增长是首要的战略任务，为此就要使生育率和出生率经过相当长时间的下降；而生育率和出生率的下降，必然导致人口年龄结构老龄化。二为老龄化要限定在合理范围之内，保证人口再生产合乎规律地进行。一定程度的人口老龄化是必需的，并不等于老龄化程度越高越好，超高老龄化可能造成社会无力支撑过重的老年负担，这样的老龄化是应当避免的。老龄化的这种双重作用，足以影响 21 世纪中国人口发展战略的抉择：一要考虑尽快实现人口的零增长，不可避免地经历较长时间的低生育水平过程和老龄化

---

① 本预测参数由田雪原、王金营讨论确定，设计、计算由王金营完成。

过程；二要考虑低生育水平必须控制在合理限度之内，防止超高老龄化的发生。将这两种考虑结合起来，最重要的，就是要为人口发展战略和相应的生育政策设置一个合理的老龄化"警戒线"。我们提出，按照国家"三步走"发展战略目标到 21 世纪中叶达到发达国家一般水平，基本的态势是"未富先老"，老龄化"警戒线"应设在不超过届时发达国家 65 岁以上老年人口比例 26% 的水平。据此并结合我国经济和社会发展实际，提出 21 世纪中国人口发展战略的基本点是：以全面、协调、可持续科学发展观为指导，通过人口数量、素质、结构的合理变动，积极稳妥地实现人口的零增长，促进人口与经济、社会以及资源、环境的可持续发展。这与 20 世纪 80 年代初确定的"控制人口数量、提高人口质量、调整人口结构相结合并以数量控制为重点"的战略相比，有表现历史继承性相同的一面，继续控制人口的数量增长；也有展现当今时代和人口变动新特点，战略重点不尽相同的一面：一是指导思想不同，那时主要是将高人口增长率尽快降下来，缓解和逐步消除人口和劳动力过剩的压力；现在是要将控制人口增长纳入科学发展观视野，推进人口与可持续发展战略的实施。二是那时突出"以数量控制为重点"，现在是在继续有效控制人口数量增长的同时，还要兼顾其他方面，尤其是人口年龄结构老龄化不应超过最高"警戒线"。三是战略目标不同，那时是人口发展战略伊始的"第一步"，以生育率下降到更替水平以下为目标；现在是"第二步"的人口零增长，还要涉及更长远一些的百年以后的理想适度人口目标。不难看出，老龄化是两个人口发展战略不同点的决定性要素，按照该发展战略的中位预测，2005 年全国人口可达 13.23 亿人，65 岁以上老年人口比例可达 7.86%；2010 年可达 13.60 亿人、8.59%，2020 年可达 14.44 亿人、12.04%，2030 年可达 14.65 亿人（峰值）、16.23%，2040 年可达 14.51 亿人、21.96%，2050 年可达 14.02 亿人、23.07%，步入峰值阶段。

老龄化对人口变动最直接的影响，表现在不同年龄组群的变动上，特别是 15～59 岁或 15～64 岁成年人口、0～14 岁少年人口以及 6～11 岁、12～17 岁、18～21 岁各年龄组群的变动。因为成年人口变动关系到劳动力的供给和社会被抚养人口比例的变动，对经济发展产生直接的作用和影响；其余各年龄组群人口的变动，决定着每年进入小学、中学和大学人口的数量，要求教育事业的发展要与之相适应。预测表明，从 20 世纪 80 年代开始劳动年龄人口所占比例不断升高，老少被抚养人口之和所占比例不断降低；进入 90 年代 15～64 岁劳动年龄人口比例更升高到占总人口的 65% 以上，老年和少年被抚养人口之和所占比例则下降到 0.5 以下，标志着人口年龄结构变动步入对经济和社会发展十分有利的"黄金时代"，或曰"人口盈利"、"人口红利"期。如以从属年龄比低于 0.5 作标准，这一"人口盈利"期可持续到 2030 年前后，每个劳动年龄人口负担的老少被抚养人口即从属年龄比，已从 1982 年普查时的 0.63 下降到 1990 年的 0.50，2000 年的 0.46；中位预测表明，2010 年可进一步下降到 0.37 的最低水平；虽然此后从属年龄比呈上升趋势，但是上升的速度较慢，2020 年可升至 0.45，相当于 2000 年水平；2030 年可升至 0.48，接近 1990 年水平。2030 ~ 2040 年间上升比较显著，2040 年可升至 0.59；2040 年以后则变动不大，2050 年略升高至 0.61，相当于 20 世纪 80 年代初期水平。机不可失，时不再来。未来 15 年全面建设小康社会期间，正值劳动年龄人口充裕、从属年龄人口比处在低谷的"人口盈利"期，我们应当充分利用"盈利"的有利时机加快经济、科技和社会发展的步伐；同时也要清醒地看到，"人口盈利"期过后便是从属年龄比上升较快的"人口亏损"期，在"盈利"期就要筹划如何以"盈"抵"亏"、以"利"补"损"的方略，不能只分享眼前的"红利"而不顾及日后的"亏损"。

第二部分老龄化与经济发展，主要分析老龄化对经济发展的制约和影响。通过构建人口—经济动态模型，对人口老龄化在经济增长中的作用作出趋势性的判断，重点阐发如下。

（1）人口老龄化与储蓄率、储蓄水平的关系。利用 1978 年以来有关人均 GDP、储蓄水平、储蓄率、人口年龄变动等时间序列数据，对人口老龄化与储蓄率和储蓄水平之间的关系进行多元回归的实证分析表明：人均储蓄水平与人均 GDP 有显著的因果关系和线性关系，与老龄化不具有线性关系；从对数模型的检验得知，储蓄水平的对数与老年人口比重之间具有弱的线性关系，反映了老年人口比重与人均储蓄水平之间具有非线性关系。通过对储蓄率与老年人口比重的双对数模型检验可知，二者之间的关系较为显著，表明它们之间具有非线性关系，参数估计可见，老年人口比重每增长 1%，储蓄率可提高 0.37 个百分点；而劳动年龄人口比重变动对储蓄率富有弹性，劳动年龄人口每增长 1%，储蓄率可提高 1.47 个百分点。因此，劳动力投入的变动对储蓄和投资的变动影响较大，而老年人口比重的变动弹性相对较小。

（2）人口老龄化对劳动参与率和劳动供给的影响。通过双标准化分析发现，我国20世纪90年代劳动参与率的降低，主要是由劳动年龄人口年龄别劳动参与模式的变动引起的，特别是较低年龄组群劳动参与率的下降引发的。在考虑劳动参与率年龄模式变动的情况下，对未来劳动力供给和劳动力资源进行预测结果显示：由于未来劳动年龄人口中25～44岁所占比例逐渐降低，而45～64岁相对较高龄劳动年龄人口所占的比例逐渐升高，即使未来各年龄组劳动参与率保持2000年水平不变，劳动参与率也将出现下降趋势。特别是在2045年以后，这种下降趋势更加明显，值得重视。考虑劳动参与模型的未来劳动供给变动趋势与以往仅仅依据劳动年龄人口变动趋势的差异，劳动力供给开始减少的时间将要提前，而下降的速度也要更快一些。

（3）人口老龄化与消费的关系。利用1978年以来人口、GDP和消费的统计数据，对含有年龄结构变量的消费函数进行检验，结果表明，1978～2000年我国人均消费水平的决定性因素是人均收入水平的提高，包括老年人口比例上升在内的人口年龄结构变动，对消费水平的影响是比较微弱的。而从对数线性模型的估计检验结果得知，在不考虑人均收入水平影响情况下，消费水平与人口老龄化程度和劳动力比重有显著的非线性关系。为了更好地分析决定消费的因素和人口年龄结构变动对消费水平的影响，本研究提出并采用标准消费人的计量方法，构建一个隐含年龄结构的消费函数。检验结果表明，采用该方法得到的消费函数更加优越，解决了老龄化对消费变动数理计算难题。

（4）人口老龄化对经济增长影响模拟。提出并构建了可计算的含人口年龄结构的人口－经济动态模型，利用该模型对未来不同人口下的经济增长进行模拟，结果显示：老龄化程度较高、上升速度较快，其对经济增长的阻力就比较大，经济增长的速度也比较慢；反之老龄化程度较低、上升的速度较慢，对经济增长的阻力就比较小，经济增长的速度也比较快。在模型模拟分析中，发现人口老龄化通过对消费的影响间接影响经济的增长，无论在何种消费函数下，都以人口低方案下的高度老龄化的产出能力为最低，中方案次之，高方案为最高。以不含滞后消费变量的消费函数为例，2020年低、中、高三种方案产出之比为1.00∶1.35∶1.35，2040年为1.00∶2.20∶2.24。从产出角度看，到2035年低方案与中、高方案相比，其产出值可相差近1倍，2050年可相差1.5倍，时间越长落差越大。虽然中方案与高方案之间产出相差不大，但是人口数量却相差不少，中方案兼顾了人口数量控制和产出的较快增长，是着眼于人口与经济共同发展比较理想的方案；而低方案人均产出增长的速度和达到的水平，远不及中方案和高方案为高。由此看来，一味地追求过低的生育率不仅为人口本身再生产的正常进行所不容许，而且对经济发展和人民生活水平的提高也是不利的，长远的生育率变动应保持在接近更替的水平上。

（5）人口老龄化与收入分配。国际社会一般将支付老年的退休金等费用占国民收入的10%或工资总额的29%定为"警戒线"，超过这一"警戒线"将使国家财政和经济发展陷入困境。中国离退休人员社会保险福利费用占国民收入的比例，已从1980年的1.4%上升到了1993年的3.7%，13年间上升了2.3个百分点；预测2025～2030年可超过10%，占工资总额可达30%左右，逼近或突破上述"警戒线"。然而此时距离老龄化峰值的到来尚有20多年的时间，足见问题之严重，对"人口亏损"必须有足够的估量。

第三部分老龄化与社会发展，阐述和分析人口老龄化对社会养老保障、科技进步、制度建设、社区发展、文化生活、婚姻和家庭等的作用和影响。从宏观的全社会到中观社区、再到微观的家庭，作出多层面、多视角的不同分析；从国外的一般经验到中国的具体国情，力求将国外成功经验与我国实际结合起来，提出相应的改革建议。尤其是以下几个方面。

其一，结合我国人口老龄化进程和经济、社会发展实际，提出逐步建立起完整的老年社会保障体系的框架和结构。在人口老龄化冲击下，西方发达国家率先建立起"从摇篮到坟墓"的全方位养老保障体系。然而由于政府财政入不敷出，福利国家的老年社会保障已经举步维艰、难以为继，暴露出种种弊端。我国一是基于"未富先老"的基本国情，没有条件实施像西方国家那样全方位的社会保障；二是鉴于当代"福利国家砍福利"的教训，也不应该走那条道路。从实际出发，我们提出走渐进式、逐步扩展的养老保障路子。前已述及，21世纪前20年为人口老龄化推进较慢时期，在此期间内逐步形成包括集养老保险、社会福利、社会救济于一体的养老社会保障框架；2020～2040年为人口老龄化加速推进并进入严重阶段，主要是完善养老保障体系和制度建设；2040～2050年人口老龄化速度减慢并趋于稳定，养老保障制度也要相对稳定，只对个别不适宜部分作出相应的调整。实施这一渐进式养老保障改革方案，关键是基本框架建立的前20年，而这20年或再长一些时间，正值人口年龄结构变动的"黄金时代"，应当说拿出"人口盈利"中的一部分构建养老保障框架是有条件的。毫无疑问，构建全社会的养老保障体系需要加大国家和地方的财政投资，政府扮演社会保障主角各国概莫能外；然而从"未富先老"的客观实际出发，还必须调动各方面的积极性，挖掘各种潜力，走改革的路子。为此，我们提出以下城乡养老保障改革建议。

（1）建立农村责任田养老基地。当前除"五保户"和个别经济发达地区外，广大农村还没有社会化养老保障，基本依靠老年人自我劳动和家庭供养。从长远发展角度观察，将来的社会养老保障要将农村纳入其中；这在国家和地方财政支持力量限制的情况下，就要挖掘其他方面的潜力。农村一般老年人个人积蓄不多，走商业化养老保险只能是少数人的事情；但是农村老年人同其他人一样，拥有一份责任田。尽管在法律上，责任田不属于个人所有，是一种使用权和经营权；但是因其具有使用价值，转让这种使用价值便可带来财富的创造，因而也可以将其视为"财产"而发挥养老保障作用。具体办法是：依据地区人均耕地面积多少，60 岁以上老年人可将其责任田的一部分或全部，入股带到农村老年责任田基地；基地是社会化养老组织，组织低龄老年人和其他志愿者从事生产劳动和经营，取得经济收入，供给基地老年人生活和消费。基地主旨是通过盘活农村土地资源，使其成为养老资产；盘活农村老年劳动力资源，用老年人口中较低年龄组群的集体劳动力量，克服老年个体体力上的不足，创立一种不需要额外投入即可实现基本养老的组织形式。

（2）创建城镇房产养老保险。同二元经济社会结构相适应，目前我国城镇中多数老年人口享有不同程度的养老保障，按时领取离退休金；也有部分城镇老年人口由于历史的原因，被排斥在离退休制度之外，不能享有离退休金。这部分老年人收入低、积蓄很少、生活比较困难。如何解决？调查表明，虽然他们现金储蓄较少，但是许多人拥有自己的一份房产，尽管房屋的质量一般不是很高。故可采取类似农村责任田养老基地办法，城镇老年人口也可以将属于自己的房屋财产投资到城镇养老保险专业公司，按照房屋的数量和质量作价入股，再按照股份多少按时领取养老金。房屋作价入股，可以采取：①出让式——老年人口将属于自己产权的房屋作价卖给养老保险专业公司，等于以出卖房产作价投保养老保险，出让后老年人将不再拥有房屋的产权和继承权；②期货式——城镇老年人口将属于自己产权的房产作价交付专业养老保险公司，但保留一定期间内的老年人的居住权（如保留到老年人去世为止），不保留房屋产权和继承权。实际上，等于专业养老保险公司预付一笔资金给老年房屋所有者作为股金投保，类似作期货交易一样；③典当式——既保留老年人口对原有房屋的产权，又保留将来的继承权，只是将若干面积的房屋出租给养老保险专业公司，保险公司以养老金形式支付给老年一定的费用。类似在当铺里典当东西一样，等到老年人口去世后，再由家人赎回来。由于房产养老方式不同，相同数量和质量的房屋入股专业养老保险公司的回报率也不同，第一种高于第二种，第二种高于第三种。

其二，在全面分析老龄化对科技进步影响基础上，论证了重视和开发老年人力资源的积极意义。迄今为止，人口老龄化对科技进步的影响和作用，认识上有很大分歧。我们认为，老龄化的影响是二重的：一方面，老年人才随着人口老龄化的加深不断增长，而老年人才长期积累起来的知识、经验和技能，具有不需要培训、成本低和实用性较强等优点，能够也应该在全面建设小康社会中发挥出更大的作用。另一方面，老龄化的加深和用在老年人口方面投资的不断加大，会影响科学、教育、技术改造投资的增长；同时老龄化不可避免地带来知识、技术的老化，阻碍着技术的进步。综合两方面的影响，最重要的，是要开发和利用好老年人力资源，充分发挥老年人才的作用。据统计，目前全国城镇4000多万离退休老年人口中有500多万各种类型人才，仅有不到20%继续奋斗在各自的岗位上，形成老年人才资源的很大浪费。我们应当重视这一人力资源，进一步开发利用好老年人才资源。

其三，通过中外对比，阐述老龄化对社区发展的影响，提出老龄社区建设新思路。人们从生产力、居住和行政等不同角度来划分社区，我国多以行政区划来划分，政府主导色彩浓厚，使之与西方发达国家有很大的不同。实践表明，社区是除家庭之外老年社会生活最主要的场所，无论生活照料、医疗保健，还是精神慰藉、文化生活，都离不开社区，老龄化呼唤社区加快发展。从我国实际出发，加快老龄社区发展除了政府重视、增加投资、动员社会各界积极参与外，当前应着重解决以下几个问题。

老年住宅建设和社区环境改造。住房要适合老年人的生理和心理特征，从楼房高度、采光到地板防滑，从门锁开关、无障碍通行到报警器装置，都要适应老年需要，力求简单、适用、方便、安全，有益于老年人的身心健康。无论是居家养老的老年家庭，还是农村责任田基地、城镇房产养老老年人聚居社区，都要有计划、有步骤地对老年住宅家庭和社区环境进行改造和整治。这种改造和整治成本不高，但却能够满足老年人生活起居、文体活动和社区人际交往等方面的需要，使社区成为老年人生活的第二个家庭。

大力发展社区志愿者服务。第二次世界大战后，志愿者服务发展很快，成为许多国家老年社区服务的主力军，1985 年联合国将每年的 12 月 5 日定为"国际志愿者日"。近年来，我国也开始组织志愿者服务活动，1994 年共青团中央领导创办"中国青年志愿者协会"，开中国志愿者服务先河。但是从总体上看，一是志愿者服务的规模小，整个社会的志愿者服务可以说是凤毛麟角；二是服务项目过少，服务的范围也有限；三是志愿者服务不够规范，活动也带有临时性质，不能持之以恒。在人口老龄化加深、家庭小型化和老年空巢家庭增多的过程中，目前英、法、德等国老年空巢家庭占到70%~80%，我国北京、上海、广州、苏州等大城市也已经占 1/3 以上，迫切需要加强社区服务。社区服务除了要有一批专业性质的"正规军"外，大量的志愿者服务队伍也是不可替代的。

试验和推进"时间储蓄银行"。20 世纪末，人口和社会学研究提出时间储蓄概念：用成年时期的业余时间为老年人提供劳务，将劳务时间记录下来并储存到时间储蓄银行，待到老年退休后再从中提取相应时间的劳务。尽管劳动有简单劳动与复杂劳动之分，单纯的时间计量不够准确；从时间储蓄银行提取劳务也不像提取现金那样方便，新的劳务提供者是否愿意、能否提供相应的劳务，还存在不少的技术问题等，但是这种转换社会劳务的时间储蓄银行（通过社区）提供一个路径：成年人口可以通过储存自己的劳务时间，有效解决未来老年的劳务需求问题。我们应当通过试验不断总结经验，大胆推进，开辟一条提供劳务转换的新路子。

其四，老龄化对老年婚姻和家庭的影响，最值得关注的是老年的再婚问题和老年家庭规模的缩小问题。人口老龄化和老年人口数量剧增，使老年婚姻问题凸显出来，特别是老年人的再婚问题。实践证明，一方面老年人特别是较低年龄组群老年人仍有一定的性需求，爱情仍然是婚姻的基础；另一方面老年人的婚姻又不完全取决于性爱，很大程度上为了消除孤独寂寞、生活互助、找个可以依靠的老伴儿而已。北京市等的调查表明，65 岁以上女性老年人口丧偶率在 40% 以上，出于找个老伴儿一起生活需要的再婚率很高。然而由于婚后子女、财产等的矛盾，造成老年离婚率持续攀升的现状；同时许多老年人再婚没有履行婚姻登记手续，而是同居补充式的婚姻，有的甚至是时来时走的"走婚"式婚姻，处于很不稳定状态。与不稳定婚姻相关联的是家庭的不稳定和小型化趋势。由于家庭小型化和家庭赡养功能的弱化，使老年单身家庭、只有老年夫妇家庭上升很快，导致传统家庭养老发生危机，甚至有的地方老年人不愿忍受子女歧视而弃家出走，许多老年人聚居在河滩、河堤上，成为自食其力的"躲儿庄"。拯救濒临崩溃的老年家庭，是社会道德建设发出的呼吁，也是社会法治化建设需要解决的问题。

其五，老龄化对文化发展的影响是深刻的，需要将其纳入精神文明建设之中。主要的，一是反映老年生活题材的小说、诗歌、散文、戏曲、电影、绘画、音乐、舞蹈等的大量增加，新闻媒体开辟反映老年生活专题如中央电视台"夕阳红"，报纸杂志"老龄之家"、"老年之友"一类专栏的大量增加。随着老龄化的加深，这类老年文化还会继续扩展，以反映老年人在全面建设小康社会中新的精神风貌。二是老龄化的加速推进，带动老年教育和终生教育的迅速发展。自20世纪20年代末英国人提出成人教育和60年代法国教育家林格兰特（P. lengrand）提出终生教育以来，包括老年教育在内的终生教育率先在发达国家发展起来，改革开放以来在我国也获得迅速发展。20世纪八九十年代老年教育发展起来，特别是雨后春笋般建立起来的老年大学，集学自然科学和社会科学知识于一堂，习琴棋书画、音乐舞蹈于一体，形成独具一格的老年大学文化，具有很大社会影响力。三是老龄化加速发展提出重新认识和评价"孝文化"问题。"孝"作为观念意义上的文化，源远流长、影响至深。我们应当继承和高扬传统"孝文化"中敬孝父母的合理内核，将其融入现代发展理念实现在更高意义上的复归；同时应当扬弃封建的糟粕，实现代际平等、代际民主、代际和谐符合现代文明道德准则和人道主义精神的新的"孝文化"。

《社会转型期老龄问题研究》序 [*]

　　20 世纪和 21 世纪，是人口、经济、社会变动和发展最为迅速的时期；而从人口变动角度观察，可以说，20 世纪是人口暴涨的世纪，21 世纪则是人口年龄结构走向老龄化的世纪。面对这一情势，发达国家忧虑少子高龄化数十年，发展中国家也逐渐体验到老龄化的含义，生育率率先下降的发展中国家已经体验到老龄化意味着什么，应当怎样做和做些什么。中国作为当今世界人口最多和发展最快的发展中国家，一方面总体人口还有一定的增长势能，控制人口增长的任务仍不能放松；另一方面由于自 20 世纪 70 年代以来生育率长期持续地下降，人口年龄结构于世纪之交步入老年型，并将以比较快的速度挺进老龄化水平较高国家行列，具有自己的一些明显特点。众所周知，人口学就是依据人口的不同年龄结构，将某总体人口划分成年轻型、成年型和老年型三种基本类型的。对于一个要实现人口零增长的国家说来，一定程度的老龄化不仅是不可避免的，而且是必需的。从这个意义上说，老龄化并不是消极的，应当积极应对。同时也必须承认，从长远发展态势观察，老龄化和老年负担系数的攀升，必然影响经济和社会的发展，带来某些方面的不利影响，需要未雨绸缪，将不利因素减少到最低限度，将有利因素提升到最大程度。

　　中国社会科学院老年科学研究中心成立以来，致力于以老年社会科学为主的科学研究。在中心常务理事和各位理事的大力支持下，发挥社会科学门类比较齐全、老学者比较多的优势，积极开展老年学研究，出了一批成果。当前，我国正面临经济转轨、社会转型、人口转变（后人口转变）的关键时期。随着经济改革的不断深入，资源节约型、环境友好型创新型社会的逐步建立，稳定低生育水平和向着人口零增长的过渡，老龄化的外部环境正在

---

　　*　本文发表于 2006 年。

发生某种变化，新问题层出不穷；与此同时，老龄化的加速推进，从一个侧面推动或延缓着上述"三转"，影响着全面建设小康社会的进程。由于以往对老龄问题，诸如老龄化趋势、老年生活保障、老年医疗保障、老年文化生活、老年婚姻家庭、老年劳动就业等研究较多，而对老龄化可能给经济、社会、科技、文化等的发展带来怎样的影响研究较少实际，近年来加强了老龄化对经济、社会发展影响的研究。奉献给读者的《社会转型期老龄问题研究》，主旨在老龄化影响的实证分析和研究，将 10 多位作者的 10 多篇文章汇集一起，尽可能突出这一主题，成为主导的体系，以推动相关研究的深入。本书有的研究应用最新数据资料作出新的中国人口变动和发展预测，概括出老龄化新的趋势和特点；提出和论证了老龄化对人口发展战略的制约，"软着陆"人口发展战略的老龄化分析；老龄化对经济增长、储蓄、投资、消费等的影响，相应的决策选择；老龄化在构建和谐社会中的作用，提出通过盘活城乡老年资产建立符合市场原则的养老保障改革建议；有的侧重中外比较研究，打开新的老年研究思路；有的应用实地调查资料，提出和阐发了新的见解。本着创新是灵魂宗旨，努力推进学术创新。

　　本书以年事已高的高龄学者为主要作者，由于水平所限，不妥之处，还望学术界同事和读者予以批评指正。

《21 世纪中国人口发展战略研究》总论*

　　20 世纪 80 年代初,托夫勒的《第三次浪潮》(中译本)在中国发行 1000 万册以上,成为知识界家喻户晓、人手一册必读的改革开放启蒙读物,足见影响力之大。跨入 21 世纪,他与妻子合著的《财富的革命》问世,中译本也开始在中国发行,其预言能否应验?他在回答《环球时报》记者采访时的一段谈话,颇耐人寻味。他说,1998 年中国国家计委官员提供这样的数字:中国有 9 亿属于第一次浪潮的农业人口、3 亿属于第二次浪潮的工业人口和 1000 万属于第三次浪潮的人口。我们没有最新的数据,但很明显,中国之后的发展越来越快,今天成千上万的中国人又加入了第三次浪潮的人口大军。只要看看有多少中国人在上网、使用电脑和手机就知道了。农业人口和城市人口之间的差距非常之大,第二次浪潮跟第三次浪潮人口之间的鸿沟也越来越深。中国面临的主要问题,是如何预防"浪潮冲突",不仅仅是农村与城市之间,也包括第三次浪潮与其他方面的冲突①。这里,托夫勒将三次浪潮归结为农业人口、工业人口、第三次浪潮人口"三大人口板块"的碰撞;再与他们的新作《财富的革命》联系起来,铺展出一幅"三次浪潮"、"财富革命"在人口不同层面分布和冲突的画卷。这给我们将人口发展战略置于世界发展大趋势背景之下,以新的启迪。

　　以 1919 年发生在北京的"五四运动"为标志,揭开中国历史发展新的一页。将近 90 年,不同历史时期中国革命和建设的指向,可以大致平分为三个阶段:1919 ~ 1949 年的 30 年,主要指向帝国主义、封建主义和官僚资本主义,用 30 年时间推翻"三座大山",民族矛盾和阶级矛盾是主要的矛盾。1949 ~ 1978 年的 30 年,经济指向以计划经济为手段、以工业化为目标;政治指向以阶级斗争为纲、全面推进社会主义革命和社会主义改造。1978

---

　　* 参见唐勇《"托夫勒预测中国未来"》,2006 年 7 月 14 日《环球时报》。

年以来又过了将近 30 年，经济指向改革开放、建立市场经济体制；政治指向民主法治建设、构建和谐社会。以第二个 30 年和第三个将近 30 年而论，前者强调的是计划经济、阶级斗争，后者强调的是市场经济、和谐社会，应了"三十年河东、三十年河西"这句话。显然，研究面向 21 世纪的中国人口发展战略，也要将人口融入市场经济和构建和谐社会之中。

1. 国际背景

迄今为止，中国是世界上人口最多的发展中国家，2005 年全国 130756 万人占世界 646475 万人口的 20.2%，比发达国家全部人口之和占 18.7% 高出 1.5 个百分点。依据联合国的预测，2030 年前后印度人口有可能超过中国，中国将心甘情愿地退居第二人口大国的位置。即使如此，届时中国仍将占世界人口的 17.6%，比发达国家占 15.3% 高出 2.3 个百分点；2050 年也占 15.3%，比发达国家占 13.6% 高出 1.7 个百分点[①]，对世界人口变动和发展仍然具有举足轻重的作用和影响。因此，中国人口发展战略离不开世界人口的变动与发展，离不开世界经济、科技、社会的变动与发展，需要将中国人口发展战略置于国际社会发展的大背景之下考察。

（1）信息化

20 世纪下半叶，国外学术界提出并论证了全球化、工业化和后工业化、城市化、信息化、区域经济一体化等重要发展趋势，但是对全球发展最具影响力的是信息化和经济全球化。1963 年日本学者 Tadao Umesao 发表"论信息产业"一文，接着卡米夏马（Kamishima）在"信息社会中的社会学"一文中首次使用"信息社会"概念，其后的讨论将"信息化"解释为在由工业化向信息化社会过渡中，信息产业逐渐占据主导和支配地位的过程。随着实践的发展，信息化研究的广度和深度不断扩展和深入，提出突破计算机化局限包括计算机化、通信现代化、网络技术现代化涵盖"三 C"（Computer，Communication，Control）的信息化；包括交换和传输的数字化、通信和网络管理服务"融合"（Convergence）等在内的"四 C"的信息化；以及包括信息环境、从有形信息产品向模拟信息产品转变过程的信息化等。尽管不同学科、不同部门对信息化所下定义有所不同，但是在基本点上则取得越来越多的共识：

① 中国为内地 31 省、自治区、直辖市，未含台湾省和香港、澳门特别行政区人口，下同。参见《中国统计年鉴 2006》，中国统计出版社，2006；United Nations, *World Population Prospects，The 2004 Revision*，New York，2005。

一是信息技术、信息产业在社会经济发展中的地位和作用不断增强。在信息化过程中，传统物质生产部门所占比重下降与信息部门所占比重上升交相互动，从事信息生产和服务的信息产业的价值得到确立和提升，成为独立和不可取代的产业，在社会经济发展中起主导和决定的作用。信息产业创造的价值和财富与日俱增，这点只要看一看当今世界富豪排行榜，就十分清楚了。在《福布斯》公布的 2006 年全球富豪排行榜中，美国微软公司创始人比尔·盖茨以 500 多亿美元蝉联首富，这已是他连续 12 次稳坐世界富豪第一把交椅；第二为美国投资家沃伦·巴菲特，拥有 420 亿美元资产；第三为墨西哥电信业巨亨拥有 300 亿美元资产的洛斯·斯利姆·埃卢，他将原居于第三位的印度钢铁大王拉克稀米·米塔尔挤到了第五位。历史发展到今天，发生了巨额财富由钢铁大王、汽车大王、石油大王等手中，向着 IT 业、电信业等信息产业主宰者的转移，信息产业集中了越来越多的财富。

二是信息资源价值不断增值。信息化意味着在商品生产和劳务中物质财富消耗不断降低，信息劳动所占比例不断升高，信息市场规模不断扩大并成为整个市场经济中越来越重要的市场，最终导致信息资源价值的增值。信息化极大地缩短了时间、拉近了空间距离，一台互联网上的计算机，可将纽约、伦敦、东京、中国香港等金融市场指数变动一览无余，将某种产品期货报价尽收眼底，搜索到世界主要国家经济、科技、文化、社会发展的动态，从而为经济和社会发展提供各种必要的动态和数据，信息资源升值当在情理之中。随着信息化向纵深推进，应用现代电子技术等手段开发利用信息资源，实现信息资源共享，提高社会的智能和潜力，已成为不可阻挡之势。

三是信息化迅速提升着工农业物质生产部门和服务业的效率和效益。信息化在推进信息产业快速发展的同时，用先进的信息技术武装工农业物质生产部门、服务业非物质生产部门、劳动和管理等国民经济和社会发展一切部门，从而使劳动生产率、社会工作效率和效益全面提高。与此相适应，经济增长转向主要依赖人的智力投资和人力资本积聚的增长，产业结构转变到与信息产业密切相关、低耗高效为主的产业上来，实现经济增长方式的根本性转变。

上述信息化及其给社会经济发展带来的一系列革命性变革，必然深刻影响人口的变动与发展，这是在研究人口发展战略时，不能不充分注意到的。

其一，立足于人口视角，信息化大大推进了人的现代化。众所周知，经济时代的划分不是依据生产什么，而是依据怎样生产、用什么样的劳动工具进行生产。据此，可将人类长达400多万年发展的历史，粗略地划分为手工工具时代、机器工具时代和智力工具时代。手工工具时代对应的是农业和农业以前诸社会形态，基本的特征是使用手工工具进行生产劳动，主要的动力来自人、畜和原始的自然力。机器工具时代开始于18世纪中叶产业革命发生后，以纺纱机、蒸汽机的发明和使用为标志。这两个时代的生产工具有着本质的不同，机器大工业与手工工具蕴涵的生产力有天壤之别；但是从人本观点看，无论手工工具还是机器工具，都是人的体能的延长，体能的物质化和外在化。锹、镐是人手功能的延长和物质化，电铲、掘土机同样是人手功能的延长和物质化；马车是人腿功能的延长和物质化，汽车、火车、飞机同样是人腿功能的延长和物质化。只不过两者之间延长的长度、科技含量多少、物质化水平高低相差比较悬殊而已。然而20世纪中期第二次世界大战结束后，发生了以微电子技术为前导包括新材料、新能源、宇航、海洋、生物工程等的新技术革命，当前又进展到以生命科学为主导学科，包括基因技术、克隆技术、纳米技术等的新发展阶段，此时出现的计算机技术已经具备了人脑具有的记忆、储存和某些思维功能，"电脑"确切地表达了计算机的含义。它已不再是人体能的延长、物质化和外在化，而是具有了人的智力某些方面的功能，发展的方向是人的智力的延长、物质化和外在化，从而把人类带进智力工具时代。毫无疑问，智力工具时代进展是否顺利，关键还在人的智力发达的程度、人力资本积累的速度，前提是人口科学、教育、文化、健康素质提升的程度。

其二，立足于劳动就业视角，信息化要求就业结构作出与之相适应的调整。随着信息技术的不断进步，包括信息资源开发、信息产品和设备的生产、信息服务的发展等在内的信息产业迅速发展起来。信息产业由信息硬件产品生产，如计算机、通信设备等的生产；软件产品的生产，主要是各种软件的开发、生产与服务；系统集成与网络集成的构建和运营组成。其中既有以微电子技术为主导的电子信息产业部门，也有以传统纸质技术为依托的传递信息的产业部门，包括邮电通信、广播、电视、数据库、广告、咨询服务等行业和部门。这些行业和部门的急剧发展和迅速扩张，必然打破原有的经济结构和就业结构，从事信息产业劳动的职工人数大量增加、所占比例迅速上升；从事传统产业劳动的职工人数明显减少、所占比例下降许多。信息产业发展不仅使该产业就业职工比例大幅度上升，而且由于信息产业对劳动者的年龄、性别、知识结构有着明确的要求，从而影响总体人口和劳动年龄人口的就业率，以及就业的性别和年龄结构和人口的城乡结构。使农业人口、工业人口、"第三次浪潮人口"之间的冲突，呈现错综复杂的情况。

中国作为当今世界人口最多、发展最快、传统工业化与信息化导航下现代工业化同时推进的发展中国家，虽然信息化发达的程度赶不上发达国家，但是较发达的东部与欠发达的中部和西部差别很大，信息化推进的速度差别很大，因此对人口变动与发展的影响要复杂得多、深刻得多。尤其在当前经济转轨，包括经济体制由计划经济转向市场经济轨道，经济增长方式由外延型转向内涵型；社会转型，由政府主导型转向社会服务型；人口转变，除了一般意义上由高出生、低死亡、高增长转变到低出生、低死亡、低增长外，在低生育水平下人口年龄、城乡、地域结构的转变——信息化在"三转"加速推进下降临，其对人口变动和发展的影响，必须作出充分的估量。

（2）经济全球化

据考证，是 T. 莱维于 1985 年最早提出"全球化"概念，用来说明在过去的 20 年中国际经济发生的巨大变化，现代技术、资本、商品、市场、服务等在世界投资、生产、消费领域的扩散，成为一种不可阻挡的发展趋势。这种扩散趋势产生不对称的国际劳动分工，而围绕生产和市场活动的分工和扩散，公司特别是跨国公司扮演着主要角色。不同学科对"全球化"的定位和解释不尽相同，政治学家侧重国际干预的扩散，国与国之间联系和交往的加强，着眼于世界新格局和新国际秩序的建立；社会学家侧重社会现象变动的过程，一国发生的重大事件和活动，足以影响其他国家的个人、群体和整个社会的变动；人文学家侧重文化视角，从不同文化相互影响、渗透中，捕捉主流文化变动和发展的趋势；经济学家侧重资本、技术、贸易、劳动力流动等经济要素的新的变动，把握打破疆界壁垒形成的经济一体化、市场一体化、金融一体化发展的新格局。

就经济全球化作为一种发展趋势而言，可以追溯到产业革命发生之后，尽管第二次世界大战前后的经济一体化有着本质的不同。众所周知，自 18 世纪中叶产业革命发生后，又经过五次重大的革命性变革。一般认为，发生在 18 世纪中叶的产业革命，以纺纱机和蒸汽机的发明和使用为标志，开辟了由英国波及法国、西班牙、葡萄牙、德国、美国、日本等，由欧洲波及美洲、亚洲、澳洲等的机器大工业取代手工业的新的时代，以机器大工业为主要标志产业的全球化时代；接着发生的，是以钢铁为主要标志产业的第二次产业革命的全球化；随后发生的，是以石油、重化工、电力为主要标志产业的第三次产业革命的全球化；再以下发生的，以汽车为主要标志产业的第四次产业革命的全球化；"二战"后，发生以微电子技术为主要标志产业的第五次产业革命的全球化；近年来由于基因工程、克隆技术等的迅速发展，发生以生命科学及其产业为主要标志的第六次产业革命的全球化。这些不同时期、不同主导产业的全球化，不仅同特定的新材料、新能源、新工艺等新的技术革命紧密相联，而且引发生产、交换、分配、消费在管理和制度上的创新，因而都是"硬件"和"软件"同时向外扩散的全球化。不过这六次主导产业的全球化，还有着不同的性质。第二次世界大战前，即前四次主导产业的全球化，是物质凝聚式的全球化，无论是钢铁、重化工还是汽车产业的扩散，基本上都是第一次产业革命机器大工业在不同领域的延伸和扩张，不同主导产业的全球化表现为机器大工业不同物质凝聚形式上的延伸和扩张。第二次世界大战后发生的以微电子技术为前导的新的技术革命，包括当前进展到以生命科学为主导学科的新技术革命，虽然 IT 技术、基因技术、克隆技术及其产业，都离不开一定的物质形式存在，但是它主要凝聚的已不是物质力，而是人的智力，是人的知识力和智慧力的凝聚。在这种凝聚形式变化的背后，蕴涵着人与自然、人与人关系的变动，把时间和空间前所未有地拉近了，从而改变着人们之间关系的性质。从这样的认识出发，"二战"之前的产业全球化还称不上真正意义的全球化；只有二战之后的全球化，才是我们所要探讨的全球化。

为什么"二战"之后经济全球化能够超越国家和民族界限加速推进，并且形成一种不可阻挡的趋势呢？首要的一条，就是发生了以微电子技术，当前又进展到以生命科学为主导的新的技术革命。包括新材料、新能源、宇航、海洋技术等在内的以微电子技术为前导的新技术革命，包括基因、克隆、纳米技术以生命科学为主导的当前最新的技术革命，使高新技术在信息、交通、通信等部门和产业的大规模应用成为可能，成本大为降低，从而为信息化带动工业化提供了广阔的平台；由于效率的提高和时空的空前拉近，各国市场在全球水平上融合变得更加容易，贸易、投资和技术转让更加便捷，大大增加了合作国之间在技术、制造、管理、销售等环节上的相互依赖性；跨国公司趁势而上，发挥它们在资金、技术、人才以及产、供、销一条龙服务等方面的优越性，加快并购步伐，最终发展为全球性质的超级公司，扮演着经济全球化的主要角色。结合我国人口经济发展实际，当前经济全球化的主要特点及其对发展的影响，作如下阐述。

其一，自由贸易成为一种趋势，全球性市场正在加速形成。经济全球化以市场经济体制为基础，是不言而喻的，计划经济不可能纳入全球化范畴。市场经济的基本特点，可归结为市场主体法人化、要素流动市场化、宏观调控间接化、经济运行法制化，核心是依靠市场实现资源的合理有效配置。要做到这一点，市场这只"看不见的手"首先就要伸向流通领域，借助市场调节产、供、销。经济全球化也是一样，先要形成更大规模的全球性市场。在这方面，世界贸易组织（WTO）的建立和发展，充分证明了这一点。世贸组织是一个独立于联合国的永久性国际组织，负责管理世界经济和贸易秩序，总部设在瑞士日内瓦，1995 年 1 月 1 日正式开始运作。2001 年 12 月 11日，中国正式加入该组织，成为世贸组织中的一员。5 年来，借助世贸组织中国加快了向经济全球化迈进的步伐，促进了经济又好又快的发展。世贸组织把国际贸易以及与国际贸易相关的各个领域纳入多边贸易体制，削弱甚至消除国家市场关税壁垒保护，要将 40% 的商品贸易变成免税贸易，其余也要大幅度降低关税，从而刺激服务和技术贸易以更快的速度增长，使之成为世界市场的主要贸易方式。中国加入世贸组织 5 年来，大大促进了对外贸易的增长，出口总额由 2001 年的 22024.4 亿元增加到 2005 年的 62648.1 亿元，增长 184.4%，年平均增长 29.9%；2005 年 7620 亿美元出口额排在德国9707 亿美元、美国 9043 亿美元之后位居世界第三位[①]。现在外贸与固定投资增长，成为拉动经济增长的主要杠杆。对外贸易拉动经济增长，拉动什么样的经济增长同外贸结构密切相关。入市以来出口商品中初级产品所占比例有所下降，由 2001 年占 9.9% 下降到 2005 年占 6.4%，降低 3.5 个百分点；工业制成品比例相应上升，其中机械及运输设备升高 10.5 个百分点，而纺织产品、橡胶制品、矿冶产品及其制品所占比例略有降低。同期进口产品中初级产品由占 18.8% 上升到占 22.4%，升高 3.6 个百分点；化学产品及相关产品、纺织产品、橡胶制品、矿冶产品及其制品等工业制成品，比例则相应地下降[②]。这种情况表明，虽然外贸结构有所改变，但是还是比较粗放的，总体科技含量仍然不够高。

其二，资本在国际流动速度加快，金融体制接轨是大势所趋。20 世纪90 年代以来，一些西方国家竭力倡导资本在国际自由流动并且出台了相应的政策，使得国际资本在更大的范围和更高的层次上，以更大的流量和更快

---

① 《中国统计年鉴 2006》，第 1030 页，中国统计出版社，2006，第 733 页。
② 《中国统计年鉴 2006》，第 756 页。

的流速在国际流动起来，远远超过商品形式物的流动和劳务形式劳动力流动的增长速度。据国际货币基金组织（IMF）提供的资料，目前货币经常性项目可兑换的国家占80%左右，少数实行固定汇率制度国家的汇率也在随市调整，实际上真正实行固定汇率制度的国家几乎是不存在的。当前金融市场国际化，不仅放宽了国内金融管制而向国际开放，为不同国家银行、企业或居民进入金融市场从事经营活动提供了各种条件和便利，而且离岸金融市场（境外金融市场）也得到迅速发展和提升。由于境外金融市场摆脱了国家金融管理部门的制约，国际货币管理机构干预的力度也很有限，所在地区的管理只能按照国际惯例行事，因而可以突破地域的限制，实现真正意义上的资本的自由流动。在这一过程中，各种金融衍生工具的出现，如期货交易、期权交易、互换交易、远期交易等形式的不断涌现，起到了催化剂的作用，为规避金融风险和推进资本流动自由化提供了相应的平台和手段。在现代微电子技术高度发达的情况下，这些金融衍生工具不断更新换代，花样翻新层出不穷，容易突破现有不合理管理办法的约束，使国际资本的跨国界交易变得更为便捷，推进了全球金融市场一体化的进程。

据联合国贸易和发展会议在其全球 FDI 状况年度报告《2006 年世界投资报告》中披露，2005 年全球外国直接投资（FDI）流入量大幅度增长到9160 亿美元，比 2004 年增长近 1/3，其中发达国家流入量占 59%，发展中国家占 36%，东南欧和独联体国家占 4%。尽管发展中国家的流入量和总额增长率都比不上发达国家，但是却创出新高，打破了主要流向少数发达国家的格局，实现了具有历史意义的新的突破。发展中国家 FDI 流入量大幅度增长，位居发展中国家 FDI 流入量首位的中国起了关键的作用。统计资料显示，2001 年中国实际利用外资 496.72 亿美元，2005 年增加到 638.05 亿美元，增加 141.33 亿美元，年平均增长 6.5%。中国加入世贸组织后，信守承诺，一方面继续吸引外资；另一方面加快金融体制改革，目前已有多家外国银行被允许在中国开展人民币业务，中国正在加速融入国际金融市场。

当前值得重视的问题，一是要进一步进行金融体制改革，促进金融业健康快速发展；二是要改变过多外汇储备继续上升的趋势，寻求一个合理的储备比率；三是要科学地看待人民币升值压力，把握好升值的节奏。客观地说，外汇储备节节攀升，人民币升值不断突破新高，是必然的，也是合乎规律的，是内外经济发展不平衡交互作用的结果。前面提到，"二战"之后发达国家加快了产业转移步伐，迎来全球产业结构调整高潮；中国改革开放适应了这种调整的需要，才变成"世界工厂"的。但是由此造成的后果之一，是加工贸易占据出口的比重过大，形成不断增大的顺差和外汇储备。加上过去主要倾向鼓励出口，实行优惠不等的出口退税政策，便形成相当规模的"加工—出口—外汇—加工"周期性"体外循环"型经济，成为支撑经济高速增长的杠杆之一。这种"体外循环"型经济对消费的刺激有限，致使国内消费需求不足，要想获得经济的快速增长，就不得不在投资上找出路。统计表明，1989 年全国固定资产投资占 GDP 的比例为 25.9%，到 1997 年提高到 32.1%，2004 年提高到 44.2%，2005 年更创造出 48.3%的新高①。到底投资与消费的比例多少为合适，20 世纪 50、60、70 年代的经验说明，一般以不超过 30%为宜，超过就有可能造成国民经济"过热"和比例失调。不过那是计划经济时代，转入市场经济轨道情况怎样，还有待进一步研究。但是无论如何，目前投资占 GDP 的比例达到 45%以上甚至接近 50%，偏高是不容置疑的。经济在投资率很高的高位上运行，消费需求严重不足，向外寻找需求动力，是自然的事情。因此，国内经济不平衡影响国际经济的不平衡，反过来，主要表现为顺差和外汇储备累进增长的国际经济不平衡，也加剧着国内经济的不平衡，是内外相互影响的不平衡。

国际资本是规模更大、投机性更强和风险更高的资本，具有高度的流动性。在开放经济背景下，国际资本和国内资本依据一定的条件而相互转化，国际资本价格和国内资本价格相互影响，国际资本流动通过汇率、收支、储备影响国内的货币供给和价格，进而影响货币和财政政策。国际资本流动除受经济景气、经济周期、国际收支状况、金融市场发育程度等经济因素制约外，还受政治、军事、外交、文化等的影响，因而具有高度的流动性和不稳定性，风险比国内资本更大。我们应该借鉴各国成功的经验，也包括吸取墨西哥特别是东亚金融危机的教训，结合我国实际稳步推进改革，成熟地踏进金融国际化新天地。

其三，产业转移加速推进，以跨国公司为主体的国际合作体系正在形成。前已论及，以纺织、钢铁、重化、汽车、微电子和生命科学为主导产业的六次产业大发展，伴随着产业升级、结构调整、产业扩散和转移同时进行。第二次世界大战后，这种产业升级、调整、扩散和转移的规模空前扩大了，速度更快了，促进了国际的分工与合作，全球性的生产体系逐渐形成。

① 《中国统计年鉴2006》，第27页。

主要发达国家生产能力转移的比例不断提高，美国跨国公司出口产品中，需要国外再加工的中间产品所占比例目前已占 70% 以上，日本所占比例不断提高，欧盟国家提高慢一些，但总的趋势也在提高。进入 21 世纪以后，国际产业转移呈现若干新的特点。一是由过去纺织、服装、鞋帽、初级电子产品等劳动密集型产业，向电子、化学、机械、交通工具等劳动密集与资金、技术密集相结合的产业转移，这些产业生产的零部件、半成品和少数成套产品，占据对外贸易额 40% 以上的比例，在我国外贸出口中要占 60% 以上，成为对外贸易的主打产业。二是在跨国总公司领导下，形成依托全球生产网络、有明确分工与合作和集产、供、销于一体的超级跨国集团，不仅深化了产业转移的内涵，而且使个别企业之间的竞争转变为经济集团之间的竞争，竞争的广度和深度都大大增强了。三是跨国公司把部分非关键生产技术、产销管理、项目研发、设计权利等转移到发展中国家，有效地降低了成本，实现了资源的合理配置。这就在世界范围内形成了规模较大的生产体系，使得国际分工由垂直向水平方向发展，跨国公司的全球化战略得以施展。如今 Google、沃尔玛、微软、可口可乐、麦当劳、通用电器、诺基亚、英特尔等世界品牌 10 强、50 强、500 强所占经济份额不断增大，通过收购、并购、资产重组等手段扩大全球范围的经营，将原本由各国经济组成的世界经济体系，改造成为由跨国公司企业主宰的世界经济体系框架，一些公司在海外的利益甚至超过本国母公司的利益，跨国公司正在实践真正意义上的经济全球化。

其四，国内外经济发展不平衡相互影响，财富分配不均日益扩大。各国经济在生产、交换、分配、消费各个环节联系的加强，跨国公司携经济一体化强有力地推进，世界经济发展不平衡越来越明显地暴露出来。主要发达国家力图通过知识产权保护控制高端技术及其产品，在经济全球化、一体化过程中赚取利润；发展中国家则发挥劳动力廉价优势，通过降低成本打入国际市场，取得外汇积累和吸引国际投资，实现快速发展的目的。但是各国情况千差万别，国内经济发展不平衡，如我国主要依靠投资和外贸拉动经济增长，导致外贸顺差和外汇储备持续增长；美国则运用国际市场，借贷消费，国际储蓄，维持其经济的发展和某种繁荣——这种国内与国外相互联系、相互制约的经济，产生内外发展不平衡的联动效应：国内经济不平衡是基础，国内经济不平衡引发国际经济不平衡；国际经济不平衡是条件，如果国内不能采取有效措施改变和调整这种不平衡，则有可能导致内外不平衡交互作用的加剧。

经济全球化加速国际一体化市场的形成，而市场总是向着资本雄厚的一方倾斜，市场非但不能改变财富分配不均，相反，它会加剧财富不均的分化。据芬兰联合大学世界发展经济研究所等的调查，全球50%的财产控制在约占人口2%最富有的人手中，最贫穷人口中的半数，仅拥有全球1%的财产。美国占人口10%的最富有者拥有70%左右的财产，法国和英国低一些，但也在50%以上。近年来联合国发布的一些报告和经济学家的分析显示，经济全球化和经济一体化的发展，使工业化国家的工人感到工作更加不稳定，发展中国家熟练工人和非熟练工人之间的工资差距拉得更大，贫富不均变得更为严重。

人既是财富的生产者，又是财富的消费者，上述经济全球化对人口生产和未来人口发展战略，必然产生和必将产生相当的影响。如经济全球化和国际市场对我国社会经济发展和人口变动的影响，外贸结构反映着产业结构和粗放型经济的基本特征，与这种结构和粗放型经济相适应，2005年就业结构情况是：第一次产业就业比重为44.85%，第二次产业为23.8%，第三次产业为31.4%；与2001年比较，第一次产业下降5.2个百分点，第二次产业升高1.5个百分点，第三次产业升高3.7个百分点①。尽管这一变动反映着产业结构在由劳动密集型向资金密集型、技术密集型转变，经济增长方式在由数量扩张型向质量提升型转变，然而劳动密集型和数量扩张型仍然占据经济增长方式的主导地位，则是一目了然的。在国外商品市场中，20世纪70和80年代日本、韩国以及中国台湾等占据明显优势，90年代特别是加入世贸组织以来，中国则取而代之，突出的一点是商品价格低廉，在价格上具有其他国家无法比拟的优势。而低廉的价格背后，是劳动力成本和价格的低廉。改革开放28年、加入WTO 5年来的发展证明，经济全球化和国际市场的开发，给中国人口就业制造了广阔的空间，平均每年新增就业人口在900万人左右，创造了世界就业史上骄人的业绩。这一点只要看一看出口贸易方式，就十分清楚了。2005年一般贸易占出口的41.3%，加工贸易占出口的54.7%，其他贸易占出口4.0%②，以凝聚劳动为主的加工贸易占据绝对优势，无怪乎有人将中国称为"世界加工厂"。从这个意义上说，经济全球化和中国加入WTO，给解决人口和劳动就业问题带来新的机遇和挑战，同人

① 《中国统计年鉴2006》，第125页。
② 《中国统计年鉴2006》，第735页。

口发展战略联系在一起。

2. 国内背景

如果说上述国际背景对人口发展战略的影响还有些间接的话，那么国内背景的影响就要直接得多，深刻得多了。国内背景除了资源、环境外部条件约束外，主要是经济发展和社会发展的背景，人口的变动与发展必须与经济、社会的发展相适应。聚焦到构建和谐社会和全面建设小康社会 20 年，最值得关注的是经济转轨、社会转型、人口转变这"三转"。

（1）经济转轨

经济转轨，一是在体制上，由计划经济体制转到市场经济体制；二是在经济增长方式上，由数量扩张型转到质量效益型。

①体制转轨：由计划经济体制转向市场经济体制

中华人民共和国成立后，借鉴当时苏联的计划经济体制，建立了高度集中统一的计划经济。一方面，国家每年和每 5 年编制和下达年度和 5 年指令性计划，各级政府、部门和企业必须保证按时完成；另一方面，则实行了从粮食统购统销到生活日用必需品按定量供应的严格计划。结果越是强调集中统一，经济活力就越减退；稍一放松，经济秩序就混乱。最终的结果，严重限制了资源的合理分配，阻碍了经济的发展，30 年的计划经济走到历史的死胡同。

1978 年岁末党的十一届三中全会的召开，揭开由计划经济向市场经济转变的序幕。从提出"有计划的商品经济"、"计划调节与市场调节相结合"，到"宏观调控下的市场经济"、"社会主义有计划的市场经济"，最后到"社会主义市场经济"，经历了 20 多年的时间，体现出"渐进式改革"的特点。一方面，这种"渐进式改革"反映出认识上的不断深化，对市场经济有一个认识的过程；另一方面，说明市场经济体制改革是"摸着石头过河"的产物和选择，是在不断总结实践经验基础上的结晶。市场经济与计划经济最明显的不同和特点，主要如下。

第一，市场主体法人化。即在市场上从事经济活动的组织和个人，主要是企业，也包括居民、政府和非营利组织，均具有独立的法人资格，对其资源拥有所有权、受益权、转让权。市场经济与计划经济最大的不同，在于对资源的所有制、经营权、使用权予以明确的界定，因而法人代表在市场上有处置的自主权。由于"三权"明确，随之而来的受益权也就明确起来，这是与计划经济的又一区别。计划经济统一分配、使用和管理资源，受益也计划分配；市场经济市场主体遵循市场法则进行交易，盈亏自负，将生产、经营、受益有效地联系起来，得以发挥在资源合理配置上的优越性。

第二，要素流动市场化。计划经济实行生产资料优先计划供应，资金、劳动力、技术、信息等统一调拨，全社会经济要素统一纳入"有计划、按比例"分配之中。按照政治经济学基本原理，计划经济是作为市场经济的对立物，作为消除个别生产的有组织性与整个社会生产无政府状态之间的矛盾应运而生的。也就是说，计划经济是按照全社会的最终消费，来计划生产、交换、分配的，主导方面是以销定产的。然而实际上全社会的消费和需求是一个很难确定的量，只好年复一年人为地去计划，加上自上而下的计划方式和方法，实际则变成以产定销式的计划分配，致使资源不能得到有效配置。市场经济能够做到以销定产，一个熟知的道理，是要通过市场实现商品的价值，通过市场传递需求信息，为生产提供需求动力。

第三，宏观调控间接化。市场经济能够更合理地配置资源、推进技术进步和经济的发展，并不意味着市场经济完美无瑕、可以无需过问地发展。相反，市场经济诱导人们以追求利润最大化为目标，因而带有一定的盲目性，克服这种盲目性需要政府这只"看得见的手"的帮助。无论是垄断占据主导但又是充分展现竞争的美国分散型市场经济，讲求效率与公平的德国社会市场型经济，还是集中决策与分散决策相结合的法国混合型市场经济，注重市场主体宏观调控的日本社会型市场经济，都少不了政府在宏观调控方面的作用。不过政府调控的手段，包括经济、法规、行政的手段，都要以市场经济为基础，按照价值规律，遵循政府宏观调控间接化原则，即主要依靠经济手段，依靠价格杠杆调节市场供给与需求；依靠税收杠杆调节收益分配，促进公平竞争；依靠信用杠杆调节货币流通量和信贷，影响投资、生产和流通；依靠汇率杠杆调节对外贸易和国际资本流动，连接国内与国外市场。

第四，经济运行法制化。通过经济立法和执法，运用法律手段调节企业、居民、政府市场主体之间的经济关系，解决矛盾和纠纷，建立健全受法律保护的市场经济秩序，保证市场平等、公开、公正、规范化运行。

市场经济体制的建立与人口有着什么样的关系，人口发展战略怎样在市场经济体制下组织实施，目前存在三种不尽相同的观点。一种认为，市场经济与人口的变动和发展是"两股道上跑的车"，各行其道，互不相干；另一种主张人口的变动和发展要与市场经济接轨，实行"指导性计划"，将人口管理"推向市场"；第三种观点认为，人口的变动和发展既同市场经济有联系，又有着本质的不同，既不能简单地说成是"两股道上跑的车"互不相干，也不能盲目地"推向市场"，运用市场经济的体制、规则、办法管理人口。本人赞同第三种观点，并且主张具体问题具体分析，高度重视市场经济对人口变动和发展的影响，谋求适应市场经济体制的改革思路。

比如，市场主体法人化是市场经济体制的基础和前提，如果按照"接轨"的意见，人口生产特别是生育孩子的数量和结构，是不是应该完全由家庭自主决定？显然不能。实行计划生育是我国的一项基本国策，由于我国人口问题本质上属于人口和劳动力过剩性质，实现人口发展战略第二个目标——人口零增长，第三个目标——未来的全方位理想适度人口，生育率和出生率在一定历史时期必须进行一定的控制，不能完全由个人和家庭自己决定。同时也要看到，个人和家庭对生育意愿的关注，对生育决定权的关注，在制定生育政策的时候，要兼顾国家和个人家庭的利益，在市场经济条件下这种利益关系的变动，使之更合理和切实可行。

又比如，要素流动市场化，如果仅仅有资本、商品、技术、信息等物质要素和金融要素的自由流动和市场化，而将人口和劳动力——人的要素流动排斥在市场之外，那么物质要素和金融要素也很难真正自由流动起来，很难实现真正的市场化。而且从根本上破坏了劳动力作为市场主体的独立法人地位，也为通过干预劳动力流动和干预其他经济活动留下缺口，劳动力市场就不可能建立起来。随着市场经济体制的进一步完善，市场经济对人口变动和发展的影响会越来越大，我们要积极推进与这种影响相适应的改革。

②经济发展方式转轨：由数量扩张型向质量效益型转变

早在 20 世纪 80 年代初提出 2000 年工农业总产值比 1980 年翻两番时，"不断提高经济效益"便作为前提条件提了出来。然而总体经济效益不高，始终是国民经济发展中的老大难问题，长期没有得到有效的解决。以 GDP 增长为主要目标，以固定资产投资增长为主要手段，以外延扩大再生产为主要方式的传统的经济发展，有两大显著特征：一曰经济效益不高，表现为高投入、高消耗、低效率、低产出；二曰忽视甚至以损害社会效益为代价，换取经济方面的效益。转变经济增长方式，就是要在这两个方面都得到转变，走出一条低耗、高效和融经济效益、社会效益、环境效益于一体的新的文明发展道路。

前已论及，我国经济高投入、高消耗、低效率、低产出外延式扩大再生产，已经发展到再也不能继续下去的地步。2005 年固定资产投资占 GDP 的

48.3%，投资总额达到 183084.8 亿元，才拉动 GDP 增长 10.2%；高消耗与低效率，是一个问题的两个方面。按现行汇率计算，目前我国 GDP 总量占世界 6% 左右，而消耗的石油却占 8% 左右，矿产资源占 10% 左右，电力占 13% 左右，煤炭占 30% 左右；单位 GDP 能源和材料消耗为美国的 2.7 倍，日本的 3.4 倍。[①] 这种粗放数量扩张型经济增长方式，必然损害到资源的合理利用，损害到环境的质量，最终损害到经济发展的社会效益。2005 年全国废水排放总量 525 亿吨，化学需氧排放量 1414 万吨，工业废气排放量 268988 亿标立方米，二氧化碳排放量 2549 万吨，[②] 在世界各国中处于首席或次席位置。因此，转变经济增长方式和节约资源、保护环境紧密联系在一起，是"十一五"以及构建和谐社会、全面建设小康社会十分迫切的任务。

转变经济增长方式和建设资源节约型、环境友好型社会，需要树立新的理念，在加强政府宏观调控的同时，充分发挥市场调节作用，改革和创建新的利益导向机制，确保提高效益和调整结构稳步推进。除了经济的、法律的、行政的等手段外，也要注意同人口变动和发展的关系，努力创造有利的人口环境。要提高作为第一次产业农业的效益，就要改变目前一多半人口搞饭吃的局面，加快农业人口和劳动力向城镇转移，让留在农村的人口和劳动力占有更多的资源，实现农村人力资本和自然资本、产出资本、社会资本的合理有效配置，大幅度地提高农业劳动生产率和增加农民的收入。要降低作为第二次产业工业的能耗和材料消耗，就要优化产业结构，用信息化带动工业化，逐步走上科技含量高、资源消耗低、环境污染少、人力资源得到充分发挥的质量效益型发展道路。归根结底，国民经济效益的提高主要取决于人力资本的积聚和增长，取决于全民族的健康、科学、文化、思想和道德素质的提高。而这诸多方面人口素质的提高，除了要以经济的发展作为基础外，还取决于社会的全面发展，取决于和谐社会建设。需要看到，投资于科学、文化、教育、卫生、体育、社区等公共建设事业不是消极的，表面上挤占了一部分财政支出，影响经济建设投资；实际上这些财政支出满足了人民群众全面发展的某些方面的需要，不断提升着人口的素质，最终起了推进经济持续增长和增长方式转变的功效。"提高效益"不应局限在经济领域，大力加强教育和科学事业，发展先进文化，加强精神文明建设等全面的社会发展，同样是发展的驱动力。我们不但要在物质文明建设中寻找提高效益的动力和

① 参见田雪原《人与自然相和谐的几个问题》，2006 年 12 月 22 日《人民日报》。
② 《中国统计年鉴 2006》，第 409 页。

手段，而且要在政治文明、精神文明建设中寻找动力和手段，向"三个文明"建设要速度、要效益。

（2）社会转型

站在社会发展全局观察，改革开放以来的发展趋势，可用"一本三化"概括。"一本"即以人为本，以人的全面发展为本。对此，本专著后面还将作出专题阐述。"三化"即市场化、城市化、现代化。市场化，如前所述，即由原来的计划经济体制转变到市场经济体制。经济体制的这一转变，必然带来人们价值观念、政策措施、社会规范、制度取向等的变化，向着效率、竞争方向转化，国家职能向着服务型政府转化。城市化，从人口学角度观察，是农村人口和劳动力向城镇转移的过程；从经济学角度观察，是三次产业结构转变的过程；从社会学角度观察，是城市理念、生活方式和管理方式扩散和提升的过程。这一过程构成社会转型的主要向度，社会阶层变动的主要催促器。现代化，包括经济、科技、社会等诸多领域的现代化，经济现代化是基础，核心是以信息化带动工业化。现代化引发经济技术结构和产业结构向高端迈进，贫困社会向富裕社会转变，"三次浪潮人口"结构和冲突随着改变，社会转型必然发生。

20 世纪 90 年代前期，在明确改革要建立社会主义市场经济体制目标后，"社会转型"被提了出来并成为媒体频繁出现的词汇之一。然而迄今为止，对社会转型的诠释不尽相同，可谓见智见仁。有学者提出："社会转型是指中国社会从传统社会向现代社会、从农业社会向工业社会、从封闭性社会向开放性社会的社会变迁和发展"（陆学艺、景天魁，1994）[①]；有学者认为，"社会转型"是一个有特定含义的社会学术语，意指社会从传统型向现代型的转变，或者说由传统型社会向现代型社会转型的过程，"社会转型"和"社会现代化"几乎是同义的（郑杭生、李强等，1997）[②]。中国科学院中国现代化研究中心、中国现代化战略研究课题组完成的《中国现代化报告2006》则称，在未来 50 年里，中国社会现代化需要完成两次社会转型，一是从农业社会向工业社会、从乡村社会向城市社会转型，二是从工业社会向知识社会、从城市社会向城乡动态平衡社会转型。

尽管对当前我国社会转型认识和观点有某些出入，但是就抽象的社会转型而言，仍应有它特定的含义。本人以为，一般意义上的社会转型，主要由

---

① 参见陆学艺、景天魁《转型中的中国社会》，黑龙江人民出版社，1994。

② 参见郑杭生、李强等《当代中国社会结构和社会关系研究》，首都师范大学出版社，1997。

如下三个方面的转变构成。

一是社会体制的转变。即所有制、劳资关系、分配制度等经济体制，国家立法、行政、监督等政治体制，以及由于受到长期传统历史文化和计划经济体制影响形成的政府职能的转变。体制的转变和创新具有本源的意义。一般情况下，转型总是从体制改革和创新开始，最后又落脚到体制的改革和创新上。

二是社会结构的转变。社会结构分成诸多方面和诸多层次，核心是人口的阶层结构，是转型期不同阶层人口地位、权利、利益的重组和改变。学术界尤其是社会学界，对此作出颇多研究，分成高等、中等、低等收入阶层，每一个阶层内部再分成高、中、低不等收入层面的子阶层，由此组成社会的不同阶层结构，研究其在社会转型中的变动趋势、彼此之间的关系和利益冲突。

三是转型的目标和阶段。社会转型，总要说清由何种类型转向何种类型。本人以为，在农业型—工业型—现代型社会转变过程中，总体上处在工业型向现代型转变过程。统计资料显示，2005 年第一、二、三次产业结构之比为 12.6：47.5：39.9，即 1.0：3.8：3.2；就业结构也达到 44.8：23.8：31.4，即 1.0：0.5：0.7[①]。这样的结构表明，总体上中国已处在工业化阶段，正在向后工业化现代社会转变。这样说，并不排除部分地区尚处在由农业型向工业型转变的前期阶段，但在比重和发展趋势上，已不占据主要和主导地位。在贫困型—温饱型—小康型—富裕型—更富裕型社会转变过程中，总体上处于由小康型向富裕型转变过程。2005 年全国食品消费占总消费的比例即恩格尔系数下降到 39.0%，其中城镇居民家庭恩格尔系数下降到 36.7%，农村下降到 45.5%[②]。虽然还有少数地区处于由温饱向小康过渡阶段，同样不占据主要和主导的地位。

社会转型期间，各阶层人口的政治、经济、社会地位急剧变动，人们的价值观念、道德意识、行为取向等，都会发生某种变化。对人口再生产中生育、死亡、流动、迁移等认识的转变，对孩子多少、性别构成、教育成才、就业方向等的价值预期，对婚姻、家庭、家族、代际等传统观念的更新，都会随着时间的推移渗透到人口生产过程中去。政府的角色也在转变。由于历史的、传统的和近半个多世纪以来政治、经济、文化发展形成的格局，政府

① 依据《中国人口年鉴 2006》，第 34 页数据计算。
② 依据《中国人口年鉴 2006》，第 347 页数据计算。

被推到各种矛盾的前沿，政府主导各种社会运动，从这个意义上说，我们的社会是政府主导型的社会。这有它的好处，一个"一竿子插到底"的政府，主要导向明确，工作效率比较高，可以集中力量办大事；无疑也有它的缺陷，诸多缺陷都同政府"抓住不放"，都由政府出面受理解决有关。当前，公共政策中一个带有方向性、方针性的问题，是如何摆正和处理好效率和公平问题。改革开放前期，强调"效率优先，兼顾公平"，是十分正确的和必要的。因为在当时平均主义根深蒂固的情况下，不强调效率就不能发展，低得不能再低的公平还能产生什么推动力?! 如今 28 年过去，经济发展取得年平均增长 9.6% 的突出业绩，人民生活总体上达到小康水平，不同阶层人口群体之间财富差距拉得相当大，再不强调公平，社会矛盾将会变得越来越突出，威胁到和谐社会的建设。由"效率优先、兼顾公平"转变到"注重公平、兼顾效率"，是经济分配领域的重大调整，必然在社会上层建筑领域发生相应的变动，成为社会转型的一个重要方面。

（3）人口转变

人口转变，一般指人口再生产类型由年轻型向成年型、成年型向老年型的转变。为了区分年轻型、成年型、老年型三种不同类型的年龄结构，人口学家给这三种类型少年人口、成年人口、老年人口所占比例设定一定的界限，还有年龄中位数等指标界限，以便判断具体的某总体人口的年龄结构类型。然而随着出生率的下降和预期寿命的延长，只能从相对的意义上认识、评价和运用这些界限指标，不能将其视为一成不变的定律。如瑞典人口学家桑德巴的"三分法"，当时将 50 岁定为老年人起点，他的划分法与现在的划分显然不同。但他将总体人口划分成少年、成年、老年三部分，依据三部分人口所占比例区分为三种不同的人口结构类型，确定不同的人口态势和增长的势能，其意义是相同的。

笔者曾言：20 世纪是人口暴涨的世纪，21 世纪则是人口老龄化的世纪。由人口暴涨到人口老龄化，是人口转变的结果。不过中国人口的转变有同世界相同之处，也有着某些不同的特点。1900 年中国人口约 4.43 亿人，2000 年增长到 12.67 亿人，100 年间净增 8.24 亿人，年平均增长 10.56‰，与同期世界人口增长率 13.22‰比较，低 2.66 个千分点。不过中国人口变动在 20 世纪前半叶和后半叶有着很大的不同：前半叶到 1950 年全国人口增加到 5.52 亿，50 年中净增 1.09 亿，增长 24.60%，年平均增长 4.41‰；后半叶净增 7.15 亿人，增长 129.53%，年平均增长 16.76‰。进一步的分析表明，如将后半叶再分成前后两个时期，前 25 年全国人口净增 3.72 亿人，增长 67.44%，年平均增长 20.83‰；后 25 年净增 3.43 亿人，增长 37.14%，年平均增长 12.71‰，后 25 年年平均增长率比前 25 年降低 8.12 个千分点。更值得关注的是，20 世纪 90 年代中期已经下降到更替水平以下，人口增长的势能大为削弱。1950～2000 年的人口数量变动，如表 1 所示[①]。

表 1　1950～2000 年中国人口自然变动

年　份	人口数（万人）	出生率（‰）	死亡率（‰）	自增率（‰）
1950	55196	37.00	18.00	19.00
1955	61465	32.60	12.28	20.32
1960	66207	20.86	25.43	-4.57
1965	72538	37.88	9.50	28.38
1970	82992	33.43	7.60	25.83
1975	92420	23.01	7.32	15.69
1980	98706	18.21	6.34	11.87
1985	105851	21.04	6.78	14.26
1990	114333	21.06	6.67	14.39
1995	121121	17.12	6.57	10.55
2000	126743	14.03	6.45	7.58

上述自 1950 年以来的中国人口变动，经历了 5 个阶段。第一阶段为 1949～1952 年的人口再生产类型转变阶段，即由高出生、高死亡、低增长向高出生、低死亡、高增长的转变阶段。按算术平均数计算，这一期间的人口出生率年平均为 37.0‰，死亡率为 18.2‰，自然增长率为 18.8‰。

第二阶段为 1953～1957 年的第一次生育高潮阶段。人口再生产转变到高、低、高类型，年平均出生率达到 34.7‰，死亡率下降到 12.3‰，自然增长率上升到 22.4‰。

第三阶段为 1958～1961 年的第一次生育低潮阶段。这是一个特殊的阶段，三年经济困难时期人口出生率下降、死亡率上升，1960 年甚至出现人口的负增长。4 年中人口的年平均出生率下降到 23.2‰，死亡率却上升到 16.6‰，导致自然增长率下降到 4.6‰的低水平。

① 《中国统计年鉴1986》、《中国统计年鉴2004》，中国统计出版社，1986、2004。

第四阶段为 1962~1973 年的第二次生育高潮阶段。12 年中人口出生率年平均高达 32.7‰，死亡率下降到 8.8‰，自然增长率达到 23.9‰，成为 20 世纪中国人口发展史上高出生率和高增长率持续时间最长的一次生育高潮。1963 年出生率达到 43.4‰，增长率达到 33.3‰，均创下历史新高。

第五阶段为 1974 年以来的第二次生育低潮阶段。自 20 世纪 70 年代以来，国家大力控制人口增长、切实加强计划生育取得显著成绩，1974~2005 年人口年平均出生率下降到 17.27‰，死亡率下降到 6.63‰，自然增长率下降到 10.6‰，可视为由高、低、高向低、低、低过渡，并在 20 世纪 90 年代中期达到低、低、低"三低"阶段。[1]

与上述人口转变相适应，人口年龄结构发生根本性改变。参见图 1。

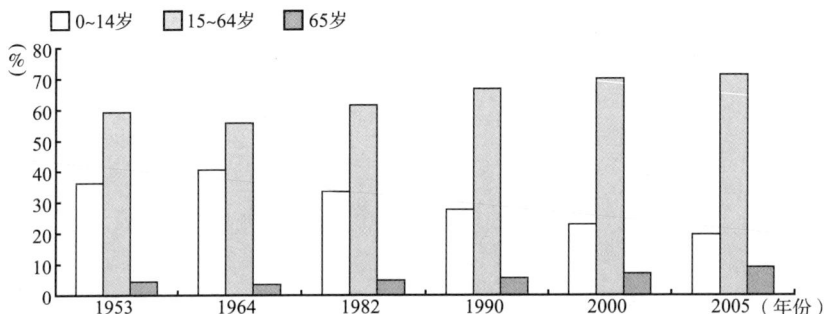

图 1   1953 年以来人口年龄结构变动

图 1 显示，我国人口年龄结构大体上在 20 世纪 80 年代中期达到成年型，世纪之交达到老年型，2005 年 0~14 岁少年人口比例下降到 19.55%，15~64 岁成年人口比例上升到 71.38%，65 岁以上老年人口比例上升到 9.07%。这说明，从本质上讲，中国人口再生产已经转变到老年型即减少型，只是由于人口增长的惯性作用，还要继续增长大约二三十年时间。基于中国人口问题的过剩性质，我们终于可以望得见人口零增长一天的到来，这是人口转变带来的最重要的成果。

3．人口发展战略宏观

中国人口发展战略研究较早，学术界在 20 世纪 70 年代末 80 年代初即

---

① 依据《中国统计年鉴 1986》第 92 页，中国统计出版社，1986；《中国统计年鉴 2006》第 99 页提供的数据，按算术平均数计算。

开始研究，笔者在 20 世纪 80 年代前期主持《2000 年的中国》研究中《2000 年中国的人口和就业》时，就曾提出和阐述控制人口数量、提高人口素质、调整人口结构，实行"控制"、"提高"、"调整"相结合，当时以数量控制为重点的发展战略。随着控制人口数量增长卓有成效地推进，人口年龄、性别、城乡、地区分布等结构方面的问题日益浮出水面，素质问题愈显重要，逐渐形成人口发展战略"三步走"的宏观思路：第一步，把高生育率降下来，降到更替水平以下，实现人口再生产由高出生、低死亡、高增长向低出生、低死亡、低增长类型的转变。第二步，稳定低生育水平，直至实现人口的零增长；这一步要充分注意到人口结构的变动和素质的提高，寻求人口数量与素质、结构变动相协调的发展。第三步，零增长以后，由于人口的惯性作用，总体人口将呈一定程度的减少趋势，再依据届时的经济、社会发展状况以及资源、环境状况，作出全方位的理想适度人口的抉择。以往的适度人口研究主要侧重人口数量方面，这里的"全方位"含义，不仅是数量的适度，同时包括人口素质和年龄、性别、分布结构等的适度，创造有利于将来社会经济发展的人口条件。

按照这样的发展战略，构建和谐社会和全面建设小康社会 20 年以及更长远一些时间人口发展战略的目标、图像和决策选择，可概括如下：人口数量处于"三步走"中的第二步，围绕中位预测"软着陆"方案，生育率保持较低水平的相对稳定，稍有回升后即基本稳定在略高于现在的水平。如此，2010 年全国人口可达 13.60 亿人，2020 年 14.44 亿人，2030 年达到峰值时为 14.65 亿人；其后转为缓慢下降，2040 年可降至 14.51 亿人，2050 年可降至 14.02 亿人。如果 1.80 的总和生育率一直保持下去，2100 年全国人口可降至 10.24 亿人。

人口素质提高显著。按照发达国家经验和国际惯例，采用联合国步长法，城镇人口预期寿命男性可从 2000 年的 73.9 岁，提高到 2010 年的 74.8 岁、2020 年的 75.5 岁、2030 年的 76.1 岁、2050 年的 77.1 岁；女性相应由 78.5 岁，提高到 79.0 岁、79.6 岁、80.1 岁、81.1 岁。同期农村人口预期寿命男性可从 68.8 岁，提高到 70.2 岁、71.3 岁、72.1 岁、73.2 岁；女性相应由 73.5 岁，提高到 74.4 岁、75.1 岁、75.6 岁、76.6 岁。婴儿死亡率由 2000 年的 28‰左右，下降到 2010 年的 15‰左右，2020 年的 10‰左右。到 2020 年这两项指标达到或接近现在发达国家的水平，届时也将大大缩小同发达国家的差距，而比世界和发展中国家的平均水平明显高出一截。15

岁以上人口平均所受教育年限，由 2000 年的 7 年左右提高到 2010 年的 9 年左右，2020 年的 11 年左右，基本上普及高中教育。提高人口政治、思想、道德、文化素质，可归结为以德育为先的文明素质的提高。重点是核心价值观念、道德规范和法治意识的提升，文明素质教育成为国民教育的重要组成部分。

人口结构变动比较合理。15～64 岁劳动年龄人口可由 2000 年的 8.67 亿人，增加到 2017 年峰值时的 10.00 亿人；其后呈减少趋势，2030 年可减至 9.89 亿人，2050 年可减至 8.62 亿人，相当于 21 世纪初的水平。劳动年龄人口所占比例，可由 2000 年的 68.70%，上升到 2009 年峰值时的 72.30%。其后转而下降，2020 年可下降到 68.97%，回落到 2000 年的水平；2030 年可下降到 67.36%，相当于 20 世纪 90 年代初期水平；2050 年可下降到 61.29%，相当于 20 世纪六七十年代的水平。总体上看 21 世纪上半叶不会发生大的劳动力供给不足的问题，下半叶的劳动力供给仍可保持在较大的规模；但是结构性劳动力供给不足、劳动年龄人口的相对高龄化是会发生的，需要引起足够重视和作出必要的调整。人口年龄结构老龄化可控制在能够承受范围之内：65 岁以上老年人口所占比例可从 2000 年的 6.9%，上升到 2010 年的 8.6%、2020 年的 12.0%、2030 年的 16.2%、2050 年的 23.1%。人口城乡结构变动比较迅速：人口城市化水平（城镇人口占总人口比例）可从 2000 年的 36.2%，提升到 2010 年的 47.9%、2020 年的 60.0%、2030 年的 72.2%、2050 年的 75.4%。

实现上述全面建设小康社会和更长远一些时间"软着陆"人口发展战略目标，需要稳定低生育水平。稳定低生育水平是一项总的方针和要求，考虑到 20 世纪 80 年代中期曾经出现过一段短暂的生育率回升，第一代独生子女进入婚育年龄旺盛期逐渐增多，一般规定双方都为独生子女者结婚可以生育第二个孩子，部分省区规定农村一方为独生子女者结婚也可以生育第二个孩子等因素影响，未来一段时间内的生育率假设，还有一定程度的微升，保持稳定中的微升。同时城乡之间、东西部之间的生育率有一定差异，总体上的稳定和地区发展不平衡，也是需要考虑的问题。稳定低生育水平要从实际出发，将低生育水平掌握在科学合理限度内。做到既使人口数量控制平稳顺利地达到零增长，又使人口素质得到比较快的提高，人口结构保持在比较合理的状态，以求最大限度地发挥人口变动对社会经济发展、统筹人与自然和谐发展的积极作用，而将可能产生的某些消极作用减少到最低限度。要随着经济的发展增加人口健康投资，建立健全疾病防控体系，合理配置公共卫生资源；要增加教育、科学、技术、文化方面的投入，提高全民族的科学教育素质，实现由人口大国、人力资源大国向人力资本大国的转变。注意未来二三十年内劳动年龄人口比例升高，被抚养人口比例较低的人口年龄结构变动"黄金时代"走势，加快经济和社会事业的发展；注意老年人口比例加速上升趋势，把握由"人口盈利"到"人口亏损"的转变，作出以"盈"补"亏"、以"利"抵"损"的决策选择。适当加快农业劳动力转移和人口城市化步伐，发挥人口城市化在推动经济和社会发展中的作用，为从根本上解决农业、农民、农村"三农"问题奠定基础。

《中国人口年龄结构变动及 老年人口问题研究》序[*]

据科学家考证，人类进化发展已有 400 多万年的历史。在这漫长的历史长河中，过去的 100 年和现在已经开始的 100 年，无疑是社会经济发展最快的两个百年。而从人口变动角度观察，可以说，20 世纪是人口暴涨的世纪，21 世纪则是人口老龄化的世纪。面对这一情势，发达国家忧虑少子高龄化数十年，发展中国家也逐渐体验到老龄化的含义，生育率率先下降的发展中国家已经体验到老龄化意味着什么，应当怎样做和做些什么。中国作为当今世界人口最多和发展最快的发展中国家，一方面总体人口还有一定的增长势能，控制人口增长的任务还没有完成；另一方面由于自 20 世纪 70 年代以来生育率长期持续地下降，人口年龄结构于世纪之交步入老年型，并将以比较快的速度挺进到老龄化水平较高国家行列，具有自己的一些明显特点。众所周知，人口学就是依据人口的不同年龄结构，将某总体人口划分为年轻型、成年型和老年型三种基本类型。对于一个要实现零增长的国家来说，一定程度的老龄化不仅是不可避免的，而且是必需的。从这个意义上说，老龄化并不是消极的，应当积极应对。同时也必须承认，从长远发展态势观察，老龄化和老年负担系数的攀升，必然影响经济和社会的发展，带来某些方面的不利影响，需要作出科学的分析和抉择。

中国宣布了"十一五"和全面建设小康社会的奋斗目标，面临经济转轨、社会转型、人口转变基本态势。经济转轨，包括由计划经济体制转变到市场经济体制，这一步已经基本完成，越来越多的国家承认我国的市场经济地位；也包括由数量扩张型向质量效益型经济增长方式的转变，现已开始并在加大实施的力度，不过解决这个"老大难"问题需要作出艰苦的努力。社会转型，由过去的政府主导型转变到公共服务型，这是一个社会观念和职

---

    * 本文发表于 2007 年。

能的转变，需要不断提高认识和深化改革，要经历一个漫长的过程。人口转变，前期由高出生、高死亡、低增长向着高出生、低死亡、高增长的转变，再向着低出生、低死亡、低增长的转变，已在 20 世纪 90 年代中期完成；现在的人口转变是进入低、低、低后的进一步转变，人口年龄结构老龄化不断加深的转变，亦可称之为后人口转变。大同小异的人口预测表明，21 世纪中国人口年龄结构变动，15～64 岁劳动年龄人口绝对数量可增长到 2017 年前后，届时可达 10 亿左右；所占比例 2009 年可达最高峰值，超过 72%。这一态势规定着劳动年龄人口的供给和人口年龄结构变动对社会经济发展的影响，社会总抚养比（从属年龄比）2030 年之前可保持在 0.5 以下，形成人口年龄结构变动的"黄金时代"或"人口盈利"、"人口红利"，我们理应抓住这一难得的机遇加快发展。同时老龄化在累进地推进，无论是老年人口比例、年龄中位数还是老年与少年人口之比，均呈加速上升趋势。预计 2020 年 65 岁以上老年人口比例可达 12%、2050 年可达 23% 左右，成为仅次于发达国家、居发展中国家最高水平的国家。面对加速推进的人口老龄化，一方面要考虑如何应对老龄化的挑战，特别是建立健全全方位的社会养老保障制度，确保安全度过老龄化严重阶段；另一方面要科学估量老龄化可能给经济、社会、科技、文化等的发展带来的影响，发挥人口转变对经济转轨、社会转型的有利影响，而将不利影响减少到最低限度。受中国人口学会委托、由姚远教授主持并完成的《中国人口年龄结构变化及老年人口问题研究》，继 2004 年《全面建设小康社会中的人口与发展》研究报告之后，又一篇理论与实践相结合研究的新作，从多视角、多层面对人口年龄结构变动和老龄问题，作出有自己独立见解的阐发，相信会在繁荣人口科学和在实践中，发挥应有的作用。

《中国人口政策60年》前言[*]

我们面前放着五本论著：彭珮云主编《中国计划生育全书》，张维庆主编《新人口礼赞——人口和计划生育工作回顾与展望》，杨魁孚等主编《中国计划生育效益与投入》，易富贤著《大国空巢——走入歧途的中国计划生育》，以及〔美〕J.艾尔德（JohnAird）的《屠杀无辜》。这五本论著从不同角度对中国的人口和计划生育政策作出阐释，却得出截然不同的结论。总体上说，前三本持肯定的态度，后两本持否定的态度，只是肯定或否定的方面、重点、程度和方法有所不同而已。

其实，除个别人由于所站立场不同外，对中国人口和计划生育政策持有不同的观点本属正常。他们或者对中国人口和计划生育政策基本不知或知之甚少，看到或听到某些违法违纪现象的报道，或听信反对派理论"权威"的宣传，感到不理解、不赞同甚至得出主要靠强迫命令推行的结论。但是一旦了解事情真相和看到实事求是的理论阐述之后，便很容易转变他们的观点，甚至成为这一政策的宣传员。举个例子，1980年5月，首次以中国人口学家代表团名义一行五人出席在美国东西方中心举办的中国人口分析会。在那次会上，J.艾尔德便手拿两份地方报纸，提出异议和质问。一是某省某村一农户因拒交计划外生育费被当地干部拿走犁、锄等农用工具的报道，质问没有了农具农民如何生产？没有办法只好变卖家当交费，证明中国推行人口和计划生育政策是政府强迫命令的结果。二是说中国的人口统计数据不可靠，认为是政府导演、为了维护国家形象人为编造出来的。关于后一点，出席会议的中国代表当即指出：中国人口数据基本上是可信的，因为中国有延续几千年比较严格的户籍制度，每个家庭都有一本"户口簿（本）"，登记造册全家人口，包括姓名、性别、年龄、民族、受教育程度、职业以及与

---

[*] 本文发表于2009年。

户主的关系等基本内容。此外，在过去二三十年计划经济条件下，还有按年或按月发放的粮票、布票、肉票、油票、购物券（工业券）等生活必需品票证，每个人都不能遗漏，遗漏了维持吃穿等基本生活资料的供给就失去保障，客观上起到人口统计的佐证作用。中国这样的人口统计和管理办法，在美国和其他西方国家是找不到的，中国的人口统计质量至少不比美国差。我们的发言赢得与会者的赞同，也引起人们对美国人口统计准确性的议论，纷纷对他们电话访谈一类调查的可靠性提出疑问。关于前一点，会议中间休息喝咖啡时，一位对中国人口问题颇感兴趣的在读博士生问我：J. 艾尔德讲的是不是事实，有没有发生那样的事情？我向她解释三点：第一，中国推行人口和计划生育政策历来强调把宣传教育放在第一位，讲清中国人口多、底子薄，进行现代化建设必须大力控制人口增长的道理；第二，中国是一个拥有 960 万平方千米陆地面积、将近 10 亿人口（1980 年内地人口 9.87 亿）的国家，且城乡之间、地区之间发展很不平衡，因此发生点儿这样那样的事情不足为怪。J. 艾尔德列举的事情可能是有的，还可能再找出第二个、第三个，但是再多能占全国 1.7 亿农户多大比例？恐怕连万分之一也占不到吧！为什么要用个别代替一般呢？这种以点盖面的做法是不严肃的，也是不科学的；第三，即使是个别的现象，中国政府和从事人口计生工作的干部也十分重视，强调各级政府要下大力量纠正。这位博士生听了我的话后，觉得很有道理，就找 J. 艾尔德辩论，弄得 J. 艾尔德无言以对。从此她对中国的人口政策有了自己的理解，后来她到中国来学习考察一年有余，用她亲身的感受讲述中国的人口政策，起了很好的宣传作用，可谓由不知论者转变到知之论者的典型一例。

基于这样的认识，实事求是地阐述中国人口政策提出和制定的社会背景、理论依据、主导思想、基本要求和实施的效果，开展不同观点的讨论和争论很有必要。因为讨论和争论，对推动真理探讨和学术进步是有益的，真理总是越辩越明嘛！可悲的是，以往包括人口在内的许多社会科学问题的讨论、争论和争鸣，实质性问题的讨论很不够，相反动辄就扣帽子、打棍子，以至于学术进步需要的学派难以形成，个人之间的偏见和成见却不少。为了扭转这种不利于学术发展的局面，老一辈经济学家孙冶方与于光远先生之间，曾经相约进行过关于价值论窄派与宽派彼此指名道姓的争论，用自己的行动带动百花齐放、百家争鸣方针的贯彻实施；然而不幸的是，争论刚刚进行一个回合，孙冶方先生便与世长辞了。笔者以为，这个问题一直没有很好解决，而不解决好这个问题，就会妨碍学术的自由讨论、发展和繁荣。总结以往的经验教训，本人主张，讨论和争论一要有一个明确的目的，为了探讨真理、推动学术进步，重点不在谁对谁错，更不在谁"左"谁"右"之争；二要有一种实事求是的精神，所言应建立在客观事实基础之上，不赞成在既不了解情况又不占有充足资料的情况下，就凭"想当然"大发议论；三要有一个科学的态度，勇于坚持真理、修正错误，以对方之长补己之短。这"三要"似乎是题外的话，但是在以往的中国人口政策讨论中，确实存在着既不了解情况又没有充足资料而大发议论的情况，以至于形成某些问题上的以讹传讹。这种不知而无畏的精神不可长，因为它违背了科学就是实事求是的基本原则，容易误导和走进误区。

众所周知，早在20世纪50年代新中国成立后不久，政府便提出了节制生育的主张，50年代后期有一场关于人口问题的大辩论，60年代前期主要在城市开展了不同程度的计划生育，1966年"文化大革命"开始后受到无政府主义冲击而处于停顿和半停顿状态，到70年代全国人口突破8亿以后，才有较大的起色，中国的人口政策在起伏跌宕中艰难起步和向前推进。1978年党的十一届三中全会重新确立了实事求是的思想路线，迎来了包括人口科学在内的科学事业发展的春天。以为马寅初先生新人口论翻案为契机，揭开人口理论拨乱反正新的篇章，人口研究空前活跃起来。不仅一批研究经济学、社会学等社会科学工作者转入人口研究，有见地的一些自然科学工作者也捷足先登加入进来，对人口变动和发展趋势作出多种方案的预测。中央对当时人口研究提出的问题和未来人口变动发展趋势研究很重视，1980年3～5月中央书记处委托中央办公厅召开人口座谈会，连续开了五次，定下中国人口发展的战略、方针和政策，这是理解和研究中国人口政策的关键和枢纽。本人作为该座谈会参与者和会议报告起草者，经历座谈会全过程，尤其对提倡一对夫妇生育一个孩子会不会引起智商下降、年龄结构老龄化、劳动力短缺、"四二一"家庭结构等敏感问题，在《报告》和《附件》中作了专门的阐发。然而本人对这些，28年来却始终守口如瓶，恪守"研究无禁区，宣传有纪律"准则。其间学术界和社会各界不断发表一些内部或公开的论著，说当年没有考虑人口老龄化严重影响者有之，说没有考虑长远劳动力供给短缺者有之，说没有考虑独生子女家庭"四二一"结构者也有之，把当时的人口决策说成过于草率，甚至是"拍脑袋"的结果。如果真的是没有考虑，那么"过于草率"的指责就是合理的、应该的；问题在于当时不是

"没有考虑"，而是考虑得比提出的问题还要多，可以说，今天提出的各种问题当时几乎都有所涉及，因而用"过于草率"、"拍脑袋"概括是不符合实际的。如今，一是人口和计划生育政策实施的效果已经显现，人口素质和结构方面的各种问题相继浮出水面，许多问题牵涉当年的决策，需要弄清历史的本来面目。二是时间已经过去将近 30 年，当年讨论的问题已无秘密可言；而且，越是弄清楚当年讨论的情况和为什么作出那样的决策选择，越是有利于对人口政策的全面了解，更好地把握未来人口变动和发展的趋势。三是参加当年座谈会的学者本来就不多，如今几位老先生已相继离开我们而去；而且参与核心工作的学者更少，有时少到只有一二个人。笔者作为参与核心工作的学者之一，有责任也有义务将当时的情况原原本本地公之于众，提供给学术界和社会各界研究参考。

"三十年河东、三十年河西"，说的是在 60 年一个甲子循环中，前 30 年与后 30 年可能呈现截然不同的情况。本人以为，一部中国现代史可用三个 30 年概括：第一个 30 年，以 1919 年发生在北京（当时称北平）的"五四运动"起至 1949 年中华人民共和国成立时止。这一时期的主要矛盾是民族矛盾和阶级矛盾，中国人民用 30 年时间推翻了帝国主义、封建主义和官僚资本主义"三座大山"，建立了人民当家作主的共和国。第二个 30 年，从 1949 年中华人民共和国成立至 1978 年党的十一届三中全会召开时止。这一时期，经济上在高度集中统一的计划经济体制下，艰难地推进工业化；政治上突出以阶级斗争为纲，在不断革命论指导下进行社会主义革命和社会主义改造。第三个 30 年，从 1978 年党的十一届三中全会实行改革开放以来至今。这一时期经济上摆脱计划经济束缚，逐步建立和完成市场经济体制改革；政治上强调民主法治建设、开辟构建和谐社会发展新阶段。以第二个 30 年和第三个 30 年比较，前者强调的是计划经济、阶级斗争，后者强调的是市场经济、和谐社会，"河东"与"河西"泾渭分明。这里，最重要的是要弄清楚从"河东"到"河西"转变的背景、原因、过程和效果，注意转变过程中中间环节的不可替代性。举个例子：改革开放初期经济学界有的同志率先提出发展社会主义商品经济、实行计划调节与市场调节相结合，应当说，这在当时是一个很大的突破；后来发展到经济体制改革的目标是建立社会主义市场经济体制，当然是更具长远意义上的突破。我们在总结改革开放 30 年的时候，就不能用后来确定的市场经济体制改革目标，要求前期的改革一步到位、早就应该提出市场经济，需知那时提出商品经济和"两种调节"是何等艰难、需要何等的理论勇气！我们不能割断历史，要用历史的眼光看待历史，评价改革开放的历史。对以往人口政策的评论也应如此，要用历史的眼光、发展的眼光，而不能运用"倒过来"的眼光和方法论。

作为曾经参与过去人口战略和人口政策工作，现今仍关心和研究当前和未来人口发展趋势和人口政策走向的一名学人，平心而论，二三十年前还没有哪一项政策有过如此开放式的民主讨论，如能将讨论的情况和作出选择的原委再现出来，对于澄清事实，促进人口政策研究的深入，总可以起正本清源、弄清政策来龙去脉的作用。笔者这样说，并不等于当年一切问题都讨论得尽善尽美、做得天衣无缝。不是的。人口同世间任何事物一样，总是不断变化和发展着的，再好的人口政策，再准确的人口预测，也要在实践中验证和不断修正完善。对以往人口政策的阐发，本人遵循尊重历史、实事求是准则，反映当年讨论和决策之原貌；重点在如何决策、怎样决策的研究上，一般情况下尽量不涉及个人。对当前和未来人口政策的阐发，主要是本人研究和本人主持的研究课题取得的成果，不代表任何组织和其他任何人，属纯学术性质的研究和探讨。

长江后浪推前浪，世上新人换旧人。笔者在 30 多年从事人口科学研究中，分出很大一部分精力研究人口发展战略和人口政策，感触颇深。古稀之年，一个愿望在心中回绕多年，就是要把亲身经历过的中国人口政策的提出、形成和发展的情况整理出来，并且纳入人口科学研究视野，将其奉献给13 亿中国人民以及国际社会关心中国人口变动和发展的各界人士。10 年前笔者所著《大国之难——当代中国的人口问题》由今日中国出版社出版发行，并且再版印刷，比较全面地分析了人口与经济关系中总体人口与消费、劳动年龄人口与就业、人口老龄化与社会保障、人口素质与科技进步、人口城市化与产业结构、人口地区分布与生产力布局的矛盾和问题，以及人口与资源、人口与环境、人口与社会发展的矛盾和问题，初步提出和阐述了解决人口问题的一些思路。《大国之路——当代中国人口政策研究》可视为它的姊妹篇，给出以往解决这些问题的政策轨迹、当前政策的具体分析和未来面临的政策选择。副标题之所以取名"当代中国人口政策研究"，是因为本人实为一名学人，全书均为站在学术视角作出的分析和探讨。不言而喻，这样的分析和探讨是否科学，能否经得住历史的检验，只能随着时间年复一年、日复一日的流转，答案也就自然地流淌出来。

英 文 论 文

Research on the Changes in Population Age Structure and Macro-Economic Development Issues[*]

With the world population rising above the 5 billion mark this year, the impact of population on economic, scientific, technological and social development has increasingly attracted wide attention. China is a country characterized by its large population and its lack of a solid industrial base. Thus, research on the impact of population on economic development appears to be of the population. Population age structure is an important though easily neglected factor which deserves extensive and in-depth research. This paper is an attempt to look at a few of the most fundamental problems that bear upon national economic development from the perspective of changes in the population age structure.

I. A Review of Changes in the Chinese Population Age Structure and Its Outlook

Changes in the population's age structure are determined by the following three factors: the number of births in each year adding to the whole population; the number of deaths of a particular age group detracting from the population aggregates; and the number of immigrants and emigrants of a particular age group adding to or detracting from the population aggregates. As far as China is concerned, immigration and emigration are rather limited. The factors that influence the changes in the age structure are primarily fertility and mortality rates. A survey

---

[*] See: *Chinese Journal of Population Science*, Volume 1, Number 1, 1989 Alleerton Press, Inc. U. S. A.

of the Chinese population's fertility and mortality rates since the founding of the People's Republic in 1949 reveals that, except for the 1958 – 1961 period, the fertility rate has maintained at a high of 32‰ – 43‰ throughout the 50's and'60's, only to decline substantially in the 1970's, from 1969's 34. 11‰ to 1979's 17. 28‰. In the'80's the fertility rate has fluctuated around 18‰. The general trend of the mortality rate is downward, except for the 1959-1961 period. In the 1970s it stabilized at 6‰-7‰. The trend of the mortality rates of all age groups is also downward. The decline in the infant mortality rate is especially apparent. These changes in fertility and mortality rates directly determine the changes in the aggregate age structure of the population. Using the 1953, 1964 and 1982 censuses for example, changes in the population's age structure are represented in Fig. 1. [1]

Fig. 1 indicates that compared with 1953, the 1964 population age pyramid appears younger: the ratio of 0-14-year-olds increased from 36. 3% to 40. 4% , whereas the ratio of the 15-year-olds declined from 59. 3% to 55. 9% , and the ratio of the 65-year-olds and older population declined from 4. 4% to 3. 7% . This trend persisted until the early 1970's. In comparison with 1946, the 1982 population age structure underwent great changes: at the bottom of the pyramid, ten age groups had contracted. The ratio of the 0-14-year-olds declined to 33. 5% . Among the adult population, except for a slight decline in the 35-39 and 40-44 age groups, the ratio of 15-65-year-old people climbed to 61. 6% . The top of the pyramid was thickening. The ratio of people 65-years-old and older increased to 4. 9% . The population age structure began to grow older.

Until recently, demographers used several different standards to differentiate population types according to age composition. One standard proposed by the Swedish scholar Sanbard divided the population into three types, taking 50 as the point of departure for calculating the ratio of elderly in the population. Later, a Polish scholar proposed using 60 as the starting point in calculating the ratio of elderly in the population and further divided the population into near aging, aging and completely aged groups according to the size of the elderly population. The United Nations adopted a dual standard: in a young population, the ratio of those 65-or-

---

[1]   Sources: *China Statistics Yearbook*, China Statistics Press, 1986 ed. *Information on China's* 1982 *Population Census*, China Statistics Press, 1985 ed.

older is less than 4% or the ratio of those 60 or older is less than 7% ; in an adult population, the ratio cf the 65-or-older population is between 4% -7% or the ratio of 60-or-older population is between 7% -10% ; in aged population, the ratio of people 65-or-older is 70% and above or the ratio of those 60 or older is 10% and above. In recent years, some demographers advanced the ratios of those 65-or-older is less than 5% , between 5% -10% and 10% and above respectively as the new standards for the three population age structures. In light of the current situation of an aging world population, a Japanese professor proposed that the ratios of those 65 or older be less than 7% , between 7% -10% and above as the new standards. Proceeding from the present reality of China's population age structure, and with reference to some of the international standards, I am of a young population type and the beginning of an adult population type. It is characterized by the following essential features: on the one hand, there is a large proportion of young people, with the median age from the 1982 Census at 22.9% , thus, with a great potential for growth; on the other hand, the aging trend of the population is already in the making. The population will reach a high level of aging in a relatively short time. For future changes in the age structure of the population as a whole, see Table 1. [1]

Table 1 indicates that until the year 2024, the percentage of 0-14-year-olds in the population will gradually decline. The mid-level forecast puts the figure at 19.3% , 14.2% decline when compared with the 1982 Census. The ratio of the 15 – 64 adult population will climb at first, only to decline later; the mid-level forecast puts the figure at 71.41% in the year 2010, compared with 61.6% in 1982. The ratio will then decline to 63.3% . The ratio of people 65 or older will decline gradually. The mid-level forecast puts the figure at 17.4% in the year 2040 as compared to 4.9% in 1982. There is a dramatic increase. The population will be aging rapidly.

---

① See Tian Xueyuan al. , ed *China's Population and Employment in the Year* 2000.

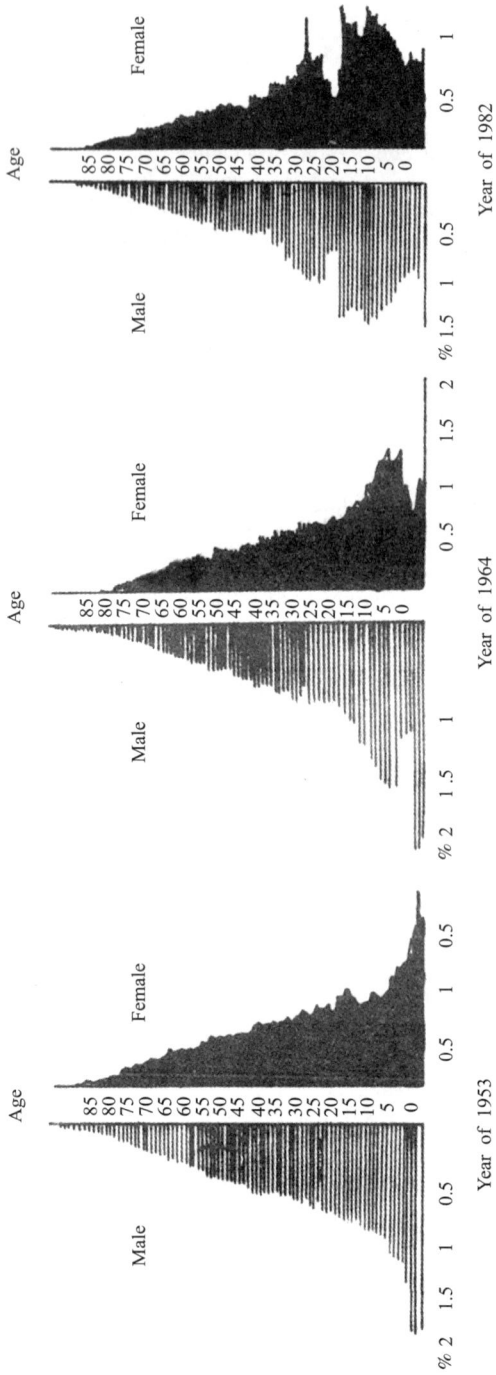

Fig .1 Age Structure of the National Population

Table 1

Age of Year	Low-level Forecast (%)			Mid-level Forecast (%)			High-level Forecast (%)		
	0 – 14	15 – 64	65 +	0 – 14	15 – 64	65 +	0 – 14	15 – 64	65 +
1990	24. 6	69. 6	5. 8	26. 0	68. 4	5. 6	27. 1	67. 4	5. 5
2000	21. 9	70. 9	7. 2	24. 3	68. 8	6. 9	25. 7	67. 5	6. 8
2010	20. 1	71. 7	8. 2	20. 7	71. 4	7. 9	21. 2	71. 2	7. 6
2020	19. 8	69. 0	11. 2	20. 8	68. 6	10. 6	21. 5	68. 3	10. 2
2030	19. 2	66. 4	14. 4	20. 1	66. 4	13. 5	20. 6	66. 5	12. 9
2040	19. 3	61. 9	18. 8	19. 3	63. 3	17. 4	19. 5	64. 0	16. 5
2050	20. 1	62. 6	17. 3	20. 5	63. 5	16. 0	20. 8	63. 9	15. 3

Research on changes in the population age structure should of course focus on population aggregates, but differences in population age structure between urban and rural areas and between different regions also deserve attention. The 1982 Census found that among the 0-14-year-old population, the rural population accounted for 35. 37%, by far the largest proportion; the township population was second, at 28. 31%; the city population was the lowest, at 26. 01%. The ratio of the 15-64-year-old population was exactly the opposite: the ratios for city, township and county population are 69. 48% and 59. 63%, respectively. The ratios of the 65-or-older population by size are as follows: county: 5. 00%; city: 4. 68%; and township: 4. 21%. This is true for cities, townships and counties across the country as a whole. Specifically, the ratio of the old population is highest in Shanghai, the largest city in the country. Beijing and Tianjing are also at the top. To measure differences in the age structure by regions, the median age reflects how young or how old a population is. According to the 1982 population census, the median age of the population is 22. 91. Shanghai has the highest median age (29. 23); the next is Beijing (27. 20) . Ningxia has the lowest median age (18. 42); Qinghai has the second lowest (18. 54);[1] As a general rule, where population density is high, the decline of the fertility rate is dramatic. And there is a relatively high ratio of older people and the median age is higher. Where the population density is low, the decline in the fertility rate is slight, there is a relatively higher ratio of young people and the median age is lower. This

---

① Sources: *Information on China's 1982 Population Census.*

results in differences in the age structure by geographical distribution: from the Northwest to the Southeast, there is a gradual increase in the median age and in the ratio of the older people. The degree of aging of the population is distributed in the shape of a flight of stairs.

II. Changes in the Productive Age Population and an Employment Development Strategy

Changes in the population age structure will influence macroeconomics development. First of all, changes in the economically productive population will have an impact on employment development strategies. From the perspective of demography, the productive age population accounts for the largest proportion in the population. Its size is larger than both the juvenile and the elderly populations. Only this age group has combined the producer and the consumer in one identity. It not only produces the wealth consumed by itself, but also produces the wealth consumed by the juvenile and elderly populations. Therefore, it occupies a dominant and core position in the whole population. From an economic point view, population has the highest order of importance in comparison with exchange, distribution and consumption. It not only determines the material contents for exchange, distribution and consumptmn, but also determines the mode and nature of exchange, distribution and consumption. Employment is the link between the core population on the one hand and production on the other. It embodies the essential nature of the relationship between the population and national economic development. As a matter of course, an employment development strategy must take into account these two aspects.

The futuer trend of change in the 15-64 age-group population was discussed earlier. Using the mid-level forecast as an example, we feel that its proportion will keep on increasing until the year 2010. The increase in its absolute value will continue for even longer. Its number will possibly increase from 683 million in 1985 to 765 million in 1990, to 858 million in 2000, to 956 million in 2010. 64 age-group population will grow by 175 million in 2000, and by 273 million in 2010, in comparison with the 1985 figure. It would be simply impossible to employ most of that population in agriculture, half of which would be in the farming industry. What should be done is to keep the annually added productive age population out of the farming industry and purposely transfer part of the agricultural labor force to other sectors. One way of doing this is to transform traditional farming to diversified agriculture. China has the necessary conditions: of 1. 44 billion mu of land, plateaus and mountainous areas (part of which is high mountain pastoral land) account for about 59% , basins and plains about 30% , hilly areas 9% and freshwater areas 2% , with great potential for the development of forestry, animal husbandry, sideline industries and fishing. The second alternative is develop town and village, industries and commerce, accelerating the process of urbanization of the population.

The recent rapid development of town and village industries in Jiangsu and Zhejiang Provinces has provided us with fresh experiences, which show that it is not only an important means for the peasants to get rich, but also an effective way to transform the agricultural labor force. As a matter of fact, in the process of modernization, some developed countries witnessed a decrease not only in the relative number of agriculture workers engaged in farming, but also a drastic decrease in its absolute numbers. From1955 to 1975, the number of agriculture workers decreased by nearly half in America and by more than half in Japan. Other developed countries also experienced the same process. The ratio of workers engaged in agriculture in France and West Germany has decreased to less than 10% . In the U. S. and the U. K. this ratio is and to its peak value of 980 million in 2015. Its decline will proceed slowly, to 977 million in 2020 and to 930 million in 2040. This means that in the next 30 years, the size of the productive age population will grow, therefore the labor force will grow dramatically, by 300 million. Even though the productive age population will decrease thereafter, its number will be above 930 million in another 30 years, 250 million more than that in 1985. The rapid expansion in the productive age population will create enormous pressure on employment from the supply side and create new challenges. In view of the needs of socialist construction and development, no efforts should be spared to bring about a shift in emphasis in the employment strategy.

First of all, the emphasis of the employment strategy should shift from farming-oriented to urban industrial-commercial oriented and diversification. In the past 30 years, newly-created jobs have been mostly in agriculture. Although there have been some changes in this situation since the Third Plenary Session of the Eleventh Central Committee of the Chinese Communist Party, until 1985 the labor force employed in agriculture, forestry, animal husbandry, fishing and the irrigation industry was more than 311. 87 million, which accounted for 62. 5% of the total labor force of 498. 73 million. This situation resulted in the low productivity of agriculture, especially in the farming industry. The per capita of cultivable land decreased drastically, by half between 1949 and 1982, and the trend is continuing. There was a large growth aggregate food production, whereas the per capita production witnessed little growth. The gross agricultural production grew quickly, but the growth of per capita net production remained slow.

According to the above-mentioned mid-level forecast, the 15-even less than 3%. The transformation of the agricultural population is still proceeding with accelerating speed. To solve the employment problem of a drastically expanded population, China has to urbanize its population. At present, there is a great need to develop small towns and let their industries and commerce flourish.

Secondly, the emphasis of the employment strategy should shift from industry and agriculture, the manufacturing sectors, to the service sectors. In the past, growth has been very slow in the commercial food industry and service sectors, as well as in science, education, culture and health, the non-material production sectors. In addition, half of the newly-added productive age population entered the agricultural sector, resulting in over-employment in the material production sector and the unproportionately high ratio of workers in those sectors. There has been too little increase in the work force in the non-material production sectors, and its ratio in the total work force is too low. As a result, some already over-staffed material production sectors and enterprises have had to take in even more people, resulting in an idle work force and low productivity. Furthermore, factories with low productivity and low levels of technology seem to have more elasticity in their ability to absorb the labor force. They seem to be able to accept as many people, as they like. This situation has seriously hampered the adoption of new technologies and blocked the way to expand production potentials. This situation must changed. In the future, the major employer of a large number of the newly-added work force should not be the production sector, but should be the service industry, i. e. the third industry. This is also an inevitable trend of modernization and development. In developed countries, the ratio between workers in manufacturing sectors and workers in service sectors is about 1 : 1. In the U. K. it is 1 : 1. 5. 1n the U. S. it is 1 : 2. 3. It is likely that the number of "white-collar" workers will exceed that of "blue-collar" workers. In view of the prospect of dramatic growth in the productive age population in the next few decades, it will be necessary to shift the thrust of employment strategies to non-material production sectors in order to provide employment to the newly-added productive age population and also to enhance productivity in the manufacturing sectors and the rapid development of the national economy.

Thirdly, employment strategies should shift their emphasis from a high employment rate to a better employment effect. China has for a long time adopted a policy of low salaries and a high employment rate. On the one hand, a high employment rate reflects fully utilized labor resources; on the other hand, it exposes the fact that behind the high employment rate is the low rate of actual labor utilization and an unsatisfactory employment effect. Using the gross industrial product of state-owned enterprises as an example, increases in production during the "first five-year plan" of 1963-1965 and the "the fifth five-year plan" were achieved primarily through enhancing "the fifth five-year plan" whereas increases during the "second five-year plan", the "third five-year plan" and the "fourth five-year plan" were realized primarily through increasing the number of work. In addition, during the second and third five-year plan, there were negative increases in labor productivity. This created a situation that promoted production through increasing the volume of labor and hampered expansion of production through enhancing productivity. In view of the fact that there will be drastic increase in the size of the productive age population in the next two or three decades, and that there will be greater pressure on the employment, the contradiction between the employment rate and the employment effect will become all the more apparent. As a general guiding principle, both aspects should be taken into account. In the past, there has been more emphasis on employment while employment effect has been largely ignored. In light of this situation, there is a need to shift the strategic emphasis to the enhancement effect. In making the strategic choice between full employment, relatively full employment, reasonable employment and under-employment, I am in favor of relatively full employment or reasonable employment. On the condition that the employment effect will continue to improve, or at least will not decline, efforts should be made to realize relatively full employment. To advocate full employment at the expense of the employment effect or to emphasize the employment effect without due regard to the fact that there will be drastic increases in the productive age population would be inconsistent with the changes in population age structure and with modernization and development needs.

III . The Population Aging Trend and Social Security of the Elderly

Apart from the emphasis on the relationship between the productive age population and an employment development strategy, changes in the elderly population and problems of their level forecasts mentioned earlier, the degree of the aging of the population will vary. But in the next 60 years, the absolute of elderly people will remain the same. This is because the elderly population is already distributed in all the age groups above 0. One can obtain the absolute number of the elderly each year by counting out the number of the dead in each age group. If we take the 50 million elderly in the 1982 Census as a base, the number will double in 28 years, reaching 100 million. In another 20 years, that figure will double again, reaching 200 million by 2030. By the year 2040, the number of elderly will reach 260 million, with 200 million more than the 1982 figure. It is noteworthy that it is not the population aggregates alone that age rapidly; the further aging of the elderly population is also fairly rapid. We can use the following formula to calculate the median age of the elderly population:

$$X_{md} = X_i + \frac{\dfrac{\sum p_2}{2} - \sum_{0}^{md-1} cx}{p_{md}} \cdot d$$

According to the mid-level forecast, the median of the elderly population will increase from 67. 6 in 1982 to 67. 7 in 1990 then to 68. 3 in 2000. It will go down slightly after 2000, to 68. 3 in 2010, 67. 9 in 2020 and 67. 8 in 2030. After 2030, the median age will climb up rapidly, to 69. 7 in 2040 and 70. 4 in 2050. The change in the median age of the elderly population is primarily determined by the number of births in the past. The baby-boom period from the mid-sixties to the early seventies is especially critical. Before this group of people reach the higher age group in the elderly population, the median age of that population is lower. When this group reaches the higher age group in the elderly population, the median age becomes higher. In research on the problems of aging, attention should be paid to these changing trends, i. e. the further aging of the aged population. Between people above and below the median age in that population there exist apparent differences in their physical and intellectual abilities. Therefore, there are differences in their abilities to take care of themselves. In our efforts to find solutions to the problems of the elderly, we must take this differences into account.

Aging is a general trend of the world population. It is sign of economic and technological progress and the longevity of human life. In addition, a certain degree of aging is necessary for the transition from a growing population to a stabilized population. It is also a necessary stage for the realization of the long-term objectives of population planning. We should adopt a positive approach, however, we cannot ignore the population aging. Faced with the trend of an aging population and a over-aged population, we must approach the problem cautiously and make sound arrangements for an elderly population four, or five times its present size. Of all the problems related to aging, the livelihood of the elderly is of the order of importance. It is the prerequisite condition for solving the problems of the elderly.

Obtaining one's livelihood is a basic problem throughout the latter half of one's life. In terms of time, from the time one enters old age to one's death, one has to be guaranteed a livelihood. In terms of space, regardless of sex, nationality, race, location, or geographic distribution, everyone should be guaranteed a livelihood in their old age. This is essential for the continuation of human life and all other activities. China has a modest level of economic development and consumption. On a scale of starvation, being fed-and-clothed, prosperity and affluence, China is in the second stage. It can be expected to reach the stage of prosperity by the end of the century. Even in the 1930's and 1940's of the next century, China will only afford a modest standard of living. In light of this reality, providing livelihood for the elderly population will remain a priority task for a long time in the future.

At present in China, care of the elderly falls into two basic categories. One is the pension system that covers workers at state institutions, state-owned enterprises, most of the urban collectively-owned enterprises and some of the rural collectively-owned enterprises. Most peasants, self-employed workers in cities and towns and workers in a small number of collectively-owned enterprises do not have a pension system. They have to depend on their children or social welfare for their livelihood. In terms of currently employed, of the two categories of people, the former accounted for about 30%, while the latter constituted about 70%. 30% of the workers in our society can live on their pensions, thus enjoying a secure life in their old age. Those who do not have pensions can also resort to some help if they have difficulties. This is a great social progress when compared with the old China, where the majority of the workers lived at a marginal subsistence level, to say nothing of having a secured livelihood in their old age. However, there are many problems in the current social security system. These problems are compounded by the rapid aging of the population. Primarily, the problems are as follows: first, there have been drastic increases in the payment of the state-owned enterprises for social welfare and benefits in 1952 was 950 million yuan, 14.0% of total wages. The payment increased to 2.668 billion in 1985, a 27.1 fold increase in 33 years, accounting for 25.1% of total wages. The workers'social welfare and benefits include many other items, but their retirement pension is by far the largest share, accounting for 42.1% in 1985. With the rapid aging of the population and dramatic increases in the number of retirees and their pensions, it is estimated that the state payment for retirement pensions will double by the year 2000. The same in the year 2030 will be 10 times more than the payment at the turn of the century. Its proportion of the total wages will also increase quickly, creating intolerable financial pressures. It is generally agreed that payment for the elderly population cannot exceed 24% of the national income, which is the "warning line". Crossing this "warning line" will create enormous financial difficulty for the economic development of the state. Some of the Western European and Nordic countries have learned their lessons. Secondly the system is incompatible with economic and technological progress. At present, it is usually the work units that pay their staff's retirement pensions. This is an enormous burden for those enterprises with an aging staff, old equipment and old products, thus hampering their replacement of fixed capital and their technological innovation. Meanwhile, since individual workers do not have to pay anything for their pensions, the society as a whole suffers from a low savings rate and the state could have difficulties in raising funds, thereby impeding investment expansion and technological innovation. Thirdly, the system is detrimental to narrowing the differences between urban and rural areas. Care for the rural elderly who have less secured income is more problematic. Fourthly, the system will not facilitate family planning and efforts to control population growth. Most of the rural laborers, especially the peasants, do not have a secured livelihood in their old age; they need their children to support them. To bear more children and to have more sons to take care of them becomes a way of securing a livelihood for their old age. Fifthly, the system is inconsistent with the trend of shrinking the family size. China has a tradition of respecting and care of the elderly. Traditional households with together are still adopted by a large part of three generation living of the population. But with the development of the commodity economy, increases in job changes, migration of the population and changes in the traditional value system, the proportion of old-couple households and the proportion of the widowed elderly have risen. There is an urgent need to strengthen the social security of the elderly.

The fundamental solution to these problems is to make the basic policy of social security for the elderly explicit and to promote reforms. In my view, the strategy should promote the Chinese tradition of reverence of, care for and support of the livelihood of the elderly, and let the traditional way of taking care of the elderly play its role. On the other hand, with economic development, we should gradually adopt a social security system for the whole elderly population and reform the current system. Its objectives should be to establish a pension fund twenty or thirty years before one's retirement, or better still, from the moment one begins working, to be contributed by the individual concerned, his work unit and the state and to be collected once the individual retires from the job. This is a detailed and very complicated task. In the United States, the pension fund system was started by the Roosevelt Administration. In the course of several decades, will pensions and disability pensions were added to the system, and they were supplemented with provisions that make these funds rise with wages and inflation. We have to accomplish the job before the number of the aged reaches a serious proportion. We have to start the reform process now and start the formulation and implementation of the strategy early.

IV. Changes in the Affiliated Age Ratio and the Speed of Economic Development

In the study of changes in the population's age structure and their influence on macro-economic development, change in the affiliated age ratio, namely, the ratio of the productive age population to the juvenile and elderly population they support is a very important issue. The aforementioned forecasts show that the proportion of the 15-64 productive age population will continue to grow until about the year 2010. Then it will slowly decreases. A direct result of this change is the decline of the affiliated age ratio, which will increase slightly only after 2010. If we take the mid-level forecast as an example, the specific changes in the affiliated age ratio are as follows: 62.3% in 1982, 46.2% in 1990, 45.3% in 2000, 40.1% in 2010, 45.8% in 2020, 50.6% in 2030, 58.0% in 2040 and 57.5% in 2050. This situation shows that in spite of the fact that the proportion and absolute number of the elderly will rise sharply, it will not offset the decrease in the number and proportion of the juvenile population. This will lead directly to the decline of the affiliated age ratio. Even though the affiliated age ratio will rise slightly in the first and second decades in the next century, the affiliated age ratio will only 58.0% in 2040, slightly lower than the current level, when aging of the population reaches the most serious proportion and the ratio is the highest.

This is an interesting trend in the population's age structure that has attracted attention. It has raised an important issue for the study of the relationship between the population and economic development, namly how to assess the influence of the decline of the affiliated age ratio on the development of the national economy. At present, there is little agreement concerning this issue in academic circles. However, it has always been my opinion that the decline of the affiliated age ratio faced by China will provide a favorable condition for the development of the national economy. On the whole, benefits will outweigh disadvantages. It will be a "golden period" of change in the population's age structure. We should make the best use of this opportunity and speed up the pace of economic development. There are several reasons for this position. First, a sharp decline in the affiliated age ratio is concomitant with the rapid aging of the population, suggesting that the decline in the absolute number and proportion of the juvenile population is even faster. Therefore there will be a substantial saving of money that the state spends on the juvenile population. It is estimated that there will be an annual decrease of more than 10 billion Yuan after 1990, and in the next two or three decades multiple billions of Yuan will be saved. If spent on the expansion of production and improvement of technological equipment, this money can play an important part in doubling agricultural and industrial output by the end of the century and speeding up the Four Modernization process.

Secondly, in our analysis of the sharp growth of the productive age population, we should adopt a historical and dialectical approach. Since there will be tremendous pressure on employment both at present and in the future, we have to speed up the pace of change in the emphasis of our employment strategy. There is a sharp contradiction between the need to expand employment and the need to enhance the employment effect. In light of this situation, it would be ideal to go without an increase in the productive age population, or better still, to have a decline in the productive age population. However. because of the relative young age of China's population's age structure, there is a greater potential for growth. It is inevitable that the population aggregate will continue to grow in the next two or three decades. The growth of the productive population will be even faster. What we can do is to slow population growth by lowering fertility rate, thereby cutting back the degree of increase in the number and ratio of the productive age population. Therefore, in our efforts to control population growth, we must face the inevitability of a sharp increase in the productive age population and make effective and full use of this population. In fact, the modernization experiences of other countries, especially that of Asian countries and regions, prove that one of the important conditions for a high rate of economic development involves taking advantage of cheap labor to improve the competitiveness of one's products, Japan and Singapore are good examples. The affiliated age ratio of China will decline substantially in the next two or three decades. The size of the productive population is large whereas the proportion of the juvenile and elderly populations is low, presenting us with a good opportunity for economic development. This is an ideal condition for the development of the national economy and quadrupling the national product. If lost, this opportunity will never return. We must grasp the opportunity that these changes in population structure present us and draw our lessons from experiences both inside and outside our country, especially the positive and negative lessons learned since the founding of the People's Republic of China. We must take advantage of the rich human resources, and make scientific use of these resources in modernization and reconstruction along the lines of reform, openness and flexibility.

Costs of Children-Benefit Theory
and Population Control[*]

The fertility and growth rates of China's population have risen in recent years. On April 14, 1989, the population in mainland China exceeded 1.1 billion. The grim situation of population in China has drawn worldwide concern. Under the circumstances of the reform and the rapid development of a market-oriented economy, new breakthroughs must be made in the integration of theories into practice and feasible and effective measures are needed in order to check population growth. In my opinion the key to the breakthroughs lies in the relationships between population reproduction and economic interests, the regulation of individual reproduction behavior by such interests and the performance of population administration departments according to the principle of economic interests.

I. About The Costs of Children-benefit Theory

In the survey of the relationships between population reproduction and economic interests, an old but still realistic question must be answered first: what factors determine the number of children people have. The answer should be given with a view on the old times and the present times as well. "old times" here does not refer only to Ancient times, but rather, to the stage in human history when people gave no thought to or were incapable of controlling the number of their children. Apparently, what governed human reproduction in this period was natural

---

* See: *Chinese Journal of Population Science*, Volume1, Number 4, 1989.

biological law. Within the period of the 408 months between 15 and 49 years of age, a normal fertile woman can have 11 children if she has an interval of 37 months between two children, including the period of pregnancy and breast-feeding, or nine children if the interval is 45 months. While this is rare nowadays, the weighted data from the sampling survey conducted in 1987 on China's elderly population aged over 60 years indicate that only 5.4 percent and 6.9 per cent of the country's elderly women have had one child or two children in their lifetime, while 11.3 percent and 25.8 percent, the highest percentage of them, have had seven, or more than eight children[1]This sufficiently proves that natural biological law governed people's reproduction behavior and the number of children they borne.

Mankind eventually freed itself from the mercy of biological law and embarked on a period when it was able to choose the number of children at will thanks to the development of economy, science technology and to new values. This is one of the greatest advances that has been made in human history. It is unimaginable what would have happened to this planet and this country, had the whole human race remained powerless against the growth of population. Therefore, family planning is a great and progressive cause related to the future of the world and the country.

What factors, then, determine the number of children people choose to have when they are able to make such a choice? There are economic, cultural, political, historical and geographical factors, of which the economic ones are essential.

It is well known that materialists believe existence determines consciousness and that social phenomena originate from economy. In the modern times since the industrial revolution, the growth of a market-oriented economy and the domination of mercantilism have led to the increasing commercialization of the society. As a result, some economists have categorized children into commodities, ones of a special kind, produced in families instead of bought at the market. Hence the theory of the costs and benefits of children, the leading exponents of which are Professor Harvey Leibenstein of Harvard University, and manpower capital expert Professor Garys. Beeker of Chicago University in the United States. Leibenstein believes that the costs of producing children consist of direct and indirect, or opportunity

---

[1]　Source: *Data of the* 1087 *Sampling Survey on China's Elderly Population Aged over* 60 *Years*, *Population Science of China*, *supplement*, 1988.

costs. Direct costs refer to those spent on children's living, education and marriage, and indirect or opportunity costs refer to the loss of potential income because of the time spent on raising children by the parents, especially the mother. Both direct and indirect costs are parents' losses, and can be called negative benefits. On the other hand, children can bring positive benefits to their parents when they grow up, mainly: 1) economic benefit earned as members of the labor force; 2) support, especially in developing countries; and 3) entertainment-family happiness. In addition, children, when they grow up, are expected to secure their families' fortunes and status.

The number of children parents choose to have depends on the benefit for which they spend money directly or indirectly: they will choose to have a child if the benefit is positive, i. e. benefit is greater than the costs; they will act according to circumstances if the benefit is zero, i. e. benefit equals costs; they will choose not to have the child if the benefit is negative, i. e. the costs cannot be compensated. Economic benefit that young people can bring to their parents tends to diminish with economic development and the increase of per capita income as does the benefit of filial support as the social security system improves, and the increase in parents' income makes it possible for them to save enough money to support themselves. Young people are also less expected to secure their families' fortunes and status. Only their function of entertainment has not changed greatly as it is not closely related to economic development. In general, as the result of economic development and the increase of per capita income, the benefit brought about by children has been diminishing and the monetary costs parents directly or indirectly pay for their children have grown. This is why the fertility and growth rates of some populations have been declining.

Becker further put forward the concept of children's net costs, i. e. the current value of the money parents spend on raising their children plus the current value of the time shadow price[1]minus the current value of the income and services children provide their families with. If the net costs are positive, it indicates that children

---

[1] Shadow price: A substitutive estimate of products, service and labor that have no market prices. Here it refers to the time parents spend on raising their children, which can be measured and included in the costs of children, although the time so spent has no market value.

cannot compensate their parents and that like durable goods. Children can only gratify their parents mentally and psychologically, if the net costs are negative, this means that like certain means of production, children can increase in value after their parents have invested on them and put them into the process of production; if the net costs are zero, children are financially, insignificant to their parents. He also suggested that on a certain level of social productivity, children's essential living expenses and the direct and indirect costs spent during a mother's pregnancy and parturition time are relatively the same and can be regarded as the children's unchangeable or quantitative costs, and the costs spent on children's health, medical care, entertainment and education can be called changeable or qualitative costs. Children's changeable or qualitative costs tend to increase with economic development and the growth of family income and, give certain substitutive relationships between the number and quality of children, parents tend to turn the children's quantitative costs into their qualitative ones. Hence the drop in some populations' fertility rate and number of children.

How should we view this Western micro-economic theory of children's costs and benefits? In my opinion, under that mercantile shell, it is in essence reasonable, having scientifically expounded on children's value to their parents and families and the impact of economics on human reproduction. China will find it impossible or will feel reluctant to apply mercantile principles to the field of human reproduction given the country's backward productivity, undeveloped economy and lack of mercantile consiousness and values. Nonetheless, it does not follow that people should give no thought to the economic benefit their reproduction will bring to them; on the contrary, people are consciously or unconsciously influenced by the thought of whether marginal children are worthwhile.

It should be pointed out that the costs to parents of their children are actual costs, while the benefit their children will bring to them is only an expected value and not the same as the benefit their children are actually bringing to them. However, such expectations are reasonable because they are based on a specific level of social productivity and education as well as traditional values.

II. The Trends in Chinese Children's Costs and Benefits

A major change in China's economic and social life since the reform started is the growth of a market-oriented economy and the enhancement of mercantile consciousness. This has made our research in children's costs and benefits not only possible but also necessary, as such research will help US find the causes for the rapid population growth and provide solutions to the problem on a theoretical basis.

The basic tendency in Chinese children's costs and benefits can be seen through a comparison of the two. First, children have brought more economic benefits than costs. According to the Western theory, when children's qualitative costs grow along with economic development, the economic benefit brought about by marginal children should diminish since, in a market-oriented economy, more economic benefit can be achieved if the extra costs of children are spent in market in return for labor. However, in spite of the rapid economic development in China in recent years, the economic benefit brought by Chinese children has generally grown instead of decreasing with few exceptions. This is mainly caused by the different conditions found in China as compared with those in Western countries. For instance, under the public ownership in urban areas and communal collective ownership in the countryside in the past, people often were not paid strictly according to the amount of their work; the practice of the "big pot", levelled distribution, was common, and households lost the function of production and were only units of consumption and human reproduction. As a result, the intention to increase the labor force through more reproduction was restrained since the economic benefit brought about through such an increase was limited. After the economic reform started in 1978, a responsibility system was established in rural areas, followed by the development of private businesses and leasing and stock systems in urban areas. The function of production has revived in many households and has been strengthened in competition. Hence the need for an increased labor force, and particularly males. While one has to experience the periods of infancy, childhood and adolescence before one becomes a mature laborer. It takes less time for a child to be considered as a member of the labor force when the levels of productivity and technology are low: a child in the early teenage years may begin to assist adults in their work, and a 15-year-old may be considered a mature laborer, so that the child can bring an economic benefit sooner than otherwise. This is currently very common in China's collectively owned businesses in urban areas. Also, the country's productivity remains low in spite of the rapid economic development of recent years. The increase in income depends largely on the increase of the labor force, and the improvement of labor's quality cannot substitute for such an increase. Therefore, marginal children can still bring about evident benefits. Finally, in a market-oriented economy that is still not fully developed, the function of regulation of a labor market is limited and the costs that have been saved by having fewer children cannot be exchanged for corresponding labor services. Under the circumstances, the economic benefit children bring has been enlarged, especially in rural areas.

Second, children render better support for their parents. According to the Western theory of children's costs and benefits, a social security system will improved with economic development so that the children's role of supporting their parents will eventually be replaced. This goal has been achieved in most developed countries. However, China's economic development in recent years has not led to the same situation because the development has been limited, and again, because of the different conditions in this country as compared with those in the West. While the change is not particularly noticeable in urban areas, rural young people are now playing a much more important part in supporting the seniors. Since the People's Commune, Which used to provide major social security to the rural elderly no longer exists, many an old age home has either disbanded or weakened in function due to a lack of funds. As a result, the role of young people in supporting the elderly has been increased. Although parents have no guarantee that their children will take on their filial responsibilities in supporting them in the future, and the risk of their investment is intensified with the shrinking of family size and the weakening of traditional values, having children is still considered to be the most important and safest way to acquire security for an old age. Therefore, the desire has been stimulated to have more children, especially to have more boys, who are supposed to be able to provide even more security for their parents.

Third, parallel to the enlargement of the above-mentioned benefits, children, particularly boys, are also more often expected to secure their families' fortunes and status thanks to the revival of the household's function of production, and to the expansion of private businesses. All this indicates the growth of expectations parents have for their children in the changing economic conditions, which is the basic reason for their intention to have more children, especially more males.

It should be pointed out that this analysis of the reasons for the rising fertility and population growth rates in the China has been made only in the basis of the impact of the change in the country's economy on children's costs and benefits. Other conditions, particularly the changes in the number of fertile women and the impact of economic measures in the State's population policy, also should be taken into consideration in analyzing the trend in Chinese children's costs and benefits. Since 1949, China underwent a baby boom between 1953 and 1957, a second boom between 1962 and 1972 and a third at the present. Of the first two booms, the first was smaller and the second was much larger, which accounts for the extremely large group of young people in the population age pyramid. The fertile women in the group will experience their reproduction peaks from 1986 to 1997, inevitably precipitating the third baby boom. All we can do is to take the best possible control of the fertility rate so as to minimize the boom.

The changes in the rewards and penalties in the State's population policy influence children's costs and benefits, as fines are intended to increase the costs of extra children and rewards are meant to make up for the loss of the benefit of extra children by enlarging the benefits of an only child. An economic lever is used here to achieve the balance between children's costs and benefits. Undesirable changes, however, have taken place in recent years. Many farmers in poverty-stricken areas are not intimidated by fines for having extra children because they cannot afford the fines anyway, nor are wealthy farmers intimidated by them as the fines are affordable to them and they would rather pay for the legitimacy of their extra children. Other penalties, such as to deprive extra children of private plots and grain rations in rural areas and to withhold extra children's grain rations and restrict employment opportunities in urban areas, are also not as intimidating and effective as before under the current new economic system. On the other hand, the bonus of five yuan per month for an only child has devalued as a result of inflation, and the priority for an only child in school admission and employment is no longer as attractive as before. The changes in value of both, rewards and penalties in the country's family planning program, and our failure to make corresponding adjustments in our policy, have worsened the imbalance between children's costs and benefits and account for the rise in fertility and growth rates of the Chinese population.

III. Family Planning Based on Children's Costs and Benefits

Confronted with the new baby boom and the current tendency in population growth, it is both of great importance and difficulty to effectively control the fertility rate in order to, as far as population is concerned, provide better conditions for the reform and the country's modernization drive. Since the 1970s, China has acquired rich experience having considerably lowered the country's fertility and growth rates and successfully carrying out the family planning program. This experience, such as that in the attention of the leadership, heavy publicity, urging contraception, statistical observation and a responsibility system, experience should undoubtedly be applied and enlarged in order to fully implement the family planning program and control population growth.

While China's experience involves administrative, legal and economic factors, I believe that the administration has played the most important part. Under the conditions found in China, this is not only necessary, but also inevitable and appropriate. For a rather lengthy period of time now, China will be plagued by a "shortage" economy and an excess of population. The State's basic policy should be to control population growth while making every effort to promote economic development.

There are two ways to lower the population's fertility and growth rates: one is the natural way, i. e. through social and economic development, increase of per capita income and the upgrading of the population's educational level, and the other is the social way, i. e. mainly through administrative intervention. We cannot choose the first solution; if we had, our population would have exceeded 1. 2 billion long ago and it is hard to imagine how long it would continue to grow. This would be detrimental to the country's development and fundamental interests. We can therefore only choose the second way. In my opinion, in dealing with the relationships between population control and economic development, we should not adopt a mechanical materialistic attitude, thinking that fertility and growth rates can only decline along with economic development and people can do nothing about them; nor should we degenerate into subjective idealism, in the belief that human reproduction is independent of economic development and solely subject to man's will. We should adopt a dialectical materialistic attitude and regulate people's reproduction both by administrative and other non-economic means and, in particular, by applying the principle of economic interests. The reasons for this are:

First, while administrative means have been adequately and effectively used in the past 20 years and should continue to be used, they have brought certain problems, often making birth control persuasion come to a deadlock. This is because administrative orders are not convincing when children bring benefits greater than the costs to their parents. In fact, many parents are not compensated for the loss of the benefits they could have enjoyed by having more children. This situation has made many administrative order less acceptable.

Second, it is important to consolidate and enlarge the achievements made in family planning since the 1970s in order to better control the fertility rate in the third baby boom. Therefore, there should be guarantee that parents who have only one child will benefit and will have secure labor compensation and support at their old age, so that they will choose not to have more children, and, on the other hand, measures should be taken so that parents who have more than one child can not benefit economically. The principle of economic interests should be applied here to help people voluntarily have fewer children.

Third, children's economic value has been drawing increasing public attention and the theory of children's costs and benefits deserve serious study now that the country's urban and rural economy has developed greatly in the past 10 years. People's minds have been freed, a market-oriented economy has been growing rapidly and people's sense of commodity has been enhanced.

Based on these arguments, China's theory and basic principle of controlling population growth and restricting the birth of extra children may be expressed as:

helping people make their choices concerning reproduction according to their interests, and gradually switching from administrative management to interest regulation to rectify the current unfavorable imbalance between children's costs and benefits. Both costs and benefits of children should be adjusted.

Thought should be given as to how to increase the benefits of an existing child while reducing the benefit of more children. The best way to do this is to improve the system of reward for those families who have only one child. In most areas, these parents receive a monthly bonus of five yuan. However, apparently in many rural areas, especially poor ones, this meager bonus is often not issued. Such bonuses are supposed to be paid by local farmers and, as the more parents who choose to have only one child, the more bonuses these farmers have to pay, it is difficult for them to have more one-child families. This situation needs to be changed. In fact, for the State, the five-yuan monthly bonus is much less than the costs it would have to bear for an extra child, because of the present conflict between a shortage economy and an excess of population. Therefore, the bonuses for single-child families should, in principle, be paid by the State. Local governments might share in the expense when the State is in financial difficulty. On the other hand, income can offset the expense, i. e. the bonuses for single-child families could be paid out of the fines levied on those who have extra children. This system should balance the government's income and expenditure. In brief, an actual reward grant should be paid to single-child families, or people are merely paying lip service when they talk about increasing the benefits of an only child.

On the basis of the bonuses, the reward system should be reformed by ensuring that it compensates parents for the loss of the benefits that they could have received by having more children. One fact is evident: a five-yuan monthly bonus or 60-yuan annual bonus that may have been of some worth in the 1970s will be of little worth in the late 1980s due to inflation. This makes it desirable to place the bonus with a fund for parents for labor compensation and old-age pension. The idea is: instead of paying parent monthly or annually, the bonus is put into an insurance company or a bank in the form of certain credit. With the current interest rate of 14 percent for State bonds, the money will grow in value in 14 years to more than 2, 600 yuan. Then the parents can receive a labor compensation for a certain period. For instance, the annual payment for a period of 15 years is more than 360 yuan. The money will be turned into a fund for old-age pension 15 years later and, in another five years, the parents will be able to receive an annual pension of more than 800 yuan until their death. This throws a new light on the great benefit brought about by the five-yuan monthly bonus awarded to single-child families, which can in this way compensate to a large degree for the benefits that might have been gained by having more children.

Similar rewards may be given to those who remain unmarried or infertile for life in order to change the irrational present situation where childless people are not rewarded. In order to increase the benefits a single child brings to his or her parents, a single-child family may be given priority in the allocation of apartments, urban residence registration, admission to quality kindergartens, schools and employment, and the child may be given lifetime life insurance.

Meanwhile, restrictions should be imposed on extra children in these areas in order to reduce the benefits they bring to their families.

The costs of having more than one child should be increased. This means it is necessary to increase fines children's parents must pay and prolong the period over which they must pay these in order to make them feel that the increased costs of having more than one child may not be made up by the benefits the children may bring in the future. On the other hand, the parent' ability to afford the fines also should be taken into consideration. The term over which they receive fines should be equal in length to the term over which a single-child family receives bonuses, i. e. 14 years. A national standard should be set for the fine. For instance, parents may be fined for each extra child an amount equal to the local per capita income. The regional amount of the fine should be set by the government of each province, autonomous region of municipality directly under the central authority. Once approved by relevant departments, the rules for the fines should be enforced as an economic law.

As mentioned previously, the increase in costs related to improving the quality of children, especially those related to children's education, is an inevitable outcome of social progress and economic development. The current situation, however, is not satisfactory and sometimes even undesirable partly due to a lack of attention paid to education and the slow increase of the State's investment in educa-tion. A more basic reason, I believe is irrational income distribution. When, as people say, a professor earns less than a street peddlar, and a surgeon makes less money than a barber, there is little incentive to send children to school. If this sit-uation does not change, it will be difficult to increase children's qualitative costs, and this in turn will prevent the increase in total costs of marginal children, as children's quantitative costs remain relatively stable. The result is the temptation to have more children.

The key to changing the situation, in addition to increasing the State's invest-ment in education, is to reform the extremely irrational distribution system under which a well-educated white-collar worker earns almost the same as, or even less than, an ill-educated blue-collar laborer. Even if the State's financial situation pre-vents a considerable increase in white-collar income within a short period of time, policies, measures and systems should be specified and implemented in favor of white-collar workers. Along with economic development, the irrational differences between the income of those who do complicated work requiring education, and that of physical laborers who do simpler work should be adjusted in order to encour-age people to be more interested in the quality than the quantity of their children and increase their children's qualitative costs by making a greater investment in their education. By using both "hard" and "soft" tactics, we should be able to create a situation in which those who have more children will find themselves pay-ing more costs while receiving fewer benefits. In the long run, people will become interested in weighing their children's costs and benefits and their own interests and will become more careful in choosing the number of children they have. A drop in the fertility rate will be a result of the people's choice and will. Correspondingly, it is possible that the State's population administration departments will be better re-ceived by the public when they safeguard the rights and interests of single children and their families, fine the parents who have extra children according to applicable laws, assist financial departments in their observations and provide information and services to those who practice birth control. This is a fundamental transformation from sheer administrative management to interest regulation——a transformation from necessity to freedom.

References

[1] Harvey Leibestein: *Population Growth and Economic Development in the Third World*, *International Union for the Scientific Study of Population*. 1973.

[2] Gary S. Becker: "An Economic Analysis of Fertility", in *Demographics and Economics in Developed Countries*, Princeton University Press, 1960.

[3] JulianL. Simon: *Population Growth Economies*, Beijing University Press, 1984.

[4] Peng Songnian: *An Introduction to Western Population Economics*, 1987.

[5] Tiall Xueyuan: "On the Strategy of Population Development", Sociology and Social Surveys, Vol. 3, 1985.

[6] Qin Fangfang: "An Evaluation of the Impact of China's Family Planning on its Fertility Rate", *The Population Science of China*, Vol. 2, 1988.

[7] Li Xiaoping "Birth Effects and Economic Solutions to Birth Control", *Population Science of China*, Vol. 1989.

[8] World Bank: *World Development Report* (1988), China Finance Publishing House. 1988.

Reform and More Flexible
Policies Promote Urbanization[*]

Since the beginning of China's reform in the late 1970s, the Chinese society
has been changing rapidly. An outcome of economic, political and cultural development, urbanization is largely determined by the progress of the reform.

I . Reform and the acceleration of urbanization

Like the rest of the world, China is becoming increasingly urbanized. This
process together with a comparison with other countries is shown in Fig. 1. [①]

Fig. 1 shows the similarities and differences in urbanization between China and
other countries. While the proportion of urban population has been increasing steadily in many countries, such proportion changed irregularly in China. These changes may be divided into three periods: the proportion of urban population increased
rapidly in the 1950s, from 11. 2 percent in 1950 to 19. 7 percent in 1960, an 8. 5
percent rise in 10 years; the proportion remained between 16. 8 and 19. 7 percent
in the 1960s and 1970s; the proportion reached 19. 0 percent in 1979 and grew
rapidly since the early 1980s. It was 10. 4 percent lower than its counterpart in developing countries in 1980, and became 4. 9 percent higher than the Latter
in 1985.

There are different explanations for the rapid growth of the proportion of

---

* See: *Chinese Journal of Population Science*, Volume 1, Number 3, 1989.

① Source: *China Statistical Publishing House*: *China Statistical Yearbook* (1986); *Department of
International Economic and Social Affairs*: *World Population Prospect*, United Nations, NewYork,
1985.

China's urban population in recent years. Some believe that the statistics are accurate and reflect the real situation. Others doubt this; they say that such growth is because China, in recent years, classified as urban areas many regions that were formerly considered rural.

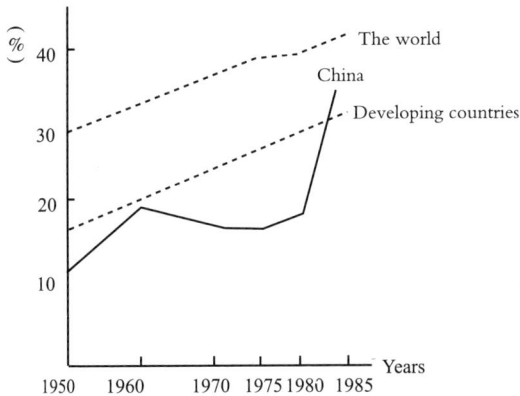

Fig. 1　Changes in the proportion of urban population in China,
the developing countries and the world

In my opinion, the second view is debatable. The urban population we refer to includes all the people within the jurisdiction of a city or township. The classification of an area as a township is subject to the approval of the government of a province, autonomous region or municipality directly under the Central Government. The standard for the size of a township kept changing: by 1963, a township was supposed to have more than 2000 permanent residents, of whom more than 50 percent should be a non-agricultural population; after 1964, a township should have more than 3000 permanent residents, of whom more than 70 percent should be the non-agricultural population or, it should have 2500—3000 permanent residents, of whom more than 85 percent should be non-agricultural residents. The definition was revised in 1984: a township must have at least one county-level government department; or it must be an administrative area with a population less than 20000 and the seat of the government must have more than 2000 non-agricultural residents; or must be administrative area with a population more than 20000 and the non-agricultural residents at the seat of the government must be more than

10 percent of the area's total population; or it must be a miniature-inhabited area, remote area, small industrial area, small port, scenic spot or a border port that is considered necessary to be classified as a township even though its non-agricultural population is less than 2000.

By the new standard, total townships increased from 2968 in late 1983 to 6211 in late 1984, a 109 percent growth within one year[1]This situation deserves further analysis.

First, except in the cases of certain specified areas, there is no considerable difference between the new standard and the old one in terms of the minimum requirement for the size of the non-agricultural population. The requirement was more than 1 000 before 1953, 2100 after 1964, and 2000 after 1984. A difference does exist: the minimum proportion required of the non-agricultural population became smaller. However, of all the township population (134474121) in late 1984, 52 282521 were non-agricultural[2]A township should have been set up earlier in an area with such a population density and such a proportion of non-agricultural residents.

Some overseas experts noticed this situation long before. A 1984 report by the World Bank on China's economic development said, "The seat of a commune government is classified as a rural area even though it may have thousands of residents, many of whom work in non-agricultural fields. In many other countries, an area with a population of this magnitude would be classified as an urban area." The report attributed China's classification to its "unusual economic structure."[3] According to the report, a township in the United States must have a population of more than 2500, or a township must be an area with a population density of 400 people per square kilometer, except for farms, railroad stations, large parks, plants, airports, cemeteries, sea and lakes. The report held that not only the seat of a commune government, but also the suburbs of a city, should be considered an urban area. By this standard, it estimated that China's urban population made

① China Statistical Publishing House, *China Social Statistical Data*, 1985; China Cartography Press: A Handbook of Chinese Urban Population.
② Ibid.
③ World Bank, *Urbanization, International Experience and Prospects in China*, Meteorological Press, 1984.

up 34 percent of the country's total. ①

Therefore, both China's old standard and foreign standards suggest that the country's standard for a township adopted in 1984 is appropriate.

Secondly, reform and more flexible State policies accelerated the country's urbanization, and resulted in the growth of urban population and the proportion of non-agricultural population. The rural economic reform that started in the late 1970s, featuring a contract and responsibility system, turned a new leaf in China's agricultural history. Farmers were released from crop growing and became engaged in forestry, animal husbandry, sidelines and fishery; many specialized households emerged; township enterprises sprang up; and new modes of agriculture developed. All this indicates that China's agriculture has been in a state of transition from farming alone into a diversified agriculture. As a result, many farmers entered commercial market and urban areas, especially small townships.

On the other hand, after the start of urban economic reform, cities felt the need for closer economic relationships with rural areas and absorbed a large amount of rural surplus labor. Rural surplus labor flooded into urban areas on a greater scale and at a higher rate than ever before. This is a major cause of the rapid growth of the urban population in recent years.

Why did the reform and the greater number of State policies accelerate urbanization? Because they greatly promoted the national economy. Fig. 2 shows the process of urbanization and the growth of national income in the past 35 years②

According to Fig. 2, the country's urbanization progressed along with the growth of national income. In the 1950s, both national income and the proportion of urban population grew rapidly. After the proportion of agriculture in the national income dropped 6. 4 billion yuan in 1959 compared with a year before and dropped another 4. 4 billion yuan in 1960, the proportion of the urban population declined in the early 1960s. During the 10-year "Cultural Revolution, "the slow growth of national income resulted in slow urbanization progress. The economy picked up again after the reform started in late 1978. From 1978 to 1985, the national income grew 1. 27 times, the proportion of agriculture in the national income grew 1. 66

---

① Ibid.

② Same as 1.

times and the proportion of industry was doubled. As a result, the country's urban population grew 1. 22 times and the proportion of urban population increased from 17. 9 percent to 36. 6 percent. It should be pointed out that because of China's national conditions, the country's urbanization cannot be achieved by exploiting farmers. On the contrary, it depends on the development of agriculture and its productivity, Urbanization should be based on economic growth.

II. Reform and Changes of the Population Structure of Cities with Different Sizes of Population

China's economic reform has had different impact on cities with different sizes of population and economic conditions. In general, the impact is strongest, on townships, less strong on medium and small cities and least strong on large cities. Inevitably, this has resulted in changes in the population structure of different cities.

The first were the changes in the population structure in cities and townships. For years, the country's urbanization remained at a low level and many townships were undeveloped and played a weak role in linking urban and rural areas. The Situation changed in the economic reform. From 1981 to 1984, township population increased from 60. 31 million to 170. 37 million, a 1. 8 time growth; the proportion of township population in total urban population grew from 31. 2 percent to 40. 7 percent, and the proportion of cities's population declined from 68. 8 percent to 59. 3 percent. In 1985, the proportion of township population further grew to 44. 6 percent, and the proportion of cities' population dropped to 55. 4 percent. The history of urbanization in most nations indicates that this process brings about a period of prosperity for small towns. This was not true in China before the 1980s. Business in some townships even declined. The situation did not change until the reform started.

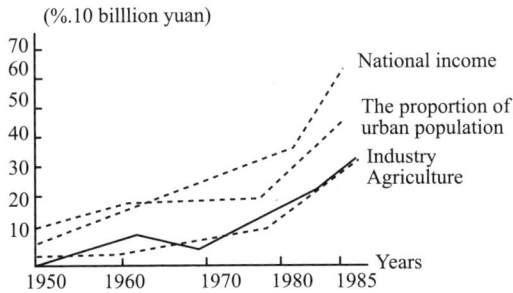

Fig. 2   **The proportion of China's urban population and the growth of national income between 1950 and 1985**

The second were the changes in the population structure in cities with different sizes of population. From 1981 to 1985, cities with populations less than 100000 decreased from 15 to 11, and the total population of these cities decreased from 1092000 to 530000; the proportion of their population in the total urban population also dropped from 0. 8 percent to 0. 25 percent; cities with populations of 100000 – 300000 increased from 86 to 93, their population increased from 16. 549 million to 19. 24 million, and the proportion of their population to the total urban population dropped from 11. 9 percent to 9. 1 percent due to the growth of the total urban population; cities with populations of 300000 – 500000 increased from 50 to 78, their population increased from 19. 551 million to 30. 4 million, and the proportion of their population grew from 14. 1 percent to 14. 35 percent; cities with a population of 500000 – 1 million, increased from 41 to 85, their population increased from 29. 33 million to 60. 61 million, and the proportion of their population grew from 21. 1 percent to 28, 6 percent; cities with populations of 1 – 2 million increased from 24 to 44, their total population increased from 29. 567 million to 54. 84 million, and the proportion of their population grew from 21. 3 percent to 25. 88 percent; there were still 12 cities with population of more than 2 million, but their total population increased from 42. 707 million to 45. 2 million, and the proportion of their population dropped from 30. 8 percent to 21. 8 percent.

From 1981 to 1985, cities with populations of 0. 5 – 1 million increased 1. 1 times (the highest rate of all cities), their total population grew 1. 1 times, and their proportion grew 7. 51 percent; cities with populations of 1 – 2 million increased

83. 3 percent, their populations increased 85. 5 percent, and their proportion grew 4. 58 percent; cities of 300000 – 500000 increased 8. 1 percent, their population increased 16. 6 percent, and their proportion grew 0. 25 percent. The proportion of population in the other three types of cities declined: it dropped 8. 99 percent in the cities with populations over 2 million, 2. 8 percent in the cities with populations of 100000 – 300000, and 0. 55 percent in the cities with populations of less than 100000.

The suburban agricultural population was not sorted out from these statistics. If only non-agricultural population is counted, the proportion of the population in cities with less than 500000 residents would grow: it would grow 2. 34 percent in the cities with populations of 100000 – 300000, 1. 54 percent in the cities with populations of 300000 – 500000, and 0. 84 percent in the cities with populations less than 100000. The proportion of the population in the cities with populations of 5 million or more would decline: it would drop 3. 16 percent in the cities with populations of 0. 5 – 1 million, 1. 52 percent in the cities with populations of more than 2 million, and 0. 04 percent in the cities with populations of 1 – 2 million.

Why is there such a big difference when the non-agricultural population is excluded? The reasons are: in the cities with populations less than 300000, suburban agricultural population grew slowly to increase the proportion of the non-agricultural population and to decrease the proportion of the cities population in the total urban population; in the cities with populations of 300000 – 500000, the cities' total population and their non-agricultural population both grew rapidly to increase the proportion of both categories; in the cities with populations of 0. 5 – 2 million, the proportion of the cities' total population and suburb an agricultural population both grew rapidly, although the proportion of the non-agricultural population declined; in the cities with populations over 2 million, the proportion of the non-agricultural population dropped and the proportion of the cities' population fell even more rapidly, since both the agricultural and the non-agricultural population grew slowly. In general, non-agricultural population grows faster in medium and small cities with populations less than 500000; agricultural population grows faster in cities with populations of 0. 5 – 2 million; and both the agricultural and non-agricultural populations grow slowly in cities with populations of more than 2 million. The growth of township population largely accounts for the changes in the proportion of urban population. Urban population structure is becoming increasingly rationalized.

Ⅲ. Reform and More Flexible Urban Policies

Urbanization in China has long been following the policy of "control of large cities, development of medium cities and prosperity of small cities. " This policy was reiterated in the State' s Sixth Five-Year Plan adopted in 1982 at the fifth National People' s Congress. So was it in the Seventh Five-Year plan, which urged to "effectively control the growth of the population in large cities but to promote the development of medium and small cities. " It suggested that cities grow to more than 400 and townships to more than 10000 by 1990. [1] I believe this policy is based on the national conditions of China and the experience of other nations. The reasons are as follows:

First, urbanization is a result of economic, political and cultural development, particularly an outcome of the development of productive forces. China has a population of more than a billion. The pace, the magnitude and the structure of the development of urban areas depend mainly on China's own economic capacity, especially the growth of its agriculture and the surplus of its farm produce. As was stated previously, whenever economy, especially agriculture, develops rapidly or slowly, So will the country's urbanization. A good example can be found in the 1960s, when agriculture declined while the number of employees, overgrew and forced the government to reduce the populations of cities. However, cities with different populations need different amounts of investment and depend on agriculture to different degrees. A smaller city is usually closer to rural areas, while a bigger one is farther away and needs an intermediary. Therefore, with a less developed economy, especially agriculture, it will be financially easier for small cities to obtain surplus rural labor.

Secondly, the prosperity of urban areas is often achieved at the expense of rural areas. Rising industry and undeveloped agriculture often result in an intensified

---

[1] *Documents of the 5th National People's Congress of PRC*, People's Press, 1983; *Documents of the 4th Plenary Session of the 5th National People's Congress*, People's Press. 1986.

conflict between urban and rural areas. The urbanization policy China adopted will help urban and rural areas develop in coordination, promote the growth of agriculture and better carry out the country's general economic policy of "agriculture as the foundation and industry as the leading factor."

Thirdly, in some developed countries, the rural population is no longer moving into urban areas as before. Those countries are currently at a higher level of urbanization. Residents tend to move out of downtown urban areas, where housing, traffic and pollution are becoming increasingly serious problems. Solving these problems requires large amounts of time and funding. China's policy of controlling the population growth in large cities while promoting the development of smaller cities will help avoid these problems.

However, this policy should not be interpreted mechanically. In fact, the policy is quite flexible, especially in large and small cities.

A city was originally an outcome of the development of business and trade. This is still true except for some politically or culturally oriented cities. When the reform promoted China's economic growth, some old regulations became unable to meet the needs of the new situation. After experiments, some provincial governments lifted restrictions and began to allow people from rural areas to stay and work in urban areas. Those people have no problem with their food supply since farmers can now sell their surplus grain to a free market after having fulfilled the State purchase quota. There are an increasing number of urban residents who do not receive the government supply of marketable grain.

Rural populations move into large cities as well as small ones; this calls up the need for population control in those cities. The country's annual total number of travellers increased 1. 2 times from 2. 53993 billion in 1987 to 5. 67092 billion in 1985. Of these, rail travelling increased 37. 6 percent, highway travelling increased 1. 9 times, travelling by water increased by 17. 2 percent and travelling by air increased 2. 2 times. [1] According to some surveys, the average daily mobile population is about 1 million in both Beijing and Shanghai; in Zhejiang Province, as many as 1. 5 million people, of whom 300, 000 are from Wenzhou, leave their

[1] *Wang Shuxin and Feng Litian*: *Beijng's Mobile Population in the Economic Reform*, *Population and Economy*, Vol. 1, 1986.

home to do non-agricultural jobs. According to a survey conducted in Beijing in 1985, few of the hotel guests in the city were farmers, but 31. 6 percent of the travelling people who stay in the dormitories of institutions were farmers; of those who stayed in people's homes, almost a half were farmers; in more than 250 farmers' markets in the city, 54. 2 percent of the farmers were from other provinces; of 2, 500 construction teams, more than 1, 800, or 75 percent, were from other provinces; 88. 9 percent of business travelers to Beijing, most of whom used to be farmers, were from rural areas①They stayed in the city for days, weeks, months or even years, and virtually became urban residents, posing a threat to the population control policy in the city.

When a large of number of farmers enter large cities, problems will arise in the supply of necessities, housing, traffic and public security. Can we block the population influx into the cities as we did before? I do not think so. Their flow into urban areas can both help the transfer of rural surplus labor and be good for urban development. Economic functions are different in large, medium-sized and small cities. Small cities have natural ties with rural economy. These ties help keep business and cultural exchanges between urban and rural areas. A large city is a center for economic, financial, scientific, educational and cultural activities, and is a hub of communications. These functions can influence and coordinate business in neighboring areas. In the economic reform, these functions will attract farmers into large cities. We should support such a great transition into large cities. Of course, it is not yet appropriate to allow farmers to enter cities freely, and the urban residence registration system should not yet be abolished, since that would bring disastrous consequences upon the urban economy.

The best way is to both support and control this trend and encourage surplus rural labor to be engaged in such urban projects as construction and services. In addition, the urban residence registration system should be used to control the mobile population in cities. Legal business activities should be protected and illegal ones should be punished in order to preserve a strong market.

---

① Same as 1.

A Macro-View of China's Elderly Population[*]

——An Analysis of the Sampling Survey in 1987 on China's Population above 60 Years of Age

"Life increases age and the increase of age ends life" —This is the subtitle on front cover of the first issue of the world's first *Elderly Journal* published in 1946. The "increase of age" that "ends life" has kept accelerating in the past 40 years. More gray-haired people are seen among street crowds, confronting mankind with a "silvery tide" —the aging of population—in addition to the rapid growth of population. Developed countries have been in the lead in becoming aging societies. Ever since the 1970s, when its fertility rate was dropping considerably, China's age structure has been changing quietly from a young type into an adult type and towards an elderly type. Given the current age structure in the country, the aging process of China's population is expected to proceed rapidly, exerting tremendous impact on the country's economy and social development as well as the population itself. The major problem is how to deal with an elderly population that will be more than four times larger than the current one, and how to meet its basic needs.

The Institute of Population Studies under the Chinese Academy of Social Sciences undertook a survey of China's elderly population and research on the social security of the elderly, a key project of the State Seventh Five-Year Plan. It also assisted the urban and rural sampling team of the State Statistical Bureau in completing in 1987 the sampling survey on China's elderly population, in order to provide a theoretical basis for the relevant State policy, the reform and the establish-

---

* See: *Chinese Journal of Population Science*, Volume1, Number2, 1989.

ment of a social security system for the elderly, and to prepare first-hand data for the country's research on the elderly population.

The survey was conducted strictly according to the principle of random samplying. A second sampling was made in cities and townships on the basis of the first that involved 150000 households, with a tolerance of ± 0. 5 percent. The survey covered 223 cities and townships, involving 17819 people more than 60 years old, and 830 counties, including 60000 regularly surveyed households, with 18936 people over 60 involved. A total of 36755 elderly people were surveyed in the urban and rural areas in all the 30 provinces, autonomous regions and municipalities in the country except Tibet and Taiwan. The survey was made on a scale larger than any other of the same kind in the world, thus ensuring its value in deducing the general situation among the country's elderly population.

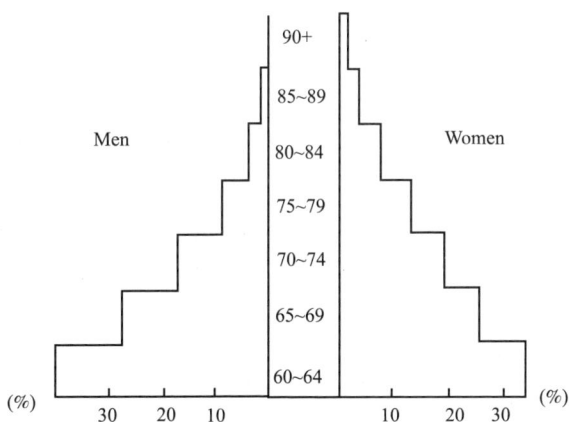

Fig. 1   Age Structure of the Chinese Elderly population in 1987

The standard time of the sampling was set on 12 midnight on June 30, 1987 and the whole survey was completed within the period from July 1st to 15th. In order to ensure the survey's quality, a trial sampling was conducted in Shanghai and Guangdong Province, and non-sampling errors were minimized through strict requirements in questionnaire design, interviewer training, form checking, computer input, logic examination and final checking and acceptance. It was proved that the sampling survey in 1987 on China's elderly population met the requirements of the designers with high quality and reliable data. Upon the basis of the survey's first lot of data, this treatise analyzes the characteristics of the country's elderly population and examines some of the most important factors that affect population, economic development and the reform of the social security system.

I . The Elderly Population's Age, Sex and Education: A Typical Pyramid Structure

（1） Age and sex strucures. Population scientists often liken a population's age and sex structure to a pyramid. This pyramid, however, is more typical among the elderly than in the whole population. This is because, excluding the effects of migration, a population's age and sex structures are generally determined by each year's newly born population and the mortality in different age and sex groups. The lower-age groups are more influenced by births, while the higher age-groups are more affected by deaths, and the population of higher-age groups is rarely more than that of lower-age groups since the mortality in different age groups among the elderly varies substantially. Although the sex ratio in the country's whole population is higher than 100—meaning there are slightly more males than females—the mortality of males is usually higher than that of females in the young or adult age groups, making the sex ratio lower than 100 among the elderly. A situation contrary to this phenomenon exists only in some 20 countries. The sampling survey in 1987 on China's elderly population indicates that the country's age and sex structures among the elderly are similar to those in most nations, i. e. a pyramid （see Fig. 1）.

Fig. 1 indicates that the proportion of both men and women decreases step by step along with age in elderly age groups, following the pattern of a regular triangle. For instance, men aged between 60 and 64 years make up 40. 4 percent of the total male elderly aged above 60 years, and women make up 33. 4 percent; the percentage of males aged above 60 years, and women make up 33. 4 percent; the percentage of males aged between 70 and 74 drops to 17. 6 and that of females to 19. 2. Men aged between 80 and 84 make up 4 percent and women 6. 7 percent; and the number of males above 90 years of age decreases to only 0. 3 percent and females to 0. 7 percent. The situation is similar in sex structure: the sex ratio among those aged between 60 and 64 is 107. 8, which drops to 82. 1 among those aged between 70 and 74, 53. 8 among those aged between 80 and 84, and 37. 5 among those aged above 90 years. In other words, the sex ratio drops as age in an elderly age group grows. the formula to calculate the median age of a total population is applicable here:

$$X_{md} = X_1 + \frac{\frac{\sum P_1}{2} - \overset{md-1}{\underset{0}{\sum}} P_1}{P_{md}} \cdot d$$

According to this formula, the median age of China's population above 60 years old in 1987 is calculated to be 67. 6. In other words, of the population aged above 60 years, those aged between 60 and 67. 6 make up one half and those aged above 67. 6 the half, which shows a rather big proportion of those of lower age among the elderly population. This is of tremendous importance in our knowledge of the status quo in the country's elderly population and in an analysis of their health, employment, self-caring ability and participation in social activities, and is of value for reference in the establishment of a new old-age caring system that meets the needs in the aging process of the population.

(2) Education. The educational structure of the elderly is also shaped like a pyramid: the proportion of the educated drops along with age growth in various age groups, whether men or women. As in the previous censuses and population registrations, the educational levels of the elderly were classified in this survey into the six categories of university, polytechnic school, senior high school, junior high school, primary school, weak literacy and illiteracy. The statistics so obtained, however, can only help in a comparison on the same level rather than on a population's educational level in general, which requires an overall and comparable index such as the population's average length of schooling. But in effect, such length is indefinite since the lengths of schooling vary from school to school and from time to time. Therefore, before the data in this field are obtained, it would be more appropriate to calculate the population's educational index on the basis of the approximate value of its average length of schooling, rather than on the length itself. Suppose the approximate value of the length of schooling is 16 years for a per-

son with university education background, 11 years for one with senior high school education, 8 years for one with junior high school education, 4 years for one with primary school education and 0. 25years for one with weak literacy or an illiterate, then the educational index of the country's elderly population aged above 60 years is 2. 00 according to the survey. The index varies considerably among different age groups, with 2. 67 among those aged between 60 and 64, 1. 57 among those aged between 70 and 74 and 1. 10 among those aged between 80 and 84.

The educational level among the elderly is lower than that of the whole population. The national educational index in 1982, obtained by using the above method, was 4. 65, 2. 3 times that elderly, indicating a low educational level in the previous years. The difference in the educational structure among the elderly between the two sexes and between urban and rural areas also deserve attention. The survey indicates a higher educational level among the elderly males than among the females. For instance, the educational index of the elderly males in cities is 5. 29, 3. 1 times that of elderly females, and the index of the elderly males in counties is 2. 13, 4. 5 times that of females. This shows the sexism in education in the old China. There is also a large gap between the educational levels among the elderly in urban and rural areas. According to the survey , the educational index among the elderly in cities is 3. 64, 2. 98 times the 1. 22 in counties, showing the backward rural education before the 1950s.

II. The Elderly's History of Marriage, Reproduction and Family: The Old-Fashioned Way

All the surveyed people were born before 1927 and most were married at an early age and have extended families with several children.

(1) Marriage. Compared with the marital status of the whole population, the elderly population has a lower marriage rate and higher rate of being widowed. For instance, the census in 1982 showed a marriage rate of 93. 9 percent among 30 – 34—year—old people and 93. 4 percent among the 40 – 44—year—olds. According to the 1987 survey, only 60. 3 per cent of the elderly were married and the percentage dropped to below 20 among those aged above 82 years; only 0. 6 percent of the 30 – 34—year—olds and 2. 5 percent of the 40 – 44—year—olds were wid-

owed, while the percentage rose to 36.6 among the 60—year—olds—or—up and 75.0 among those aged above 80 years. The "low and high" characteristic is mainly a result of higher mortality among the elderly, especially among males; it becomes even more noticeable as age grows and is especially true among women. In general, the marriage rate of adult females is only slightly higher than that of males and there is little difference before 50 years of age. The gap becomes quite large among the elderly. For instance, in the age group of 65 – 69—year—olds surveyed in 1987 in Chinese cities, the marriage rate was 88.3 percent among males and 57.7 percent among females; and it was 42.9 percent among the males above 90 years of age and only 3.7 percent among the females of the same age group. In contrast with those aged between 65 and 69 years, where the widowed were 10.2 percent of males and 39.6 percent of females, 50.0 percent of the males aged above 90 years and 92.6 percent of the females of the same age group were widowed. This accounts for the fact that women make up a majority of the widowed elderly. In this sense, elderly women deserve special attention.

Table 1 A Comparison on the Age of the First Marriage
Between Those Aged Above 60 Years and Those Above 15 Years

First Marriage Age (Years)	People Aged Above 60 Years	People Aged Above 15 Years
15 – 19	47.0	7.5
20 – 24	35.2	72.8
25 – 29	11.8	15.8
30 – 34	4.2	2.8
35 +	1.8	1.1
Total	100.0	100.0

Note: The first marriage age of those aged above 15 years was obtained in 1986. Source: *Data of the Sampling Survey on the Changes in Population*, 1986.

The major difference between the marriage rate among the elderly and that among the whole population is the earlier marriage age of the former. Table 1 shows the seriousness of early marriage among the elderly: 47.0 percent of those aged above 60 years were married between 15 and 19 years of age, while in 1986, only

7. 5 percent of those aged above 15 years were married within that age peri-od. Among the elderly, the older one, the more likely one' is to have been married at an early age. Of those first married between 15 and 19, 43. 8percent are aged between 60 and 64 years, which is lower than the average (47. 0 percent) among the total elderly population; 46. 0 percent are aged between 65 and 69 years, which is close to the average, and 49. 4 percent are aged between 70 and 74 years, which is higher than the average. The percentage rises to 50. 8 among those aged between 75 and 79 years, 53. 8 among those aged between 80 and 84 years, 54. 3 among those aged between 85 and 89 years, and 61. 0 among those aged above 90 years. Correspondingly, the percentage of those first married at an early age declines along with the growth of age. For instance, those married between 20 and 24 years of age make up 37. 1 percent of 60 – 64—year—olds, 33. 7percent of 70 – 74—year—olds, 33. 3 percent of 80 – 84—year—olds and 26. 4 percent of 90—year—olds.

（2）Fertility. Closely related to early marriage in the elderly population is an early age for having children and a larger number of children. According to the sur-vey, 14. 5 percent of the elderly women began to have children before 20 years of age, 75. 1 percent before 25 years of age and only 24. 9 percent after 25 years of age. In contrast, a survey in 1986 shows that among15 – 49—year—old women, who are considered fertile, those who gave birth between the ages of 15 and 19 made up 2. 6 percent, 11. 9 percentage points lower than what the survey of the elderly shows; those who gave birth between 15 and 24 years of age accounted for 53. 9 percent, 21. 2 percentage points lower than the figures in the survey on the elderly; and those who began to have children after 25 years of age amounted to 46. 1 percent, 21. 2 percentage points higher than the sampling of the elderly women.

An early marriage is often followed by productiveness. According to the sur-veys, women who have one child make up 5. 7 percent of those aged above 60 years, but 10. 2 percent of those between 30 and 34 years of age, a gap of 4. 5 percentage points; women who have two children amount to 7. 3 percent of the elderly, but 44. 9 percent among the 30 – 34—year—olds, a difference of 37. 6 percentage points; women who have three children account for 9. 3 percent of the elderly, and 25. 0 percent of the 30 – 34—year—olds; those who have four children make up 12. 2 percent among both elderly women and 30 – 34—year—olds; and those who have five or more children, however, make up 65. 5 percent of the elderly women in contrast to the 7. 7 percent among the 30 – 34—year—olds. Those who have eight or more children make up 27. 1 percent of the mothers aged above 60 years. (Source of the 1986 statistics: *Data of the Sampling Survey on the Changes in Population*, 1986)

On the other hand, the number of children each elderly woman had is closely related to their educational background. Of all the elderly women surveyed, those who have received higher education make up 22. 6 percent of the women with three children; those with senior high school background make up 22. 0 percent of the women with four children; a majority of those with junior high school education have three, four, five or six children, with mostly three or four on the average; those who have received only primary education and literate women account respectively for 19. 5 and 26. 5 percent of the elderly women with eight or more children. In general, the more education a woman receives, the smaller number of children she is likely to have.

(3) Family. The formation and development of a family, a basic unit of population reproduction, indicates the characteristics of such reproduction. So does the family of an elderly person. There are as many similarities as differences between the families of the elderly and those of young and middle-aged people. A comparison will help us understand the evolution of family relations over the past 100 years. The 1987 survey of China's elderly population indicates that in spite of the existence of a large number of extended families among elderly people, the extended family has been affected by the new trend and that many such families are disintegrating. This can be felt through both the size and structure of the families.

According to the survey, the average size of the families of the elderly is 4. 9 persons, 0. 5 person more than the national average of 4. 4 from the 1982 census, and 0. 7 persons more than the 4. 2 persons as found in the sampling made in 1987 of 1 percent of the whole population. Currently, five-member families are the majority among the elderly, making up 18. 9 percent in the 1987 survey, while four-member families are the majority of the whole population, making up 19. 5 percent in the 1982 census. Next are six-member families among the elderly, making up 16. 7 percent in the 1987 survey, and five-member families in the whole population, making up 18. 4 percent in the 1982 census. Occupying the third place are four-member families among the elderly, making up 14. 1 percent in the 1987 survey, and three-member families among the whole population, making up 16. 0 percent in the 1982 census. The elderly have a slightly higher percentage of two-member families, but a lower percentage of one-member, three-member and four-member families in comparison with the whole population. The proportion of five-member families is far higher among the elderly than in the whole population. The bigger size of families of the elderly, however, is still relative. According to historical records, the Chinese families had an average of 5. 5 members in the early Ming Dynasty (1368 - 1644) and 5. 2 members in 1912. The family size at both times is bigger than the current family size of the elderly, and ever bigger than the average of the whole population. (*Source*: *Statistics in China's Census Records*, *Land Ownership and Land Taxes Through the Ages* by Liang Fangzhong, Shanghai People's Publishing House, 1982)

Table 2   A Comparison Among the Per Capita
Monthly Income in Cities, Townships and Counties

Per capita monthly income (Yuan)	Cities (%)	Townships (%)	Counties (%)
Total	100. 0	100. 0	100. 0
No income	20. 0	24. 1	0
Below 15 yuan	3. 2	5. 8	9. 4
16 – 25	4. 1	8. 4	26. 7
26 – 45	8. 7	11. 4	44. 6
71 – 100	20. 9	16. 2	3. 3
101 – 150	16. 7	14. 2	0. 8
151 – 200	7. 0	4. 3	0. 2
Above 201 yuan	3. 6	1. 1	0. 1

Closely related to family size, three-generation families are the majority among the elderly, making up 50. 0 percent in the 1987 survey; the second place is occupied by two-generation families, which make up 29. 2 percent, and the third by single-couple families, which account for 12. 9 percent. Single-member or four-or-more-member families make up respectively 3. 4 and 3. 1 percent. This indicates that the families of the elderly generally have been freed from the big extended family structure that was common in the feudal times. The survey also shows that two-member and three-member families make up respectively 34. 6and 36. 9 percent in cities and 31. 1 and 37. 6 percent in townships. In these two areas, however, nuclear families have not yet become the majority, as among the whole population, and that extended families are still transforming into two-generation or single-couple families, although two-member families among the elderly already have a higher percentage among all families. This shows that the extended families of the elderly have been shrinking at an increasing rate along with the development of a market-oriented economy and the process of modernization. Therefore, the reform of the social security system for the elderly deserves adequate attention.

III. Economic Conditions and Support of the Elderly: the Co-Existence of Agricultural and Industrial Types

The traditional respect for the elderly in China, as well as in other parts of the Orient, has won admiration from some Westerners. How, then did such tradition take shape? Does it have any economic basis? I believe it does. The basis for this respect is the traditional agricultural economy. In an agricultural society, such as old China, that was short of a market-oriented economy, production techniques developed slowly and experience became a key factor that determined a person's technical level. Since experience often accumulates along with the growth of age, the elderly became the symbols of experience and techniques and the authorities in production, as is expressed in the Chinese saying: "An overgrown ginger is hotter. " As a result, the elderly won respect from both their descendants and the public, and it became right and proper for young people to show filial piety to their seniors and support them.

The situation is entirely different in an industrial society. Tough business competition and rapid progress of science and technology have greatly devalued the experience that the elderly acquired in an agricultural society. Unable to keep up with technological developments and the swift tempo of life, many elderly people have fallen behind as technical authorities. Their superiority has been replaced by age discrimination and an inferior and unfavourable position. Consequently, a new system to support the elderly came into being in modern society.

In a developing country like China, low productivity and the deep influence of the traditional agricultural economy in rural areas on one hand, and rapid industrialization and growth of a market—oriented economy on the other, are bound to have a joint impact on the economic conditions of the elderly. The 1987 survey shows such an impact, which has helped shape new economic conditions and support for the elderly in the current period.

(1) Economic conditions (see Table 2). Table 2 shows that nearly half of the elderly in cities have a monthly income between 46 and 150 yuan, and that more than 85 percent of the elderly in rural areas have a monthly income between 16 and 70 yuan. Suppose monthly averages of less than 45 yuan, between 46 and 100 yuan, and more than 101 yuan are considered low, medium and high levels of income. The medium income earners make up the highest percentage in cities and townships, with 36.7 percent in cities and 30.7 percent in townships, and 80.7 percent of the rural people are low income earners. The second highest percentage is high income earners in cities (27.3 percent), low income earners in townships (25.6 percent) and medium income earners in rural areas (18.2 percent). Next is low income earners in cities (16.0 percent), medium income earners in townships. (19.6 percent) and high income earners in rural areas (1.1 percent). Although the wide gap between the monthly income of the elderly in urban and rural areas can be deducted when the difference of prices and commercialization in the two areas are taken into account, there is no doubt that the rural elderly have lower incomes and their economic status in their families is lower than those in urban areas. Therefore, they need more economic security. This is an indubitable conclusion reached in the 1987 survey.

According to the survey, 41.5 percent of elderly people in cities, 39.9 percent in townships, 18.7 percent in counties and less than half in rural areas than in townships have the final say in their family economy. The elderly who have no say in their family economy account for 18. 5 percent in cities, 20. 5 percent in townships, 49. 7 percent in counties and 2. 5 times as many in rural areas as in townships.

(2) Support. The economic conditions of the elderly are determined by their income sources and support. According to the 1987 survey, the elderly in urban areas depend on their own salaries, pensions, support from their spouses, support from their childen, support from their relatives and government subsidies. The sources of support for the elderly in rural areas include their own income from work, support from their spouses, children, relatives, government and the collective. Those who depend on their pensions make up 56. 1 percent in cities and 47. 5 percent in townships; those who depend on their 4 children account for 22. 4 percent in cities and 27. 8 percent in townships; and 13. 0 percent of the elderly in cities and 14. 3 percent in townships depend on their spouses. These three categories make up approximately 90 percent of the sources of support for the elderly in urban areas, and the other three account for the rest. Therefore, pensions and support from children and spouses serve as the "three pillars" in the living expenses of the elderly in urban areas.

The situation in rural areas is very different: 67. 5 percent of the rural elderly depend on their children, 26. 2 percent on the income from their own work and 5. 0 percent on their spouses. The three sources, serving as the "three pillars" of the support of the elderly in rural areas, make up 98 percent of their living expenses, while the other three account for no more than 2 percent. In short, the elderly in urban areas mainly depend on the government and their former employers, while these in rural areas largely depend on their families, particularly their children. The social security system in the whole country is characterized by the transition from the "agricultural type" to the "industrial type. "

IV . The Elderly Population's Employment: Self—Support and Contribution

The above-mentioned facts indicate that some elderly people support themselves by their own work. This tendency, which is growing along with the progress of the country's modernization program and the improvement of the elderly people's health, deserves thorough study.

(1) Employment. In this study, the employed elderly are those in urban areas who continue to work, first begin to work or resume work after retirement, and those in rural areas who continue to work. In this sense, the employment rate among the elderly population, as shown in the 1987 survey, is 15.0 percent in cities, with 20.4 percent among men and 10.2 per cent among women; 11.6 percent in townships, with 17.9 percent among men and 6.0 percent among women. and 31.5 percent in counties, with 53.0 percent among men and 12.4 percent among women. The total employment rate is higher in rural than in urban areas, and men's employment rate is from twice to four times as high as women's. More than half of the elderly men above 60 in rural areas are still doing jobs of different intensity. This indicates that on the one hand, elderly people in rural areas still have to earn their own living, given the nation's low productivity and backward agricultural production and, on the other, the involvement of the rural elderly in economic activities will affect both the country's economic development and the elderly people themselves.

The pro-retirement employment among the urban elderly tend to increase along with the progress of the reform of the country's economic system and the employed personnel system. The survey shows that the pro-retirement employment rate is 18.0 percent in cities, 3.0 percentage points higher than the general employment rate among the elderly there, and 13.2 percent in townships, 1.6 percentage points higher than the general employment rate among the elderly population there. The situation helps to increase elderly people's income, improve their sociability and diversify their lives, although it also has created certain social problems, such as worsening job shortages, a problem that will become increasingly serious in the next two or three decades when China will be confronted with a surplus of labor.

After having been able to make ends meet, the Chinese people are becoming comfortable. The employment of the elderly during this transitional period is basically intended for survival. This is especially true in rural areas. In urban areas, 34.0 percent of the elderly in cities—the highest percentage—work to meet basic economic needs; the percentage is 32. 6 in townships, where 36. 6 per cent of the elderly claim to work for personal development, apparently as a result of the rapid growth of townships that provide more job opportunities.

In Western countries, people are categorized into "white collar" or "blue collar" workers by the nature of their jobs. As China's economic structure and employment structure are undergoing a change, it will be oversimplifying the matter if we also divide people into merely "white collar" or "blue collar" workers. Therefore, a transition is needed. Suppose professionals, officials and office workers are considered "white collar workers. " business and service people are considered "gray collar workers" and industrial workers, farmers, foresters, herdsmen and fishermen are regarded as "blue collar workers. " Then the employment motive of the biggest proportion (approximately 40 percent) of the elderly "white collar" workers is personal development, while for the biggest proportion (approximately 42 percent) of the elderly "gray and blue collar workers," it is for the basic economic needs for survival.

(2) Occupations. The survey divides the employed elderly into eight occupational categories. In the order of percentage, the elderly are employed in cities as industrial workers (22. 9 percent), office workers (17. 6 percent), professionals (16. 5 percent), service people (14. 3 percent), officials (9. 8 percent), business people (7. 1 percent), farmers, foresters, herdsmen and fishermen (0. 4 percent) and others (11. 6 percent), and in townships as office workers (21. 8 percent), industrial workers (17. 9 percent), professionals (17. 9 percent), service people (12. 8 percent), business people (12. 1 percent), officials (10. 3 percent), farmers, foresters, herdsmen and fishermen (0. 5 percent) and others (6. 0 percent) . This shows that a large proportion (approximately a third) of elderly employees in both cities and townships are involved in production as industrial workers and professionals, while business and service people account for no more than a quarter. The rural elderly's involvement in production is even more noticeable. The survey shows that farmers, foresters, herdsmen and fishermen still make up 86. 5 percent of the employed elderly there. Nonetheless, the employment structure has changed considerably. In cities, the percentage of industrial workers, officials and professionals has been declining and that of service and

business people and office workers has been on the rise. Of all the industrial workers who have transferred into other occupations, 34. 4 percent have transferred into
services, and, respectively, 13. 4 percent and 13. 1 percent have transferred into
offices and businesses. Of all the officials who have transferred into other occupations, 51. 2 percent have become office workers and others have become industrial
workers and professionals. Of all the professionals who have transferred into other
occupations, 45. 3 percent have become office workers and 17. 0 percent have
become service people.

Table 3

The Elderly Population's Medical Expenses (%)

	Nation	Cities	Townships	Counties
Total	100. 0	100. 0	100. 0	100. 0
Paid	71. 72	6. 7	45. 1	94. 7
Partially paid	9. 9	22. 1	19. 2	3. 1
Free	18. 4	51. 2	35. 7	2. 2

Although a large proportion of elderly employees are still involved in production, these changes represent the tendency of employment among the elderly population. They have opened new fields where the elderly can continue to contribute to
the society, and have suggested a solution to the problem about the competition in
the production labor market between the elderly and younger people. If properly
guided, the problem regarding the employment of the elderly can be solved properly, which is beneficial to both society and the elderly themselves.

V. Medical Care, Health and Activities of the Elderly Popula-
tion

(1) Medical care (see Table 3)

Table. 3 indicates that of all the elderly in the country, the ratio of those who
enjoy free medical care, those who pay part and those who pay all of their medical
expense is roughly 2 : 1 : 7. However, there is a big difference between urban and
rural areas. Most of the elderly in urban areas enjoy at least partially free medical

care. Those who have free medical service or pay parts of their medical expenses make up 73. 3 percent in cities and 54. 9 percent in townships, while a majority of the rural elderly people pay their own medical expenses. Those who enjoy free or partially free medical service account for only 5. 3 percent of the elderly in rural areas, while the remaining 94. 7 percent need to pay all of their medical expenses. Correspondingly, 25. 4 percent of the elderly in cities and 14. 9 percent in townships need not worry about medical expenses, 19. 8 percent in cities and 17. 0 percent in townships pay no more than 10 yuan of medical expenses each year, and 23. 0 percent in cities and 27. 6 percent in townships pay an annual total of 11 - 50 yuan for medical care. The three categories of the elderly make up 68. 2 percent in cities and 59. 5 percent in townships, who are considered as having no or little burden of medical expenses. Only a small number of people feel overburdened: 14. 3 percent in cities and 20. 3 percent in townships can hardly afford their medical fees. This indicates that medical service is generally guaranteed for the elderly in urban areas. In counties, 54. 7 percent of the elderly pay no more than 10 yuan each year for medical service, and 29. 8 percent pay an annual total of 11 - 50 yuan for such service. Those who pay an annual total of more than 51 yuan make up 15. 5 percent of the rural elderly, which is considered a burden given the undeveloped economy and low income level in rural areas. Of all the 18936 rural elderly peoples surveyed, 61. 8 percent said it was difficult for them to pay medical expenses. Apparently, medical service is still a problem for most rural elderly people, and needs to be solved as soon as possible. The age-specific difference in medical fees for the elderly deserves particular attention (see Fig. 2).

According to Fig. 2, about 10 percent of the elderly in the whole country pay part of their medical fees regardless of their age. However, along with their growth in age, the number of those who pay all of their medical fees increases, while the number of those who enjoy free medical service decreases. For instance, among those between 60 and 64 years old, 65. 4 percent pay their own medical fees, and 18. 4 percent enjoy free medical service; among those aged between 70 and 74 years, 76. 5 percent pay their own medical expenses and 13. 7percent have free medical care; among those aged between 80 and 84 years, 82. 4 percent pay their medical fees and 7. 8 percent enjoy medical service for free; and among those aged above 90 years, 86. 5 percent pay for their medical service and 3. 7 percent enjoy free medical care. In short, the older one gets, the more medical expenses one needs to pay. Therefore, it is important to ensure the medical security of the elderly, particularly the oldest.

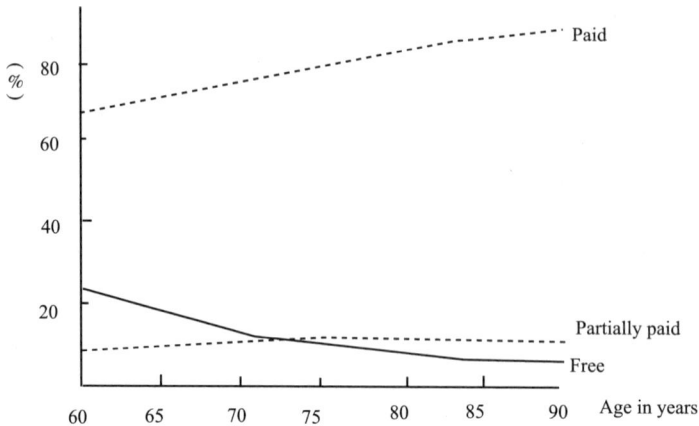

Fig. 2 Age – Specific Medical Expense of the Chinese Elderly in 1987

（2）Health. The 1987 survey shows that 16. 3 percent of the country's elderly are in excellent health, 28. 3 percent are good, 27. 9 percent are fair, 17. 6 percent are poor, 9. 3 percent are very poor and the condition of 0. 7 percent are unknown. Generally healthy elderly people make up more than 70 percent of the total. As a result, 83. 8 percent of the elderly can take care of themselves, and there is little difference between urban and rural areas—the percentage is 86. 6 in cities, 85. 6 in townships and 82. 2 in counties.

However, men's health conditions are better than women's. For instance, in cities, those with good health make up 49. 4 percent among men and 42. 3 percent among women, a gap of 7. 1 percentage points; in townships, 49. 5 percent of men and 42. 7 percent of women have good health, a gap of 6. 8 percentage points; and in counties, 47. 7 percent of men and 40. 4 percent of women have good health, a difference of 7. 3 percentage points. In contrast, of those who have poor health, there are 5. 6 percentage points more women than men in cities, 5. 4 percentage points more women than men in townships and 4. 1 percentage points more women than men in counties. Elderly women's health cannot be effectively improved without finding out the reasons for their poor health. At first sight, the reasons may include the bigger proportion of women among those of high age, who generally have worse health than younger people; the higher income of elderly men than of women's, which affects one's living and nutrition conditions; and the greater opportunity of men to receive medical care and more respect from the public. In the efforts to improve the health conditions of the whole elderly population, the improvement of the health of elderly women should be given the top priority.

(3) Activities. According to the survey, elderly people spend the biggest amount of their time sleeping—8.6 hours in cities, 8.9 hours in townships and 9.3 hours in counties; the second biggest amount of time is spent on housework—3.5 hours in cities and townships and 3.0 hours in counties; and the third biggest amount of their time is spent by those in urban areas on watching television—1.8 hours in cities and 1.5 hours in townships, and by those in counties on working (2 hours) . Elderly people in urban areas spend the fourth biggest amount of time on working—1.4 hours in cities and 1.3 hours in townships, and those in counties on visiting friends (1.9 hours) ; and elderly people in urban areas spend the fifth biggest amount of time on public activities—0.9 hours in cities and 1.2 hours in townships, and those in counties on entertainment (0.5 hours) . These statistics indicate that elderly people's division of time on sleeping, working (including occupational jobs and housework) , studying and entertainment generally follows the ratio of 9 : 5 : 4 : 3 in cities and 9 : 5 : 1 : 9 in rural areas. The most noticeable difference between the daily activities of elderly people in urban areas and those in rural areas is that the former spend three more hours each day on studying and entertainment, including watching television. The big difference between the cultural life among the elderly in urban and rural areas accounts for the fact that 31.4 percent—the biggest percentage—of the surveyed rural elderly listed the lack of cultural facilities as the "biggest problem. " which indicates the acute need of the rural elderly for variety in their cultural life. We should examine the change among the rural elderly from the viewpoint of the 1980s.

Elderly people have become considerably more sociable along with the implementation of the State's more flexible policy, the development of a market-oriented economy and the improvement of people's livelihoods and health conditions. In the 1987 survey, cities and townships were set as the boundaries of urban residence areas, and villages the boundaries of rural residence areas. Those in cities stepped out beyond their boundaries an annual 0.6 times per capita, those in townships 1.0 time and those in rural areas 6.3 times. Although the scopes of activities of urban and rural elderly are not exactly comparable, these statistics do indicate that it is no longer appropriate to consider elderly people only sticking to their homeland. While Chinese elderly still infrequently leave their homes and their purposes for going out are very different from those of the elderly in developed countries, such purposes have some distinct characteristics. First, going to rural fairs makes up 48.4 percent—the highest percentage—of the trips of the rural elderly, indicating the close ties between their activities and an increasingly market-oriented rural economy. Secondly, in terms of percentage, travel as a new out door activity now ranks the second (16.5 percent) in townships and the third (13.8 percent) in cities of all the out door activities of the elderly. Even in the countryside travel accounts for 0.6 percent of the rural elderly's out door activities, It is quite a new phenomenon that some elderly people who were never away from their homes now travel for sightseeing, which indicates a change in the activities of the Chinese elderly that is bound to occur in an increasingly modernized society.

Integrating Theory
with Practice to Promote
Population Science*

The third plenary session of the 11th Central Committee of the Chinese Communist Party, held in December 1978, turned a new leaf in the history of socialism in China by shifting the Party's focus to the modernization program. The adoption of the ideological guideline: "seeking truths from facts", helped emancipate the country's thinking, ushered in a spring season in scientific development and brought life to the country's population studies, which have flourished since then in an unprecedented manner. It should be admitted that such a shift in focus, and the adoption of the new guideline, were prerequisites to creating a climate propitious to the development of population studies in China.

The economic growth brought on by the shift in the Party's focus brought many existing problems in production, consumption and employment to the surface. As people began to ponder the rapid increase in population, questions were raised concerning the population theories and policies of the three decades following the founding of the People's Republic in 1949. Therefore, it is of particularly far-reacing significance for Chinese population scholars to commemorate the 10th anniversary of the third plenary session of the Party's 11th Central Committee.

It is well known that China's population studies were active in the early 1950s. Unfortunately, however, this active period did not last long. The unfounded criticism of noted economist Ma Yinchu's essay "A New Theory on Population" withered the new branch of science before it was able to develop. Population re-

* See: *Chinese Journal of Population Science*, Volume, Number4, 1989.

search in China did not revive until the 1970s, and particularly not until after the third plenary session of the Party's llth Central Committee. In the past 10 years, population science has grown into an independent research area in China. This is evident from the facts that the number of population scholars has increased, specialized research institutions have been set up, dozens of articles on population have been published, some 40 magazines on the subject have been founded, a large amount of census or survey statistics and other data has been provided and tremendous progress has been made in research methodology.

The growth of China's population studies in the past 10 years has distinct characteristics. As expressed in the ancient Chinese saying; "Reviewing the past helps one to understand the present and the future", reviewing and summarizing these characteristics will undoubtedly help promote the future development of the population research in China. The characteristics include the following:

First, Marxism had been taken as a guideline in population research. As popu-lation studies had long been a "troubled area", many people maintained lingering fears, even in 1979, when the research began to thrive. Under the circumstances, it was natural for them to start with the study of Marxist theories on population, including those on the "two kinds of production" (material production and human reproduction), in order to find patterns of population development in a socialist society. It needs to be clarified that the adoption of Marxism as a guideline should mean the study of Marxist viewpoints and methodology in population research, rather than a contentment with quotations from Marxist predecessors. While Marx, Engels, Lenin, Stalin, Mao Zedong and other revolutionaries expounded many principles on population, they did not, nor was it possible for them to, provide ready solutions to all problems related to population, especially those in a socialist society. We must keep to historical and dialectical materialism in their fundamental stand, viewpoints and methodology.

Second, great importance has been attached to surveys. A large number of in-depth surveys including censuses, samplings and surveys on special subjects have been conducted in the past 10 years. Nationwide studies of this sort include the following:

(A) The census of 1982. This was the third census since the founding of the

People's Republic, and the largest in the world; covering more than a billion people. This survey had 19 items, many more than the previous two surveys had. 13 of these items were filled out by individuals, and the remaining 6 by households. In order to minimize the error rate, the survey was checked and appraised on each level throughout the sampling according to preset standards. For the first time, electronic computers were used to treat the statistics.

(B) The sampling survey of 0. 1 per cent of the country's population on fertility, organized by the State Commission of Family Planning. A total 815 work units and 1017574 people were selected as samples, and 310485 women aged between 15 and 67 years were surveyed. The standard time for the survey was set at zero hours, July 1, 1982, and the actual survey was completed between September 1 and 15 of the same year. A post-survey check showed that the error rate of the sampling survey was 1. 07 per cent, which is considered to be very low.

(C) The survey on the basic conditions of Chinese children, sponsored by the United Nations Children's Fund and conducted in 1983 by the Department of Society of the State Statistical Bureau. A total of 179000 children aged between 0 and 14 years were surveyed and data were obtained on the children's education as well as their physical and mental health.

(D) The nationwide sampling survey on the handicapped, conducted by the Ministry of Civil Affairs, and the State Statistical Bureau, from April 1 to mid—May 1987 in 29 provinces, municipalities and autonomous regions. The survey covered 424 counties, 369816 households and 1579314 persons; 1. 5 percent of the country's total population. It was learned that there were 51. 64 million handicapped persons in the country. The statistics obtained categorized those who were handicapped in hearing, speech, sight, body or mind.

(E) The sampling survey on the nation's elderly population aged above 60 years. This project was listed in the State's Seventh Five-Year Plan and was undertaken by the Institute of Population Studies under the Chinese Academy of Social Science with the assistance of the Urban and Rural Sampling Team of the State Statistical Bureau. The survey covered 233 cities and townships, 830 counties and 36. 775 elderly people aged above 60 years in 28 provinces, autonomous regions and municipalities, not including Tibet and Taiwan. The standard time of the survey was set at zero hours on June 30, 1987. Comprehensive and systematic data were abtained on patterns in the elderly population's age, sex, education, marital status, fertility, families, income, employment, means of support, medical care, health, activities and family economic status.

(F) The sampling survey on China's fertility and contraception, started on July 1, 1988 by the State Commission of Family Planning. The survey has been completed and the statistics obtained are being processed and analyzed. The survey involved more than two million people in all 30 provinces, municipalities and autonomous regions. Comprehensive and systematic data will be obtained on the pregnancy, parturition, contraception, marriage, and mortality of the female population aged between 15 and 57 years.

(G) The survey on China's ethnic minorities, which was started in 1984 by China Population Information Center, and is not yet complete. Data have been collected on 10 ethnic minorities, including the Uygurs.

Other large-scale population surveys on provincial, municipal and regional levels include: a) the survey on the migration of populations in 74 cities and townships, listed as a key project in the State's Seventh Five-Year Plan and undertaken by the Institute of Population studies under the Chinese Academy of Social Sciences, b) the survey on the country's fertility, conducted in April 1985 by the State Statistical Bureau in the provinces of Hebei and Shaanxi and in Shanghai, and c) the 1982 survey on families and marriage in five cities, including Beijing.

These surveys have furthered China's population studies by allowing us to acquire first-hand data on major aspects of the status quo in the Chinese population, and to fill many gaps in the research. Much information has been provided to the relevant government departments. Also, personnel has been trained on computer use in the process of the surveys.

Currently, overseas scholars are more impressed with China's population surveys than with their analysis. Now that China's population is nearing 1.1 billion. A deeper understanding of the country's population, careful surveys and indepth analyses are needed. Follow-up surveys and surveys about special subjects should also be done. The best possible use should be made of data obtained through these surveys. More final products from rough data are needed in population research.

Third, research on basic theories has gone hand in hand with that on applied population science. Not long ago, there was practically no population research done in China. In the past 10 years, research on basic population theories has developed rapidly. More than a dozen works, as well as textbooks and reference books have been published. Meanwhile, progress has also been made in research on the practical aspects of population science. The population question is a major factor in studies dealing with contemporary China's national condition. The hindrance of a large population to China's modernization drive has been analyzed in the research on how to control population growth. Family planning departments, supported by statistics, have expounded the necessity of family planning as a basic national policy. Techniques for the prediction of population development have been improved. Contraceptive methods have been bettered by adapting techniques discovered overseas to the special requirements and preferences of Chinese women. Remarkable progress has been made in research on China's strategies and goals in population control, the country's population capacity, future tendencies in population development and prediction of the population in the year of 2000.

Research on the quality of the country's population has promoted the combination of population studies with research on eugenics and efforts to raise the nation's educational level beneficial analyses have been made on the population's mortality by medical workers and population scholars.

Not only the population's quantity and quality are being studied, but its age structure as well, especially the tendency of the population's aging process and the urban / rural distribution of aging. Chinese scholars have acquired a clear understanding of the status quo of the country's elderly population and the population's aging process, and are now able to offer suggestions for an overall strategy for the development of Chinese population, and for appropriate measures to be taken concerning the aging process, laying a foundation for further research on the elderly population.

It is encouraging that there have been such remarkable achievements and that such rapid progress has been made in China' s population studies in the 10 years since the third plenary session of the Party's 11th Central Committee. Still, people should be aware that as we are dealing with a population of more than a billion people, the number of population scholars in China is not big enough to meet the needs of socialist modernization, that there has been little or no research on many population issues and that the research on certain issues has been done on a low level. Looking ahead, we can see that we shoulder heavy responsibilities. We must take on the responsibilities entrusted to us by history, and carry on the research on population science. As we commemorate the loth anniversary of the third plenary session of the Party's 11th Central Committee, it is of particular importance to recall the speech made at the session by Comrade Deng Xiao ping on freeing the mind, seeking truths through facts and looking ahead in unity. The rapid progress of population studies since the session must be attributed primarily to the emancipation in thinking achieved by the adoption of the materialist guideline that practice is the only criterion in judging the truth. Without this emancipation, the case over *A New Theory on Population* by noted economist Ma Yinchu, severely criticized in the 1950s, would not have been reversed. Without this too, the goal to limit the country's population to within 1. 2 billion by the end of the century would not have been set, nor would the policy have been made to request each couple to have only one child. Eugenics would not have received as much attention as it has and the country's population policy would not have been gradually improved. Every breakthrough in China's population studies is in some way a result of this emancipation of the mind.

Of course, people's minds need to be further freed in order to deepen the country's population studies and promote research on the theoretical and practical aspects of population science, as well as on how to combine them. Many new questions have arisen with the changes caused by the rural and urban economic reforms and the implementation of the more flexible policies. For instance, while the economic boom brought about by the reform will result in a decline in the fertility rate in the long-term, did it lead to a growth or a decline in the fertility rate in the short-term? What are the conditions and criteria for the growth or decline of this rate? There have also been changes in causes of death: the development of a market-oriented economy and the increase in the mobility of the population have led to an increase in accident-caused deaths. The rapid increase in the mobility of the population and its migration, as well as the progress of urbanization are both results of the development of a market-oriented economy and have had a profound impact on the growth of the national economy and are even related to current inflation rates. Certain sensitive population issues such as marriage, family and the changes in women's status in the family and in society, have also been affected by the reform and deserve more research. The tremendous impact of the changes in the composition and age structure of the population on economic and social development is not to be ignored. The accelerating process of aging of the Chinese population requires corresponding adjustments in the country's systems of production, consumption and social security in order for it to be prepared to deal with the peak of the process which will occur in four or five decades.

Seeking truths through facts is the principle of the necessary emancipation of thought. Research should be conducted on the basis of the current reality in China in order that it be of the best quality and practical value. The accomplishments and scientific methodologies of overseas population studies should be introduced into practice in China. Population scholars of different generations, research areas and schools, and those with different views, should respect and learn from one another to help further research. As Comrade Deng Xiaoping said 10 years ago, we should "look ahead in unity. "

The Third Population Boom and Corresponding Macro-Policies

Eight new age groups, distributed in 5-year intervals, were noted at the bottom of the age—structure pyramid of China's population to the 40th anniversary of the People's Republic. The uneven distribution of population within the groups will exert a crucial impact on future population development. Although each age group has its own impact, the birth peak that occurred between the early 1960s and the early 1970s, and two following peaks, to be referred to as the "third population boom" in this essay, deserve the most attention, due to China's problem of surplus population. This problem is the key to China's long-term population growth.

I. A Peak in China's Population Growth

In spite of the inadequacy of data for certain historical periods, the picture of Chinese population growth is generally clear. Two periods are particularly noteworthy. The first stretches between 1685 and 1830, when the country's population grew from 100 million to 400 million: a four-fold increase within 145 years, with an average annual growth rate of 1.0%. This constituted the basis for the country's huge population in subsequent years[1].

The second period lasts from 1949 to 1989, when the Chinese population increased from 540 million to 1.11 billion, with an annual growth rate of 1.8%. This second period stands out even more sharply in terms of the rate of increase and its magnitude, despite several fluctuations (Figure 1).

Figure 1 indicates a 2% annual rate of increase in Chinese population between

1949 and 1952. This period saw a transition in the pattern of population growth from a high fertility rate, high mortality rate, and low growth rate, to a high fertility rate, low mortality rate, and resulting high growth rate. The growth in the 1953 – 1957 period may be considered as a small population boom, during which population grew at an annual rate of 2.38%. The rate dropped to 0.46% between 1958 and 1961, and jumped again to 2.56% between 1962 and 1973: the biggest population boom in the 40 year since 1949. The 1974 – 1985 period, however, saw a drop in the annual population increase rate to 1.37% : the longest low fertility rate period since 1949. Finally, birth and growth rates rose again after 1986, featuring an annual growth rate of 1.43% in the first 3 years. This indicates the beginning of a third population boom that may extend until 1996.

The curves of China's population growth over the past 40 years are clearly marked on the age-structure pyramid of the country's population, and are expected to exert a crucial impact on the future development of Chinese population. The 12-year-long population boom that occurred between 1962 and 1973, the most influential in the past 40 years, deserves particular attention due to its surplus population characteristics.

The above-mentioned population boom was the biggest and longest one of the past 40 years; the one between 1953 and 1957 lasted only 5 years. There was also a large difference in the number of births: 105.82 million during the first peak and 317.94 million during the second. The birth rate fluctuated between 31.90‰ and 37.97‰ during the 1953 – 1957period, and between 28.07‰ and 43.60‰ during the 1962 – 1973 period. The arithmetic mean of the annual birth rate was 0.30‰ higher in the second period than in the first, and the birth rate remained over 37.22‰ between 1962 and 1965.

The difference in mortality rates is even more notable. The country's mortality rate fluctuated between 10.80‰ and 14.00‰ during the 1953 – 1957 period, and between 7.08‰ and 11.56‰ during the 1962 – 1973 period. The mean annual mortality rate was 4.45‰ lower in the second period than in the first.

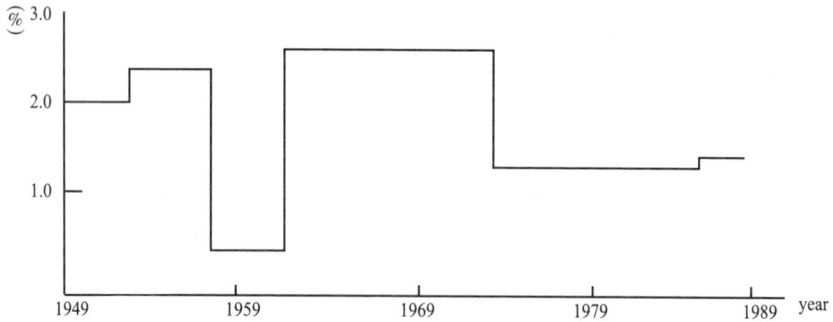

Source: China Statistical Yearbook (1989), China Statistical Publishing
House. 1989.

**Fig. 1 Growth of the Chinese population in different
periods between 1949 and 1989.**

This inevitably resulted in an apparent difference in the population's natural
growth. While the absolute population increase totalled 67. 85 million between 1953
and 1957, with an annual increase of 13. 57 million, the absolute population increase reached 238. 90 million between 1962 and 1973, with an annual increase of
19. 91 million. The difference between the totals was 171. 05 million and the difference between annual increases was 6. 34 million.

The population's natural growth rate was 2. 03% – 2. 48% between 1953 and
1957, and 2. 10% – 3. 35% between 1962 and 1973. Moreover, the annual average growth rate was 0. 18 percentage points higher in the second period than in the
first. In particular, the natural growth rate remained above 2. 57% between 1962
and 1970, reaching 3. 35% in 1963. That situation exerted, and will continue to
exert, a tremendous impact on the country's population development.

II. A Two-Fold Impact

The impact of the first population boom manifested itself in a birth rate increase and a new population boom that started in the mid-1980s. Its impact was also
felt in the new pressure on the job market of the work force whose prolonged and
continuous growth began in the late 1970s. This impact on both population control
and the job market characterizes the current second population boom.

Of the 320 million people born between 1962 and 1973, more than 150 million were females. Most of them passed the age of 15 years between 1977 and 1988 and embarked upon their reproductive years. They have passed, or will pass, 20 years of age, which is the legal age of marriage for women in China, between 1982 and 1993, and have reached, or will reach, 23 years of age, or the peak of their fecundity, between 1985 and 1996. In particular, more than 11 million women have reached, or will reach, their twentieth birthday each year between 1982 and 1993. Within this period, an annual total of more than 12 million reached or will reach this age in 8 of those years, and an annual total of 13 million in 3 of those years. More than 11 million women reached or will reach the age of 23 each year between 1985 and 1996. During this period, an annual total of 12 million reached or will reach this age in 7 of those years, and an annual total of 13 million in the first 3 years of the 1990s. These women make up a fecund population, unprecedented in size, that predicts an inevitable new population boom. In my opinion, this boom deserves adequate explanation and a correct evaluation on which to base a scientific analysis, in order to design strategic policies.

A comprehensive analysis of the emerging population boom reveals that it will feature a lower peak than that between 1962 and 1973, but a strong tendency of growth. In the past 4 years, the population's annual average birth rate was approximately 21. 05‰, the annual growth rate approximately 1. 44%, and the annual net increase approximately 15. 54 million. [1] Obviously, neither the birth rate, nor the growth rate, nor the net increase in these years reached the level of the 1962 – 1973 period. Given the current age structure of the Chinese population, particularly that in the category of fertile women, the country's birth rate, natural growth rate, and net increase may reach a high level in 1992, the peak year of the current population boom. They will not, however, be as high as in the last population boom, thanks to the government's tremendous effort to curb population growth through the family planning program, the considerable change in people's attitudes

---

[1]   According to China's Statistical Yearbook (1989), in 1989, the country's birth rate was 21. 60 per thousand, the mortality rate was 6. 60 per thousand, and the natural growth rate was 1. 50%. These statistics were estimated on the basis of the current number of fertile women and the age composition of fertility levels.

towards reproduction, and the remarkable improvement in people's material and cultural life as a result of the rapid economic growth of the past 20 years, and, more particularly, of the past 10 years.

Nonetheless, the absolute increase of the country's population may be gigantic because of the huge size of the Chinese population. The Chinese population grew by 374 million between 1963 and 1986. As a result, the same birth rate and growth rate will yield greatly different population increases. Although the number of births and the absolute value of the population increase in the past few years did not reach the level attained during the last population boom, they did exceed the annual average level of the 1953 – 1957 period. Just as the last population boom, the current one will last for approximatly 12 years and may not slow down until 1996.

Given this situation, the government's planned limit for the country's population growth—1.2 billion by the year 2000—may be exceeded. According to the 3 predictions presented in China's Population and Employment in 2000 (i. e. low—level—1.20 billion, medium level—1.25 billion, and high level—1.28 billion), the Chinese population has been increasing in line with the upper medium level

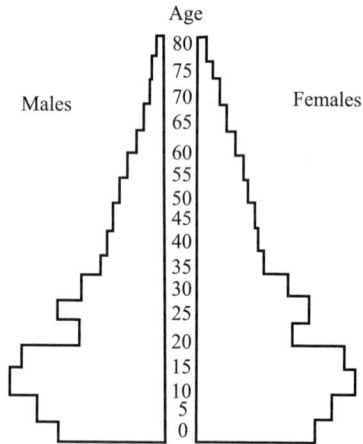

Fig. 2 Age structure of the Chinese population in 1982.

Source: China Statistical Yearbook (1988), China Prospects Publishing House, 1988.

"China's Population and Employment in 2000. " (Tian Xueyan, Editor-in-chief, Qiu Cangping and Lu Zhipiang Associate Editors-in-chief)

prediction in the past 4 years. As a result, the country's population is expected to reach 1.5 billion by the middle of the 21st century. Therefore, the seriousness of the current population boom deserves adequate attention.

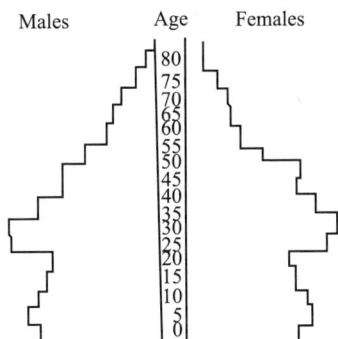

Fig. 3   Age structure of the Chinese population in 2000 (predicted)

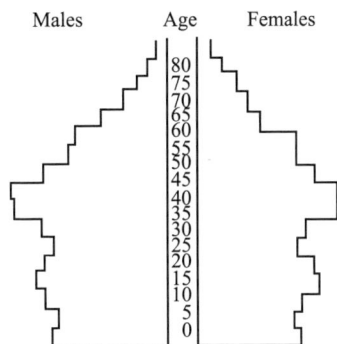

Fig. 4   Age structure of the Chinese population in 2010 (predicted)

Source: China Statistical Yearbook (1988), China Prospects Publishing House, 1988, "China's Population and Employment in 2000." (Tian Xueyuan, Editor-in-chief; Qiu Cangping and Lu Zhiqiang. Associate Editors-in-chief).

In brief, the current population boom is an inevitable outcome of the age structure that took shape during the last boom. Controlling population growth in China remains an important goal in both this century and in the future. A correct strategic policy is to keep population growth under tight control by implementing the family planning program and reducing the peak in this boom to its minimum. Any suggestion to loosen population control for any reason runs counter to the country's fundamental interests. Of course, "tight control" does not mean that the stricter the population growth limit, and the harsher the penalties, the better it will be. Rather, it requires that limits and measures be worked out to the greatest extent possible to be acceptable to the public. It is of primary importance at this time to maintain the consistency and stability of the current policy, since any changes would be acutely felt and could result in excessive births, worsening the situation.

Another characteristic of the second boom of the Chinese population in the past 40 years is the rapid increase in the working-age population, which progresses simultaneously with the growth of the general population. This is demonstrated through population age—structure pyramids（Figs. 2，3，and 4）.

Figure 2 shows that the 300 million people born between 1962 and 1973 reached the working age in the late 1970s. and have all passed the age of 15. By the year 2000，this huge group will reach 27 – 38 years of age，According to Figure 3，the groups of 25 – 29，30 – 34，and 35 – 39 year—olds are particularly large，and most will reach the ages of 37 – 48 by 2010. Figure 4 indicates that the groups of 35 – 39，40 – 44，and 45 – 49 year—olds are particularly noticeable. This tendency shows that the proportion of the working population is expected to increase appreciably between the late 1970s and 2010. Moreover，the absolute number of these people may keep growing until 2020. More specifically，the proportion of the working population between the ages of 15 and 64 is expected to increase from 61. 5% in 1982，to 68. 8% in 2000，and to 71. 4% in 2010，while their absolute number is expected to grow from 625 million in 1982，to 765 million in 1990，to 858 million in 2000，to 956 million in 2010，and to 977 million in 2020. Although the second population boom fluctuated，and will continue to fluctuate，between the mid-1980s and mid-1990s because of its social impact on fertility，the increase in the working population is unlikely to fluctuate as most of those who will join the working population by 2010 have already been born. Therefore，the situation expected to extend from the 1980s to the 2010s has already taken shape：the working population will grow rapidly，and the pressure of inadequate employment will continue to increase. This is a very serious problem in China's population and economic development，that deserves due attention.

The growth in the proportion of the working population means a drop in the proportions of dependent young and elderly people. The support-dependence ratio may drop from 0. 63 in 1982，to 0. 46 in 2000，and to 0. 40 in 2010，and may grow back to 0. 46 in 2020. These ratios are considerably lower than previous ones. Such changes in the population's age structure may be regarded as a "golden age" for the country's economy. During such a period when the support-depend-ence ratio drops considerably，the burden on society becomes lighter，and labor is abundant and inexpensive. These constitute great advantages for an economic take-off in developing countries. Since 1983，I have written several essays on how to take advantage of such an opportunity to boost the country's economy[2]. In fact, experience acquired during the modernization process in certain other countries and regions, especially those in Asia, such as Japan and Singapore, indicates that in-expensive local labor helps to enhance the salability of local products, and is one of the important conditions for rapid economic growth. We should make the best use of domestic and foreign experience, especially of the experience we have acquired in the past 10 years, and also of the abundant labor, in our modernization drive.

On the other hand, we should be ready to bear increasing employment pressure, given the country's population surplus, working population surplus, and labor force size. In other words, advantages and disadvantages, potential for economic growth and pressure, and opportunities and challenge coexist. Our strategy should be to make the best use of the advantages and try to mitigate the disadvantages; to make full use of the labor force, and reduce the drawbacks of the huge working-age population. In order to meet this global requirement, a strategy that incures full and reasonable employment, and that accords with both population and economic development, should be worked out. In addition, labor should be rationally distributed in state-owned, collectively-owned, and privately-owned enterprises, as well as in various trades.

The relationship between employment rate and employment effect is where to start in working out China's employment strategy. It is the focus of the conflict between population and economic development as far as employment is concerned. In general, a country's employment rate is determined by the age composition of the country's population, the level of its economic and technological development, as well as its employment policy. Most developed countries have an employment rate of over 45% owing to a variety of employment opportunities, an old-age type structure of their population, and a large proportion of working-age population. On the other hand, because of a high educational level, 25% – 30% of the working-age population are studying in schools. This accounts for the relatively low employment rate (usually below 75%) among the working-age population.

The situation in developing countries is just the opposite. Most of these countries have a young age structure, a lower proportion of working-age population, and an employment rate of approximately 35% of the total population. Because of a low educational level, only a small proportion of the working-age population is attending schools, and the employment rate among this population group is generally above 85%.

Let us consider the case in China. In 1987, China's employment rate of the total population was 48.8%, and the employment rate of the working-age population was 74.2% [3]. Both rates are in the range of developed countries. The high employment rate is attributed to the country's socialist system, and is also related to the long-standing policy of low wages and high employment rate. There are both advantages and disadvantages to this situation. The biggest disadvantage is the slow growth of productivity. In agriculture, for example, according to calculations based on comparable prices, China's total agricultural output value between 1952 and 1988 grew at an annual rate of 3.7%, while agricultural labor increased at an annual rate of 2.2%. This means that some 60% of the increased agricultural output value was achieved through the increase in labor, and only 10% was attributed to growth in productivity. The amount of grain yielded by each farmer increased little, and was not much higher than that during the best periods in ancient times.

It is generally acknowledged that the growth of productivity is a condition of economic and social development. The growth of productivity should be a basic principle for the increase in employment. However, this principle alone is not enough. It is both unrealistic and unfeasible to place excessive emphasis on the growth of the employment rate irrespective of the explosion of the working-age population. Excessive emphasis on the growth of the employment rate regardless of a huge unemployed population not only means, generally, a tremendous waste of labor and a serious social problem, but also, in particular, cannot solve the problem of the increasing employment pressure resulting from the addition of another 200 million people to the working-age population in the coming 20 years. Therefore, the need is for full employment on the condition of continuous productivity growth.

This twofold employment strategy is difficult to carry out. Further reforms of the country's employment system are required in order to achieve a reasonable distribution of employees in state-owned enterprises and in urban collectively-owned enterprises has been increasing, while that of self-employed individuals has been decreasing considerably. The ratio of employees in state-owned and urban collectively owned enterprises to urban self-employed individuals was 24 : 6 : 1 in 1957 and 497: 137: 1 in 1978. In effect, the proportion of self-employed individuals in the total urban working population dropped drastically from 3. 4% to 0. 2% during that period.

The situation has changed appreciably since 1978. In 1988, the ratio of the three types of urban working population was 15 : 5 : 1. The self-employed made up 4. 8% of the total urban working population, the highest percentage in the past 30 years[4]. This is a result of the reforms and of the effort to increase employ-ment opportunities. Increasing the proportion of employees in collectively-owned enterprises and of the self-employed in order to tune in with the level of economic development is another major policy dealing with the rapid increase of the working-age population and employment pressure.

Employment in various trades has been similar along with the changes of the ownership structure. Agriculture absorbed a much larger amount of labor than industry and services until 1978. From 1978 to 1988, the country's agricultural labor decreased by 11. 2 percentage points, while industrial labor increased by 5. 0 percentage points and service labor increased structure, and of the shifting of the employment focus of the newly increased working-age population, both of which are indispensable in carrying out the two-fold employment strategy. Some of the new rural labor should transfer from farming to forestry, animal husbandry, fishery and various sidelines, changing the previous situation in which agricultural productivity grew slowly because new agricultural labor was mainly engaged in farming. In addition, some of that labor force should transfer to urban industries. Generally, the transfer should be accelerated, although agriculture's surplus production capacity, and the urban areas' capacity for these people should be taken into consideration. Still other rural laborers should transfer to services. Finally, such transfers should be based on the development of agriculture and industry.

III. The Challenge of Aging

Figure 4 shows the aging trend in China's working-age population. The proportion of the 40 – 44 year—old age group ranks the highest of all age groups. In the next two to three decades, these people, and those born between 1962 and 1973, will be over 60 years old, meaning that the peak of the third population boom is aging. The population's age structure in the peak years of the aging process is shown in Figure 5.

Figure 5 depicts an increasingly rapid rate in China's aging process. According to predictions, the country's population aged over 65 years is expected to grow from 492. 75 million in 1982 to 1. 05417 billion in 2010, 1. 98162 billion in 2030, and 2. 56533 billion in 2040. This means that in 48 years, China's population aged over 65 years will have quadrupled, with the total in 2040 5. 2 times higher than in 1982. In the meantime, the proportion of those over 65 years old is expected to increase from 4. 91% in 1982, to 6. 93% in 2000, to 13. 51% in 2030, and to 17. 44% in 2040. According to the United Nations, it usually takes approximately 80 years in a developed country for the proportion of its population over 65 years old to grow from 7% to 17%. In China, it is expected to take only 40 years. The rate continues to accelerate, and the proportion of those over 65 years old is expected to increase 1% every 10 years from 1982 to 2010, 3% every 10 years from 2010 to 2030, and 4% every 10 years from 2030 to 2040. It is believed that this increase will slow down after 2040.

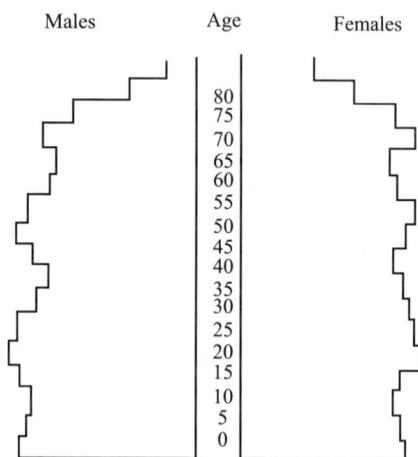

Fig. 5 Age structure of the Chinese population in 2040 (predicted).

The aging process of the Chinese population will exert a series of effects on the country's entire social life, including its economic, political, and cultural dimensions. The impact will be particularly profound on economic development, including production, consumption, technological progress, and economic structure. It is of special significance that, so far, all the countries that have become aging societies are developed countries. China will be the first developing country to undergo this process. The challenge of an aging society at a low level of economic development is a difficult one. How to support the elderly is a particularly difficult question. Welfare policies are in a predicament in many Western countries. In this country, the traditional means of supporting the elderly have been shaken with the growth of a market—oriented economy, and nuclear families are becoming widespread. The traditional value of supporting the elderly is undergoing a severe test. In the third population boom, unlike in the first two, dealing with the challenge of the aging process to make sure that the elderly are taken proper care of is an urgent task. This should be the basis for a macro-strategic policy. In order to work out such a policy, it is undoubtedly necessary to become familiar with the scientific observations reported in foreign research on elderly populations, and study the positive as well as the negative experiences of the aging process in developed countries. It is even more important to summarize our own experience, and to investigate the situation of the country's population, economy, and society.

Let us here again examine the situation in China. According to the sample survey of the Chinese population conducted in 1987 for those above 60 years of age, of all the 10 types of income of the Chinese elderly (including salaries, pensions, savings, insurance, social welfare, income from financial assets, funds provided by children or other family members, sale of property, and gifts from friends), the weighted total of pensions, funds provided by children or other family members and salaries constituted the "three major pillars" making up more than 90% of elderly people's total income. On the basis of this information, the basic idea in establishing a new support system for the elderly may be to develop social welfare, encourage help from family members, and assist the elderly in supporting themselves.

The development of social welfare is an important hallmark of economic development and social progress. Along with the growth of the national economy, we should gradually increase the number of people who enjoy State-provided welfare, and improve the retirement system. However, as a result of the second population boom, those who enjoy pensions in urban areas alone, compared with the present time, will increase by some 2 million every year in the 1990s, and by more than 3 million in each year between 2000 and 2030. The State will be overburdened with little room for improvement. Reforms provide a solution. To that end, successful overseas experiences should be examined. A system featuring joint fund-raising by the State, institutions, and the individuals themselves should be established, and scientific management methods should be adopted with the aim of providing the State with more funds on which to expand social welfare.

Help from children occupies an important place in China's elderly security system. According to weighted data from the 1987 sample survey, of all the families that have elderly members, 3-generation households make up 50%, and 2-generation households make up nearly 30%, totalling 80%. This means that it is still feasible for children to support their elderly parents. Although this practice is being weakened by the trend towards nuclear families and is being overshadowed by the retirement system, the traditional means of support is still deeply rooted among the Chinese people. This type of support for the elderly is particularly helpful when social welfare can help only a part of the elderly population.

Assisting the elderly in supporting themselves constitutes a supplement to the two above-mentioned types of support. According to the 1987 sample survey, 44.6% of the country's elderly population are in good health and are capable of working. As a result, the employment rate among the elderly is 15.0% in cities, 11.6% in townships, and 31.5 in rural areas. The income they earn through their work is a major financial resource. In spite of the fact that employing the elderly may somewhat worsen employment pressure as the elderly compete with younger people for jobs, proper guidance may help to transfer elderly people from production sectors to services, so that their competition with the younger work force may be eased.

References

[1] Zhao Wenhn and Xie Shujun: *A History of Chinese Population*. People's Publishing House, 1988.

[2] Tian Xueyuan. "Promote the Modernization Drive by Taking Advantage of the Change in the Population's Age Structure. " *People's Daily*, June 15, 1989. "A Study on the Change in the Population's Age Structure and Economic Development. " *Population Science of China*, first issue, 1987.

[3] *China Statistical Yearbook*, (1989) .

[4] Ibid.

[5] Ibid.

The Virtuous Cycle of the Population and Economic Development *

——Experience After the Reform
and Opening-up in China

1. In the present-day world, there exits two kinds of population issues, belonging to two kinds of cycles between different population and economic deve-lopment. One is categorised by a population surplus, belonging to the high fertility rate—low labour productivity—high fertility cycle model; the other is categorised by a demographic and labour productivity deficiency, belonging to the low fertility rate—high labour productivity—low fertility rate cycle model. The latter could be seen as the high-level cycle model of the population and economic development. However, taking the world as a whole, among the world population of 1990, that of the developing countries accounted for about 77. 2% , total fertility rate (TFR) was 4. 6 (not including China, the same for the following figures), birth rate was 35 per thousand, and natural growth rate was 2. 4%. The per capita GNP for 1988 was 870 US $, basically belonging to the primitive cycle model of high fertility rate—low labour productivity—high fertillity rate. Developed countries and regions accounted for about 22. 8% of the population of the world. Its total fertility rate was 2. 0, birth rate was 15 per thousand, natural growth rate was 0. 5%. The per capita GNP for 1988 was 15. 830 US $, entering into the high—level cycle model of low fertility rate—high labour productivity—low fertility rate . Clearly, looking at the predominant aspects, the demographic problem of the world is mainly that of the population surplus, fast growth, which are not corre-

---

* The Article for "International Seminar on Population and Development 1991", Xian, China.

sponding to the economic development, therefore belonging to the previous category of primitive cycle between the population and economic development.

2. China is the most populous country in the world, at the same time, a developing country. The nature of the Chinese population issue also belongs to the previous category. i. e . the stage of primitive cycle. As is known to all, before the founding of the Peoples's Republic of China in 1949, the demographic reproduction was in a status of high birth rate, high mortality rate and low growth. Following the birth of the People's Republic, the national economy was rapidly rehabilitated and developed, medical-care and health conditions improved, people's livelihood enhanced and mortality rate drastically reduced. Before 1949, the mortality rate was above 20 per thousand, but decreased to 17 per thousand in 1952, and 14 per thousand in 1953, while the birth rate was still maintained at a high-level of 37 per thousand. Therefore, the natural growth rate of the population increased drastically and demographic reproduction quickly entered into the category of high birth rate, low mortality rate and high growth rate. Immediately following this, there was a baby boom in the mid-50s. Afterwards, due to several rises and falls in the national economy, and the influence of anarchy during the 10 years of chaos, measures were adopted to enforce family-planning and population control in the mid-70s. Demographic reproduction was demonstrated by a low fertility ebb in 1958 - 1961, another baby boom in 1962 - 1973, another low fertility ebb in 1974 - 1985 and a new baby boom starting from 1986 and will last into 1997 or later. Although drastic changes happened in birth rate, mortality rate and natural growth rate in the past 40 years or more, the present population growth rate in China belongs to the lowest category among the developing countries. However, the total population (not including Taiwan, the same for the following figures) increased from 541, 670, 000 in 1949 to 1, 143, 330, 000 in 1990, a net growth of 601, 660, 000 in 41 years' time with an annual average growth rate of 1. 84 per thousand, still tended to be high. Indeed, remarkable successes achieved by the state in the mid - 70's to vigorously control the population growth and enforce the family-planning have laid cornerstones for the population and economic development to change from the primitive cycle into the high-level cycle. However, on one hand, China has a weak economic foundation, despite of

the great changes taken place in the 41 years, the productivity is still not developed; on the other hand, the population has increased by folds, which has consumed a part of the newly-added national income to a large extent, and putting us
basically into a stage of primitive cycle of the population and economic development. If the past "6th Five-Year-Plan" and "7th Five-Year-Plan" were considered to be the 10 years with fastest growth in the national wealth and largest attain-
ment of tangible benefits for the people, GNP calculated in terms of the price of
that year, was increased from 447, 000 million RMB Yuan in 1980 to 1, 740,
000 million RMB Yuan in 1990; an increase of 1.36 times in terms of comparable
price; at the same time, national income increased from 368, 800 million RMB
Yuan to 1, 430, 000 million RMB Yuan, an increase of 1.31 times in terms of
comparable price. However, due to an increase of the population from 987, 050,
000 to 1, 143, 330, 000 during the same period, which was an increase of
15.8%, the GNP was only increased by 1.04 time in terms of comparable
price. 32% of the newly-increased GNP was divided up by the newly-added population; per capita national income was only increased by 99.17%, the remaining
31.8% was also derided up by the newly-added population. Although there was a
rather large decrease in the birth rate and natural growth rate in past 10 years in the
"6th Five-Year-Plan" period, the annual average growth rate was decreased to
1.41% and in the "7th Five-Year-Plan" period, it was decreased to 1.55%.
However, in general, we still could not rid ourselves of the passive situation with
population squeezing the productivity, nor could we extricate ourselves from the
primitive cycle of the population and economic development.

3. Here, a question calls for discussion, i.e. the definitions of the per capita
GNP, national income and other quotas in China and the problem of making international comparisons. If in terms of exchange rate between RMB and US $, 100
US $ in 1980 was equivalent to 160 RMB and 100 US $ in 1990 was equivalent to
520 RMB, then the per capita GNP for 1980 was 283 US $; and per capita
national income was 234 US $; the same for 1990 was 293 US $ and 241 US $
respectively. Therefore, in 10 years time, the per capita GNP was only increased
by 10 US $, an increase of 3.5% while per capita national income was only in-
creased by 7 US $, an increase of 3.0%, it is apparently not compatible to the

reality. This is mainly caused by a continuous downward adjustment of RMB against foreign exchange rate. If taking the comparable price of 1980, the per capita GNP should be 577US $ and national income 465 US $ for 1990 in China. Due to the irrationality in comparable price, estimations from home and abroad on China's per capita GNP and national income vary greatly, some even drastically different, ranging from 300 US $ per capita to 1, 000 US $ per capita. However, according to the materials provided by the Population Advisory Bureau of U. S. A. in "World Population Data 1990", the per capita GNP in developing countries and regions has already reached 870US $ in that year with China ranking in the medium level or between the medium and rather low level among the developing countries. With a low labour productivity, China is in transition from high fertility rate low labour productivity—high fertility rate cycle model to low fertility rate—high labour productivity—low fertility rate cycle model, but basically belonging to the previous stage of primitive cycle model.

4. Then, how could the transition be accelerated and a path be found to obtain a virtuous cycle of the population and economic development? From the concrete conditions of China, it is of paramount importance to vigorously develop the economy and to strictly control the population growth and combine closely these two factors. Here, certain analysis will be made on how to control the population growth through economic means in the main and by combining the above-mentioned two factors.

5. Historical materialists consider that existence determines consciousness, productive forces determine production relations and economic foundation determines superstructure. Demographic changes are finally determined by economic changes. In the final analysis, population issue is that of the economic issue. The two possible cycles between the population and economic development mentioned above are finally determined by the level of social economic development besides different traditional and cultural influences of various countries and their different population policies. The fundamental reason for the high fertility rate—labour productivity—high fertility rate cycle model of the population and economic development is due to the fact that under the condition of a low level of productive forces, high fertility can bring greater economic results to the parents and family. Here it is nec-

essary to explain, in a general way, the theory of beneficial results—the costs of upbringing the child. Since the outbreak of the bourgeois Industrial Revolution, and with the establishment of capitalist productive relations and the development of the overall commodity concepts, some micro-demographic economists look at demographic reproduction from the perspectives of commodity production, putting forward the theory of beneficial results—the costs of upbringing the child. They indicate that the production costs for a child could be composed of two parts: direct cost, i. e. direct money expenses to raise a child and indirect realistically significant to reveal the universal law of economic dominance over fertility behaviour. The important aspect of the universal law is the transition from the primitive cycle into the high-level cycle, and change of child cost-benefit theory during the transitional stage. On the issue of cost, under certain conditions in the level of social productive forces, direct or indirect costs on the basic living expenses of the child and during pregnancy and delivery time remain relative stable, constituting constant costs or quantitative costs of the child; while expenses of medical-care to enhance the physical quality of the child and that of education to raise his cultural quality are increasing continuously, constituting variable costs or qualitative costs of the child. On the issue of benefit, due to technological advancement and the increase of economic income of the parents and family, which does not mainly depend on the increase of the quantity of the labour force, but on the improvement of their quality, sophisticated labour increases cost, i. e. time spent on the child by the parents, especially the mother which reduces their income. However, the child is also beneficial to the parents, most importantly his labour-economic benefit; support for their old age-insurance benefit; consumption-entertainment benefit; benefit of inheriting the family property, risk-taking benefit to revitalize the family business and benefit of providing security and safeguard. Among the 6 benefits, the first 3 are most important. Then, whether the parents want benefits, the first 3 are most important. Then, whether the parent want to produce an edge child would depend on the cost benefit put into the child: if cost is larger than benefit, they feel it unnecessary and if cost is smaller than benefit, they would feel the necessity. Cost versus benefit would depend on random factors. It should be pointed out that the child cost-benefit theory has its limitations and different schools of the bourgeois demographic economists have different views. However, by linking the human fertility behaviour with economic gains and losses and making quantitative studies, it is by folds against simple labour. The economic benefit of labour from the edge child is constantly decreasing. How is the support for the old-age-insurance benefit from the child? On one hand, due to social economic development, it becomes possible for the state to allocate more capital on the social security works for the aged; on the otherhand, with the social economic development and increase of the family income, people have already accumulated a deposit of old-age pension before they enter into the old-age, so as not to rely on their children for support; thirdly, the government carries out an universal pension system by combining social pension support with private deposit, an old—age pension fund would be set up by the government, enterprise and individual to contribute a certain part of their capital to the fund, thereby reducing rapidly the insurance benefit from the child to support the old. Others like inheritance benefit benefit to reshape the family business and benefit of security and safeguard also tend to decrease to various extent with the social economic development. There is no definite conclusion only no consumption-entertainment benefit, the changes in this respect are not very clear. Therefore, from the perspectives of development, drastic increase in child costs, especially the qualitative cost of child, notable decrease in child benefit, especially economic benefit, and people's choice prone to change from quantitative cost or constant cost of the child to qualitative cost or variable cost of the child have enabled fertility rate to decrease, and will gradually accomplish the transition from high fertility rate—low labour productivity—high fertility rate into low fertility rate—high labour productivity—low fertility rate drastically reducing the birth rate of the population.

6. As discussed above, in general, the present-day China is in a stage of primitive cycle of the population and economic development and the production of one more edge child can bring clear economic benefits. However, I believe, due to the vast territory of China, and rather imbalanced economic, cultural and social development, great differences exist between the cities and countryside and among the regions. Developed cities and regions have already entered into the stage of high level cycle while certain regions are in the transitional period into the high—level

cycle. This could be seen in the following chart, showing the relationship between per capita national income and birth rate of the population.

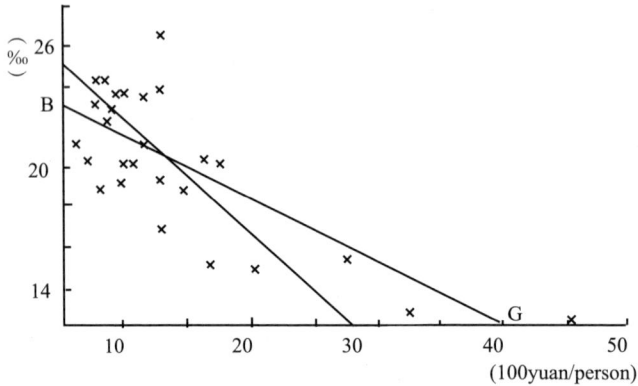

Fig 1　Per capita national income and birth rate in different regions in China. 1989.

Sequence indicated in the chart from left to right: Guizhou, Guangxi, Yunnan, Tibet, Sichuan, Jiangxi, Henan, Gansu, Shaanxi, Hunan, Anhui, Ningxia, Inner Mongolia, Shanxi, Qinghai, Hebei, Hainan, Hubei, Fujian, Jilin, Shandong, Heilongjiang, Jiangsu, Zhejiang, Guangdong, Liaoning, Tianjin, Beijing, Shanghai, Xinjiang (absent)

7. In chart 1, axle X represents the per capita national income, axle Y represents the birth rate of the population, curve BG is the regression model which indicates the change of the national (except Taiwan and Xinjiang) birth rate Y with the change of the per capita national income X. In 1989, the per capita national income of China was 1, 189 RMB yuan. Besides Xinjiang, 11 provinces and cities under direct jurisdiction of the central Government such as Shanghai, Beijing, Tianjin, Liaoning, Guangdong, Zhejiang, Jiangsu, Heilongjiang, Shandong, Jilin, and Fujian had a higher average national income. The other 18 provinces and autonomous regions were below the national average level. The birth rate of the population for the whole country was 20. 83‰. For the 11 provinces and cities under the direct jurisdiction of the Central Government which had a higher per capita national income, with the exception of Fujian, the birth rate of the 10 provinces and cities was below the average national level. Among them, the per capita national income of Shanghai reached 4, 599 RMB Yuan and birth rate decreased to 12. 53 per thousand: the per capita national income of Beijing was 3, 248 RMB

Yuan and birth rate 12. 84 per thousand; that of Tianjin 2, 738 RMB Yuan and birth rate 15. 48 pre thousand respectively; that of Liaoning 1, 989 RMB Yuan and birth rate 15. 04 per thousand respectively; that of Zhejiang 1, 660 RMB Yuan and birth rate 15. 20 per thousand respectively, it was not only Beijing Tianjin and Shanghai as cities under the direct jurisdiction of the Central Government, whose per capita national income clearly proved to be in negative relationship to the birth rate, but also developed regions, especially the coastal developed provinces demonstrated the similar situation with clarity. For the regions which had a per capita income below the national average level, in general, their birth rate was higher. Among the 18 provinces and autonomous regions whose per capita national income was below the national average level, 12 of them had a higher birth rate than the national level, e. g. per capita national income for Yunnan was 771 RMB Yuan, and birth rate reached 23. 07 per thousand; per capita national income for Tibet was 778 RMB Yuan, and birth rate was 24. 17 per thousand; per capita national income for Henan was 836 RMB Yuan and birth rate was 24. 25 per thousand. However, due to the impact of the demographic age structure, or relative good results from implementing the population policy or other economic, social and cultural factors, there were 6 provinces and autonomous regions whose per capita national income was below the national average level and their birth rate was also below the national level. Nevertheless, from a general survey of the 29 provinces, autonomous regions and cities under direct jurisdiction of the Central Government indicated on the chart, it is very clear to see the negative relationship between per capita national income and birth rate of the population. Its correlation coefficient is − 0. 764, belonging to the scope of strong correlation. The general tendency is, higher the per capita national income, lower the birth rate of the population; the reverse is lower the per capita national income, higher the birth rate of the population. The regression model of the changes in birth rate with the per capita national income is indicated by curve BG:

$$Y = -0.318X + 24.648$$

8. Due to strong correlation existing between birth rate and per capita national income, and vast difference in per capita national income between cities and countryside and among regions such as the per capita national income of Shanghai in

1989 was 3. 7 times that of Fujian, 5. 1 times that of Anhui, and 7. 4 times that of Guizhou, different stages of cycle exist in population and economic development. At present, in extra-large cities like Beijing, Tianjin and Shanghai or in large or medium cities with rather developed economy and culture, or in a small number of medium and small cities and a few village townships rapidly grown up during the reform and opening-up, the costs to bring up one child, mainly that of variable costs or qualitative costs of the child increase drastically while the labour-economic benefit and support for old-age-insurance benefit from the edge child remarkably decrease. Special emphasis should be made about a decrease in seeking support for old-age-insurance benefit from the child, which constitutes the initial motivation for continuous fertility at present. Due to the fact that these regions have basicaly solved the problem of old-age social securities, popularized the system of setting up a pension fund and eliminated apprehensions in old-age support and securities in a fundamental way, solid foundation could be laid for family-planning and eugenics. Such cases could be easily found in almost all the cities and they also exist in some of the economically developed rural townships. The author made an inspection tour to the South of Liaoning Province in October 1990. Examples could be cited about Sifangtai Village, East Anshan Township in Anshan city. The village has 280 households with a population of 1, 004. The whole village live in a large compound consisting of 7 building blocks with 7 storeys. The buildings are fully e-quipped with running-water and gas-cookers similar to that of the Anshan city proper. The situation is even better than some of the residential quarters of certain institutions and enterprises. The per capita income of the whole village is 1, 596 RMB Yuan. The rent for the housing is covered by the township with many other special treatments. Male retires at 60 years old and female at 55. They are given a 330 Yuan pension allowance per year after retirement. Plus their previous savings, they are free from economic apprehensions in their old-age. Under such circumstances, support-benefit from the children decreases to a great extent. As indicated by the people there: "with running-water, we have been compensated like having half of a child. " They no longer worry about having nobody to fetch water for them. Some people voluntarily hand back the quota for allowing them to have the second child since they are single-girl families. The concept of fertility for the people there is "fewer, better and bring up a useful person. " They have realized the transfer from the input of quantitative costs on the child to that of the qualitative costs and reduced fertility rate through a natural process.

9. However, after all, examples like the Sifangtai Village are still few. Looking at the predominant aspects, the qualitative costs or variable costs of the child have not been increased together with the economic development and income rise in the recent years, and correspondingly, the child-benefits have not been decreased either. On the contrary, disadvantageous slanting has occurred. We have seen a rapid rise in the livelihood of the residents: in the 10 years from 1980 – 1990, real consumption level has been increased annually by 5. 9% in average. However, the costs for the edge child, especially qualitative costs or variable costs for health and education have not been correspondingly increased. Policies and mechanisms are lacking to stimulate the increase of variable costs for the child. Concerning the issue of child-benefit, on one hand, due to the implementation of contract responsibility system to link enumeration with output and the practice of township economies with individual or joint ventures, the productive and management functions of the households which were dormant for a long time in the past have been brought back to a large extent. It becomes rather urgent for the household-economy to acquire labour force, especially the male labour force, thereby enhancing drastically the labour-economic benefit of the child, and stimulating the motivation of fertility, especially the increase of the male babies.

10. On the other hand, under the old People's Commune System in the countryside, a set of social security mechanisms for old-age characterized in the main by "5 categories of households under favourable treatment scheme" and "old peoples' home" were of high standards and systematically rather comprehensive for a relatively under-developed economy and they played an important role in supporting the old-age people with no children or with few children. With the economic structural reform and the establishment of the new rural power structure, some of the original social security organizations for the old-age people were retained, but some of them were disintegrated or abolished. In general, they were weakened rather than strengthened. From practice, people have realized that relying on the children for old-age, at present circumstances, is still the best way with greatest

security coefficient, and supporting the old-age by the children-insurance benefit has also increased in value.

11. The above-mentioned disadvantageous slanting of the costs of child-benefit in most of the countryside and economically under-developed townships provides clear economic benefits to produce one more edge child, stimulates initiatives in fertility and seriously hinders the population and economic development from trandition into the high-level cycle. However, from the point of view of the dialectic materialists, the hindrance meanwhile also contains elements to eliminate the hindrance itself. The method is to find ways to increase the costs of the children, mainly the qualitative costs and to reduce the child-benefits.

12. Concerning the costs of the children, first, it is necessary to raise the costs on extra children. Adequate consideration should be given to increase the penalty for extra children. The old once-for-all penalty practice for extra children should be changed and the time of penalty should be about 14 years, as long as the bonus for the single-child families. The amount and time of the penalty should serve one general objective: making the parents of the extra children realize clearly that the costs they spend on their extra children could not be fully compensated by the benefits from their future children and that costs are greater than benefits. Secondly, it is necessary to effectively raise the qualitative costs of the children, especially educational expenses on children be steadily increased. Relevant policies and mechanisms need to be readjusted to correspondingly compensate or even double the compensation of the intellectual investment on the children by parents.

13. Concerning the issue of child-benefit, firstly, it is necessary to raise the benefit of the single-child or children within family-planning system to their parents. Due consideration should be given to increase the bonus on the single-child and guarantee to honour the commitment on time. At the same time, labour market should be developed to provide labour services to no-children or single-child families or social communal services could be developed to make up for the loss in labour-economic benefits due to no-children or few children situations. Measures and methods should be adopted to gradually carry out an old-age security system to the parents of the single-child or children within the family-planning scheme including

changing the single-child bonus into a pension fund or providing insurance to the single-child to raise the supporting old-age-insurance benefit of single-child or children within family-planning scheme. Considerations should also he made to provide preferential policies to the single-child such as enrollment in nurseries and schools. Employment, transfer the rural household registration into non-rural status, allocation of housing, etc. and to create a rather favourable external circumstance to the growth of the single-child and to enhance his risk-benefit to inherit the family business and maintain the family status. Secondly, through necessary restrictions on enrollment into nurseries and schools, employment, transfer rural household registration into non-rural status, allocation of housing, etc. on extra-children, their labour-economic benefits and supporting the old-age-insurance benefits to their parents would be reduced and it remarkably weakens the benefits of the edge child, not sufficient to make up for the costs which the parents spend.

14. It must be pointed out that corresponding policies and measures adopted towards child-costs and child-benefits discussed above are the key to a virtuous cycle of the population and economic development. This is extremely important for the 90's as a whole starting from 1991. However, we should never forget that the economy is the base and the continuous development of the national economy is only the foundation to enter into a virtuous cycle. It is only the continuous development of the national economy that could raise a higher demand on the labour force, thereby on the qualitative costs of the child and for people to be able to increase the qualitative costs of the child. Meanwhile, only when the economy is developed, tool of production improved, the quality of the labourers appearing to be more important than the quantity, can the labour-economic benefit of the child be gradually reduced; and only when the economy is developed, and when society, enterpries and labourer himself are capable of setting up a fund as future deposit for the old-age, can supporting the old-age-insurance benefit of the child be rapidly reduced. Therefore, continuous development of the economy serves both as the basis for effectively raising the costs of the marginal child, and also the basis for reducing various benefits of the child. From this point of departure, to ensure a stable, sustained and coordinated development of our national economy is not only the central task to realize the second-stage strategic objectives of the next 10 years,

but also highly relevant to realize the transfer from high fertility rate—low labour productivity—high fertility rate to low fertility rate—high labour productivity—low fertility rate. It is the objective foundation to achieve, the virtuous cycle of the population and economic development.

References

［1］ Liu Guoguang, *Strengthen ecological economic studies and promote coordinated development of the economy*, *society and ecology Economic Studies* No. 4. 1991.

［2］ Peng Pei-yun-Vigorously, *strengthen the grass-roots family-planning scheme*, *strive to accomplish the demographic plan in the 8th-Five-Year-Plan* Population Trends No. 1. 1991.

［3］ Tian Xueyuan, *Develop the economy*, *Promote the transfer and Seek a virtuous cycle of the population and economic development* China's Social Sciences No. 3. 1991.

［4］ *Zeng Yi and others Several issues in the process of future demographic development of China*, *China's Social Sciences*

［5］ Lester R. Brown et al. , *State of the World* 1991. *A Worldwatch Institute Report on Progress Toward Sustainable Society*, W. W. north and Compant, New York, London.

［6］ United Nations, *World Population Prospcts* 1988. *U. N. New York* 1989.

［7］ World Bank, *World Development Report*, 1990. *China's Finance and Economic Press.* 1990.

［8］ United Nations Environment Programme: *Environmental Data report. China's Science and Technology press.* 1990.

Develop the Economy, Initiate Changes and Promote the Benign Cycle of Population and Economic Development [*]

——Implications of the Development of Population and Economy in the Coastal Areas of China

Since the implementation of the policy of reform and opening to the outside world ten years ago in China, there have been rapid development in social productivity and unprecedented vigorous economic activities. Concurrent with such epoch-making developments, some traditional ideas are being transformed. All this has made, and will continue to make a decisive impact on population. This impact is particularly noticeable in the coastal areas which serve as the front lines of reform. The coastal areas include 12 provinces, autonomous regions and municipalities directly under the Central Government. They are Beijing, Tianjin, Hebei, Liaoning, Shanghai, Jiangsu, Zhejiang, Fujian, Shandong, Guangdong, Guangxi and Hainan. It is of considerable strategic significance to the interior and the entire China to study this impact by relating theory with practice and seek the inner workings of development. It should be admitted that there is great variation in the development among these 12 coastal regions, but they do have much in common. As far as the relation between population and economic development is concerned, it is most important to point out a direction where by economy stimulates demographic change and develops in concert with population dynamics. This direction is: develop economy and elevate the level of science and technology to bring about the transition from the quantitative cost of having more children to the quali-

---

  * See: *Chinese Journal of Population Science*, *Volume*, *Number* 1, 1992.

tative cost of raising children. The improvement of the educational quality of population further advances technological progress and economic development in a benign cycle of low fertility—high educational quality—high labor productivity—low fertility.

I . Basic Theory and Practice

The relation between population change and economic development, and the way in which economic development constrains demographic change are not only a basic theoretical issue in population economics, but also real issues to be seriously addressed in looking for solutions of population problems in China. Since the implementation of reform and opening to the outside world, the development in population and economy, particularly in some coastal areas, have provided many useful experiences that deserve our attention. According to Marxist materialism, existence determines consciousness, forces of production determines the relations of production, economic basis determines superstructure and the economic interests of people act as the ultimate driving force of population production and reproduction. As the capitalist commodity economy develops and pan-commodity ideas dominate, a number of capitalist economists and demographers, particularly micro economists have done extensive studies in this area. In the United States, Professor Leibinstein of Harvard University, Professor G. S. Baker of Chicago University and others proposed the more comprehensive "children's cost-benefit theory". Regarding children as a commodity and population reproduction as the process of commodity production, they maintain that the costs of producing children are both direct and indirect. Direct cost refers to the expenses of living, education, marriage and so on in raising a child. Indirect cost or opportunity cost refers to the reduction of income due to the loss of time by parents especially the mother, in raising a child. The benefit of children to their parents is primarily manifested as the labor-economic benefit, old age support-insurance benefit and consumption-pleasure benefit provided by children to their parents when they grow up. In providing the labor-economic benefit, children earn income for the family. The old-age support-insurance benefit has to do with the fact that in developing countries, the support of parents has to depend on their children to a large extent. As far as the consumption-pleasure benefit is concerned, children, as a unique object of consumption, satisfy the psychological needs of parents and bring them joy and happiness. In addition, children can also provide the benefits of bearing risks for the rise and fall of the family fortune, inheriting and protecting the family status and safeguarding the family. On this account, the number of children that parents desire is determined by the direct or indirect cost of children. If the net cost is positive, it means that extra children will not compensate for the cost incurred on the parents. Such marginal children are not desired by the parents. If the net cost is negative, this means such marginal children, who will yield more benefits, are desired by the parents. If the net cost is zero, whether more children are desired will be determined by random factors, and to a large extent by the state of mind of the parents. From a dynamic perspective, there is a tendency of gradual decline in children' s labor-economic benefit and old-age support-insurance benefit as economy develops and the per capita family income increases. But how about the consumption-pleasure benefit? Studies have shown that there is no inherent relation between this benefit and economic and cultural development. Studies have also shown that children's benefit in bearing the risk for the rise and fall of the family fortune and succeeding to and maintaining the family status will also be reduced. In terms of the cost, G. S. Baker points out that the basic living expenses of children and the direct and indirect expenses incurred by the mother during her pregnancy and parturition are relatively stable under the given development level of the social force of production. As such, they are the invariable cost or quantitative cost of children. On the other hand, the expenses on children's health care and education, which are continuously increasing, are the variable or qualitative cost. The more society advances, the more the variable or qualitative cost of children should increase. This increase leads to the decrease of the invariable or quantitative cost of children. Parents' preference turns the quantitative cost to qualitative cost, which will give rise to the decline of fertility and drastic decrease of the birth rate.

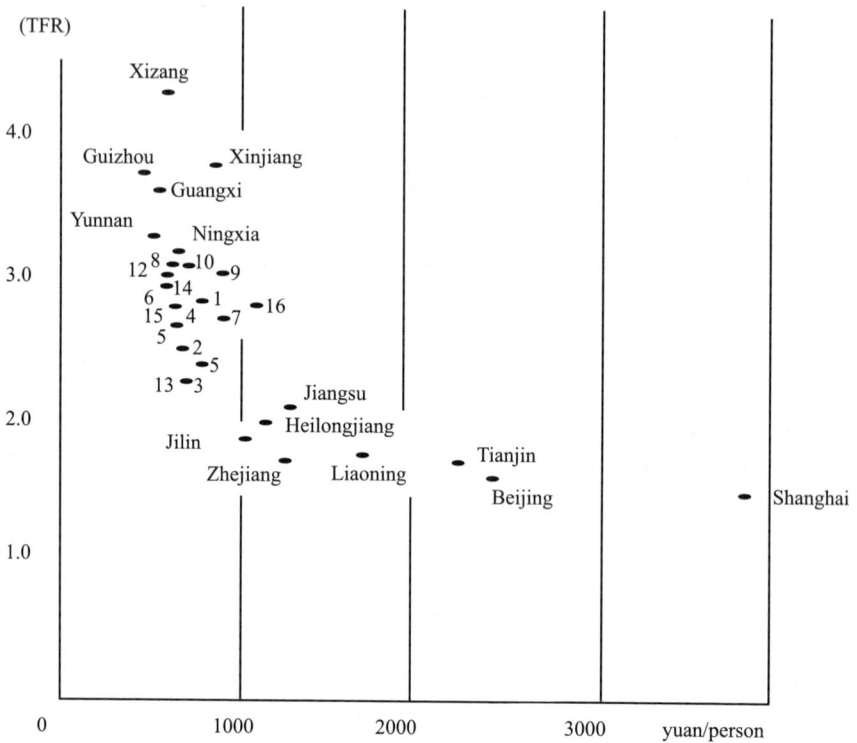

Fig. 1 Gross fertility rates（TFR）and per capita income in various regions in 1987

Note: 1. Hebei, 2. Shanxi, 3. Neimeng, 4. Anhui, 5. Fujian, 6. Jiangxi, 7. Shandong, 8. Henan. 9. Hubei, 10. Hainan. 11. Xizang, 12. Shanxi, 13. Gansu, 14. Qinghai, 15. Hunan, 16. Guangdong.

Undoubtedly, the cost-benefit theory discussed above has its limitations and is not generally accepted in the field of the population economics elsewhere in the world, but it reveals the relationship between reproductive behavior and the choice of interests. It provides us with experiences for reference in our search for solutions of population control. Due to the underdevelopment of commodity economy and blunted commodity concepts that has been the norm over a long period of time in China, population production has naturally not been conceived of as falling into the category of commodity production. However, this does not mean that the reproductive behavior of people is not controlled by interest adjustment. Frequently, we hear observations such as: somebody raised a son in vain, and somebody gets

benefit from his children. "In vain" refers to the fact that the investment of the
parent in a child is not returned as it is expected such that the child would not allocate part of his income to his parents or the child ignores and refuses to support his
parents after he gets married. "Getting the benefit" is just the opposite, referring
to the fact that the investmentof the parents in the child is returned as it is expected, yielding obvious labor-economic benefit or old-age support-insurance benefit
or other benefits. "Raising in vain" and "getting the benefit" are conclusions
reached after the cost-benefit of a child is assessed. It is a conscious or unconscious
assessment of the economic interests of the reproductive behavior as well as a motivation that determines the number of children to have.

In practice, the relationship between economic development and fertility is
evident. as shown in Fig. 1[1]

This figure clearly indicates the following findings. First, the gross fertility
was above the replacement level (TFR > 2. 1) in the 22 provinces and autonomous regions where the per capita income was below 1000 yuan in 1987 (which
included Shandong and Hubei where the income level was higher and Guizhou and
Yunnan where the level was lower) . Second, with the exception of Guangdong,
the gross fertility was below the replacement level in 8 provinces and[2]municipali-
ties directly under the Central Government such as Beijing and Liaoning, where
the per capita income was above 1000 yuan. The gross fertility declined to 1. 46 in
Shanghai which had the highest per capita income in the country and to 1. 58 in
Beijing, which was second only, to Shanghai. Third, provinces and autonomous
regions with the highest fertility were all the regions that had the lowest per capita
income. The gross fertility was 4. 3 in Xizang, which was the highest in the nation
and its per capita income was only 598 yuan, ranking the fourth lowest in the nation. The gross fertility in Guizhou ranked third, and its per capita income was the
lowest. The gross fertility in Guangxi ranked fourth and its per capita income was
the second lowest. How about the situation in the 12 coastal regions (Taiwan is not
included due to the lack of information)? The per capita income was 872 yuan in

---

① See *statistic Yearbook of China.* 1989, China Statistic Publishing House, 1989.
② P. 33 and Yearbook of Vital Statistics of China, 1989, Science and Technology Press, 1989,
pp. 132 – 133.

1987. These are eight provinces and municipalities in the coastal areas that exceeded this level. These were Beijing, Tianjin, Shanghai, Liaoning, Jiangsu, Zhejiang, Shandong and Guangdong. Four provinces were below this level. These were Hebei, Fujian, Guangxi and Hainan. The gross national fertility was 2.6. In the coastal areas, eight provinces and municipalities of Beijing, Tianjin, Shanghai, Liaoning, Jiangsu, Zhejiang, Fujian and Guangdong were below this level, while Shandong, Guangxi, Hainan and Hebei were above this level. The per capita income was above the national level and gross fertility was below the national level in 7 out of these 12 regions. In two regions, either the per capita income was above the national level or the gross fertility was below the national level. Overall, in the coastal areas, the per capita income is higher, economy is more developed, the decline of fertility is more rapid, the level reached is lower, which agrees with the general law that fertility declines as economy develops. Admittedly, the decline of fertility in China is mainly the result of the population policy, but we cannot rule out the role of the economic factors. In fact, the above results have been achieved as a consequence of the interplay of these two factors.

II. Cost Transition

Under the same population and birth policy, fertility is lower in the coastal areas and areas where economy is highly developed. In some such areas, the transition from the invariable or quantitative cost to variable or qualitative cost has been effected. This is both the cause and effect of economic development and technological advancement.

First of all, developed economy and technology put an end to the era of manual labor whereby workers rely on their arms. Economic and technological development is determined not by the number of laborers, but by their quality and their scientific and technological level. Under these circumstances, the cost of an extra marginal child is relatively stable, but the economic benefit of the marginal labor the child brings to the family and his parents is drastically reduced. With the development of commodity economy and the strengthening of commodity concepts, traditional ideas are giving way and families are increasingly becoming small. Against this background, the decline of the marginal labor-economic benefit provided by the marginal child is inevitable. Economic and technological development sets higher demands on the quality of laborers, particularly their scientific and educational quality. It is only when the child is trained to become a well-educated worker that he can earn higher income and provide more labor-economic benefit for his family and parents. This makes the family and the parents face such a decision that they are willing to spend money more on the variable or qualitative cost than on the invariable or quantitative cost, thus initiating the transition of the cost of children.

Second, as the economy develops and the per capita income increases, the old-age support-insurance benefit of children also tends to decline. This makes people hesitate to desire more children and reduces the invariable or quantitative cost. This may be explained from both the social and the individual's perspectives. From the social perspective, economic development and enhanced productivity of labor gave increased social wealth accumulation. In any case, out of whatever purpose, the government and enterprises will provide fund to set up the annuity system, sponsor more old-age welfare services. In the extreme case, the government may even opt for a welfare state. From the perspective of individuals, economic development will certainly produce a big increase in their income so that they can save for their retirement. Various retirement plans are particularly attractive because they exempt retirees from paying income tax on their pensions and at the same time provide high interest, making individual savings an important source and component of pension. Under these circumstances, the role of children in providing for their parents in their old age is vastly reduced. In developed countries, such a role is reduced to the minimum, which gives more impetus to people to make the transition from investing in having more children to investing in the quality of children.

In addition, the rapid development in modern science led by micro electronic technology has not only advanced the industrial revolution, ushering in an upsurge in the so-called "post-industrialization", and giving a powerful impetus to economic development, but also introduced modern science and technology into the family and every sphere of social life, widening people's vision and enhancing their tastes. To some people, the benefit of children in providing emotional pleasure is reduced and so is their benefit in bearing the risk for the family fortune. All these have contributed to varying degrees to the transition from the emphasis on quantity to the emphasis on quality.

What about the situation in China? Since the implementation of reform and opening to the outside world, rapid headway has been made in our economy and economic technology. The gross national product increased from 999. 8 billion yuan in 1979 to 1, 578. 9 billion yuan in 1989 with an increase by 1. 41 times calculated according to the comparable price[1]. This undoubtedly has a tremendous impact on fertility and population reproduction. However, due to the general low level of productive forces and some particularities in the reform of the economic system, this role is somewhat compromised.

On one hand, the impact is pronounced in cities as previously analyzed, especially in large and medium-size cities, and in some rural areas with a well developed economy. That is, with the development in economy and technology, the benefits of children in providing labor, income, old-age support and insurance have been on the steady decline and there has begun the transition from the emphasis on quantity to the emphasis on quality. Numerous examples can be cited from the coastal areas. A number of studies have demonstrated that in the open coastal areas with highly developed economy such as Beijing, Shanghai, Tianjin, Shenyang, Guangzhou, Jiangsu, Zhejiang, Fujian, Guangdong, the proportion of children who can provide their parents with labor and income or the proportion of parents who rely on their children for support are very small. On the contrary, the proportion of children who are married and set up their own family, but still need financial support from their parents is high. Moreover, there is a large proportion of old people in cities who receive pensions. According to a sampling survey in 1987, such people amounted to 63. 7% in cities and 56. 3 in towns. Most people no longer depend on their children for old—age support, which makes the benefit of children in providing financial support and insurance for their parents in their old age considerably reduced. Such examples are not lacking in the countryside either. For in-

---

[1] See *Statistic Yearbook of China*. 1990, China Statistic Publishing House, 1990.

stance, in the village of Sifangtai in East Anshan Township of Anshan City in Liaoning Province, its 1004 villagers live in 77-story buildings with a spacious compound. The per capita income of the village in 1989 was 1596 yuan. Housing is free
and equipped with running water and gas stoves as is the case in cities. At the
Double Ninth Festival (9th day of the 9th lunar month), the elderly were taken
on 8 trip to visit the Water Cave, a scenic spot in Benxi City. They are provided
with a 25 yuan monthly stipend. People in the village are reluctant to have more
children and some even gave up their quota for a second birth. Another case in
point is the Houshi Village in Hangzhou District of Dalian City where the transition
from the emphasis on quantity to that of quality has been completed. Fewer but better births have become the aspired goal for the people.

However, there are some recent developments which are unfavorable to the
decline of fertility and even encourage fertility to rise. First of all, the implementation of the responsibility system in the countryside and the development of private
enterprises in urban areas, particularly small towns, have restored the function of
the family as a unit of production and economic management that had been lost for
more than 20 years. The need for labor, especially male labor, in the family has
become very acute, which has greatly increased the benefit of children in providing
labor and income and consequently stimulated the economic motivation for more
children, particularly sons.

Second, the system of collective old-age care in the rural area with wubaohu
(childless and infirm old persons who are guaranteed food, clothing, medical
care, housing and burial expenses by the people's commune) and old people's
home as the core established under the former commune system has been a sound
and high-level old-age security system in areas where productivity is low. It has
played an important role in alleviating the fears and anxieties of old people who
have no or few children. With the reform and the establishment of the new administrative and economic systems, the original old-age care institutions were either
abolished or greatly weakened such that the reliance on children has reemerged as
the safest measure for old-age care. The benefit of children in providing old-age
support and insurance is thus increased.

The major benefits of children are increased to varying degrees in the vast countryside and areas with underdeveloped economic technology. If the cost of children is simultaneously increased, fertility will not be significantly affected. However, such simultaneous increase in the cost of children never happened. The above analysis demonstrates that the quantitative cost of children is relatively stable at given level of economic development and the qualitative cost of children is on the continuous rise with the progress in economic technology. Exceptions do occur however, under given historic conditions. This is mainly the result of the limited benefits from the qualitative cost of children. Statistics indicate that for individuals employed in state-owned units in 1989, the highest-paid occupations were geological survey and exploration enterprises with an average annual per person salary of 2563 yuan. Transportation, postal and communications industries were the second highest-paid occupations with an average annual per person salary of 24490 yuan. Next comes the building industry, whose average annual per person salary amounted to 2414 yuan. The average annual per person salary was only 2123 yuan in scientific research fields and comprehensive technological services where scientists are concentrated, 1899 yuan for educational and cultural establishments and only 1875 yuan for Party organizations, government departments and mass organizations. The reversal of mental and manual work in terms of remunerations, which is even more staggering in the case of private enterprises, depreciates mental work and causes the erroneous conception that academic study is useless. In some places, the problem of dropouts from middle and elementary school is serious. There are people who think it is more profitable to do business than go to school and better to make money by doing transportation business than spend money on education. All these have seriously hindered the increase of the qualitative cost of children. It is thought that the increase in the quantitative cost of children will bring more economic benefits.

The unfavorable tilting of the cost-benefit of children in the countryside and underdeveloped small towns, coupled with the environmental factors, has diminished the effect of the economic policy of fertility. It is known to all that under the economic system of the former People's Commune, rural areas had adopted the centralized management in economy, production, exchange, distribution and consumption. In addition, such management had been incorporated with government administration, assuming an extraordinary authority. Under this authority, the implementation of family planning policies, including various measures of award and penalty, had been easy. Furthermore, the validity of various rules and measures was sufficient to influence individuals' reproductive behavior. In some places, for example, unplanned children were refused grain ration and private plot, which was enough to affect the livelihood of an entire family. Together with other forms of penalty and public opinion pressure, it made individuals pay a very high price to have unplanned children. However, things have been different since the start of reform such that the authoritative entity integrating government administration and commune management has been abolished and centralized production management has been given way to the economic activity with the family as the basic unit. Various rules and measures of award and penalty have lost the power they used to have. For example, the withholding of grain ration and private plot from children born not as planned is now meaningless and fines have no effect on well-to-do farmers because they do not mind paying the fine. For those who are still poor, fines do not have an effect either because they will not be able to pay anyway. It is the view of materialist dialectics that internal causes are the basis for change, while external causes are the conditions for change. Since the implementation of reform, a number of factors in the changes in the economic system in rural areas have increased the benefits of children to parents and the family. In urban areas, these factors have mainly to do with the changes in the opening to the outside in small towns. However, the cost of children, primarily the variable qualitative cost, has not similarly been increased. In terms of the external environment, the changes in the system have weakened the function of social control mechanisms. Besides the constraints imposed by the age structure of the population (there will be a new baby boom between 1986 and 1997), the changes in the internal and external cause are important factors for the pickup of fertility in recent years. However, the age structure of the population is not expected to change in a short period of time because it is the result of the changes in births, deaths and migration over the last several decades and even over the last century. In order to effectively control the growth of population to make it fit the economic development, all we can do is to focus on the above- mentioned external causes that affect fertility. Unfortunately, however, this is extremely difficult when the level of economic development is low. This is where the real difficulty is.

III. The Benign Cycle of Reform and Endeavor to Develop

The above analysis indicates that there are two types of cycles between population and economic development. One type is that when the level of the development of productive forces is low, economic development relies mainly on the more input of labor, which leads people to desire more children and maintains the invariable or quantitative cost of children at a high level. The other type of cycle refers to the fact that the tremendous progress in industrial revolution, especially in modern and contemporary scientific development, continuously advances industrial revolution and increases productivity as never has before with the consequent result that economic development relies mainly on the enhancement of the quality of labor rather than excessive input of human labor. These are the two models of cycle for population and economic development: families adopting the former model rely on the heavy input of the cost of children in order to obtain more economic benefit from children when the level of science and technology and labor productivity is very low. The lower the technological makeup and the more flexible is its absorption of labor, the more lower the technological makeup and the more flexible is its absorption of labor, the more investment people will make in having more children. Conversely, families adopting the latter model invest more in the quality of children to obtain more economic benefit from them when the level of science, technology and labor productivity is high. The higher the technological makeup, the less flexible its absorption of labor, the more it will encourage people to turn from the number of children to the quality of children, thus making the qualitative cost rise. Obviously, these are two diametrically different models of cycle for population and economic development, which may also be called the elementary and advanced developmental cycles. Our goal is to work hard to initiate the transition from the elementary model to the advanced model.

The reduction of fertility is the key to the promotion and completion of the transition. In its turn, the reduction of fertility rests upon the education of the benefits of children in providing labor-economic benefit, old age support-insurance benefit and upon the transition between the emphasis on the invariable or quantitative cost to the emphasis on the variable or qualitative cost. It took a fairly long time for most countries in the West to complete this process. The transition to low fertility and high labor productivity has been made gradually in responding to the needs of social and economic development. A new problem has emerged following the completion of the transition in most developed countries today, that is, the shortage of new labor force that results from the exceedingly low fertility. This shortage affects the benign cycle of population and economic development, although its impact is only beginning to exert itself. The situation in China is completely different from that in the West. The major problem at present and for a considerable time to come is the population surplus. We should do our best to promote the transition of population and economic development from the elementary stage to the advanced stage and to effect the change from high fertility and low labor productivity to low fertility and high labor productivity. We need to promote this transition and effect the change from the point of the view of the reform and on the basis of the reality in China. Strategically, decisions are to be made at three levels.

First, we should seriously implement the basic national policy on population control, stabilize the existing family planning measures and make reference to past experiences that have proved to be successful. This is because the reduction of fertility in China is through a different channel from that in the West where fertility reduction depends on economic development and natural decline. In reducing fertility in China, the family planning policy formulated by the government plays a key role. This will remain a major avenue for fertility control and reduction in the future. What is crucial at the present time is to stabilize existing policies, because any shift in the policies, either relaxation or tightening, will cause people to lose confidence in the government and unfavorably spur fertility to pick up. The application of previous experiences is equally important because many practices in the several decades of family planning in China have proved effective and suitable for the country. These experiences include the importance attached by leaders, close coordination among various departments concerned in carrying out the basic national policy, reinforcing of population management, installation of the system of responsibility for birth planning, integration of family planning with other tasks, setting up of key households that need to be monitored, integration of family planning with the assistance with the poor, strengthening of facilities at the grass roots level and so on. In so doing, we should particularly learn from the experiences in the coastal areas where population control is more successful and economic development is more rapid.

Second, in order to explore the internal causes for the decline in fertility from a long-term and fundamental perspective, we need, in the spirit of reform, to take effective measures in both aspects of cost and benefit to gradually effect the transition in the choice of interests of the reproductive behavior by individuals and the transition from the control by administrative measures to the control by the adjustment of interests.

In terms of the cost of children, we should mainly work to increase the cost of having unplanned children by appropriately raising the fine for people who have unplanned children. Instead of one lump sum, the fine should be applied for about 14 years, the same length of time during which parents who have only one child are awarded. The measure is taken to make parents clearly realize that the benefits to be brought by having extra children will not compensate for the cost of raising them. This will also effectively increase the qualitative cost of children, especially the expenses of education. This requires us to gradually correct the unreasonable income distribution between mental and manual work in order to increase the return of the investment in the intellectual abilities of the population. Parents should be made to realize that their investment in the quality of their children will be compensated by the benefits to be brought by their children so that they will be encouraged to shift from investing in more children to investing in high quality.

As far as the benefits of children are concerned, we need to increase the benefits of one child for his parents and make sure that parents receive the bonus award for having only one child. We should make up, through labor markets and community services, for the labor-economic benefit parents lose because they do not have many children. We should also make up for the old-age support-insurance benefit that parents lose because they do not have many children by providing the old-age insurance for parents with one child. In addition, we should give preferential treatment to single children in admissions to kindergartens and schools, employment and transfer from the farmer's status to worker's status. We should provide life insurance for single children to increase their benefit in assuming the risk for the rise and fall of their family fortune and maintaining the family status. Another measure that may be adopted is to impose restrictions on unplanned children in admissions to kindergartens and schools, housing assignment, employment, government subsidies, transfer from the farmer's status to the worker's status so as to reduce the value of these marginal children to their parents.

The above measures adopted in the cost and benefits of children will lead to such a situation that whoever has fewer children and whoever spends less in the quantitative cost of children will receive more benefits and conversely, whoever has more children and invests more in having more children will receive fewer benefits or will even suffer a loss. As time goes by, people will turn from the concern about their interests, i. e., the cost and benefits of their children, to the concern about the quality of their children. Consequently, they will choose to have fewer but better children. Studies carried out in some economically developed coastal areas indicate that there have been a considerable number of families that are on this track. Corresponding to this, the mechanism of population management by the state can also turn from the present emphasis on the administration of population targets to the management that is aimed at safeguarding the rights of single children and families that have planned children, and collecting necessary fines from families that have extra unplanned children, in order to enforce the law. The state should be devoted to providing direct and desired service for the vast masses of people and institute the transition from administrative management to interest adjustment.

Third, we should develop economy and advance technology to lay a sound foundation for the transition of children's cost and move to the benign cycle of population and economic development. It is recognized by all, both at home and abroad, that the population policy of the Chinese government has played a key role in fertility reduction in the last several decades in China. Moreover, the fertility control in the future will also be largely determined by the ability of the state to adjust and control, as is discussed in this paper. However, the role of the infrastructure is not to be overlooked. It is only on a sound economic and social basis that policy can produce good results. In fact, the success of the family planning policy in China is closely related to the level of national economy, to the nature of economic structure and relations of production, and to the superstructure. On this account, population issues are in the final analysis economic issues. It is only when economy and technology are developed, labor productivity raised, income in general increased that the dependence of parents on children for support can be eliminated and their expectation of the benefits of their children be lowered. Likewise, it is only when the level of economy and technology is elevated, the overall requirements of workers in the level of science, education, and technology are raised that the qualitative cost of children, especially the qualitative cost on the education of children, can be raised accordingly and the transition from quantitative cost to qualitative cost be accomplished. With regard to the development of economy and advancement of technology, we should depart from reality, act on the basis of our capacity and develop accordingly. In terms of the constraints of demographic conditions on economic development and technological advance, we must realize that under the limited natural resources and economic development, our population is overgrown and has a strong momentum of growth in the considerable period of time in the future. Besides, our consumption is extensive and vast. Under these circumstances, we should not allow too much accumulation, too large and broad investments and we should not require our national economy to develop too fast. The quality of our population, especially the educational quality of population, is low, the proportion of people who have had schooling from colleges, high schools, polytechnic schools, junior high schools and elementary schools correspond to the age makeup of the population, displaying a typical pyramid. In addition, there are about 200 million people in China who are illiterate and semi-illiterate. The number of workers is insignificant in high-tech industries, slightly higher in advanced or medium-level-tech traditional industries and the highest in the industries of manual labor and semi—mechanized labor, displaying a similar pyramid structure of economy and technology. For this reason, economy and technology can only be developed in a coordinated and protracted way with long-term stability as its goal. This is a quick, rather than slow, way because it fits our demographic conditions. As such, it is also the way to steadfastly encourage the decline of fertility and the transition from quantitative cost to qualitative cost of children. This will lead to the benign cycle of population and economic development characterized by low fertility, high educational quality and high labor productivity.

References

[1] Liu, Guoguan, Some Theoretical Issues in the Economic Construction in China, Jiangsu People's Publishing House, 1986.

[2] State Statistic Bureau, ed. Economic Studies and Statistics of the Economic Development in the Coastal Areas, China Statistic press, 1989.

[3] Tian, Xueyuan, Demographic Perspective of the Strategy of Economic Development in coastal Areas, *Economic Studiess*, Vol. 8, 1988.

[4] Zeng, Muye, Coastal New Tide and Reform in Guangdong, Guangdong High Education Press, 1989.

[5] Zhang, Minru, et al, Population Migration and Management in China's Coastal Areas, China Broadcasting and Television Press, 1989.

[6] Beeder, Gary S., An Eeconomic Analysis of Fertility, Princeton University Press, 1960.

[7] Simon, Juham L., The Economics of Population Growth, Princeton University Press, 1977.

[8] Brown, Lester R. et al., State of the World 1990, A Worldwatch Institute Report on Progress Toward Sustainable Society, W. W. Norton and Company; New York, 1990.

Technological Advances and the
Transformation of the Cost of Children[*]

Poverty creates population. [①]Population growth and economic development have proved the truth in this axiom put forward by Karl Marx more than 100 years ago. Demoeconomists often attribute this phenomenon to the low marginal cost of children, especially low support cost, under poverty conditions. While this approach is correct and significant in providing guidance for reproductive behavior, I consider it inadequate since technological advances are not taken into account in the analysis of the cost of children and the characteristic differences under different technological conditions are usually not examined in the analysis of the marginal benefit of children. This inadequacy prevents further study on the cost and benefit of children, especially the study on the transformation of the fixed or quantitative cost of children to the variable or qualitative cost of children.

I . Two Types of Circle

Despite frequent regional conflicts and wars after the World War II , the global population and economy have in general developed hand in hand and the world population has been developing under relatively stable and peaceful conditions. According to the United Nations Department of Economic and Social Affairs, during the 40-year period between 1950 and 1990, the world population doubled from 2. 5 billion to 5. 3 billion, marking perhaps an era of the fastest population growth since the human race came into being. Meanwhile, the world economy has

---

 * See: *Chinese Journal of Population Science*, Volumes, Number 1 , 1993.

 ① Kar Marx, *Das Capital*, People's Publishing House, Vol. 3 , p. 243 , 1975.

developed rapidly and per capita gross national product (GNP) has been increasing along with the growth of population. A further analysis will reveal, however, that situations vary considerably from country to country. The World Bank states the following in its 1990 *World Development Report*: In the 1980s, many developing countries were not only unable to move forward along with industrialized nations, but also saw a decrease in the absolute value of their income; millions of people in Latin America are living under worse conditions than early 1970s; and people's livelihoods in most areas in Africa to the south of the Sahara Desert have lowered to the level in the 1960; to those people, the 1980s was a decade of desertion. ①This was determined by the pace of economic developing countries. Take the decade of 1980 – 1990 as an example: total fertility rate (TFR) was 3.53 on the world average, 1.91 among developed countries and 4.07 among developing countries. The latter two figures not only mark a great difference but also have different characteristics: TFR in developed countries has been lower than the replacement level and their population is expected to decrease if the current situation persists; in contrast, population has been growing rapidly in developing countries, which is expected to continue. Between 1980 and 1990, the gross domestic product (GDP) increased at an annual rate of 2.5% in developed countries and 2.3% in developing countries; negative increase was seen in the Africa to the south of the Sahara Desert, Latin America and the Caribbean, and the development in the Middle East and North Africa Was stagnant. ② This situation illustrates two types of circle in today's world between population growth and economic development: one is low fertility rate—high per capita income—low fertility rate, which is seen mostly in developed countries; the other is high fertility rate—low per capita income—high fertility rate, which is common in developing countries. It should be noted, however, that the situations vary considerably among different developing countries.

Apparently, different types of circle between population growth and economic development is based on different productivity, since low productivity brings about low income while high productivity may yield high income. It is commonly known that the level of productivity may be raised by either intensifying work load or im-

①　World Bank, 1990 *World Development Report*, China Financial and Economic Press, 1990.
②　United Nations, *World Population Prospects* 1990, World Bank, 1990 *World Development Report*.

proving technology, the first having been replaced long ago by the latter. Therefore, the circle between population growth and economic development is based on a certain technological level. The description of the above-mentioned two types of circle can thus be modified as: the low-level circle features high fertility rate—low technological level—low productivity—low per capita income—high fertility rate, and high-level circle is characterized by low fertility rate—high technological level—high productivity—high per capita income—low fertility rate. This is a universally applicable inference based on many phenomena in the relationships between population growth and economic development. One may wonder whether government interference can change or improve these two types of circle. In my opinion, the answer is generally "no." Government interference can only help seek the maximum expectation threshold value within a certain type of circle. For example, in a low-level circle, the population problem is usually demonstrated by excess population and labor that puts pressure on productivity, and the goal of government policy is to seek the maximum possibility of lowering fertility rate under the low levels of scientific and technological development, productivity and income. It is difficult, however, to reduce fertility rate to a very low level, e. g. , below the replacement level, or to maintain fertility rate at a low level for an extended period of time. This opinion supports rather than disparage the role of government policy in population growth and scientific, technological and economic development. Policy is a guideline adopted by a political party or state under its political principles in order to further its goal. Such guideline must be formulated and implemented within, and not without, the limit permitted by reality. Policy should not be a product of whims, but should reflect the reality. No policy can have an effective impact, or play any significant role, or allow any flexibility, unless it presents an accurate picture of the real world.

While its population policy is universally considered very successful, China has not been able to break through the above circle among population growth and scientific, technological and economic development. For example, although China's fertility rate (TFR) was 5. 44 in the 1940s, 5. 87 in the 1950s and 5. 68

in the 1960s, it declined rapidly to 4.01 in the 1970s, 2.45 in the 1980s,[1] and 2.25 in 1989, the lowest in developing countries. However, it remained above 2.20 even in the 1970s and 1980s and never dropped below 2.10, the replacement level. China is currently in the process of transition from a high fertility rate to a low one, but has not yet reached the stage of low fertility rate.

Despite the drastic fluctuations in its national economy since 1949, China's economy has in general developed rather rapidly and the country's economic strength has been enhanced substantially. The Chinese economy has been growing at a particularly high rate since its economic reform started more than 10 years ago, benefiting the Chinese people immensely. According to a calculation based on fixed prices with China's national income in 1952 as 100, the country's national income was 1133.4 in 1989, an annual increase of 6.8%; the annual increase rate was 10.7% between 1979 and 1989 and 11.2%, between 1981 and 1989, making China one of the economically fastest growing nations in the world.[2] However, China's per capita income remains low due to the low starting point of the Chinese economy and the substantial increase of the Chinese population. The Population Reference Bureau, Inc. in the United States estimates that in 1988, the per capita GNP was $ 3470 in the world, $ 15830 among developed nations, $ 710 among developing nations and $ 330 in China. In its 1990 *World Development Report*, the World Bank estimates that China's per capita GNP was $ 340 in 1988. Estimates of China's per capita GNP by foreign countries and multinational organizations vary considerably, ranging from $ 300 to $ 1000. The $ 300 figure was apparently influenced by the continuous drop of the exchange rate of RMB versus hard currencies and does not accurately reflect the reality in China. Based on the 1980 exchange rate of RMB versus hard currencies and deducting the factor of inflation in the previous 10 years, China's per capita GNP in 1990 was approximately $ 577, even lower than the average among developing countries, making China one of the countries with the lowest per capita income.

---

[1] State Family Planning Commission, Table and Charts of the Sample Survey on the Fertility Rate of 1‰ of the Chinese Population, 1984; China Demographic Yearbook 1989, Scientific and Technological Documents Press; Data of the 10% Sampling from China's 1990 census, China Statistical Press, 1999.

[2] *China Statistical Yearbook* 1990, China Statistical Press, 1990.

Universities, high and elementary schools and vocational schools have been growing rapidly in China in the past four decades and have produced an increasing number of graduates. However, the level of scientific, technological and cultural development should be viewed in the perspective of the educational level of the entire population and should be indicated by a universal quantitative index. Several years ago, this author put forward the concept of educational level index (ELI),[1] which refers to the average years of schooling among a particular population group, the index being 16 years among university graduates, 11 years among senior high school (including vocational school) graduates, eight years among junior high school graduates, four yeas, among elementary school graduates, and 0.25 year among illiterates and semi-literates. According to these classifications and the census data, China's ELl was 2.41 in 1964, 4.38 in 1982 and 5.18 in 1990, the index being more than doubled in a quarter of a century. While this demonstrates a remarkable growth of the national level of education, an index of 5.18 is rather low after all, which in turn affects labor productivity.

In sum, China remains primarily in the low-level circle between population growth and scientific, technological and economic development, featuring high fertility rate—low level of scientific and technological development—low productivity—low per capita income—high fertility rate, albeit it is in the process of transition from a low-level circle to a high-level circle. Certain anomalies, however, should be kept in mind: the transition with regard to fertility rate has progressed faster than other aspects and is close to the level in developed countries, while science, technology, productivity and per capita income has been developing more slowly, at a pace typically seen among developing countries. This suggests that in order to complete the strategic transition from the low-level circle to the high-level circle, it is necessary to focus on the development of science, technology, productivity and per capita income while maintaining a slow population growth and low fertility rate.

---

① Tian Xueyuan , *A Report on the 1987 Sample Survey on China's Elderly Population Above Sixty Years of Age*, Population Science of China, Special Issue I, 1988.

II. The Key Role of Technological Advances

Population growth, scientific and technological progress and economic development are closely related and a change in any one of them is bound to affect the other two. For example, a decrease of new births will help reduce the consumption of national income and increase the accumulation of funds needed for further economic growth and scientific and technological development as well for distribution among the current population; and economic growth and increase of per capita income provide the material basis for population control, upgrading of the educational level, and the improvement of a social security system for the elderly necessitated by the aging of the population and decline of fertility rate. In other words, the development of national economy and increase of per capita income are basic guarantees of China's national policy of controlling population growth, upgrading the level of education and adjusting the population structure. While the decline of China's fertility rate despite the low level of the country's scientific, technological and economic development has brought about excellent social benefit. It will be rather difficult to further reduce the rate within a short period of time. The growth of economy and per capita income is subject to the limitation of various conditions and cannot be expected to achieve an ultra-high speed. Under these circumstances, the key role of scientific and technological development in lowering fertility rate, raising productivity and increasing per capita income becomes increasingly evident.

First, scientific and technological advances help lower fertility rate by stimulating the growth of marginal cost of children, especially marginal qualitative cost of children, and reducing marginal benefit of children. Along with the development of the capitalist market economy and permeation of mercantilism, certain micro-demoeconomists put forward the theory of cost and benefit of children by studying human reproduction from the perspective of commodity production and exchange. They suggested that the cost of a child is composed of direct cost, i. e. , monetary expenses in rearing the child, and indirect cost, i. e. , reduction of the income of parents, particularly the mother, in rearing the child. When social productivity is low, a child's basic living expenses and the mother's direct and indirect expenses during the periods of gestation and delivery are relatively stable, constituting the child's fixed or quantitative cost, while the expenses on the child's health care and education keep growing and can be regarded as the child's variable or qualitative cost. Of course, parents not only incur expenses in rearing their children, but also receive benefit after incurring such expenses. A child's major benefit for the parents and the family comprises economic benefit (labor), security benefit (future parental support) and entertainment benefit (family happiness); other types of benefit include property inheritance, preventing the family business from declining and household safety. Whether parents need to have a certain marginal child depends on a cost-benefit balance regarding the child. i. e. , they will not have the child if the cost outweighs the benefit, but will have the child if the opposite is true; their decision will depend on random factors if the cost equals the benefit. This theory of a child's cost and benefit undoubtedly has its limitations, and even demoeconomists in capitalist countries do not agree on the theory among themselves. Nevertheless, the theory is of immense significance to our population study since it provides a quantitative survey on the relationship between human reproductive behavior and their cost and benefit and illustrates a tendency of growing variable or qualitative cost and decreasing benefit of marginal children along with scientific and technological progress. The key point here is the role of technological advances in causing the loss of balance between a child's cost and benefit.

On the one hand, technological advances lead to the transformation of a child's fixed or quantitative cost into variable or qualitative cost and a change of reproductive attitude from favoring a greater number of children to favoring a better quality of children. In agricultural and early industrial societies, a laborer's strength lies in his physical energy, and a family acquires a qualified laborer once a child has come of age after healthy growth. Since the cost of children is low and the marginal cost of children is even lower, people tend to prefer a larger number of children, their fixed or quantitative cost being more important. Technological revolutions symbolized by the steam engine, diesel engine, electric motor and primary controller have kept improving means of production and upgrading technical levels, demanding a higher educational levels. The new, postwar technological revolution pioneered by the microelectronic technology and followed by such technologies as computer, astronavigation, laser, marine technology, new materials and biological engineering have not only revolutionized the traditional industries but also created new industries, requiring even higher level of education. Workers cannot meet their job requirements without acquiring modern scientific and technological knowledge. This situation has strongly stimulated the increase of marginal variable or qualitative cost of children, shifting the focus on fixed or quantitative cost of children to variable or qualitative cost of children.

On the other hand, technological advances have decreased the marginal benefit of children. As a result of technological progress, the increase of family's income depends more on the upgrading of its members' quality than on the growth of the number of its members, thus considerably decreasing the marginal benefit of children. Moreover, technological advances, the improvement of productivity and increase of societal and personal income make it possible for the society to establish more elderly social security programs and for individuals and households to have more savings for elderly support; the extensively established elderly social security system based on individual and societal resources further reduced the marginal benefit of children for elderly support, inheritance, promotion of family business and household security. Theoretically, the lower the technological level, the looser the connection between the labour and the work tools, the easier for laborers to be absorbed and the easier to materialize the marginal benefit of children; conversely, the higher the technological level, the closer the connection between the laborer and the work tools, the more difficult for laborers to be absorbed and the harder to realize the marginal cost of children. Technological advances have mercilessly shattered the tradition of favoring more children and presented in its place the advantage of breeding fewer but stronger and more intelligent children who are to receive better education.

Secondly, scientific and technological advances promote productivity and help increase income by combining technological advances, the subject of labor and work tools. Chinese economists have been debating on the theories of "two key elements" and "three key elements." As a matter of fact, any production process involves specific a subject of labor regardless of whether there are two key elements (labor force and the means of production) or three key elements (labor force, the subject of labor and the means of production), and the new meaning of the subject of labor is bound to receive increasing attention along with the progress of the new technological revolution. The reasons are various: a combination of new technology and the subject of labor will allow more exploration of utilization of natural resources; new technology can be adopted by raising the resource utilization rate, allow better use of the subject of labor, promote the quality of production, help develop new materials such as synthetic materials and increase profit.

The combination of technological advances and work tools has always been the major means by which productivity is improved and economy development promoted. As is well known, the division of the stages of economic development depends on how to engage in production and what work tools to use rather than what is produced. The ever-developing new technological revolution has been changing the traditional mode of production and life styles on a tremendous scale and at an astonishing speed; not only high technology industries as a result of the new technological revolution have been springing up, but new technologies have been used to renovate such traditional industries as metallurgical, coal-mining, automobile and textile industries, which came to be known as "reindustrialization." creating the highest ever productivity rate. These developments accout for the continuous and rapid growth of per capita GNP and per capita income in industrialized countries after World War II. Today a supercomputer is capable of handling a workload far beyond the capacity and speed of human calculation. Under these circumstances science, technology and other key elements of productive forces are transformed into actual productive forces at a much higher rate and with far greater impact. The "energy" of science and technology as the first productive forces is being released with an unprecedented magnitude.

That technological advances have the dual effects of lowering fertility rate and substantially raising productivity is manifested clearly in today's China. According to the 1990 census, the ELI among the national population was 5.18 in that year, the TFR 2.25 and per capita income 1189 yuan at the end of 1989. Of the 18 provinces, autonomous regions and municipalities whose ELIs was higher than the national level, in nine of such areas, the ELLs were much higher than the national level the TFRs much lower than the national average and per capita income much higher than the national average. Take Beijing as an example: the ELl was 7.65 in that city, 1.5 times higher than the national level; the TFR was 1.33, 59.9% of the national rate; and the per capita income was 3248 yuan, 2.7 times as much as the national figure. In Liaoning, the ELI was 6.28, 1.2 times as high as the national level; the TFR was 1.51, 67% of the national rate; and the per capita income was 1989 yuan 1.7 times as much as the national figure. The ELIs were slightly higher in six provinces and autonomous regions than the national level, and their TFRs and per capita income were close to the national level. In three provinces and autonomous regions, the ELIs were higher than the national level, but their TFRs were much higher than the national rate and the per capita income in two of them was considerably lower than the national figure. The situations in the three areas are: in Xinjiang, the ELl was 5.59, the TFR 3.16, and the per capita income 1232 yuan; in Hainan, the educational level was 5.45, the TFR 2.93, and the per capita income 1131 yuan; in Henan, the ELI was 5.23, the TFR 2.88, and the per capita income 836 yuan. Why do we have these unusual phenomena? The main reason is external interference, such as the policy of favoring population growth among the ethnic minorities in Xinjiang, the greater proportion of migrant population and the lack of control of population growth in Hainan, and the less rigorous enforcement of the family planning program in Henan. Therefore, these irregularities are without general significance.

While under the low national educational level, the fertility rate and per capita income in certain areas whose ELIs are slightly higher than the national level do not conform with the "high ELI, low fertility rate and high per capita income" pattern, it is generally true that fertility rate is higher than the national average and per capita income is lower than the national level among 12 provinces and autonomous regions whose ELIs are lower than the national level. For example, in Xizang, the ELl was 2.23 in 1990, 43% of the national average; the TFR was 4.22 in 1989, 1.87 times as high as the national rate; and the per capita income was 778 in 1989, 65% of the national average. In Guizhou, the ELI was 4.08, 79% of the national average; the TFR was 2.96, 1.32 times as high as the national rate; and the per capita income was 625 yuan, 53% of the national average. The only exception is Sichuan, where the ELl was 5.12, slightly lower than the national level; the TFR was 1. 76, only 78% of the national rate; and the per capita income was 809 yuan, 68% of the national figure. Why does Xizang Province have a low fertility rate despite their low level of scientific, technological and economic development? Perhaps it is the result of rigorous enforcement of the family planning policy.

Understanding the key role of technological advances in population growth and economic development has another implication. While the current administrative means of controlling population growth is necessary, it often creates confrontations and resistance since many concerns of people are not addressed. On the one hand, the administrative means need to be strengthened in order to avoid the loss of control of population growth; on the other hand, confrontations and resistance are after all undesirable and should be dealt with by reforming the current family planning program. One solution is to lower fertility rate through technological progress, i. e., to make available various options that increase the benefit of having fewer but better-quality children and that discourage having more children. This will help people determine the number of their children on the basis of their own interests and voluntarily choose to have fewer children, thus shifting the focus from the fixed or quantitative cost of children to variable or qualitative cost of children. It will ensure the transition from the circle of high fertility rate—low scientific and technological level—low productivity—low per capita income—high fertility rate to the circle of low fertility rate—high scientific and technological level—high productivity—high per capita income—low fertility rate, and will result in the best control of population growth.

III. Speeding up the Transformation of the Cost of Children

When it announced its ambitious goal of modernizing the country's agriculture, industry, national defense, science and technology, the Chinese government correctly pointed out that science and technology are key links to and education serves as the basis for, this process. In other words, the development of education in order to upgrade the population's educational level is the starting point for scientific and technological progress. As far as the subject of this article is concerned, during the transition from the low-level circle of population growth and economic development to the high-level circle, the development of education directly increases the variable or qualitative cost of children and thus relatively lowers the fixed or quantitative cost of children. Furthermore, by improving productivity and per capita income, the development of education provides material basis for the control of population growth, causes fertility rate to decline and help shift the focus from the quantitative cost of children to qualitative cost of children. Thus, how to effectively raise the variable or qualitative cost of children. i. e. , upgrade children's educational level, is the key to the transformation from the circle of high fertility rate—low scientific and technological level—low productivity—low per capita income—high fertility rate to the circle of low fertility rate—high scientific and technological level—high productivity—high per capita income—low fertility rate.

To many people, the development of education means increasing investment on education, e. g. , building more schools, hiring more teachers and purchasing more equipment. This is certainly correct. In fact, these were exactly what most developed countries did during their transition from the low-level circle to the high-level circle, and these are also what we will do. However, the increase of investment on education is limited by the increase of the national revenue and is therefore unlikely to be very fast. Between 1979 and China's expenditure on economic development grew 83% from 76. 159 billion yuan to 139, 7 billion yuan, a 183% growth; defense spending dropped 2. 09% from 22. 266 billion yuan to 21. 8 billion yuan; administrative cost increased 3. 31 times from 6. 305 billion yuan to 27. 16 billion yuan; expenditure on arts and education increased 2. 32 times from 17. 518 billion yuan to 58. 118 billion yuan, of which the spending on education grew from 11. 145 billion yuan to 44. 353 billion yuan,[1] one of the fastest growing category of government expenditure and second only to the increase of administrative cost. The author is by no means suggesting that the State has made enough investment on education so that no additional investment is necessary; rather, the author cautions that any increase of investment should be based on reality, i. e. , the country's financial capability, and that it is more important to pay attention to

---

[1] *China Statistical Yearbook* 1990.

the efficiency of investment than merely complaining about a shortage or slow increase of investment. In 1987, there were 4,118 million university professors and 59,316 million university students in the world, with a faculty – student ratio of 1:14; the ratio was 1:10 in Japan, 1:13 in the Soviet Union, 1:18 in the United States, 1:19 in India (1979), 1:23 in Canada, but only 1:5 in China. ① China must have 1.8 times as many as university students as it does now in order to catch up with the world's average level, 2.5 times as many students in order to reach the faculty-student ratio of the United States, and 3.5 times as many students in order to catch up with Canada. This suggests low efficiency of China's investment on education. Therefore, we must not only increase investment, but also tap the potential of the currently available resources, which is particularly important now, and seek proper solutions through reform.

Both the increase of investment and tapping the potential of currently available resources are but external conditions for upgrading the educational level of the Chinese population and shifting the focus from the fixed or quantitative cost of children to variable or qualitative cost of children. While these external conditions are important, effective mechanisms are needed for bringing people's initiative into full play. Such initiative depends ultimately on the effect of the variable or qualitative cost of children and on the corresponding mechanisms that regulate people's interests. Suppose the marginal variable or qualitative cost of a child is c, the benefit that may be yielded by the child after the parents have incurred the cost is b, then there are three possibilities:

1) $c > b$, i.e., the child's net marginal variable or qualitative cost is positive, meaning that the parents are unable to recoup from the benefit provided by the child the expenses they incurred in the child's education and other aspects of the child's life. As a result, people are unwilling to make any more investment than they have to on the child education.

2) $c = b$, i.e., the child's net marginal variable or qualitative cost is zero, meaning that the child provides enough benefit for the parents to recoup the expenses they incurred in the child's education and other aspects of the child's life. The

① *Ibid*

parents may feel encouraged to invest on the child's education, but they may not, depending largely on the family's financial status and the parents' understanding of the importance of education.

3) $c < b$, i. e. , the child's net marginal variable or qualitative cost is negative, meaning that the parents benefit more from the child than they have spent on the child's education and other aspects of the child's life. Naturally, parents will be more interested in investing on education.

Of these three situations, the second ($c = b$) is the necessary condition for the shifting of the focus from the fixed or quantitative cost of children to variable or qualitative cost of children, and the third ($c < b$) actually triggers the shifting. In other words, only when $c \leqslant b$ will the shifting actually occur, resulting in the upgrading of a population's educational level. This formula is of universal significance and nonconformity carries a price. For years, especially during the Cultural Revolution, when knowledge was considered a source of counterrevolutionary ideas, $c > b$ was true, stripping the incentive to shift the focus from the fixed or quantitative cost of children to variable or qualitative cost of children. While this abnormal phenomenon was ended after the Cultural Revolution was over, new problems deserve attention that have arisen during the economic reform, and the rapid development of a market economy. For example, although many schools expanded and equipment and faculty increased remarkably along with the development of the national economy, the number, of enrolled high shool students decreased from 54. 031 million in 1987 to 52. 61 million in 1988 and 50. 54 millon in 1989; enrolled elementary school pupils began to decrease as early as mid-1970s from approximately 150 million to 140 million in the early 1980, 130 million in the mid-1980s and 120 million in the late 1980s. ① While this was partially due to the change in population's age structure as a result of declining fertility rate, the main reason is the failure of the variable or qualitative cost of children to yield corresponding benefit, i. e. , $c \geqslant b$. This situation can be described well by the population sayings such as "a professor's pen is less profitable than the arm of a street peddlar's steelyard" and "those who use scalpels earn less than those who use

---

① *China Statistical Yearbook* 1990.

hair-clippers". In 1989, the average annual salary was 1, 935 yuan across the country, 2, 558 yuan among geological prospectors, 2, 288 yuan among employees in transport and post and telecommunications industries, 2, 171 among construction workers, 2, 118 yuan among scientists and engineers (only 183 yuan more than the national average) 1, 883 yuan among professors, teachers, artists and employees in the broadcast and television business (52 yuan) lower than the national average), and 1, 874 yuan among employees of the government, the Communist Party and other social organizations (61 yuan lower than the national level). This irrational distribution of income is the ultimate reason for the rampant elementary school dropout, and growing loathing against schools and must be rectified through reform. The current $c \geqslant b$ situation must be turned gradually to $c \leqslant b$ in order to ensure that the shifting of the focus from the fixed or quantitative cost of children to variable or qualitative cost of children can yield corresponding or greater benefit. Correspondingly, mechanisms should be set up so that adjustment of personal interests will replace administrative enforcement, variable or qualitative cost of children will increase gradually, fertility rate will decline continuously, and a transition will be completed towards the high-level circle of low fertility rate—high educational level—high productivity—high per capita income.

References

[1] Becker, Gary S. , *An Economic Analysis of Fertility*, Princeton University Press, 1960.

[2] Brown, Julian L. , *The Economics of Population Growth*, Princeton University Press, 1997.

[3] Brown, Lester R. , *et al.* , *State of the World* 1991: *A Worldwatch Institute Report on Progress Toward Sustainable Society*, W. W. Nortor & Company, New York, 1991.

[4] Peng Peiytn, Strengthen the Grassroots Im plementation of the Family Planning Program and Strive to Realize the Goal of Population Control Set Forth in the Eighth Five-Year Plan, *Population Bulletin*, January 1991.

[5] Zeng Yi, Several Issues in China's Future Population Development, *Social Sciences in China*, March 1991.

[6] Tian Xueyuan, Promote Economic Development, Transition and the Positive Circle Between Population and Economic Development, *Chinese Journal of Population Science*, Jan-

*uary*1991.

[7] A Ten-Year Program of Economic and Social Development and an Outline of the Eighth Five-Year Plan of the People's Republic of China, *People's Daily*, April 16. 1991.

[8] World Bank, 1990 *World Development Report* , China Financial and Economic Press. 1990.

Report on the Sample Survey on Household Economy and Fertility in the Ten provinces and Municipalities in China [*]

——To develop the economy is the highway to birth control—a universal conclusion that is proved again by the sample survey on household economy and fertility in the ten provinces and municipalities in China——the author

I. Background and plan design

According to the CPR/90/PO6 agreement that was concluded between the Chinese Government and the United Nations Population Activities Fund, the Institute of Population Studies of the Chinese Academy of Social Sciences, together with the Population Research Center of the Academy of Social Sciences of Hebei province, the Family Planning Commission of Liaoning Province, the Institute of Population Studies of Shanghai Academy of Social Sciences, the Institute of Population Studies of Hangzhou University, the Institute of Population Studies of the Academy of Social Sciences of Shandong province, the Population Research Office of the Academy of Social Sciences of Jiangxi province, the Institute of Population Studies of the Academy of Social Sciences and the Urban Investigation Team of the Statistics Bureau of Guangdong province, the Population Research Office of the Academy of Social Sciences of Sichuan province, the Institute of Economics of the Academy of Social Sciences of Guizhou conducted, in the first half of the year 1992 a sample survey on household economy and fertility in the above ten provinces and

* The Article for the "International Symposium on Household Economy and Fertility in China", Oct 25 – 30. 1993, Beijing. China.

municipalities. I, director of this project, put forward this report on the basis of the primary generalization of the data gathered from the sample survey.

The reform and opening to the outside world of China had been carried out for ten years by the end of the 80s when the second period of support by UNPAF was to conclude and the third period was about to begin. This decade was not normal and it witnessed the fastest economic development with people getting the most benefits. At that time the idea was not yet raised clearly to establish a socialist market economy, but it is not difficult to find that from the implementation of the family contract responsibility system in rural areas and the rapid development of joint ventures, the tide of commodity economy was knocking at the door of market economy. This has exerted a direct influence on the development of the national economy but also has a deep influence on the material, cultural and spiritual life of the whole society and its influence on population reproduction is becoming more and more obvious. To explore the influence on economic growth of population reproduction under the new situation, the difficult point being household economy and fertility changes, to find new ways for control over population increase, and to develop and promote scientific research through on-the-spot investigation and verification and through absorbing the rational elements in the micro population economics in Western countries, we chose as our research project "household economy and fertility studies in China". In line with the requirements of the project plan, we began, after theoretical preparation and project verification, including inviting Chinese as well as overseas experts to give lectures in seminars, to carry out the sample survey on household economy and fertility in China.

The plan design for the sample survey on household economy and fertility in China was divided into five levels. ①

A. Sampling scope. In light of the focal point this project was to make breakthroughs, 25 provinces, autonomous regions and municipalities (excluding the five provinces and regions of Neimeng, Xinjiang, Xizang, Qinghai and Hainan, that are mainly inhabited by minority nationalities and the minority autonomous pre-

---

① Mr. Gao Jialing, associate research fellow, was in charge of the sample survey plan and the parts l. 3 and l. 4 of this report were written on the basis of the paper plan for the Sample Survey on Household Economy and Fertility in China.

fectures in bordering areas in the 25 provinces, autonomous regions and municipalities) constitute the sampling areas. The total number of households was
283339184 (as in 1991). The number of households surveyed actually was
223908687 if the households in city suburbs (for the city sample was not fit for
agricultural households) were excluded.

B. Different levels and different groups. The survey was conducted at the four
levels of cities, towns, developed counties and underdeveloped counties. In cities
the object of the survey was non-agricultural population, in towns, the non-agricultural population while in counties, the agricultural population. To make the four
levels relatively concentrative to facilitate the survey, the 25 provinces, cities and
districts were divided into five groups according to the seven indexes of per capita
national income, the average per Capital income in rural areas, the average per
capita consumption in urban areas, the average per capita consumption in rural
areas, the proportion of urban population, the total fertility rate and the woman
literacy rate; group of highly developed areas, including Beijing, Shanghai,
Tianjin and Liaoning; the group of mediocrely developed areas, including Guangdong, Jiangsu, Zhejiang and Fujian; the group of ordinarily developed areas, including Heilongjiang, Jilin, Shandong and Shanxi; the group of relatively underdeveloped areas, including Hebei, Hubei, Hunan, Sichuan and Shanxi and the
group of underdeveloped areas, including Anhui, Jiangxi, Henan, Guangxi,
Guizhou, Yunnan, Gansu and Ningxia. Sampling was taken out at the same time at
the four levels in these provinces, cities and districts.

C. Sampling at different stages. The method of unequal probability sampling at
different levels in different stages was used. At the first stage on the basis of divid-
ing the 25 provinces and cities into different groups, the samples at the provincial
level were taken out and the PPS method was used to take out two provinces or
municipalities: Shanghai and Liaoning in the group of highly developed areas,
Guangdong and Zhejiang in the group of mediocrely deve loped areas, Shandong
and Jilin in the group of ordinarily developed areas, Sichuan and Shaanxi in the
group of relatively underdeveloped areas and Jiangxi and Guizhou in the group of
underdeveloped areas. Jilin was replaced by Hebei later. At the second stage, with
the PPS method, two cities, two developed counties and two underdeveloped

counties were taken out of the 10 sample provinces and municipalities and according to the random sample principle, two towns were taken out in the areas where the tourcounty governments are located respectively. At the third stage, streets and xiangs and towns were taken out, according to the PPS method, in the sample cities and counties. At the fourth stage, the PPS method was still employed to take out neighbourhood committees and village committees in the sample streets and xiangs and towns. At the fifth stage, the households to be surveyed were taken out from the sample neighbourhood committees and village committees.

D. Distribution of samples. To meet the requirements of the plan design and giving consideration to the compatability between these provinces and cities, the number of households to be surveyed was 1400 in each province or municipality: 500 households in cities, 300 in towns, 300 in developed counties and 300 in under – developed counties. The number of samples to be taken out in the neighbourhood committees and village committees was 20 to 30.

E. Two-phase Survey. To raise the reply rate to the question aire, Surveys were not conducted on the sampled households that would give no satisfactory answers due to various reasons. A two-phase survey was carried out. That is to say, an overall investigation was made in the chosen neighbourhood committees and village committees to find out the proportion of the households that would render a satisfactory reply and then the sample households were taken out from those investigated and who would meet the requirements of the survey, on the analogy of this, the overall survey analysis was made in cities, provinces and across the country. Practice shows that the two-phase survey was very limited in percentage because the design in various areas had taken into full consideration of the basic requirements of the sample survey.

Design effect and precision. This survey was a complex sampling of many stages and therefore it is impossible to get its precision with certain equations. As to the design effect, equals to the actual variance of complex sample to the variance of simple random sample on the condition of equal quantity of samples. The design effect was 2 to 3 of empirical data sampling of many stages and so the simple random sample equation was used to get its precision. The result of the calculation of sex in this sample survey shows that the corollary value precision is about 98 percent at the national level, 92 percent at the level of provinces and municipalities, 80 percent at the level of cities and towns and 75 percent at the county level.

II. Household economy and fertility level

In the present population theories in the West, there are a great many influential theoretic works and hot debates on the issue of fertility rate. These theories can be divided macrolly into two types: economic school and sociological school. The former holds that the determinant factors that have a bearing on the changes of fertility rate are in economy while the latter stresses the role in the drop of fertility rate of social factors such as nationality, culture, women's status, social structure and the like. In my view, the changes of fertility rate result from the influence of both economic and social elements, but their respective influence and position in the changes of fertility rate are different. Economic elements are the source and may condition the changes of fertility rate while social elements can exert a more direct influence. What is more important is the relations between economic elements and social elements. An important reason for the endless debates between the two schools is that both of them emphasize their own role in the change of fertility rate (mainly drop of fertility rate) while giving little attention to the relations between them. I think that the fundamental features of social elements are decided, in the final analysis, by economic elements, by the economic development level and by the nature of the economic structure. For instance, viewed from the macro point of view, the cultural quality of the population of a country can never be parted from the development level of the national economy and the given economic structure; and viewed from the micro point of view, the education level of one family basically tallies with the income level, economic structure and especially the nature of the occupation of the adults of the family. Therefore, the emphasis of the sample survey was laid on the relations between household economy and fertility rate, with an attempt to make break throughs.

The family is the social cell unit bonded by marriage relation, blood relation or adopting relation. Economic strength is needed for the movement of this kind of social cell and therefore where there is a family, there is family economic activities and hence, family economy. It needs further studies as to how to differentiate the family economic types under different historical conditions. In my opinion, it suits the past as well as the present that family economy may be roughly divided into production-type family economy and non-production-type family economy. The former includes the whole process of production, change, distribution and consumption and it is an epitome of social production. The self-sufficient natural family economy, the current household contract responsibility system economy and the individual economy in urban areas all fall into this category. As to the non-production-type family economy, the family itself is non productive, its economic resources mainly come from wage income and its family economic activities are marked obviously with consumption character. However, no matter what type a family economy might be, the complete family economic activities should be possessed of: regular income and that main family members are engaged in certain occupational activeties. The sample survey illustrates that these two pillars in the family economy have close relations with fertility level.

Debates still exist on the role of per capital income, a budgeting index in the family economy, on fertility, and among the debates, the theory of the so-called "critical point" is influential. According to this theory, when the per capita imcome does not reach the "critical point", the increase of the per capital income stimulates fertility and it restrains fertility when the per capita income surpasses the "critical point". However, our sample survey shows clearly the inverse ratio between the family per capita income and fertility rate, no matter inside or outside the "critical point". That means that the lower the monthly per capita income, the more children in the family and the earlier the first marriage and pregnancy and the higher the monthly per capita income, the fewer children in the family and the later the first marriage and pregnancy. The weighted generalization of the country may be seen in Table 2. 3

The per capita income level is a comprehensive index reflecting the family economy, but is not the sole index. The nature of the occupation of the main family members, the kind of industry they are engaged in not only mirror the type of industry of the family economy but also are indexes that have an obvious bearing on the changes of fertility rate. Our sample survey illustrates that among the eight

Table 2. 3   Situation of the Monthly per Capita Income
and Fertility of the Family of the Country
(weighted generalization, 1991)

Monthly per capita income (Yuan)	Number of children	Age at first marriage	pregnancy age	Note
121	2. 13	22. 05	23. 15	National average
0 – 25	2. 64	21. 39	22. 65	
26 – 50	2. 55	21. 16	22. 17	
51 – 75	2. 43	21. 34	22. 39	
76 – 100	2. 14	12. 09	23. 25	
101 – 200	1. 91	22. 79	23. 88	
201 – 300	1. 95	22. 79	23. 99	
301 – 400	1. 84	22. 09	23. 01	
401 – 500	1. 59	21. 74	22. 72	
501 +	1. 93	22. 79	23. 57	

occupation types of professionals, cadres over section chief level, workers in production and transportation, office workers, workers in commerce and catering trade, individual labourers, workers in agriculture, forestry, animal husbandry and fishery and other workers, those who have more than one child were mainly workers in agriculture, forestry, animal husbandry and fishery. The weighted generalization shows that in the occupation composition, 52. 0 percent of those male populace over 15 years of age surveyed were workers in agriculture, forestry, animal husbandry and fishery and their proportion rose to 70. 2 percent in the distribution of having a second child after the first boy, 18. 2 percent increase over the 52. 0 percent. For workers of other occupations except for other labourers whose proportion in the above survey remained balanced, their respective proportions fell to varied degrees and the biggest drop was 2. 6 percent of the proportion of cadres over section chief level. The more than one child phenomenon happened in families of workers in agriculture, forestry, animal husbandry and fishery. This reflects the reality of the low-level income and technological composition in rural areas, especially in economically backward rural areas, and the reality of the low cost of the marginal child and his relatively high utility. Here lies the difficulties of the work in

China to control population growth and to implement family planning, hence the focal point of our work. Further analysis is to be made later in this report. See Table 2. 4:

Table 2. 4   A Comparison of Occupation Structure of Men Over 15-year-old Surveyed and of the composition of Having One More Child After the First Boy in the Country (weighted generalization)

Occupation	Composition (%)	Composition of having one more child after the first boy (%)
professionals	4. 3	3. 4
Cadres over section chief level	4. 2	1. 6
Workers in production and transportation	9. 6	7. 2
Office workers	4. 5	3. 6
Workers in commerce and catering trade	2. 6	2. 0
Indiviedual labourers	4. 6	4. 0
Workers in agriculture, forestry animal husbandry and fishery	52. 0	70. 2
Other workers	5. 6	5. 4
the unemloyed	12. 6	2. 3

III. The composition of child cost

Prof. H. Leibenstein, Harvard University and Prof. Gary S. Beckers, University of Chicago, of the United States can be said to be the authoritative in the West for the theory of child cost-utility. Prof. Leibenstein divides child cost into two parts: direct cost, i. e. the expenses paid, from the pregnancy of the mother to the independence of the child, for clothing, food, living, medical treatment, education, marriage and the like of the child, and this part is the direct monetary expenditure; indirect cost, i. e. the loss of opportunities of the parents for education, promotion and of earning income due to the spending of time of the mother on raising the child, and therefore it is also called opportunity cost and it is the indirect monetary expenditure that may be calculated by the shadow price ① On the basis of the theory by Prof. Leibenstein, Prof. Becker introduces the theory of consumer equilibrium and family consumption restriction line. This is to say, on the premise of a commodity price and the income of a consumer, the consumer purchases more than two pieces of commodities and will make the optimum realignment of the commodities or to maximize their utility. This is introduced into the child cost-utility. The quantitative elasticity of the child is small like other durable consumer goods and the child is easy to be satisfied while his qualitative elasticity is endlessly great. The result of people seeking the maximum utility of the child will lead to changes from the input in the invariable cost or quantity cost to the variable cost or quality cost, and consequently to the fall of fertility rate. Our sample survey drew the rational and scientific results from these theories and proceeded from reality of China. Now we have well in our hand the present situation about child cost, which may provide scientific basis for analysis of fertility decisions.

The exact data of child cost needs to be further examined by other departments concerned. Here, I would like to point out the nature of child cost mainly through, a comparative analysis of the deviation of the child cost composition in rural areas.

A. The child cost deviation of different economic income levels and compositions of different families. What is the child cost? It refers to the input of the family in the process of the production of a child, including monetary input and working time input, i. e. direct cost and indirect cost. Therefore it has close relations with the input capability——the economic income level and composition. The child cost for those not-at-school or living apart (being enlisted, family breaking up, women being married to their husbands' home and so on) as divided according to the monthly per capita income of the family (weighted generalization in rural areas from the sample survey in the ten provinces and cities shows that the direct (monetary) cost increased in direct proportion with per capita income. The child direct cost of families with the monthly per capita income between 301 to 400 Yuan was 2. 7

---

times more over the average level, and 7. 8 times more over that of families with a monthly per capita income below 50 Yuan. Indirect (time) cost did not, however, have regularities and generally speaking it was close to the average level. Child cost also had relations with income source composition: the child direct cost of families with a non-agricultural income source was 68. 8 percent more than that of families without a non-agricultural income source and indirect cost dropped slightly. The weighted generalization of data of the ten provinces and cities can be seen in Table 3. 1:

Table 3. 1   The Not-at school or Living apart Child Cost as Divided According to Family Per Capita Income Level and Composition in Rural Areas (weighted generalization) of the Country

Monthly per capita income (Yuan)	Direct cost (Yuan)	Indirect cost (Days)
The average	229	11
0 – 25	79	
26 – 50	82	11
51 – 75	150	10
76 – 100	144	11
101 – 200	253	14
201 – 300	401	13
301 – 400	620	6
401 – 500	610	1
500 +	1247	19
With a non-agricultural income	319	9
Without a non-agricultural income	189	13

B. Deviation of child quality (education) cost. The variable child cost or quality cost in prof. Becker's theory mainly includes expenditure on medical treatment and health and intelligence investment in education for the child. The latter is most important: it increases with income increases, i. e. the change from family input in the variable child (quantity) cost to variable (quality) cost is critical to the further drop in fertility rate. From the survey we can find that the deviation was obvious of the quality cost for the education of the child and particularly great that of child direct (monetary) cost while indirect (time) cost changed slightly and had no regularities. The direct monetary cost for the at-school or living apart child in rural areas was 575 Yuan for primary school, 677 Yuan for middle school, 901 Yuan for high school, 969 Yuan for technical secondary school, 1289 Yuan for the three-year period colleges, 878 Yuan for university and 503 for post graduate school. From the deviation comparison we may find that the cost for middle school increased slightly over that for primary school, that for high school and for technical secondary school increased by a big margin over that for middle school, the cost reached the highest for the three-year period college, that for university was much less than that for the three-year period college while that for post graduate school dropped again by a big margin from that for university. It seems, on the surface, to be a strange phenomenon, but it can be explained if family education cost is taken into account. Some students in technical schools and three-year period colleges are paid by themselves, thus increasing expenditure; while there are scholarships and grants-in-aid in universities and postgraduate schools and therefore family expenditure decreases. Nevertheless, we have gained some enlightenment from the structural changes of family education cost for the at – school child in rural areas: there was little obstruction for the child to continue his school days at a middle school from the primary school; it was most difficult for him to continue his study at a high school or a technical school; there was again little obstruction to entering a university and so to revive high school education is the difficulty to be o-ver-come. See Fig. 3. 1

In Chart Fig. 3. 1, (1) represents primary school; (2) represents middle school; (3) high school; (4) technica secondary school; (5) represents three-year period college; (6) represents university and (7) postgraduate school.

C. Deviation of child cost of different ages and sexes. Different needs of the child in the growth process and different inclination for the sex of the child bring about the deviation of child cost of different ages and sexes. The sample survey shows that the deviation was slightly small of the direct (monetary) cost for the child not-at-school, that was big for the at-school child, and the cost increased with the growing up in age due to the influence of child education cost: and that indirect (time) cost for school age children were not very different except for the

big difference for infants. The deviation of boy child cost, manifested in sex, was u-
niversally higher than that of girl child cost. The average direct (monetary) cost
was 229 Yuan for children not-at-school or living apart in rural areas, that was 237
Yuan for boys and 207 Yuan for girls; the average for children at-school or living
apart was 867 Yuan, with 871 Yuan for boys and 859 Yuan for girls. The average
indirect (time) cost was 11 days for children not-at-school or living apart, 12
days for boys and 10 days for girls; the average indirect cost for children at-school
or living apart was 15 days, 20 days for boys and 4 days for girls. On the whole,
the child direct cost or monetary cost and indirect cost or time cost for boys were all
higher than that for girls and there existed certain sexual deviation, which reflected
the sexual inclination of the family, Meanwhile, it is not difficult to find that the
sexual deviation value of the child cost and the degree of sexual inclination are becoming less and less and some are getting close. The ideas of equality of the sexes
is penetrating into all family cells.

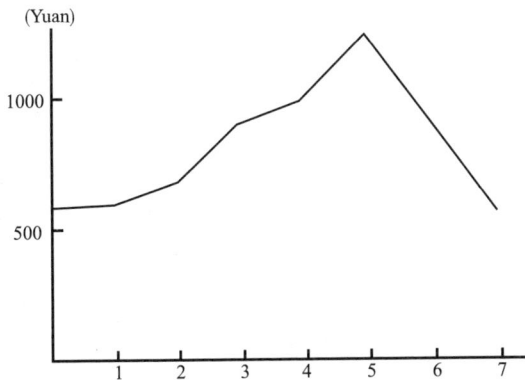

**Fig. 3. 1　A Comparison of Direct Monetary Costs
for Children At-schools or Living apart in Rural Areas
(Weighted generalization)**

The above mentioned survey on the various child cost deviations is a generalization of the results of the snapshot of those surveyed and it reflects the present
child cost level and different aspects of the structure. However, with economic
development, technological progress and changes of traditional ideas of family,

child cost is always changing. The anticipated child cost is an important variable and has a direct bearing on the changes of fertility in the future. Having taken full notice of this point, the sample survey has achieved expected data on child cost from many angles. In the analysis of these data, much attention was paid to the fundamental trends that will influence child cost—mainly direct (monetary) cost in the future.

A. The trend of extension of the cycle for child-raising. The weighted generalization illustrates that the child-raising cycle was under 18 years for 9.5 percent of those surveyed, 73.7 percent of those surveyed agreed to the cycle between 19 to 24 years; and 16.8 percent agreed to the cycle over 25 years. It was the choice of most families to support their children well over 20 years old.

B. The trend of increase of quality cost for the child's education. The weighted generalization prepared eight levels onto which those surveyed would raise their children: the levels of primary school, middle school, high school, technical secondary school, three-year period college, university, postgraduate and no demand and the percentages were 3.6, 18.8, 9.6, 6.5, 29.2, 3.1 and 12.3 respectively. People surveyed who would support their children to the level of university graduation took the biggest proportion, in the second place was the proportion to support the children to the level of middle school and in the third place was that at the high school level. This tells us that though there is the phenomenon that mental work gets less paid than physical work under the present market economy condition which affects the intelligence investment of some families, Chinese people still pin great hope on their children and wish their children to get a higher education. This is very encouraging to the realization of the change from input in child invariable (quantity) cost to variable (quality) cost.

C. The trend of complete independence of the child. The most explicit messages are starting a career and getting married. The weighted data generalization shows that 32.2 percent, 44.0 percent and 23.8 percent of those surveyed would bring their children up till the time of their being capable to work, to be employed and no consideration respectively. People were not just satisfied with the low standard of supporting their children to the level of their being capable to work, and rather they would support their children until the latter find a suitable job. For the five lev-

els of raising their children to the time of engagement, marriage, child – bearing,
longer time and no consideration, the proportions of those surveyed were respectively
1. 3 percent, 59. 2 percent, 4. 8 percent, 10. 9 percent and 23. 6 percent. The majority of the people under survey would support their children till the time of their
marriage and even after the children have their own children or longer. Few people
would support their children only up to the time of their engagement.

It is known to all the population policy has played a critical role in the drop of
fertility rate in China since the 70s. The population policy has as its main part to
conduct propaganda, education and ideological work and it is supplemented with
necessary economic measures, which constitute the added cost and added utility of
the child. [1]Contents in the aspect were designed in the 1992 sample survey. The
weighted generalization shows that the average amount of money was 870 Yuan that
was collected on parents that had a second child outside plan. This amount was
62. 1 percent of the 1401 Yuan, of the per capita national income in 1991. Fairly
speaking, this amount is not very big. The amount was even more than that was
collected on parents having a third child, but it was often collected at one time and
it took less than 30 percent in the total child direct (monetary) cost. The addition
of the expenses for parents having more than one child to the direct (monetary)
cost of the marginal child has helped, without doubt, to change the unfavourable
slope of child cost-utility, but the result is not very satisfactory and new ways out
should be found.

IV. A comparison of child utilities

Discussions inside and outside China about the utilities that children provide
to the family can be generalized into the following six aspects:

A. Labour-economic utility: Children grow up to become a labour force member and they are engaged in certain work or certain occupational work as a family
member and increase the economic income for the family.

---

[1]   It was once called cost and utility of the fertility policy in papers written by the author. It ismore accura-
    teto call it added child cost and added utility because it is added and because of the limited influence of
    thet policy on child cost and utility.

B. Old age support-insurance utility: The underdeveloped social insurance for old age leaves the task of supporting the aged to the children and later generations of the family.

C. Consumption-enjoyment utility: Children are possessed, as durable consumer goods, of spiritual attribute which is absent in material commodities and may bring about "family happiness" to their parents.

D. Continuation-extension utility: Children have the function of reproduction for the family.

E. Inheritance-risk utility: Children inherit the legacy left over by the parents . Children decide, by their basic quality, the rise and fall of the family in the next generation and shoulder some risks.

F. Security, defense and other utilities.

The sample survey designed a questionaire that included the above mentioned utilities and achieved a whole set of data. The following points, closely related with population growth control, are well worth notice:

A. Child utility composition. The weighted generalization of various child utilities shows: 18.3 precent of child utility was to provide labour and economic income, 21.3 percent was to provide old age support, 9.3 percent, for spiritual enjoyment, 22.2 percent for generation continuation and family extension, 16.7 percent, for legacy inheritance and shouldering risks and 12.2 percent for security, defense and other utilities. Utilities for generation continuation and old age support took the biggest proportions, which is, explicitly, a basic characteristic of the child utility of developing countries.

B. Family income utility, of child utilities, the proportion of providing labour and economic income took the second place. It had a great bearing on the family economic situation and income and it was particularly so in rural areas. In the family utilities provided by children not-at school or living apart in rural areas (weighted generalization), corresponding to the annual average 47 Yuan was families with a per capita income below 25 Yuan, corresponding to 120 Yuan was families with a monthly income between 26 to 100 Yuan, corresponding to the 254 Yuan provided was families with a monthly income between 101 to 200 Yuan, corresponding to the 249 Yuan provided, was families with a monthly income between

201 to 300 Yuan, corresponding to the 606 Yuan provided, was families with a monthly income between 301 to 400 Yuan······The general tendency was that the higher the economic utility provided by children, the more the income of the corresponding families. In the source structure of children providing utilities, it was similar to that of child cost: children with a non-agricultural income provided 90 Yuan more than those without a non-agricultural income. A comparison on utilities provided by children of different sexes tells us that male children provided 119 Yuan more which was almost twice as much as that by female children.

C. Occupation structure effect. The sample survey illustrates that there was a big difference between children of different occupations who provided utilities to their families. For instance, of the children not-at-school or living apart in rural areas, those working in commerce and catering trade provided the most as economic utility with as average of 260 Yuan every year; in the second place was individual laboueres who provided an average of 224 Yuan each year; in the third place was workers in agriculture, forestry, animal husbandry and fishery who provided an average of 216 Yuan every year; in the fourth place was office workers who provided 215 Yuan while scientific professional provided 140 Yuan and cadres only provided only 50 Yuan. The reason for this is that it has close relations with the providing ability of the child, i. e. his income level, and at the same time it has relations with the consumption level of the child himself, for example, workers in agriculture, forestry, animal husbandry and fishery, though with a low income level, provided more economic utilities to their families.

V. The ways to reform child cost-utility and the interest-regulation of population control

The purpose of investigating and analysizing the marginal child cost-utility changes is to find out the start of the motive in fertility decision and ways to solve the problem. when talking about this issue, Prof. Becker introduces the concept of net cost: it is equal to the direct (monetary) cost prepaid by the family for the marginal child plus indirect (time) cost (through the shadow price) spent by the parents minus the present value of the anticipated income and of labour provided by the marginal child. If the net cost is a positive value, then the marginal child is only equivalent to an ordinary durable consumer goods and the family can only get the utility from this child of psychological satisfaction. If the net cost is a negative value, then the marginal child is equivalent to a durable consumer goods and he can bring about increase of value for family. In this way, families can make their decisions for fertility in the light of the estimate of the net cost of the marginal child. In our sample survey, the indirect (time) cost of the marginal child was quite near to the labour utility provided by the child and so the calculation of the net cost of the marginal child cost-utility was made with no regard to the time cost-utility.

The child cost-utility data in the weighted generalization show that the net cost of the child in the monetary form was obviously a positive value and it had begun to turn to be a positive value in rural areas. For instance, the direct (monetary) cost was 229 Yuan that was spent by families with children not-at-school or living apart in rural areas in 1991, and the child, in turn, provided 203 Yuan for the family with a net cost of 26 Yuan. As for the net cost for children at-school or living apart in rural areas, it was as high as 806 Yuan. But why do people still want to have such a child at a loss? The answer can be looked for in the total utilities composition of children: the labour and economic utility was 18.3 percent and on this basis, the total utility value that was provided by the child should be 1109 Yuan; if the present value (calculated according to the shadow price) of indirect (time) cost was added to the original cost, then the net cost of the child turned to be several hundred Yuan in negative, hence the increase of the value of the child. This is exactly the motive for further fertility.

It should be pointed out that in the comparison between the year's direct cost for the child and the monetary income utility provided by the child for the family with workers in agriculture, forestry, animal husbandry and fishery, utility was higher than cost, that is to say, the net cost was minus 50 Yuan. This shows that the child net cost was still a minus in th families of those working in agriculture, forestry, animal husbandry and fishery, under the premise that total net cost was a positive value of the child not-at-school or living apart in rural areas, why so? This is because the low technological composition of agriculture, forestry, animal husbandry and fishery led to low cost of children who would be workers in these industries. Another reason is that technological composition is in inverse proportion to the elasticity of absorbing workers: the lower the technological composition, the greater the elasticity of absorbing workers and the earlier and more remarkable of the display of utilities, hence the contrast of the net cost of the child. This unfavourable contrast stimulates strongly fertility composition and it has become an important reason for the backwardness in economy and technology and for the high fertility rate in the areas where agriculture, forestry, animal husbandry and fishery are the dominant industries.

The only way to change this is to develop the economy and promote technological progress. This is because on the one hand, when the economy gets developed and the technological composition is enhanced, the demand will be raised for the cultural and technological level of workers. The increase in income in the family depends mainly on the quality instead of quantity of the worker, thus lowering the labour-economic utility of the marginal child provided to the family. Meanwhile, economic development and productivity increase will lead to the increase of social wealth and the government and the society are capable of running more security undertaking for the aged people, workers themselves and families can also deposit their money in a bank against old age and consequently the old age support-security utility of the marginal child will drop to a great extent. Other child utilities such as risk-shouldering utility, will also drop to varied degrees. On the other hand, to develop the economy is to bring along technological progress which in turn promotes economic development. Families should be well aware that they can achieve utilities as long as they make necessary intelligence investment for the child, thus raising the child cost, mainly the quality cost that is spent in education. The rise and fall of child cost-utility will promote the family to change its input in the quantity cost for the child to quality cost. The fertility model will change from more fertility and more children to less fertility and more efforts on the child and eventually fertility rate will drop continuously. Up to date, this has been proved correct by economic development and drop of fertility rate in Western developed countries and also by the successful practice in areas with a higher level of economic development and technological progress since the reform and opening to the outside world. To develop the economy is a highway for birth control and it is also a radical measure in the population policy strategy.

That does not mean to let economic development to solve the population problem spontaneously. The population, resources, economic development level and other basic conditions in China decide that the population problem, particularly the population quantity control do not permit the "basic settlement" by merely developing the economy and instead "parallel work" must be done. That is to say, while the economy being developed greatly to lay a solid foundation and create conditions for the drop of fertility rate, the basic national policy of family planning should be implemented conscientiously, and administrative, economic and legislative measures should be employed to control population growth. What, is more important at present is to stabilize the current policy and to make full use of the past successful practice and experience. The relative stability of the population fertility policy is more important since any policy change can bring about agitation and results in harmful consequences. To make use of past successful practice and experience, particularly the whole set of experience and practice of the establishment of the socialist market economic system, the target management responsibility system and the strengthening of the construction of the grass root contingent should be combined with reality. New problems can be studied and resolved in this way and ways for reform may be found out.

How can we get a new balance between child cost and utility by properly increasing interest regulating weight and achieve the goal of further and effective control over population growth? I would like to propose some ideas for reform, on the basis of the results of the sample survey.

A. To readjust distribution for mental work and physical work and to encourage intelligence investment. It is very popular today that a doctor earns less than a barber and a professor get less paid than a small pedllar. This kind of distribution is unfair. This will affect greatly the development of the national economy and the modernization construction and will be unfavourable to the population growth control. The sample survey demonstrates that even if the children at-school were bypassed, the child not-at-school provided an economic utility that could not compensate for the direct (monetary) cost expenditure the family spent for him and this was more serious with the rise in degree of education level. For instance, the year's net cost was 7 Yuan for primary school, 37 Yuan for middle school and 249 Yuan for high school for the child not-at-school or living apart. According to the theory of "flow of wealth between generations" by Prof. J. C. Caldwell, a well-known Australian expert of population studies, an abnormal phenomenon appears that the more intelligence investment made for the child, the more wealth flown from parents to the child. This is unfavourable to the drop of fertility rate and to turn this trend, there should be a big policy: to bring into reality the principle of distribution according to work: complicated work should be paid times more over simple work, to increase the income of mental workers, and to make sure that the education quality cost the family spends for the child can bring about the corresponding or additional economic utility. The inclination of people to have more children should be changed to pursue the quality of the child and the inputs in quantity cost should be directed to quality cost.

B. The added utility should be brought into play and the security for old age should be reformed. It has been said earlier that the author has, in combining the reality of developing countries and particularly the reality of China, put forward and demonstrated the child social added cost and added utility. To study the start of the level of child cost – utility to control population increase, efforts should be spent on the aspect of reducing the cost of the only child and children within plan, increasing their utility and increasing the cost of children outside plan and reducing their utility. And here the cost and utility naturally refer to the social added parts. At present, it is a common practice across China that the only one child gets 5 Yuan or 10 Yuan award. This added utility is too slight and it can not play its expected role. At the same time our sample shows that in the total child utility composition, old age support-insurance utility took 21.3 percent, which was in the first place and it was even the focus of anxiety of the parents with the only one child. Sichuan province has started the "two-aspect insurance" for the one child and the old age support insurance for the parents. That is to say, the money award for the only one child is used to pay for the injury and death insurance for the child and this will be transferred, 14 years later, to the old age support insurance for the parents, and in this manner, all anxieties can be solved and good results have been obtained. Mme. Pend Peiyun, state councilor and Director of the State Family

Planning Commission, pointed out in her speech: "This method organically combines family planning with social insurance for old age support. It has found a new way for the implementation of the basic national policy of family planning and it is a reform measure for resolving the population problems in a comprehensive way in China. " Moreover, to increase the added utility of the only child and children within plan, preferential policies should be adopted in the aspects for enrollment of the child in a kindergarten, in a school, medical treatment, housing allocation in urban areas, employment in township enterprises and change of residence card from agricultural to non-agricultural in rural areas and so on, on equal conditions and compensation should be made for the loss of child utility for those for no more fertility.

C. The cost for more children outside plan should be increased and the unbalance of utility should be changed. It is an established policy that parents having children outside plan are charged. But how much may restrain fertility as an added cost while parents can afford? Our sample survey shows that parents having a second child outside plan paid less than 900 Yuan, that having a third child paid 3 plus more over that amount. This is not much, generally speaking. Nevertheless, there are big economic differences between urban and rural areas and there should not be only one standard for the whole country. What is critical is that the amount levied and methods to be adopted in various areas should be scientific. In 1989, the project team on population countermeasures of the Institute of Population Studies of the Chinese of Social Sciences put forward in a report, the view that the amount of money to be collected as charges for having more children should be equivalent to the per capita income level of the locality and also the method of levying for 14 successive years. We have found that it is feasible from the survey. In the first place, the level is not very high and ordinary people can afford. Secondly, the psychology of the parents having one more child of "temporary agony (to be charged once) with life enjoyment (utility provided by the child) is changed. Parents will feel the heavy burden of this added cost, thus restraining fertility. Besides, on equal conditions, policies should be adopted that are unfavourable to child outside plan for enrollment in a kindergarten, in a school, medical treatment, housing allocation in urban areas, employment in township enterprises and the change from agricultural to non-agricultural of residence card in rural areas and so on. Such a policy will reduce the utility provided by the child to the family and consequently will change the present unbalance state.

D. The idea of fertility should be changed and the tradition of following the father's surname should be reformed. In the child utility composition, the utility of reproduction and extension for the family took 22. 2 percent in the first place. This shows that the influence of the idea "he who produces no descendents for the family is most unpardonable" is deep-rooted. Naturally, the descendents here refer to male children only and this is the very reason for people's inclination for boys. Therefore, it is still a long-term and difficult task to do away with the private fertility idea, to acquire a public and scientific and progressive idea of equality of the sexes. Apart from propaganda and education, the issue of affirming the position and role of female in population reproduction needs to be explored and solved. The greatest obstacle is the tradition to follow the father's surname that has been passed down for ages. This tradition has obliterated so much the role of women in population reproduction that some families want to have boys at any price. One way for reform is that the child adopts a compound surname, i. e. the child follows both the surnames of the father and mother and children of the third generation may choose either surname of their parents with compound surnames. In this way, the daughter can also play the role of extending the family surname. This is a simple and feasible method and the obstruction lies in the traditional idea. So long as we have a clear understanding, proper propaganda and the conveniences for residence registration, it is indeed feasible.

References

[1] H. Leibenstein, A Theory of Economie-Demographic Development, Princeton University Press, 1954.

[2] G. S. Becker, An Economic Analysis of Fertility, Princeton University Press, 1960.

[3] R. A. Easterline and E. M. Crimmins, Fertility Revolution: A Supply-Demand Analysis. University of Chicago Press, 1985.

[4] J. C. Caldwell, Theory of Fertility Decline, London Academic Press, 1982.

[5] Liu Guoguang and some others, "Report on Further Effective Control over Population Growth in China" in The Economic Reform and Development in the 80s in China, Economic Management Publishing House, 1991.

[6] Tian Xueyuan, "On the Child Cost-Utility Theory and Population Control", in Collected Works of Tian Xueyuan, China Economy Publishing House, 1991.

[7] Peng Songjian, Introduction to Population Economics in the West, Beijing University Press, 1987.

[8] Li Jingeng (chief editor), Contemporary Population Theories In the West, Shanxi People's Publishing House, 1992.

[9] Tian Xueyuan (chief-editor) and Zhong Kan and Xu Gailing (deputy chief-editors), The Theory and Practice of the Only One Child and the Parents Old Age Support Insurance, Sichuan University Press, 1992.

[10] Jiang Yiman (chirf editor) and Zhu Huizhu, Peng Xizhe, Zhu Yuncheng, Chen jian and Qian Rusheng (deputy chief-editors), Out of the Marshland—The Origin and Countermeasures for More Fertilities, Meterology Publishing House, 1993.

"Intermediary" Population Control and Comprehensive Community Development

The English word "community" is usually translated as a commune, a group or a common community. Although people make various definitions to this concept, they are increasingly aware of the role it plays in the transfer of fertility, especially its key role in the "intermediary" population control in China as well as in other developing countries.

I. Basic fields of "intermediary" population control

In the present world, population growth has been put on the agenda of global concern of the mankind and is most noticeable. Intertwined with issues of food, resources, industrialization, environment and others, it has become one of the most heavy obstacles that impedes the economic take-off of the developing countries. More and more countries have taken the option of population control which could be divided into three levels: macro policy intervention, intermediary community services and micro family planning. The three levels are mutually related, different countries and regions lay different emphasis on different levels at different periods. Since the 70's when China took drastic measures to control the population, it has achieved remarkable successes with TFR decreased from 5.81 in 1970 to 2.25 in 1990, more than 50% in 20 years. [1] It is recognized by people both home and abroad that China's success in population control is mainly due to the fact that

---

[1]   "*China Population Yearbook* 1986", Social Science Documentation Press, 1987: "*China Statistics yearbook* 1991".

Chinese government has formulated a rather strict policy guideline, enforcement of birth control, i. e. the result of carrying out a macro population control objective. Without doubt, in the 20-odd years, China witnessed great development in economy, education, science and technology and culture, especially rapid development after the reform and opening-up to the outside. People's concept of fertility also went through some changes which played certain role in the micro control of population. What about intermediary control? Although some of the region in China did some creative work, the function of community as the major field of intermediary population control is still not clear, comparatively speaking it is a neglected level.

The population science has been greatly concerned with the population change in births, deaths, and migration; population structure of age and sex; urban and rural distribution and regional population distribution and stratigic studies on population and economy, science and technology and social coordinated development. A series of works have been published in these aspects. The macro research in these aspects become the main stream of research since the revitalization of the population science in China. In micro-studies, certain progress has been made in the research of China Statistics Press 1991: family and marriage; in the recent years studies have been done on the supply and demand of children, and great breakthrough has been made in the research of the inherent law of the fertility behaviour and the number of children revealed by the child cost-effectiveness. Assisted by UNFPA, representatives organized by the Institute of Population Research under CASS did sample survey in 10 provinces and municipalities out of the 25 provinces, municipalities and autonomous regions not including the 5 remote and border provinces and comprehensive and systematic data have been obtained concerning the present urban and rural family economy and its relation with fertility. In order to clarify the present status of child cost-benefit and explore the inherent law of constant decrease in fertility, new micro research should be done in terms of the transfer of personal fertility behaviour and the transition of population control mechanism from taking administrative means to that of regulation by benefits. The weak link is the research on intermediary population control. Some of the research such as the "central households" of birth control in Liaoning Province and single-child and parents' pension insurance in Xizang Province and other regions all lack of the aspect of community as the main field of intermediary population control although it touches upon the research of the community development. It also lacks serious research in combining theory with practice. In a way, it has reflected the present status in China's population research of heavy emphasis on macro control, looking down upon micro control and lack of intermediary control. This state of affairs do not suit the upsurge of the reform and opening-up and the population situation that we face in the 90's. While continuing to pay attention to the macro studies, we should strengthen micro studies and fill up the vacuum of intermediary research.

Research of intermediary population control is basically aimed at community as its field of study. However, people give different definitions to the issue in different disciplines: the emphasis is either laid on culture transition, or on economic activities or on social life. I personally believe that community could be defined as a specific geographic region with certain similar political, cultural and social features based on common economic interests. This definition has expressed the basic intention of the community concept: community is based on the common interests of its members, primarily of economic interests, therefore it has an inherent centripetal force and code of conduct shaped by this centripetal force. It also expressed the extension of the concept: the specific geographic region determined by the common interests and the strength of the centripetal force. However, the geographic region could either by identical or not identical to the administrative geographic region. With such understanding and in respect to the basic field of intermediary population control and a clear subject for demonstration sense the main battlefield of population control in China is the community. I believe the establishment of the subject is mainly determined by the position and role of the community in the population control.

Firstly, the similar income level of the community member determined by the community economic development level has basically contained the fertility level of the people. As is known to all, the fertility behaviour and the number of children are determined by various social factors such as economic, political, cultural, ethnical and religious, but all in all, it is determined by economic factors. The population issue, in general, is an economic issue. Since the income level of members of the same community is rather similar in general, fixed cost of numerical cost for the same marginal child is also rather similar so the cost-effectiveness of the marginal child is on the same level. Therefore, it contains the number of fertility of the family. Meanwhile the economic development level of the community also influences the level of the means of supplying contraceptive techniques, governing the realization of the birth control, generally speaking, the birth rate is in direct ratio to the level of economic development of the community.

Secondly, since the community is composed by the members with common economic interests, the fertility of each member does not only have a direct bearing over his own self interest, but also over the vital interest of other natural resources in the community as specific region are relatively limited and the growth of populations means the reduction of resources in per capita terms, encroaching upon the interests of other members of the community. It is not only forbidden by the state policies, but also contradictory to the common interests of the community members. It provides the government with evidence to formulate development policies to control the population and safeguard coordinated development between population and environment, which has a good mass foundation like giving incentives to the single-child family and punishment to the excessive children's family.

Thirdly, since the community plays the role of a natural "cell organ" in the social organization, it becomes a "welding" bond between the state's macro population control and micro control of the number of children in the family. The scale of community could be large or small. The large communities are similar to the scope of grassroots organizations of the state power and become the basic units for government to promote birth control, e. g. the urban neighbourhood and rural township government, in general, have appointed special work staff to be in charge of birth control; the small community would not have the grassroots power organizations, but they are usually linked to them through unofficial or semi-official organizations, and naturally become the "cell" linking the grassroots power organization with the households. The state policies to control the population and various measures promulgated by the government could be implemented and infiltrated into household through these large or small "cells" and accomplish the welding between the macro control and micro control.

Fourthly, since the community has its traditional characteristics, it has shaped the fertility concept and level of fertility of people while forming its mini – culture rims including the culture of fertility. The community has been formed during the history of economic, culture and social development. Although different communities have common traditional culture of Chinese nation, which constitutes the basic tone of the community culture, the degree of the traditional culture is varied. In communities, where the reform and economic development bring great changes, the culture difference is quite drastic. In less open region where economy and culture are backward, the community members are still bound by the belief the "more children will bring more happiness" and "continue the family line", whereas in mere open communities with a rapid developing economic and culture atmosphere, the fertility concept of many people has been changed into fewer births and eugenics, the same preference for girls as well as for boys, a few people even do not like to have babies and enter into the "non-fertility culture rim" as proposed by some people in the western society.

II. Population and different types of community development

Community plays a decisive role in the intermediary population control while the solution to population issue exerts an important impact on the community development, the two are interactive and influence each other, forming a specific population community development model. From the concrete condition of China, the degree of the development of the population communities could be classified into three types:

Type one is the traditional agriculture type. The community is in a closed or semi-closed status. The community members mainly engaged in primary industry with backward means of production. They basically engage in manual labour and semi-mechanized labour with low labour productivity and low per capita income. They are in a transitional status from low level of sustenance. Under such economic situation, the cost for the marginal child is low and the child's labour-economic effects and old-age support-insurance efficiency and other effects could be displayed earlier with remarkable results, and it is difficult to realize the transfer from input of numerical costs of the child to that of the qualitative cost. Therefore, in population production, basic characteristics occur in high birth rate, high natural growth rate and low health and culture qualities of the population. Population control and economic development of community are interactive and a vicious circle of "low labour productivity——high birth rate——low labour productivity" appears, which could best be described as "more poverty more babies and more babies more poverty". With the development of the reform and open-up, different changes have taken place in many of such population communities; but in the hinterland, especially in the remote mountainous areas, there are still quite a number of such communities, population and community development are in a backward situation of traditional agriculture type.

Type two is the modern industrial structure type. Such communities are in the forefront of the reform. If they engage in agriculture, forestry, animal husbandry, and fishery, they have already basically gone onto the path of specialized commodity production with a market-oriented economy. Most of them have extricated themselves from the lop-sided agriculture production. Township enterprises have extensively with industrial production in a superiority position in the economy of the community. A rational structure for primary, secondary and tertiary industries have been initially established. They have advanced means of production with a high level of modernization. The labour productivity and per capita income both reached a rather high level, even to prosperity. More than 10 years of reform and open-up has already brought up a group of such communities especially in the Pearl River Delta, the Yangtze River Delta and the Minjiang Delta; Shandong Peninsular, Liaodong Peninsular and the whole of the coastal open region. Daqiuzhuang in Jinghai County, Tianjin is such a typical community. In the 13 years since the reform and open-up, the growth rate of its production value has been increased 10,000 times, entering into the well-to-do status 10 years ahead of the schedule and 7 times in overfulfilling its production targets, it has now already reached the standard for prosperity. Fundamental changes have been taken place in its industrial structure: the rural labour force was reduced from 1200 in 1978 to the present 8 persons, others have been transferred to the industrial enterprises, breaking a new path of joint development of industry and agriculture. Taking grain production as an example, the output of each Daqiuzhuang peasant is 650000 kilos of grain, 400 times that of the average level of a peasant in the country, creating an amazing productivity. ①These community has a common feature, i. e. without exception, they rely on science and technology to get rich. The impact on the population is to stimulate the drastic rise of the qualitative costs of the child especially the costs on education while the labour-economic effectiveness of the child to the family mainly depend on the quality and not quantity of the child. Meanwhile due to the development of the community insurance welfare including that of the old-age insurance and increase of the private savings, child's old-age support-insurance effectiveness is on the decline. As to other benefit and risk benefit and others, they are weakened to different extent with the development of the community economy, culture, science and technology, welfare and security. Such an orientation of benefits has led community families from the input of the quantitative costs of the child to that of the qualitative costs. The option that people take has changed from seeking the quantity of the children to that of the quality and then to the decline of fertility. Therefore, contrary to the traditional agricultural type, the communities with modern industrial structure, its population control and community development has the circular model of "high productivity-low fertility-high productivity", entering into the benign circle of population and community. Sifangtai Village in Donganshan Township in Anshan city of Liaoning Province is typical of such communities. The village has a rather high per capita income level. Over 1000 people live in a seven-storyed building without having to pay the housing rent. The old people there are given an old-age pension with tap water and gas supply just like in the cities and they are subsidized for using them, which greatly weakened child's effectiveness especially the old-age support-insurance benefit, so it has led people to transfer from the input of the quantitative costs of the child to that of the qualitative costs. Some of the community members voluntarily give up their quota for having the second child and fewer children, eugenics and better upbringing have become popular objectives that people seek.

Type three is the transitional industrial structural type, i. e. between the above-mentioned two types. For this type of community, the door of reform, and

---

① "On the path to prosperity", *Guangming Daily Sept.* 30. 1992. by Han Xiuqi development.

open-up is already wide open, and it is in the process of changing from single-sided agriculture into multiple management and the means of production is also changed from manual labour to mechanized labour and automation with increasing labour productivity. The per capita income is continuously on the rise and it is in the process of changing from basic sustenance to that of well-to-do. In this situation, the quantitative and qualitative costs of the marginal child are both on the increase, its labour-economic effectiveness and old – age support-insurance effectiveness experience a process from rise to fall and the population and community development is quite complicated. But in general, the trend of population and community development in the transitional industrial structural type is a circular transition from "low labour productivity——high fertility——low labour productivity" to "high labour productivity——low fertility——high labour productivity" except that different population communities in the transitional stage vary greatly, some of them have just rid themselves of the traditional agricultural type and some have already approached modern industrial type.

If the population communities are divided in terms of scale, they could be divided into three basic types of large, medium and small sizes. The small population communities could take after the "central households for birth control" as in some localities. Among scores of households, one household with high cultural quality, enthusiastic about population control and rooms for activities could be chosen as the central household and it would radiate to organize the neighbouring households mainly women of child-bearing age to study the theory of population and knowledge of birth control, launch contraceptive services, allocate responsibilities to the households and individuals meanwhile developing cooperation in production and in daily life among the households, opening up cultural and science and technological education and help each other to aim at prosperity. It is proven by practice that the "central households for birth control" could combine population control with economic development and social services as one, small in scale, and flexible in activities. With the assistance from the government, it displays a strong vitality and plays its role in the small population community. Such small communities generally correspond to the sizes of village residents' groups and the urban neighbourhood committees with features of flexibility and convenience.

The medium population communities are mostly natural villages in the country-side and residential quarters in cities. Using the definitions of this paper, they could not reach the standards of population community so the medium population communities referred here mainly are those clearly demarcated regions with population concentration and the space where population management is closely related to economy, culture and other aspects. From the present situation, such communities have certain economic entities and community members share common economic interests; or they are naturally members share common economic interests; or they are naturally linked by the traditional culture including religion, the community members share a strong bond of linkage.

Large population communities are communities basically divided by village townships in the countryside and streets in the cities. They are not only large in size but also closely linked with the grassroots power organizations of the state therefore greatly contained by administrative regulations. However. whether it could constitute what we define as communities would first be judged by its economic foundation whether it has strong economic entities to link the common economic interests of the community members together; secondly, it would be judged by its organizational leadership, publicity and education, technical services and other aspects of population control, and whether it could form a closely linked network. It is proven by experience over the years that it would be difficult to maintain such large communities through administrative means and it could only be developed and consolidated by a strong economic, demographic and cultural centripetal force.

The structure of the population community in certain historical stages is closely related with the demographic, economic, cultural and social conditions, mainly determined by the social economic development level and its structure. The present situation in China is as follows: On the one hand, since the reform and the open-up, the national economy has been greatly developed and the township enterprises as the pillar of the community economy have witnessed drastic development with a great momentum of further advancement and laid a new foundation for the formation and development of the population communities; on the other hand, in overall terms, the level of the national economic development is still not yet high with fair-ly backward economic technological level while the agriculture still takes the main form of separate management of the household responsibility contract system, which constrain the formation of the communities and their structure types. The present situation is that most of the population communities are those in a process of transition from traditional agricultural type to that of the advanced industrial structural type, second most would be those of traditional agricultural type and the third would be those of advanced industrial structural type. In terms of scale, most of the population communities are medium and small scaled communities. The proportion of large-scaled population communities such as based on rural townships and urban streets is relatively low. They should proceed from the concrete situation of China, sum up experiences earnestly and strive to cultivate, develop and perfect the population communities. In order to make use of the opportunities provided to us at present by the reform and the open-up, and accelerate the pace of community construction while actively developing new population communities, we should study the theory of these issues earnestly and learn from the successful experiences of the developed countries and the developing countries alike and sum up our own experiences earnestly to create population communities that suit the concrete conditions of China and with our own characteristics. In this respect, the comprehensive development of the population communities in Hainan Province provides us with some fresh experience.

Ⅲ. Inspirations drawn from the pilot population communities in Hainan

Hainan island is situated to the North of the South China Sea and in the sub − tropical region with an area of 33920 square kilometres. The population census for 1990 was 6557482 persons. It has rich natural resources and good geographic conditions. However, its economic development was fairly backward for a long time in the past. Although the reform and open − up brought great changes to the region, the economy was far from developed until 1988 when Hainan became a province. It was in the medium-lower level with low cultural qualities of the population and fairly high birth rate and growth rate. Population issue became one of the issues that impeded the economic development of the special economic zone. In order to solve the problem, and promote the coordinated development of the population with economy, science and technology and the society, a pilot population community for comprehensive development was set up in Hainan Province in the beginning of 1991. It included Maoyang Community covering Maoyang Township of Tongshi City and area under its jurisdiction, three townships in the middle of Qiongshan County-Lingshan Community , Yunlong Community and Hongqi Community under its jurisdiction and the rural township communities with Quilingyang farm as the main community. The common features of the 5 communities were that they were all centered around townships and covering adjacent rural areas. The difference was that their economic level was uneven: Maoyang Community was the lowest with a per capital income of 282 Yuan in 1988; Lingshan, Yunlong and Hongqi were in the middle income level and Quilingyang Community was relatively higher. The fertility situation was quite similar to the economic situation: in 1990 TFR in Maoyang Community was 3.5; Lingshan, Yunlong and Hongqi Communities were around 3.0 while the TFR of Quilingyang was reduced to 2.5. [1] For the past two years, the five communities strove to realize the general development plan for 1991 – 2000 and achieved initial success. Their main success lies in their efforts to incorporate the complete solution of the population issue into the community construction and break the path for combining the population control with comprehensive community development and important inspirations could be drawn from the following basic issues:

Firstly, coordination of the population control mechanism with the reform and open-up. Hainan Province as the largest special economic zone of China is on the outpost of the reform and the open-up. It has made large strides in the economic reform and carried its work along the socialist market economic system including the public ownership economies and individual economy, private economy and foreign capital economy, all entering into the market and competing on equal terms and seeking joint development. Corresponding to the establishment and operations of the market economic structure, reform of superstructure and other fields is also being carried out and policies being readjusted. In light of the principles of separating the administration from enterprises and streamlining and unity of the structure, Hainan

---

① Ed. ZhanChangzhi "Bulletin for Population and Community Development" No. 3. April 1992.

Province has put forward the idea of "small government and large society" so as to change the function of the government and achieved initial success.

Under such a new situation of economic and political reform, a divoice occurs in the intermediary population control between the macro state population control and micro family fertility behaviour: the divoice caused by some methods not adapted to the market-oriented policies. Pilot population communities for comprehensive development have been born, on one hand, to solve the problem of divoice between the macro control and micro "welding"; on the other hand, to create conditions for the transition from using administrative means as the mechanism for population control to that of the regulation through incentives and the transfer of the options for benefits in the personal fertility behaviour so as to give more weight to the regulation through incentives in the population control by means of developing community economy, personnel training and strengthening community services. Besides assisting the government in realizing the regulations on the regards and punishment in the family planning, they give priorities to the single-child families and the birth-control families in technical training, in recommending workers to the "joint-venture" enterprises and in running economic entities to help the poor regions get rid of poverty and head for prosperity so that they could enjoy better treatment and benefits economically, politically and culturally than the families that have more children. The incentive-oriented measures like this have features of market regulation to certain extent and have grasped the key factor of the fertility behaviour determined by the cost-effectiveness of the child and solved the problem of coordinated development between the population control and reform and open-up in the intermediary field.

Secondly, combining the quantitative control of the population with the improvement of the quality of the population, besides the high fertility rate in the pilot communities which should be controlled, illiteracy and semi-illiteracy also account for a high percentage with low proportion for intermediary education and very few for high education in a small proportion. How should the quantitative control of the population be combined with the improvement of the quality of the population and make them mutually promote to each other? On one hand, the pilot population communities have launched workshops and seminars for the basic education on the state policy of population control such as the "state-policy gates" and the "state-policy rooms" and strengthened the population consciousness of the community members and changed the education departments, they have run "vocational schools of the pilot population commuinities in Hainan" to provide cultural courses and vocational technical training to the youth before employment. Since the schools practices the principles of" setting up courses upon requirement "and" recruitment on behalf of the enterprises", most of the graduates could enter into "joint-venture" enterprises and their opportunities for employment have been widened. Good effects have been achieved in combining the quantitative control of the population with the improvement of the quality of the population.

Thirdly, mutual advancement of the population control and the community economic development. The Hainan pilot population community for comprehensive development has always put the community economic development in the center of its work and treated it as the base to solve the population problem. They have opened vocational technical schools to promote the economic development of the community and also introduced personnel, technology and capital from Beijing, Shanghai, Nanjing, Anhui and other places in assistance to the office of the pilot community. Proceeding from the concrete conditions of the community, they help to explore the local agricultural by-products in developing the economy and trade of the region and assist the poor communities to get rich; or help to run economic entities with clear superiority in developing high-tech industries, tourism and actively participate in the market competition so as to promote the community economy to develop more rapidly. The community economic development could help to do more concrete services to the transfer of the input of quantitative cost of the child to that of the qualitative cost so as to open the way for the benign circle of the population and economic development of the community to operate.

Fourthly, coordination between the population control and the community services. Quantitative control is the primary issue in the population of the pilot community, however, it is not the only issue. The problems exist in the improvement of the quality of the population and the population aging with the increase of the old-aged population. Therefore, like the general problems faced by China in the population issue, the pilot community has to solve its population problems thoroughly including control of the quantity of the population, improvement of the quality of the population, readjustment of the population structure, especially the aging of the population structure and other aspects and the policy of combining control, improvement and regulation should be implemented. In terms of quantitative control, some of the people still have the traditional concepts of "continuing the family line" on one hand; on the other hand, the single-daughter families, and sonless families are faced with some concrete difficulties in their lives, most importantly the difficulty in caring for the aged. The concept of "having sons to prepare for one's old age" still has its deep ideological and economic roots, and it is specially true in the poor regions. In consideration of these cases, the pilot community has incorporated the problem of old-age support into the agenda of the "programme" of the development plan and is now vigorously preparing to establish a "Hainan community services center", It is also ready to develop comprehensive services in the urban residential quarters and rural communities including services for the aged population; it will set up an "International SOS Center", old people's homes, recreational homes for the aged and rehabilitation centers for the disabled persons, etc, with the aim to alleviate the worries of the old people who have single-child or who are birth-control families. The community services will be combined with the population control and implement the population control objectives in a concrete way while welcoming the challenge of the population aging and seeking comprehensive development of the future population and community with strategic perspectives.

Preface: Ma Yinchu and His Population Theory[*]

Tian Xueyuan

China is the most populous country in the world. Throughout the history, many philosophers, statesmen, and military strategists have discussed the population issue and left with us lasting theses on this subject. Nevertheless, in the long past of the Chinese feudal society, the pro-nationalist ideas such as "More sons mean more happiness" and "of the three kinds of unfilial conduct, the most serious one is to have no heir" have dominated the thinking of the ruling classes in all dynasties and dictated the fertility behavior of the common people. The trend had been one-sided. Occasionally some advocated a control of population growth, but that was merely an insignificant adverse current in a sea of torrential flood.

The western demography was introduced to China in modern times. In the 1920s and 1930s, a few sociologists advocated the control of population growth. However, as China was still a semi-colonial and semi-feudal society, demography could not be developed under that circumstances. After the People's Republic of China was founded in 1949 and in the late 1950s when the country was in a state of national recovery, an old scholar involved himself very actively in the fields of economics and demography. It was Mr. Ma Yinchu.

Mr. Ma was born on 24 June 1882 (or 9 May according to the Chinese lunar calendar) in Shaoxing City, Zhejiang Province. In 1898 when 16 years old,

---

[*] See: *Ma Yinchu's collected papers on population*, 1997.

Mr. Ma went to study in Shanghai and later to Tianjin attending the Beiyang University majoring in mining and metallurgy. In 1906, he went to the United States and was enrolled first in Yale University and later in Columbia University where he received his doctoral degree. In 1916 he came back to China and was appointed as Professor of Economics in Peking University, and later as Dean of Teaching.

During 100 years from the late Qing Dynasty to the time he passed away, Dr. Ma had gone through all major political upheavals. His political as well as academic views had also undergone along process of development. During the Anti-Japanese war (1937 – 1945), Dr. Ma Yinchu saw with his own eyes the total corruption of the nationalist government. He was a progressive thinker and was against the Jiang jie shi Clique and its dictatorship, against the exploitation of the Four Families, against the bureaucratic capitalists that monopolized China's economy, and against those who created the hyperinflation and made great fortunes. He was not afraid of telling the truth out of a sense of justice, but was jailed by the Jiang jie shi Clique and put into the Xifeng concentration camp in December 1940 and later to the Shangrao concentration camp. Mr. Ma was released from the jail in August 1942, but was immediately placed under house arrest in Geleshan in Chongqing. His lofty patriotism and dauntless spirit were respected by people of all walks of life, and praised highly by the Chinese Communist Party.

In 1941 on his 60th birthday while Mr. Ma was still in jall, Mr. Zhou Enlai (later the Premier), Mr. Dong Biwu (later a vice-President of China) and Madame Deng Yinchao (wife of Premier Zhou Enlai) presented a poem to celebrate his birthday:

Absent is the God of Longevity at his birthday celebration;

But he enjoys a long life with the company of books and music.

The *New China Daily*, the newspaper of the Chinese Communist Party in Chongqing also published a poem to mark Ma's 60th birthday praising warmly his bravery and noble quality:

Unyielding and dauntless are his natural characters;

Dare to speak and to anger show his inspiring spirit.

Mr. Ma Yinchu valued highly these two poems and had kept them carefully for decades.

After Japan was defeated in 1945, Mr. Ma took an active part in the patriotic and democratic movement hoping to prevent the out-break of the civil war and to promote peace and democracy in the country. He went to teach in the China College of Industry and Commerce in Shanghai and participated in the patriotic movements for democracy. He severely denounced the "Sino-U. S. Treaty on Commerce and Trade" signed between Jiang jie shi's Government and the U. S. , which actually sold out China's national sovereignty. In May 1947, the secret agent of the Nationalist Party tried every means to stop Mr. Ma from delivering a speech at the Central University Student Association in Nanjing. The agent even declared that Mr. Ma would be assassinated if he insisted on going there. Mr. Ma paid no heed to the death threat and went ahead with a will prepared before his departure. In 1948, when his life was endangered in the Nationalist-ruled areas, Mr. Ma went to the Liberated Areas controlled by the Communists by way of Hong Kong with the help of the underground Communist organizations. In September 1949, Mr. Ma attended the first session of the Chinese People's Political Consultative Conference (CP-PCC) held in Beijing.

Since the People's Republic of China was established, Mr. Ma Yinchu had supported strongly the leadership of the Chinese Communist Party and socialism, and contributed greatly to the socialist revolution and reconstruction, particularly to the development of education, culture and economy. He was elected a member of the first and third CPPCC and a member of the Standing Committee of the second and fourth CPPCC, a deputy to the first National People's Congress (NPC) and a member of the Standing Committee of the second NPC. He was named Vice Chairman of the East China Administrative Council, Vice Chairman of the Commission of Finance and Economy of the Central People's Government, President of Zhejiang University as well as Peking University.

During the turmoil of the "Cultural Revolution", it was our respected late Premier Zhou Enlai who gave orders to protect the aged Mr. Ma and to care for his health. This protection prevented this ninety-year old gentleman and scholar from persecution by Lin Biao, the "Gang of the Four" and their group. After regaining his reputation in 1979, Ma was elected a member of the Standing Committee of the Fifth CPPCC and became Honorary President of Beijing University.

Mr. Ma Yinchu has paid his attention to the issue of population quite early. He wrote an article in 1920 on "Mathematics on the Calculation of Population" in which he discussed the application of mathematics in population studies. In his 1928 speech on "Modern New Economic Policies", he expressed his "shock" at the rapid growth of population and advocated "controlling births to reduce population growth".

After the founding of the New China, particularly after 1955, Mr. Ma wrote many articles and talked on various occasions about the balance between the population growth and the development of national economy. He placed population issue at the focus of his attention. But why studying population? The remarks he made in 1957 in his interview with a correspondent from *Wenhuibao* could be used to represent his views on this topic. He said, "Just take a look at what a miserable life people lived in the past. Many were on a state of half starvation. In famines, they could hardly find anything to eat and had to turn to grass roots and tree barks for food. So many people died of hunger and beggars were everywhere." He continued to say that since the Liberation, people's living standard had been limitedly improved. One of the important reasons for the limitation was our population was large and its growth was fast. Therefore, he studied the population issue and advocated the control of population growth. Not worrying about his old age, Mr. Ma took every opportunity to visit factories and rural areas. He discussed with factory workers, farmers and administrative cadres on the population issue. He visited Zhejiang Province three times in 1954 and 1955 and learned in details of the growth of rural population and of food there. In 1955, Mr. Ma wrote a drafted speech on the "Control of Population Growth and Scientific Study" with the collected data, and submitted it to the Zhejiang Group of NPC for discussion. Since most people paid little attention to the population issue at that time, some even branding his views as the Malthusian doctrine, he had to withdraw his draft from discussion. At the Supreme State Council Meeting in February 1957, Mr. Ma expressed his views on the population issue again and aroused the attention of Chairman Mao Zedong, Premier Zhou Enlai and other leaders. In June, he explained systematically his views on population at the fourth session of the first National People's Congress. The full text of his speech was published in the *People's Daily* on 5 July. This was his "New

Population Theory", his most representative work on population issue.

Although Mr. Ma's "New Population Theory" and his other speeches and articles on the population issue were not lengthy, they were characterized by their clear-cut viewpoints and convincing facts. Contrary to the doctrine in the Soviet textbooks which stated that rapid population growth was the population law of socialism, Mr. Ma's writings dismantled the fallacy that "It's good to have more people." His fresh views had also started a heated debate. Unfortunately, Mr. Ma was later criticized severely as if he were Mr. Dean Acheson, the U. S. Secretary of State at that time and the debate turned into a political attack on Mr. Ma himself, who was accused of "attacking the Chinese Communist Party and socialism using the pretense of academic study", "serving imperialism, feudalism and capitalism" and "opposing the Chinese Communist Party, socialism and Marxism". As a result, his New Population Theory was condemned to eternal damnation.

However, practice is the sole criterion for the examination of truth and also for the examination of population theories and population policies. It is irrefutable that decades of practice have proven that the principles of Mr. Ma's "New Population Theory" were correct and all the accusations against him were false and should be thrown out.

Mr. Ma's theory was correct for the following reasons:

First of all, Mr. Ma Yinchu made a correct assessment of the development of China's population in the 1950s on which his new population theory was based. According to the 1953 national population census, China had a total population of 601, 938, 035 persons, a birth rate of 37 per thousand and a rate of natural increase of 20 per thousand. A few years later after the census, Mr. Ma took notice of the possible errors in the population estimation as the population growth might have been accelerated. He gave seven reasons to explain his concerns: 1) An increase in the number of marriages, which would lead to an increase in births; 2) The decline of the infant mortality rate resulting from the improvement of medical, health and all kinds of social welfare services; 3) The drop in the old age deaths. In the past, it was rare to see people survive to seventy years but now more people could live to seventy years old and over; 4) It was a stable and orderly society, and few died unnatural deaths; 5) Most monks and nuns returned to a secular life, and the problem of prostitution which could not be solved in the capitalist society was basically solved; 6) The feudalistic thinking of "More sons bring more happiness and a longer life" and "Prosperity in five continuous generations" were deeply rooted in the minds of people; and 7) The government rewarded those women giving multiple-births. Mr. Ma felt that, "These were the causes that contributed to the increase in birth rate and the decrease in death rate." Therefore, "In the past four years the rate of natural increase could have been well over 20 per thousand." Statistical data collected later on indicated that the rate of natural increase was 24.8 per thousand in 1954, 20.3 per thousand in 1955, 20.5 per thousand in 1956 and 23.2 per thousand in 1957. The average rate was 23.2 per thousand for these four years and was higher than the 20 per thousand in 1953. Clearly, Mr. Ma's analyses of the growth rate and the causes for the rapid increase were scientific and true.

Second, through his analysis of the contradicting relationship between the rapid population growth and the development of national economy, Mr. Ma explained the central thesis of his New Population Theory: to control the size of population and to improve the quality of the people. This thesis pinpointed the fundamental problem of our population.

The major contradictions between China's rapid population growth and the development of the national economy were: 1) between the rapid population growth and the acceleration of capital accumulation; 2) between rapid population growth and the increase in labour productivity ; 3) between the rapid population growth and the improvement of people's living standards; and 4) between the rapid population growth and the development of sciences.

Mr. Ma held that there were population problems in size as well as in quality. He linked population size and population quality together and explained that the control of population growth and the improvement of population quality were closely related and mutually promoted. He proposed unequivocally "to raise the standard of education," and "to raise the quality of population". In his *My Philosophical Thoughts and Economic Theory*, Mr. Ma said that "In this impoverished country where we have many people but limited capital, it would be a good thing to organize the people and turn them into resource. But just keep in mind the disadvantage of having more people. More people represent a great resource, but they are also an enormous burden. My New Population Theory is to retain the advantages and to do away with the disadvantages. Efforts must be made to keep this great resource and to get rid of the burden through improving the quality of the population and controlling its growth. "

Mr. Ma, by applying the first-hand survey data, demonstrated the imbalance development between population growth and economic development and the contradicting relationships between population growth on the one hand and capital accumulation, consumption patterns and scientific development on the other. He was very worthy of our esteem for making such a prudent analysis as early as in the 1950s. His views on controlling population sizes and improving population quality were strategic and foresighted. He had suggested a fundamental solution to China's population problems in a positive manner. His view was correct then and is correct today as we are still facing the arduous task to control the population size and to improve the quality of the people.

Next, all measures suggested by Mr. Ma to control population growth were practical and workable. In order to effectively control population growth, the first step was to "publicize the control of population", to help people breaking away with the traditional concept of family continuity and the residuals of feudalistic thoughts such as "To have a son quickly", "To wish such prosperity of having five generations living together" and "Of the three kinds of unfilial conduct the most serious one is to have no heir. " The second step was "to revise the Marriage Law when the publicity began to gain some success" in order to promote late marriages. "It appeared that the age of 25 for men and 23 for women were proper ages for marriages. " The third step was "to introduce more powerful and effective administrative measures if population control is not working well after the revision of the Marriage Law".

He proposed that couples who gave births to only two children should be rewarded, to three children be taxed and to four should be heavily taxed. The taxes collected would be used as reward money and the national budgets would not be affected by such a programme.

The above were the basic views and positions of Mr. Ma's New Population Theory. Nevertheless, these were distorted as "genuine Malthusianism" and Mr. Ma was branded as the Malthus in China. He was thought to look on people only as consumers and not in the first place as producers. He saw people's mouth instead of their two hands. The logic of the" human hands "was that the more people the more labourers, the more things produced the more capital accumulated and the faster the society developed. Therefore it seemed the more people the better. This logic was said to be the true Marxist concept on population. Some even went so far as to say that the Chinese term of population, *renkou* or man-mouth was Malthusiastic and should be replaced by *renshou* or man-hand. The logic seems rather ridiculous today but was" authoritative" and popular at the time when Mr. Ma was criticized and repudiated. As a matter of fact, anyone who was not biased would agree that Mr. Ma's theory was different from Malthus population theory and he had criticized and refuted Malthus seriously. Mr. Ma pointed out that Malthus' advocation of wiping out or reducing the existing population by means of wars, plagues and hungers was "definitely reactionary." He further said that the improvement in production and in the standard of living of the people since the founding of the New China were eloquent enough to destroy the fallacy of the arithmetic progression in food production. He again said that although the natural conditions, "might impose certain restrictions, but the scientific advances are boundless" and Malthusian's underlying principles had been bankrupted long before. However, Mr. Ma's new theory was arbitrarily equated with Malthusianism and his criticism of Malthusianism was purposely distorted as "true dissemination under the disguise of criticism".

Mr. Ma Yinchu was in an extremely difficult situation when the long debate on his new population theory continued. But he stood firmly because he believed that truth was with him. In his "Supplementary Statement", he said, "Although I am nearing 80 years old and aware of the situation in which I am hopelessly outnumbered, I am ready to take up all the challenges and to fight until I die. I will never surrender to those who can not convince anyone but only use force to submit others." "Because I have full confidence in my theory, I have to stick to it and to defend the dignity of knowledge. I refuse to make self-criticism." It was precisely the thoroughness of his theory or the "dignity of knowledge" that determined his political staunchness. Those who had experienced the great debate would have remembered Mr. Ma's scientific and truth-pursuing attitude, the dauntless spirit and the insistence until the very end of the debate.

There is fine old Chinese saying that "Where the hills and streams end and there seems no road beyond, amidst the shading willows and the blooming flowers another village appears" After the defeat of the "Gang of Four" in the late 1970s, the Communist Party Committee of Beijing University announced, with the ap-proval from the Party Central Committee, the decision to completely reverse the verdict of Mr. Ma Yinchu's case and to recover his reputation. The accusations which had been imposed on Mr. Ma for more than two decades were finally reversed and his "New Population Theory" was fully accepted. This was not only a big e-vent to Mr. Ma, but also of great importance to the theoretical study of China's population. The event has helped us to clean up the disruptions coming from the ex-treme left, to sum up correctly what have been learned in history and to fulfill the strategic goal of controlling the growth of China's population.

Time passes. At the 40th anniversary of the publication of the New Population Theory and the 18th year after Mr. Ma regained his reputation, we are welcoming the convention of the 23rd Conference of the International Union for the Scientific Studies of Population (IUSSP) in Beijing. This convention is the "Olympics" for demographers of the world to get together once every four years. It is also an impor-tant occasion for Chinese demographers to learn from the experiences of other coun-tries and to conduct academic exchanges on different demographic subjects. At the invitation of the Zhejiang People's Publishing House, I select Mr. Ma's writings on population from the *Complete Works of Ma Yinchu* entitling them *Ma Yinchu's Collected Papers on Population* (English) and present it to the 23rd Conference of IUSSP. This volume is also served as a commemoration to the memory of Dr. Ma Yinchu.

The Promising Prospect for the Large Population Country—China

Tian Xueyuan

Member of the Chinese Academy of Social Sciences General Deputy President of the Population Society of China

The history of demographic transition and population development has fully demonstrated that 20th century had a rapid population growth, while 21st century is a century of population aging. In the past 100 years, the world population is increased from 1. 6 billion in 1900 to 2. 5 billion in 1950 and to 6. 1 billion in year 2000, with the increasing 56. 3% and 281. 3% respectively. However, with the decline of fertility rate lasted from 1970s, the population growth rate decreased from 1. 9% in the mid -20th century to 1. 3% at the end of the century and the age structure appears that the elderly people has occupied a large proportion of the total population. As a developing country with the largest amount of population, China's population rose from 0. 42 billion in 1900 to 0. 54 billion in 1950 and to 1. 27 billion in year 2000, with the increasing 28. 6% and 202. 4% respectively, over the same period of time above. The fertility rate has decreased continually since the 1970s. The population growth rate decreased from 2% in the middle of the century to 0. 8% at the end of the century which means around 0. 4 billion babies' birth has been controlled. As the result, the World Population Day of Five Billion has been successfully postponed for two years, and the World Population Day of Six Billion postponed for three years. Although the momentum of population growth is inevitable, it has been weakened effectively. The "Three Population Peaks" will arrive ahead of time at different extents.

(1) The peak of total population size will appear ahead of time. In 2030, the population will be 1. 465 billion and the zero growth can be carried out at the same year. Fig. 1 shows the three (low, medium and high) population projection scenarios.

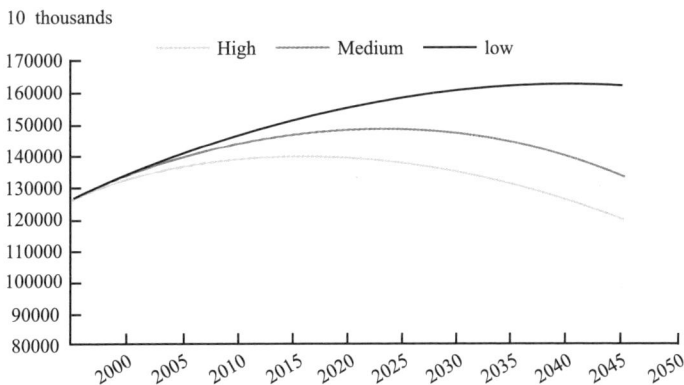

10 thousands

Fig. 1   Three Predictions (low, medium and high)
of The Population's Development. 2000 ~ 2050

Notes: orange-high, purple-medium, yellow-low.

(2) The number of working age population will increase slowly, which can reach its peak one decade later. Adult working people aged 15 – 64 has increased from 644 million in 1980 to 867 million in 2000, and it is predicted to reach the peak of about 1 billion in 2017. A trend of reduction can be foreseen, which shows the working age population will reach 988 million in 2030, and 858 million in 2050. It's proportion in the total population was 64. 5% in 1980, 68. 7% in 2000 and it will reach its peak at 72. 4% in 2009. There will be a reduction afterwards, accounting for 69% in 2020, 67. 4% in 2030, and 63% in 2050 (See Figure 2) .

(3) The aging population is increasing rapidly. The peak of population aging will arrive in the first period of the 21st century. According to the prediction, the proportion of the elderly people over the age of 65 will increase from 7% in 2000 to 8. 6 percent in 2010, 12% in 2020 and reach its peak of 23. 1% in 2050. Compared with the 25. 9% of aging population in developed countries in 2050, the ag-

ing population proportion in China will still be 2.8% lower, compared with the 15.9% and 14.3% of aging population in the whole world and in developing countries in 2050, the aging population proportion in China will be 7.2% and 8.8% higher. (See UN: World Population Prospects: The 2002 Revision. P. 38 – 42). It is obviously at a high level in the world and at the highest level among developing countries. (See Figure 3).

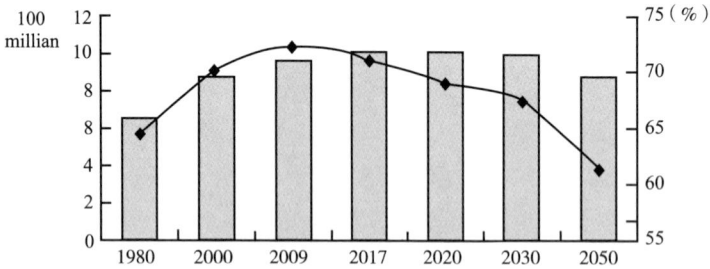

Fig. 2   Population Change among Working-age People aged 15 – 64 (green/Total Population/; red/percentage)

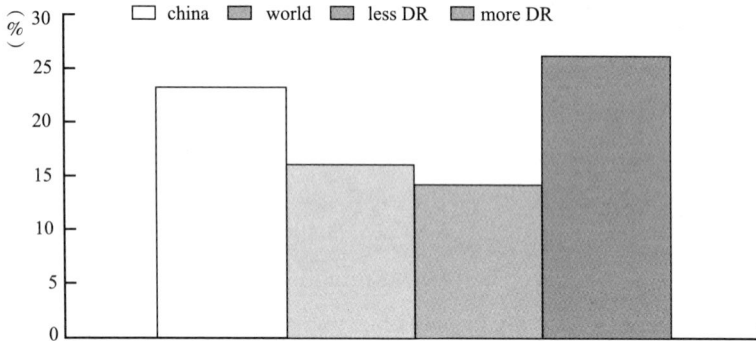

Fig. 3   The comparison of the proportion of Elderly People Aged over 65 in China and Around the World 2050

The problem of China's population is characterized by the pressure of population on productivity. In order to solve China's population problem, a "Three Stages" development strategy has been made out. The first step is to make the fertility rate lower than the replacement level, realizing the goal of the demographic transition from "high birth rate, low mortality rate, and high growth rate" to "low birth rate, low death rate and low growth rate". This stage had been done in the mid 1990s. The second step is to stabilize the lower fertility rate until the zero growth of population is realized. It is expected to be realized about 2030. We are currently at this stage. The third step is to set an ideal goal for moderate population based on the factors such as the development of economy and society as well as the conditions of resources and environment in 2030 when zero growth is realized. This ideal goal for moderate population should be comprehensive, which includes an appropriate quantity, high quality, suitable age and sex structure.

附　录

《中国民族人口》出版发行[*]

    本报北京 4 月 11 日讯   记者丁伟报道：集民族人口研究成果于大成的系列专著《中国民族人口》今天在京正式出版发行。全国人大常委会副委员长、中国人口学会会长彭珮云为该书题词并作序。

    《中国民族人口》是全国社科规划重点项目，由著名人口学家、中国社会科学院学术委员田雪原研究员担任主编。该书由中国人口出版社出版，分6集，约 1000 万字，以翔实的资料、深入浅出的分析，分别论述了我国 56 个民族的起源与变迁、规模与分布、身体与文化素质、婚姻与家庭、生育与死亡、人口与发展等方面的内容，为新时期民族人口研究打下了坚实的基础。

---

* 2002 年 4 月 12 日《人民日报》。

中华民族人口研究的恢弘巨著[*]
——《中国民族人口》出版

本报讯（通讯员莫丽霞报道）全国社科规划重点项目，集民族人口研究于大成的一部力作《中国民族人口》近日由中国人口出版社出版发行第1集。

我国是有56个民族的多民族国家，加强民族人口研究是做好人口与计划生育工作的重要任务之一。整套《中国民族人口》共分6集，约1000万字，可称得上是中国民族人口文献中的恢弘巨著。《中国民族人口》第1集共160万字，以世居在华北、东北的满、蒙古、朝鲜、锡伯、达翰尔、鄂温克、鄂伦春、赫哲族为主，每个民族独成一卷，按照民族人口起源与变迁、规模与分布、身体与文化素质、年龄与性别结构、婚姻与家庭、生育与死亡、人口与发展等章节规范撰写，特别是贯彻党的民族政策和计划生育基本国策取得的突出成绩，生育率的下降，人口身体素质和文化教育素质的提高，劳动就业条件的改善，养老保障事业的发展等，是集民族人口研究于大成的一部力作，是研究人口学、民族学、人类学以及民族地区人口、经济、社会、资源、环境发展不可多得的论著。

著名人口学家、中国社会科学院学术委员田雪原研究员担任主编并作绪论。全国人大常委会副委员长、中国人口学会会长、《中国民族人口》名誉主编彭珮云题词并作序。全国人大常委会副委员长布赫，全国人大常委会副委员长铁木尔·达瓦买提，原全国人大常委会副委员长、著名社会学家费孝通分别为本书题词；国家计生委主任张维庆、国家民委主任李德洙等担任顾问。

---

[*] 2002年4月15日《科技日报》。

《人口·经济·社会可持续发展》出版[*]

　　田雪原主编的《人口·经济·社会可持续发展》一书，已由中国经济出版社出版。目前，关于可持续发展问题，一般是将其作为一种发展战略或行动纲领提出和阐述的。该书的特色在于，以理论探讨为开篇，力求从理论与实践的结合上展开论述。作者认为，以人为本的发展观及其理论，构成了可持续发展的理论基础，但研究发展观和发展理论应首先弄清发展的含义。就词语解释，发展是指事物由小到大、由简单到复杂、由低级到高级的变化过程。但这样的解释偏重于外在形态变动的描述，没有揭示发展的内在变动，而研究可持续发展更需要后一个方面的挖掘。因此，该书提出，一切发展都可归纳为资源的物质变换，如人们采掘铁矿石炼成钢铁，制成各种器具，推动冶金、制造业的发展；进行经济体制改革，实现人、财、物等资源的合理配置，推动经济和社会发展等。从这样的定义出发，该书阐述了以人为本的可持续发展观及其理论的含义。

（李经）

---

[*]　2004 年 4 月 8 日《人民日报》。

控制数量　提高质量　调整结构[*]
——《人口·经济·社会可持续发展》出版

　　《人口、经济、社会可持续发展》是我院"九五"重点课题的结项成果。全书在合理评介和借鉴国内外已有研究成果的基础上，刻意进行学术创新，从理论与实践的结合上，阐发了人口、经济、社会可持续发展的理论、战略目标、行动计划与决策选择。资料翔实，理论色彩浓厚，实证研究针对性强，逻辑分析层次清楚，体现了理论指导实践，通过实践再上升到理论的研究准则，展现了理论研究与实证研究相结合的学术研究价值。

　　全书共分绪论、人口可持续发展、人口与经济可持续发展、人口与社会可持续发展四个部分。"绪论"在前期及当代可持续发展理论的基础上，提出以人为本的可持续发展理论及其理论体系。阐述了建立在这一理论框架基础上的可持续发展战略结构，即人口是可持续发展战略的关键，资源是可持续发展的前提，环境是可持续发展的目的，人口、资源、环境是可持续发展的调节器，是实现可持续发展的途径。"绪论"部分勾画出了可持续发展的独立的理论体系，奠定了全书的理论基调和篇章结构。

　　该书通过对人口变动的历史回顾，到目前的人口现状与特点，未来的发展趋势，阐明了当前存在的人口数量持续增大、劳动年龄人口增长突出、人口年龄结构变动速度加快、人口素质提高显著但水平仍较低、人口城市化道路曲折、人口地区分布失衡等主要问题。由此得出以全方位适度人口论作为理论支撑的人口可持续发展战略。并提出可持续发展的人口目标、行动计划和决策选择，稳定低生育水平和寻求机制转变的具体建议；提高人口文化教育素质的改革思路，西部大开发增强人力资本积聚的建议；调整人口年龄，城乡、地域结构所需要谋求的可持续发展的养老保障体系、适当加快人口城

---

　　*　中国社会科学院，2003 年 11 月 11 日《院报》。

市化步伐、科学界定人口地域分布的建议。这些改革和建议贴近实际，锐意进取，具有较强的可行性和可操作性。

在人口与经济可持续发展的部分，重点探讨人口与资源、人口与就业、人口与消费、人口老龄化与养老保障、人口流动与城市化、人口素质与技术进步的关系，可持续发展的目标与决策选择。借鉴了诸多当今人口经济学研究成果，如人口承载力学说、经济适度人口论、消费函数理论、退休经济理论和产业结构、就业结构与人口城乡结构理论等，紧密联系中国实际，分析和阐述了人口与经济可持续发展的战略目标、行动计划与决策选择。还对人口城市化水平落后于就业结构、就业结构又落后于产业结构以及加快人口城市化进程进行了分析并提出了全新的观点。

作者从人口社会学视角，追踪社会进化与人类自然观升华的历史进程，探讨现代社会价值要素变动的规律，论证了社会可持续发展的终极性质，是可持续发展战略的最终落脚点。在综合评介已有研究成果的基础上，提出将社会可持续发展的理论方法和指标体系建立在社会分层、社会文明、社会调控、社会进步"四大支柱"基础上。社会分层分为社会管理层、社会中间层、社会弱势层三个不同层面，强调合理的阶层结构是现代社会可持续发展的重要条件；社会文明、社会调控、社会进步分解为人文发展、社会效能、社会安全等 9 项指数，不仅使社会可持续发展的度量成为可能，而且为找出在社会可持续发展中存在的问题以及解决这些问题提供了科学的理论方法。

人口与可持续发展问题的系统研究[*]

——《全面建设小康社会人口与可持续发展报告》简评

人口问题和可持续发展问题，都是事关我国全面建设小康社会全局的重大问题。田雪原主编的《全面建设小康社会人口与可持续发展报告》一书（中国财政经济出版社出版），把这两个重大问题结合起来加以研究，通过考察人口的变动和发展与经济、社会、资源、环境的变动和发展之间相互影响、相互制约的关系，对人口问题和可持续发展问题的理论与实践进行了深入探讨，并提出了一些政策建议。

提出和论证了可持续发展理论的框架。该书认为，可持续发展的目的是为了满足人的全面发展的需要；在发展问题上，应遵循以人为本和代际公平原则，既把满足当代人发展的需要放在首位，又不能损害后代人满足其需要的能力；可持续发展的根本驱动力在人力资本；为了实现可持续发展，应寻求人与自然的和谐，促进人口、资源、环境协调发展。在此基础上，该书提出和论证了由稀缺资源论、全方位适度人口论、生态系统论、总体经济效益论、社会协调发展论"五大支柱"构成的可持续发展理论的框架。

阐述了人口与经济可持续发展、社会可持续发展、资源可持续发展、环境可持续发展的关系。在人口与经济可持续发展问题上，该书通过揭示人口变动与经济发展之间的基本关系，提出了以积极老龄化、健康老龄化、轻量老龄化来应对人口老龄化挑战的策略；通过系统解析人口容量、人口荷载、人口压力指数等指标，得出了我国东、中、西部地区的人口压力指数以及人口与经济发展的可持续性和协调性状况。在人口与社会可持续发展问题上，该书提出了建立阶层利益整合机制、改革收入分配制度从而遏制收入差距扩

---

* 原载《人民日报》2006年9月27日。

大，以及建立城乡一体化、加速人口城市化的社会机制，从根本上解决"三农"问题等政策建议。在人口与资源可持续发展问题上，该书认为，我国资源消耗大，主要是粗放型经济增长方式的结果。也同人口增长特别是人口城市化的加速推进加大了人均资源消耗的"加权效应"分不开。因此，控制人口数量、提高人口质量是实现资源可持续利用的重要途径。在人口与环境可持续发展问题上，该书指出，保护环境必须转变经济增长方式，而经济增长方式转变同人口数量、质量、结构特别是同人口科学文化素质的提高和城乡结构的调整有着密切关系。应通过提高人口素质，调整城乡人口结构和三次产业就业结构，促进经济增长方式转变。

（皮专胜）

始终发扬艰苦奋斗的精神*

——增强节俭意识对话录（节选）

对话人：《人民日报》记者　马宏伟　张怡恬

中国人口学会常务副会长　田雪原

中国社会科学院研究员　金碚

中共山东省昌乐县委书记　王树华

　　"要进一步增强节俭意识，始终发扬艰苦奋斗的精神"。这是胡锦涛同志在今年两会上强调的增强"三种意识"的内容之一。在物质财富越来越充足、人们越来越有条件享受富裕生活的今天，我们是否还需要节俭？如果需要，那么，需要什么样的节俭意识和节俭行为？怎样使节俭成为一种社会风气？日前，记者就这些问题与中国人口学会常务副会长田雪原、中国社会科学院研究员金碚和中共山东省昌乐县委书记王树华进行了对话。

　　没有节俭，就没有积累和经济增长。增强节俭意识是由我国人口多、资源和环境承载力有限的客观实际决定的，是一个带有根本性和长期性的原则问题。

　　记者：节俭是中华民族的传统美德，也是一个古老的话题。那么，在现代社会，在物质财富越来越充足的今天，我们应该怎样看待节俭的价值呢？

　　田雪原：我们应当站在经济社会可持续发展的高度来认识节俭问题和树立节俭意识。增强节俭意识是由我国人口多、资源和环境承载力有限的客观实际决定的，不是权宜之计，而是一个带有根本性和长期性的原则问题。我国人均耕地面积不足世界平均水平的1/2，人均淡水资源不足1/3，人均林地面积不足1/4，人均矿产资源不足1/2。未来二三十年，我国人口还将再增加1.5亿左右。随着工业化、城镇化的推进，人口增长对资源消耗的"加权效应"将会更加明显地表现出来。与此同时，环境恶化的形势非常严峻。长期以来，粗放的经济增长不仅消耗了大量资源，而且加剧了环境污染，对人民群众的健康构成了威胁。实施可持续发展战略，要求继续控制人口数

---

　　* 参见《人民时报》2007年4月23日。

量、提高人口素质、调整人口结构，要求节约资源、提高资源利用率、转变经济增长方式，要求将人类活动纳入环境生态系统、依法保护和改善环境。这些方面都同节俭意识密切相关。特别是要将人口增长对资源消耗的"加权效应"控制在合理范围之内，从根本上理顺人与自然的关系，将增强节俭意识纳入人口素质提高的范围。

政府部门以及各级领导干部的行为，对全社会能否形成节俭意识和节俭行为具有至关重要的影响。建设节约型社会，应从领导干部做起，从建设节约型政府做起。

记者：胡锦涛同志强调各级干部特别是领导干部要进一步增强节俭意识，对此应如何认识呢？

田雪原：我国现在经济总量位居世界第四，对外贸易额位居第三，外汇储备位居第一，过去"一穷二白"的状况有了根本改观。面对财富较快增长而制度、管理、监督还不能及时跟上的复杂局面，各级领导干部能否正确对待和使用社会物质财富，就成为关系党和国家事业发展的大问题。所以，现在强调增强节俭意识，首先是针对各级干部特别是领导干部讲的。如果搞劳民伤财的"形象工程"、"政绩工程"，如果不计成本地挥霍浪费现象刹不住，改革开放的一部分成果就会被白白浪费掉，党同人民群众的血肉联系就会受到伤害。建设节约型社会，应从领导干部做起，从建设节约型政府做起。

节俭并不是资源的消极闲置，不是封库守财。用之当用，物尽其用。珍惜民财，耗有所值，才是现代社会的积极节俭意识。

记者：有人对提倡节俭存有疑问：这是不是又要"勒紧裤腰带"过苦日子？提倡节俭和拉动内需是不是有矛盾呢？

田雪原：节俭乃节制、节省和俭朴、勤俭之意，树立节俭意识并不意味着抑制消费。我们发展经济的目的就是为了满足人们的物质和文化生活需求，促进人的全面发展。而且，当前经济生活中的一个突出问题是内需不足、消费不振。因此，增强节俭意识不是抑制消费，而是倡导合理消费。应当看到，在我国经济社会发展的新阶段，节俭有新的含义。高耗低效一直是我国经济增长中的老大难问题。我国人均资源不足，而单位 GDP 能源和材料消耗约为发达国家的 2 倍，转变经济增长方式的任务非常紧迫。在这样的背景下提出增强节俭意识，应把生产节约包含在内，努力实现单位产品能源和材料消耗的下降，以节约推动生产的发展。所以，需要从可持续发展的高度来认识和树立节俭意识。

经济学家追踪*

经济科学出版社协办

著名人口经济学家、中国人口学会常务副会长田雪原（1938—）教授日前在接受采访时，自述他 40 年前读大学就和《光明日报》"结了缘"——对此我并不吃惊，因为我早就知道他 20 世纪 60 年代初就在《光明日报》的《经济学》专刊发表了一篇不下 5000 字的大文章（题为《关于中国近代国民经济史分期的几个问题》）、只是没想到他当时还只是一名在校大学生！尤其值得一提的是，在北京大学经济系读书期间，他就觉得社会上批判北大老校长马寅初的"新人口论"有什么地方"不对劲"，可当时的环境又怎样允许他"唱反调"？十数年后，被调到中国社会科学院经济所搞研究时他终于"憋不住"地想说些什么了，于是，积多年之研究撰写了一篇题为《为马寅初先生的新人口论翻案》的长篇论文，并于 1979 年 8 月 5 日刊登在《光明日报》的显著位置上。了解那段历史的人都知道，这是当时党报上系统论述马寅初人口思想的第一篇重要文章，其影响是可想而知的。田雪原从此也就与人口经济学结下了不解之缘。

迄今，田雪原教授共出版了《新时期人口论》等著述（含主编）16 部，发表论文 300 余篇。在承担众多科研课题、带博士生的同时，田雪原还主编《中国人口年鉴》，同时又是全国社科规划人口学科组组长、中国人口学会副会长、中国老年学会副秘书长、国家计生委人口专家委员、国际人口科学联盟成员，等等。目前，他主编的《中国少数民族人口研究》进展顺利，所主编的《人口学》也基本脱稿，所主持的国家项目"人口与可持续发展问题研究"也完成了最终报告。可他显然闲不住，这不，关于人口老龄与社会保障、人口因素对经济发展的影响，以及西部大开发中的人口和人才问

---

* 2000 年 3 月 21 日《光明日报》。

题，他正准备写点什么。

在人口问题研究中，田雪原总是以一种平和的心态把枯燥精深的理论和晦涩难懂的公式，化成具体生动的事例和幽默朴素的语言娓娓道来，从而使人口学这曲"阳春之雪"走出学者的书斋，进入了"寻常百姓家"，为更多的普通人所接纳后，很快又加印和再版，总印数已高达 32000 册，学术著作能成为畅销书，这显然与他的治学努力是密不可分的。

进入 2000 年，田教授喜讯不断：中国经济出版社出版的《田雪原文集（三）》销售看好，《大国之难——当代中国的人口问题》又被译成日文在日本出版！这是日本首次翻译出版的中国人口学方面的专著。日本新社在出版该书时，还特意聘请日本同行在书后作"解说"，详细介绍了田雪原早年在马寅初"新人口论"翻案和近年为出版《马寅初文集》所作的努力，以及他在人口理论拨乱反正、中国人口政策和人口战略目标的制定、人口与资源环境的可持续发展研究等方面取得的成果和研究。前不久，《马寅初全集》出版座谈会在人民大会堂召开，许多与会者在缅怀马寅初先生对中国人口发展的杰出贡献时，也对田雪原在此方面所取得的突出成果给予了高度评价。

（萧　吟）

天行健，君子以自强不息[*]
——记国家级有突出贡献专家、人口学家田雪原

随着岁月的钟声把我们带进21世纪，中国人口科学发展也由幼年步入成年时期。这是学术界众学人前仆后继、不断开拓进取的结果。走在这支拓荒者队伍前列的领军者之一，便是现任中国社会科学院学术委员、国家级有突出贡献专家、博士生导师田雪原研究员。是他，率先举起人口理论拨乱反正的大旗；是他，早在1980年起草中央人口座谈会报告时对诸多疑难问题作了经得起历史检验的论证和诠释；是他，较早地阐发了比较完整的"三位一体"的人口发展战略和"三位一体"的养老保障体系；是他，在将西方人口学理论与中国实际相结合研究中，提出并阐发了社会附加孩子成本—效益理论，人口文化素质指数概念和计算方法……《易经》云："天行健，君子以自强不息；地势坤，君子以厚德载物。"田雪原正是以这种自强不息、不断进取和勇于开拓的精神，活跃在新世纪的人口科学战线上。

报国之志立少年

田雪原出生在素有"煤铁之城"之称的辽宁省本溪市郊区，那时尚在日本侵略者的铁蹄蹂躏控制之下。在他幼小的心灵中，洋鬼子的战刀高出头项一大截，自然最痛恨的莫过于那些鬼子了。上小学三年级的一天，作为教师的哥哥带回一本书来：方志敏烈士的《可爱的中国》，他便囫囵吞枣般地读起来。读着读着他眼睛湿润了，当看到帝国主义列强用一根根管子吸着祖国母亲的血液，母亲在痛苦中呻吟的时候，他再也抑制不住内心的悲愤，泪

---

[*]　原载《动在千秋——中华人口奖十年》，中国人口出版社，2003。

水打湿衣衫，立志长大要保卫母亲，为祖国母亲的强大而献出一切。可是为什么母亲总受别人欺侮呢？他还找不到答案。上中学学习历史，他明白了一是清政府腐败无能，二是经济技术落后、国力虚弱的结果。在五星红旗下长大的他，第一个原因已不复存在，第二个原因却依然没有多少改变，于是他立志发奋学习，以便将来报效有门。20 世纪 50 年代的教育倡导全面发展、又红又专，他身体力行，初中他以各门功课全 5 分的成绩毕业，高中以全市最高分考进北京大学；他是校合唱队主要成员，"一二·九"全市文艺汇演他们团获总分第一名；体育不仅通过"劳卫制"，而且乒乓球、篮球、100 米、1500 米跑等还达到三级或二级运动员标准；"勤工俭学"、"大跃进"不甘示弱，下乡同农民一起春种、夏锄、秋收，井下一起同矿工挥锹，高炉前给工人师傅当小工一起读《铁水奔流》；在校办工厂，他锉出的"卡钳子"屡屡受到教师的赞许……至今回忆起来，他深感得益于全面发展的教育方针：报国之志给了他无尽的力量，身心健康的学校生活使他过了花甲之年丝毫没有感到记忆力减退，100 米跑尚在 15 秒以内。

学坛驰骋有中年

1959 年秋，满怀报国之志的田雪原来到北京大学攻读经济学。第二年学习中国经济史，使他进一步明白了中国经济贫弱的深层次原因；同时感到当时的学术讨论有些问题，于是便查找资料，写出"关于中国近代国民经济史分期的几个问题"的论文，《光明日报》以半版篇幅全文发表，引起师生关注，是年刚刚 20 岁。这一期间最大的事件是批判马寅初的"新人口论"，全国报刊发表数百篇文章，大字报铺天盖地而来，批判声讨之声不绝于耳，一时间掀起一场轩然大波。田雪原摸不着头脑，便躲在期刊阅览室里找到发表的一些文章读了起来。那些批判文章读来读去除了扣政治帽子之外，却很少讲出多少道理；相反倒是马寅初的文章讲得头头是道，而且那种为真理而献身的精神深深地感染着他。他把搜集到的一些文章保留了下来，成为后来他为马寅初翻案和出版马寅初《新人口论》一书的原始素材，田雪原也因此同人口科学结下不解之缘。

1964 年田雪原大学毕业后被分配到国家机关工作，但他一直没有忘记 20 世纪 50 年代后期至 60 年代初的那场关于人口问题的辩论。粉碎林彪、江青反革命集团后，特别是党的十一届三中全会的召开，实事求是思想路线的恢复，使他看到正义战胜邪恶、真理驱散谬误的曙光，他积极投身到那场拨乱反正的理论斗争中去。1979 年他连续在《光明日报》理论版头条发表"调整是目前国民经济全局的关键"，"大会战是组织经济建设的好形式吗？"等分量较重的经济理论文章；同时集中精力梳理材料，撰写为马寅初平反的文章。1979 年 8 月 5 日《光明日报》以将近整版篇幅发表他的"为马寅初先生的新人口论翻案"重头文章，报社还加了"编者按"，作为报社对五六十年代批判的一种检讨和反思。这是第一批为马老平反文章之一，并且是公认的最有说服力的权威性文章；在第二次全国人口科学讨论会上他以此为题发言，博得全场最热烈和持续时间最长的掌声。他以确凿的资料，层层入理的解析，义正辞严的论证和犀利的笔锋征服了读者和与会各界人士，由此他也成为人口学界冉冉升起的一颗新星。

为马寅初翻案是人口理论拨乱反正的关键之举，以此为契机，"人口越多越好"论逐步退出历史舞台；直面中国的人口问题，田雪原把研究的重点首先放在了人口发展战略上面。在宋健等与他合作的自然科学与社会科学合作研究小组进行人口预测基础上，1980 年 3～5 月他出席中央召开的人口座谈会，力陈大力控制人口增长的观点，同时担负着会议向中央起草报告的任务。他白天参加会议，晚上整理记录和准备提交会议讨论的材料，经常是通宵达旦地工作，致使 5 月他作为首次中国人口学家代表团赴美参加会议时，开始时声带竟然不能发出一点儿声音来。不过他为改革开放后党和国家领导人这种科学的、认真负责的精神所感动，虽然夜以继日地工作却十分兴奋。当他在起草中描绘中国人口发展战略、目标、决策选择以及人口与经济、科技、社会发展蓝图时，更是兴奋不已，仿佛一个强大的中国已经屹立在世界的东方，少年时代的梦想即将变成现实。但他知道，作为学者，他的任务是科学论证。当他受命在《报告》后面以他个人名义对提倡一对夫妇生育一个孩子多长时间为宜、劳动力供给、老龄化、人口素质、城市化、家庭结构等问题写出《附件》时，他以实事求是、极端负责的精神作了诠释，现在来看也是经得起历史检验的。

跨进人口学行列的田雪原深知，经济学与人口学虽属近邻，但是"隔行如隔山"，他必须补上人口学这一课，否则便没有资格呆在人口学界，更不消说作带头人了。机会来了，1982 年 5 月～1983 年 6 月他到美国作高级访问学者，利用作项目余下时间系统地学习了几本人口学著作，并有机会向到那里同样作高级访问学者的著名人口学家，诸如美国普林斯顿大学的 A. 柯尔，芝加哥大学的 G.S. 贝克尔和 F. 豪泽，布朗大学的 S. 哥德斯坦，伦敦大学的布拉斯，日本大学的黑田俊夫，澳大利亚国立大学的考德维尔等请教和探讨，了解他们各自擅长的领域和主要的学术观点，打下比较扎实的人口学基础。回国后不久，让他主持中国社会科学院人口研究中心的工作，第一项任务是参加国务院发展研究中心组织的"2000 年的中国"国家项目研究，并以他为主主持完成该项目第一篇研究报告"2000 年的中国人口与就业"。前面谈到，1980 年中央人口座谈会讨论并定下我国人口发展的方针大计，田雪原备受鼓舞；但要在 2000 年全国人口控制在 12 亿以内，除非实行更严格的生育政策，否则不大可能。他本着"研究无禁区，宣传有纪律"原则，在这分内部报告中，大胆而又严谨地提出和论证了 12.0 亿人、12.5 亿人、12.8 亿人低、中、高三种方案的人口预测发展目标。其中中位特别是高位预测目标受到不少指责，包括来自有的领导和某些权威人士的指责；但他坚持不动摇，实践最终作出了符合他们预测的正确结论。

　　驾驭人口变动与发展趋势，为解决中国人口问题出力献策，在解决了总体发展战略之后，还必须对主要由人口数量控制带来的问题进行深入研究。一方面，他在 1980 年人口座谈会《附件》基础上对比较重要的可能发生的人口问题继续作出研究，并陆续写成论著发表；另一方面，对其中的关键问题立项作出专题研究。"七五"时期他主持国家重点项目"中国老年人口调查与老年社会保障改革研究"，在国家统计局调查队协助下，进行了首次全国老年人口抽样调查，向社会各界提供数据资料，提出建立集社会供养、家庭供养、老年劳动自养，"三养"结合、互相补充、三位一体的养老保障体系，受到党和国家领导人、著名专家学者的高度评价。"八五"时期他主持国家重点项目"中国家庭经济与生育研究"，作了全国 10 省市的抽样调查，立足于孩子成本—效益并结合中国实际展开研究，同样将调查资料提供各界开发应用，《资料》、专著和国际交流成果引起国内外人士的密切关注。人口控制中一个不大被重视但却是很重要的一角，是少数民族人口问题，于是"九五"时期他承担了"中国少数民族人口研究"国家重点项目。这是一个特别困难的项目，要在调查研究基础上对 56 个民族均完成 15 万字左右的完整论著，谈何容易！在领导、副主编、编委会和相关省、区、市领导、计划生育委员会等部门的大力支持下，经过不懈努力，硬是完成了东北、华北第一集的出版，其他 4 集也大都完稿，近期内可望全部完成，留下 20 世纪中国民族人口变动与发展的完整的历史记录。近年来，长期积沉下来的另一个心病——生育率大幅度下降后出生性别比升高问题重又泛起。中国是当今世界人口最多的国家，任何人口失误都可能酿成严重社会问题；同时中国也是一个性别偏好比较强的国家，性别比升高自应引起格外重视。于是他又通过可能渠道力陈主张，受到党和国家领导人、有关部门的重视，加大了治理的力度，可望获得有效的解决。

20世纪70年代以来中国推行计划生育和控制人口增长，先后提出过"计划经济决定论"、"两种生产论"等不同的理论解释；而随着发展和时间的推移，这两种理论都表现出一定的局限性。90年代以来他与其他同志一道主持国家、中国社会科学院"人口与可持续发展研究"重大和重点项目，研究中他提出并全面地阐发了以人为本的可持续发展理论及其理论体系，包括全方位的适度人口论、稀缺资源论、生态系统论、总体经济效益论和社会协调发展论。这样的理论概括，在国内外尚属首次，也为实施计划生育基本国策找到了可持续发展的理论依据，获得广泛认同，产生积极的理论影响和实践效果。

开拓进取不言年

如果从20世纪60年代初田雪原发表第一篇学术文章算起，至今已过去42个春秋。同许多有学之士一样，在"文化大革命"十年中他空怀一腔报国之志得不到施展，不同之处在于他没有忘记所学专业，在动乱中保存下来不少珍贵资料。粉碎"四人帮"后迎来科学发展的春天，他常说："天时很重要，不得天时再好的种子也不能开花结果"。不过同时代的人为什么有那么大的不同呢？自然同一个人的思想境界、意志品质、治学态度密切相关。强烈的报国之志，顽强的自强不息精神，深入实际和务实创新的治学态度，是他不断取得成功的"秘密"所在。田雪原1984年4月～1998年12月任中国社会科学院人口研究所（中心）所长（主任），《中国人口年鉴》、《中国人口科学》主编，现任中国社会科学院学术委员会委员，中国社会科学院老年科研中心常务副主任，研究员，博士生导师，国家级有突出贡献专家；主要社会兼职有：国务院学位委员会专家评议组成员，全国社科规划人口学科组长，中国人口学会常务副会长，中国老年学学会副会长，中国社会经济文化交流协会副会长，国家计生委人口专家委员，国际人口科学联盟成员等。所有这些职务均属学术性质。他认为，站到学科前沿是任职的前提条件，眼光向着未来，永远的开拓进取，是做学问毕生应当遵循的准则。他是这样说的，也是这样做的。初步统计，20 世纪 70 年代以来共发表《新时期人口论》、《中国老年人口（人口、经济、社会三卷）》等专著 18 部（含主编），论文"论人口与国民经济的可持续发展"、"中国人口科学发展的昨天、今天与明天"等 360 多篇（含 20 多篇英、日、俄文），研究报告 50 余篇，发表论著总字数在 500 万字以上。论文代表作，收集在《田雪原文集》一、二、三中。20 世纪 80 年代以来主持国家重大和重点项目 5 项，联合国、美、日等国际合作项目 5 项，在人口理论拨乱反正、人口发展战略、中观人口控制与社区、家庭经济与生育、人口老龄化与养老保障、人口与可持续发展等领域，发表了独立见解和比较系统的研究成果。他创造性地吸纳国外先进成果，结合中国实际在吸纳莱宾斯坦、贝克尔等的孩子成本—效益理论基础上，提出并阐发了社会附加孩子成本—效益理论和计算的理论方法；将西方的社区理论与中国的实践结合起来，提出社区是中观人口控制基本领域的理论；在可持续发展研究中，在参考了国内外大量研究成果基础上，构建了人口、资源、环境、经济、社会可持续发展理论框架；鉴于人口文化教育统计只有大专、中学、小学、文盲和半文盲人口数或所占比例，不同省、区、市之间不好比较，他提出了相当于平均所受教育年限的人口文化教育素质指数概念，设计了相应的计算方法。由田雪原主编，李竞能、翟振武副主编力求站到学科前沿并具有中国特点的《人口学》，也即将面世。《大国之难——当代中国的人口问题》一书，全文在日本翻译出版发行；在美、日、荷、比、澳等国作多场学术报告，受到普遍欢迎和好评；在国内，给上自省部级领导下至基层干部作不同类型报告几十场，受到各界重视并产生实际推动作用。1984 年授予国家有突出贡献的中青年专家，1988 年获国家科技进步成果一等奖，1991年英国剑桥国际名人中心授予"国际知识分子名人"，颁发证书并在《成功的人》中作了事迹介绍；1995 年美国传记协会列入"世界五千名人"，颁发证书并在《名人录》中作了业绩介绍；1996 年获第二届中华人口奖（人口最高奖）；精神文明建设"五个一"工程奖；2001 年获国家图书奖；科研成果中还有 20 来项获部委级特别荣誉奖、一等奖。对于这些，田雪原从不在人前提及；他以为，这些都已成为过去，对于已过了花甲之年的他，用他自己的话来说，就是"科学家的眼睛应当永远向着未来，永远自强不息、开拓进取"。

（李嘉岩）

2002 年 7 月

创造中国人口质量的辉煌[*]

——记中国人口学家田雪原

长城象征着中国历史的悠久，文化的坚韧，观念的统一。它表现了几千年来祖祖辈辈炎黄子孙胼手胝足、辛勤勇敢和卓越贡献。尽管中国历经盛衰兴亡，有广大的地域和多种方言，屡经内战与朝代更迭，但贯穿历史的只有一个中国。从马寅初到田雪原，不正是人口学家连绵延续的长城吗？

田雪原，一个对于当代大部分中国人来说并非耳熟能详的名字，然而在中国当代立德立功立言者的史册中，田雪原的名字光彩夺目。在新世纪，随着他在新闻界频频出现的音容笑貌和陆续问世的华章宏论，带给我们兴趣盎然的话题：关于21世纪中叶中国将拱手让出世界人口大国"第一把交椅"，关于人口国略与"银色浪潮"，关于时代精神与学者风骨……这是一首充满哲理和生活气息的诗歌，也是一段引人入胜的仍在进行的历史。

让我们沿着时代的轨迹，走近田雪原的精神世界和现实生活，并从这一视角寻找折射出的历史、思想和文化。

历史的帷幕并没有落下

我徘徊在美丽的燕园与"天下第一街"起点建国门之间，欲寻觅曾深深扎根于这片沃土上那些先哲们的伟岸身影。我惊奇地发现，从当年的百岁学士马寅初到后起俊彦田雪原之间，有着某种必然的联系。

短短一个世纪，历史似乎已模糊，人也有些淡忘。悠悠数十载，"横看成岭侧成峰，远近高低各不同。"无论横侧远近，人生的评说仍是那般依稀朦胧，蓦然回首，恍如隔世黄花。不过，有些人死了，却依然活着。身为教

* 原载《大众生活报》2003 年 4 月 23～30 日。

育家，马寅初的血液已延续到那些出类拔萃的后起之秀的血管里奔涌。作为红色经济学家和中国人口学家"第一把交椅"，马寅初的灵魂已铭刻在新中国的思想丰碑上。"我虽然年近八十，明知寡不敌众，自当单身匹马，出来应战，直至战死为止，决不向专以力压服不以理说服的那种批判者们投降。"马氏一言九鼎，道出中国政治经济文化百年动荡的大环境，也道尽在此环境下每一位有良知的学人不可逃避的命运。每每饮泪泣读，历史犹历历如昨。百年前先哲们经历种种思想苦旅；百年沧海桑田，新世纪的朝阳已冉冉升起，然焉知今日田雪原是否感受着与前贤相似的命运？想到这里，我止不住流下了一行伤感、落寞的清泪。我不知以这样的感怀描述是否无愧于历史和时代，是否对得住鞠躬尽瘁于祖国繁荣昌盛的良师？此时此刻，我沉浸在马寅初与田雪原之间那浓浓的百年惊梦中不能自拔。

历史的帷幕并没有落下。在中国历史上，出现过不少杰出的思想家。他们以自己的思想、理论和学说丰富了世界文化宝库，对各自时代发生过深远的影响。中国人口学说从它诞生起，就同中国政治经济文化息息相关，成为犀利的理论武器。马寅初逝世 20 余年，他创立的学说至今仍具威力，影响遍及全球。要了解马寅初为什么具有如此深远的影响力，就应当了解后继者田雪原和他的创新理论。

随着历史揭开 21 世纪新的一页，中国人口科学经过数十年的发展也由幼年步入成年时期，日臻完善。这是科学界众学人前仆后继、不断开拓进取的结果。走在这支拓荒者队伍前列的领军者之一，便是现任中国社会科学院学术委员、国家级有突出贡献专家、博士生导师田雪原研究员。是他，率先举起人口理论拨乱反正的大旗；是他，早在 1980 年起草中央人口座谈会报告时对诸多疑难问题作了经得起历史检验的论证和诠释；是他，系统阐发了"三位一体"人口发展战略和"三位一体"养老保障体系；是他，将西方人口学理论与中国国情有机结合，提出并阐发了社会附加孩子成本—效益理论，人口文化素质指数概念和计算方法，丰富和发展了马寅初之后的中国人口理论；在新世纪，是他，全面阐发了以人为本的可持续发展战略及其理论体系，包括全方位的适度人口论、稀缺资源论、生态系统论、总体经济效益论和社会协调发展论。其全新的理论框架，受到国内有关人士的高度评价，也为实施计划生育基本国策提供可持续发展理论支持，产生积极的理论影响和实践效果。在众多的社会科学家和人口学家中，田雪原的贡献非同凡响。田雪原不愧为那一辈人中高山景行的学者，同时又是最为成功的社会科学家和人口经济顾问。而且他还证明了教授和学者完全可以成为善良、和蔼的好心人。很少有社会科学家能像田雪原那样兼具学术和名望。他是作为跨世纪的人口理论家和为现代化事业奋斗的国家有突出贡献的专家获得人口最高奖——"中华人口奖"而载入史册的。他的科研成果曾荣获国家科技进步成果一等奖、国家图书奖和"五个一工程奖"，并被世界公认的两大国际名人中心分别列于英国剑桥"国际知识分子名人"和美国传记协会"世界五千名人"。

梁启超说过："中华五千年文明史中立德立功立言者只有两个人：范仲淹和曾国藩。五千年历史中事业有继、衣钵得传者只有曾国藩。"梁氏的话不无启发。

一个人能够取得卓越的成就绝不仅仅因为他有才华，不是每朝每代都有一些才华横溢的人慨叹自己生不逢时吗？但同时又总是有一些人能够把握时机，驾驭命运，实现自我，作出造福当代，功泽后世的事业来。这期间的重大落差不是世道不公，而是除了机遇以外，每个人的处世哲学和人生态度使然。今天看来，田雪原无疑是一位成功的实践者。

田雪原在春节曾作过一副对联，高屋建瓴，将大志与艰辛一起咏唱出来，颇有几分高山流水之感：

大国之难难不难基本国策家喻户晓奏世纪凯歌任重道远

寒窗清苦苦非苦崇尚真理脚踏实地作强国文章知难而进

世界大文豪歌德写道："辽阔的世界，宏伟的人生，长年累月，真诚勤奋。既安于守旧，又乐于迎新，人类前进了一程又一程。"曹操有诗云："老骥伏枥，志在千里。烈士暮年，壮心不已。"《易经》释义："天行健，君子以自强不息；地势坤，君子以厚德载物。"如同一个不知疲倦的车轮，田雪原在高速飞转，以自强不息和勇于开拓的精神感召着迈进新时代的学人。田雪原认为如果抱残守缺，不努力创新，就等于失去了社会科学理论的生命，创新是艰难的，不仅要有理论勇气，而且要付出艰辛劳动，迸发出生命的全部活力。创新的天地无限宽广，创新的道路永无止境。

这位年过花甲的多产思想家，面对严峻挑战，迎难而上。他的精神状态仿佛刚过而立之年，就在前不久召开的全院运动会上，他参加100米跑竟然冲进决赛圈，成为参赛年龄最大的运动员。世界超级灵魂工程师雨果和从凡人走向成功波峰的"交际旋风"卡耐基及东方富翁李嘉诚英雄所见略同：人的精神是最为宝贵的。难能可贵的是，田雪原无论何时都一直保持着胜过海洋明朗、天空辽阔的美好心灵，并将这颗真善美的心灵涌现的激情化做语言文字，送到人们面前，成为拉开下一个帷幕的力量。

小荷才露尖尖角

"火树银花不夜天，弟兄姊妹舞翩跹。"1959 年，国庆十周年天安门广场庆典之夜。在金水桥畔载歌载舞的人群中，有一位来自辽东半岛山城，刚刚跨进北京大学校门的青年，他就是田雪原。随着悠扬起伏的乐曲，田雪原和大家一起边唱边跳，诉说衷肠，他那东方之子特有的淳朴、儒雅和热情给师生们留下了深刻的印象。

1984 年，时过 25 个春秋，当礼炮的轰鸣揭开国庆 35 周年帷幕之际，田雪原作为国家有突出贡献的中青年专家，登上天安门西观礼台，目送工、农、兵、学、商各路游行队伍昂首阔步走过，思绪万千，心潮难平。

2002 年，岁月又划过 18 个寒暑，第八次全国人口科学讨论会暨会员代表大会在北京召开。会后田雪原同外来教授一起登上天安门城楼，百年风云、五十余年沧桑和奔向现代化未来的激情一齐涌上心头，百感交集，留给他严峻的思考……

田雪原出生在辽宁省本溪市。他少年时代就好学乐思，第一本打开他心灵天窗的读物是方志敏烈士的《可爱的中国》。书中字里行间燃烧着爱国主义烈焰，深深感染着他。当读到帝国主义列强瓜分中国，祖国母亲在痛苦中呻吟，联想到幼年记忆中日本侵略者挥舞大刀横行时，泪水便夺眶而出，一种难以抑制的悲愤和渴望祖国强大的激情在他心中呐喊，并且一直成为支撑他在人生道路上不懈奋斗的巨大力量。

1959 年，田雪原以优异成绩考上北京大学经济系，从此叩响科学大门。他认为，人口众多的文明古国惨遭帝国主义蹂躏，原因有两条：一是旧中国反动阶级腐败无能；二是经济技术落后，国家实力空虚。新中国的诞生结束了旧中国丧权辱国的历史，东方睡狮觉醒，但要实现繁荣富强，必须走科教兴国的道路。田雪原把攻读经济学与报效祖国、探索强国之路联系在一起。于是，从未名湖畔开始，未满 20 岁的他开始了与共和国同兴衰、共荣辱的漫漫征程。在北大读书期间，他不仅认真攻读马列主义经典经济学理论，而且对西方经济学研究成果颇有兴味；不仅对经济史和经济学说史予以关注，尤其重视中国现实的政治经济文化问题。逐渐形成了他的兼容并蓄、博采众长和理论联系实际的学风。早在大二时，田雪原就在《光明日报》发表题为《关于中国近代国民经济史分期的几个问题》的长篇论文，引起北京大学师生们的反响，包括当时已经遭到批判的老校长马寅初先生的注意。

"在科学的入口处，正像在地狱的入口处一样，必须提出这样的要求：这里必须根除一切犹豫；这里任何怯懦都无济于事"马克思的警言给了田雪原探索科学的勇气和力量。就在他考入北大不久，便遇上所谓"理论权威"康生导演的对马寅初先生的批判，把马先生的《新人口论》说成是"中国的马尔萨斯主义"，谁提控制人口，谁就会被扣上这顶帽子，人口问题和人口学研究实际上成了无人敢于问津的"禁区"。田雪原对此困惑不解，一个学术问题怎会遭来劈头盖脑的批判？他丢弃"犹豫"和"怯懦"，一头钻进图书馆，捧读在《新建设》上刊登的老校长的文章："中国最大的矛盾是人口增长太快，而资金积累似乎增长太慢……过多的人口拖住了中国高速工业化的后腿，使我们不能大踏步地前进"，"控制人口，利国利民"……马先生公开就人口增长速度问题与传统观点展开辩论，坚持中国人口规模必须加以控制。读着读着不仅为马寅初的观点所征服，而且为他那种"言人之不敢言，言人之不能言"的精神所打动，他坚信真理的光辉是掩埋不住的，总会有一天历史将作出公正的裁判。这是田雪原第一次接触人口问题，由此他领悟到，富国强国除了要发展经济、科技和教育外，还有一个亟待解决的重大课题——中国人口问题。为了尽快改变贫困落后面貌，一方面必须发展生产力；另一方面必须控制人口的过快增长。这成了他后来转向人口学研究的潜在的动因。

1964年8月，大学毕业后的田雪原未能如愿，被分配到国家机关工作，但仍改变不了他的初衷，"身在曹营心在汉"，田雪原注定要做一名学者，一名社会科学家。粉碎"四人帮"以后，多年的夙愿终于实现，田雪原"归队回家"，调到中国社会科学院经济研究所。"似曾相识燕归来。"田雪原如鱼得水，如鸟投林，他从心里接受自己的角色，热爱自己的角色，并想通过这一角色实现少年时代便埋在心底里的报效祖国的夙愿。在经济研究所，他得到刘国光等一批著名经济学家的指点，热情的鼓励和支持使他进步很快，并逐渐形成了自己的研究风格和特点。

当中国人民经历一个漫长的、灾难的、动荡的10年以后，田雪原的智慧花蕾一朵朵绽放了，他立即成为中国人口学界的重要代表。遗憾的是时光不能倒流，如果没有这十余年漫长的知识空白时期，今天的中国还会送给世界怎样的惊喜是难以想象的。同样，对于经历和才学都处于旺盛期的田雪原，他还将获得怎样的收获也是不可斗量的。

尽管今天我们经常听到某些人历尽坎坷，但由于个人的志向矢志不渝，终于成为非同凡响的一代雄才；但与此同时，我们却很难想象究竟有多少人由于长期的磨难而最终丧失了他们本来可以取得更好成就的可能，而后者的数目累积起来比前者的数目要大得多。《红楼梦》唱出了人情冷暖、世态炎凉的人间真谛："叹人间，美中不足今方信，纵然是齐眉举案，到底意难平。"

不仅仅是田雪原，与他同时代成长起来的大多数知识分子同时发现，他们真正的生命，富有创造性的生命，是从中年以后开始的。客观地说，40岁应该是人生由盛转衰的关口，但对于田雪原这一代中国人来说，残酷的现实剥夺了他们在如同早晨八九点钟太阳的生命旺盛期耕耘的机会，所以当他们面对40寿辰的时候，只有让生命在秋天重现辉煌。

20世纪50年代初，国内有一批与马寅初学识不相上下的社会科学家，他们也和先生一样有热情有能力在科教兴国征途上干一番事业，谋一番成就。但到了20世纪60年代，这些人有的被打成右派，下放劳动，彻底失去了探索社会科学问题的条件，在风雨中停滞，在泥泞中消失，人生的路越走越窄；有的被接二连三的政治斗争扰乱心态，无力再搞研究，担心学识为自己招来杀身之祸，他们真正沉默了，放弃了，所以他们错过了，被超越了。"十年动乱"对中国学者造成的灾难是无法衡量的，这种灾难的开始并没有一个确切时间，它巨大的杀伤力显示了千百年来在这块土地上孕育着的那股暗流。在中国的第一个大一统的国家秦朝，始皇帝就兴起了文字狱。但在残酷的"焚书坑儒"中，他毕竟还保留了"法家"，因而在大多数学者蒙难之时，还有那么一部分幸免于难者。到了明清代，"文字狱"越发使人心惊胆战，在穿越这一时空时，许多灿烂一时的古文化就此寿终正寝。可就在这种情况下，仍有一门学问——理学，不仅没有萎缩，反而发展了，同时还留下了千古文明的小说，比如《红楼梦》，还留下了郑板桥。

由此可见，"文化大革命"是集千古威猛于一身，割断文化，割断科学，却没有留下文明。幸而这场浩劫在20世纪70年代中后期结束了，否则，田雪原的心仍无归宿。值得庆幸的是，当我们的民族又一次从低谷中走出的时候，田雪原和他这一代不幸却又执著的知识分子们，还是赶上了这班车，并且把半生积攒的智慧和心血全部奉献给了这个属于包括他们自己在内的一代人的辉煌。

如果田雪原在 20 世纪 70 年代末的时候没有利用宝贵的改革开放带来的春光，如果他稍微放松一点、懒惰一点，那么现在他一定不会是这个著名的、有成就感的、不可替代的田雪原。

乐于创新，注重实际，是田雪原从事社会科学研究的一大特点。"小荷才露尖尖角，早有蜻蜓立上头。"1979 年他连续发表《调整是目前国民经济全局的关键》、《为社会主义的"托拉斯"恢复名誉》、《按需生产是社会主义经济活动的基本原则》等实证研究文章，以积极参与经济领域理论上的拨乱反正，支持调整的方针而崭露头角。不过田雪原的主要精力还是致力于人口科学研究。以为马寅初《新人口论》平反为契机，首先展开中国人口问题和人口发展战略的研究，发表了一系列有较大影响的论文，一开始便站在了高起点之上，引起有关部门和领导的重视。在思想解放的大背景下，田雪原愤然挥毫写出《为马寅初先生的新人口论翻案》的长篇论文。1979 年 8 月 5 日《光明日报》予以全文发表，并加注编者按语，作为报社对 20 世纪五六十年代批判的检讨和反思。在第一批为先生平反的文章中，田雪原的文章被公认是最具有说服力和影响力的，在海内外引起强烈反响，日本厚生省人口研究所翻译后发表。田雪原以此为题在第二次全国人口科学讨论会上作主题报告，博得会场经久不息的掌声。接着，他又搜集整理马寅初先生有关人口问题的谈话、文章等资料，编辑成《新人口论》，由北京出版社出版，并在两年内连续再版三次，为人口科学的拨乱反正、正本清源，起到开路先锋的作用。从此田雪原与人口学研究结下不解之缘，一颗新星在人口学地平线上冉冉升起。1980 年 3 ~ 5 月，中央召开 5 次人口问题座谈会，有 20 来个部、委、办领导和少数学者参加，田雪原参加并受命起草向中央书记处的报告。这次座谈会讨论热烈，在重大问题上取得共识，但也提出一些需要回答和解决的问题。如中国民间有一种说法，老大憨，老二聪明，老三为"猴仁儿"（最聪明），如果提倡一对夫妇生育一个孩子都"憨"起来怎么办，会不会引起智商下降？田雪原同与会学者一道，查找资料和论证。得出结论是：第一，虽然民间的这一说法"无风不起浪"，但是并无科学根据，生育次序与聪明不聪明并无必然联系。由于旧社会多生多育，老大就要显出作大哥大姐的样子，给人的印象比较憨厚。第二，虽然 1980 年中国经济体制改革处在"摸着石头过河"阶段，但是要打破以往高度集中统一的计划经济体制，大力发展商品经济则是确定无疑的。发展商品经济，交换价值升值，泛商品观念渗透到婚姻家庭领域，传统的婚育观受到冲击，婚外恋、非婚生育、人工流产、离婚率等将会上升。提倡生育一个孩子留下来的，不是第一次所怀胎儿的比例将会升高。结论是：提倡一对夫妇生育一个孩子不会出现"老大憨"，不会引起智商下降。正因为作出这样的论证，才敢于提出生育一个孩子的动议。又如，提倡生育一个孩子以后，少年人口减少、老年人口增多到何种程度，会不会出现老年人口为四、成年人口为二、少年人口为一的"四二一"结构，提倡一对夫妇生育一个孩子能够坚持多长时间？会议领导责成田雪原以个人名义写一附件附在向中央的《报告》之后，田雪原深入研究和计算后提出：提倡一对夫妇生育一个孩子主要是控制一代人的生育率，而控制好一代人的生育率，也就影响到下一代人的生育率，取得良好代际效应。提倡一对夫妇生育一个孩子既非权宜之计，短期的三年五载难以明显见效；也非永久之计，几代人连续生育一个孩子，必然造成人口年龄"倒金字塔"结构；社会负担过于沉重，是不能够接受的。据此提出一对夫妇生育二个孩子的时间为25至30年为宜。一代人过后，独生子女结婚应当允许生育二个孩子。无需多言，这样的论证在后来的实践中体现了应有的价值。中国实行计划生育少出生3亿多人口，人口年龄结构由年轻型过渡到老年型初期，大大削减了人口增长的势能，为全面解决我国人口问题奠定了基础，无疑是党中央英明决策，全党全国人民共同努力的结果。这中间也包含着科学家们的辛勤劳动，凝聚着他们科研成果的结晶。

1982年初，田雪原出版了他的第一部专著《新时期人口论》，论证了以控制数量为重点的人口发展战略，在海内外引起强烈反响。《人民日报》、《中国日报》、香港《大公报》等发表书评。《大公报》影印该书封面的述评称："这是1957年马寅初发表《新人口论》以后第一部全面研究我国现代化人口问题的专著。著者积多年研究工作的成果，写成是书……资料丰富，联系实际，观点新颖，深入浅出，是一部学术性，资料性和知识性兼备的著作。"同年，出版宋健等同志与他合著的《人口预测与人口控制》，多方位探讨了中国人口发展趋势，从动态意义上阐述了中国人口问题的严重性，受到自然科学界和社会科学界的高度重视。这一期间田雪原研究的重点主要是人口问题和人口发展战略，力图为国家的宏观决策提供有科学价值的研究成果。

俗话说："隔行如隔山"。田雪原原本学习的是经济学，清楚没有系统学习过人口学的缺陷，这一课需要补上。机会来了，1982年5月到1983年

6月，他应邀赴美国东西方中心作高级访问学者，使他很好地"充了一次电"。在那里，他结识了多位来自世界各国的资深学者，有的则是当代人口学界的泰斗。诸如美国普林斯顿大学的 A. 柯尔，芝加哥大学的 G.S. 贝克尔和 F. 豪泽，布朗大学的 S. 哥德斯坦，伦敦大学的布拉斯，日本大学的黑田俊夫，澳大利亚国立大学的考德维尔等。田雪原虚心求教，他想，如果能从一位大师那里学到一种特长，报效祖国的本事就大大增加了。他边学英语边博览群书，终于比较系统地了解了当代西方的主要人口理论，开阔了他以后研究的方法和思路。

1983 年回国后，他参与大型国家攻关项目"2000 年的中国研究"，并负责第一专题"2000 年中国的人口与就业研究"。他审时度势、实事求是地开展研究，针对当时将 2000 年人口控制在 12 亿以内的目标，在这份内部报告中，大胆而又谨慎地提出和论证了 12.0 亿人、12.5 亿人、12.8 亿人低、中、高三种方案。对于中位和高位预测，引来不少指责，包括来自有影响权威学者的指责；但他坚持不唯上，不唯书、只唯实，毫不动摇，最终由实践作出了公正的结论。可以说，田雪原的研究始终保持着中庸大雅的风度，他既不张扬，轻易地否定这个那个，也绝不观点暧昧，勇于阐发自己的主张，并且在没有充分的证据证明错误的时候，绝不放弃自己的观点。在这点上，他有与先师马寅初共同之处，也有某种不同，田雪原将其归结为时代进步的成果。

田雪原的故事浓缩了一代人的命运。

20 多年来，田雪原站在世纪风云变幻和中国改革开放潮头，成为众多"弄潮儿"中的一员，辛勤的汗水换来公平的回报；出版专著 18 部（含主编），论文 360 余篇（含 30 多篇英、日、俄文），研究报告 50 余篇，代表作搜集在《田雪原文集》（一、二、三）中。20 世纪 80 年代以来主持国家重大、重点研究项目 5 项，与联合国、美、日等国合作项目 5 项，在人口理论拨乱反正、人口发展战略、中观人口控制与社区、家庭经济与生育、人口老龄化与养老保障、人口与可持续发展等领域，发表了独立见解和比较系统的研究成果，得到国内外学术界和相关各界的广泛承认，得到诸多奖励。相关各界也把国务院学位委员会专家评议组成员、全国社科规划人口学科组长、中国人口学会常务副会长、中国社会经济文化交流协会副会长、中国老年学学会副会长等头衔加于其上。田雪原呢？则把这些头衔视为"干活的平台"，出力报效的场所而已。

科学社会主义理论鼻祖马克思认为，经济活动是人类一切活动中最基本的活动，经济动因是人类社会发展的根本动因。如果说，经济学被当代人称为"社会科学皇冠"，那么对于中国这个举世瞩目的第一人口大国来说，人口经济学则是皇冠上的明珠。中国人口增长成为全球的难点和焦点。

田雪原无疑是这一焦点的一个"热点"人物。人口数量控制和素质提高关系着祖国前途、民族命运，人口学家在这一伟大历史进程中担负着生死攸关、举足轻重的神圣使命。

中国自古就有 60 秉烛的说法，几千年来也不乏其例。如果从个人的治学历程和整体的理论高度来看，国内确实出现了一个"人生从四五十岁开始"的科学家群体。这些人以极大的勇气和勤奋燃亮了 20 世纪最后 20 年的中国天空，到目前为止，他们所取得的成就也许比起 21 世纪的后来者们是不足称道的，但他们用自己的身躯，用自己的思想所铺起的这一跨世纪的桥梁，足以让后世的人们永世不忘。

田雪原还在坚定地走他自己的路。他并不计较未来史书对他的评价，回顾 60 余载人生历程，他留下了太多太多的遗憾，但有一分最大的安慰，那就是：他抓住了也许是人生最后一次机会，让生命闪耀出令他和他所热爱的事业欣慰的光芒。无论何时，无论何地，无论面对何人，田雪原都可以坦然地说："我付出了我应该付出的一切"。

这就是一个中国人的故事，一个中国社会科学家的故事，一个经历了历史更替的中国人口学家的故事。

（周毅）

新中国 60 年人口政策回顾与展望

——访中国社会科学院学部委员、研究员田雪原

《马克思主义研究》记者

田雪原，男，1964 年毕业于北京大学经济学系。先后在教育部等国家机关工作，1979 年后在中国社会科学院经济研究所从事人口经济研究，1984 年始任中国社会科学院人口研究所（中心）所长（主任），现任中国社会科学院学部委员、研究员、博士生导师，国家级有突出贡献专家。主要社会兼职有：国务院学位委员会学科组成员，全国社科规划人口学科组长，中国社会经济文化交流协会副会长；曾任中国人口学会常务副会长（1998～2007），中国老年学学会副会长（1997～2004），国家人口计生委专家委员，国际人口科学联盟（IUSSP）成员等。

自 20 世纪 70 年代以来发表专著 28 部（含主编），论文 500 余篇（含30 多篇英、俄、日文），研究报告 30 余篇。

▲（采访者简称▲，下同）：目前，中国是世界人口第一大国。国内外有关预测表明，到 2030 年中国人口达到 14.65 亿以后才能实现零增长，才能把人口第一大国的这把交椅让给印度，方能心安理得地退居次席。田委员，您作为我国人口学研究方面的专家，请您给我们谈谈新中国 60 年来的人口问题、政策和理论。

●（被采访者简称●，下同）：好的。中国人口问题属人口压迫生产力，即人口和劳动力过剩性质；如今人口零增长这一天的到来依稀可见，这一成绩的取得实属不易。一方面，经济的发展和社会的进步是基础，是人口转变的基础；另一方面，旨在以降低生育率为主线的人口政策长期卓有成效地实施，则起到了关键的推动作用。然而学术界和社会上还存在某种歧义，特别对 1980 年中央提倡一对夫妇生育一个孩子决策的出台存有各种猜测，有的甚至以讹传讹。我以亲历者并立足人口学以及人口与经济、社会发展的视

野，对 1980 年人口决策出台的前前后后，当前的人口政策选择，谈一些观点和建议。

一 舆论准备：为马寅初先生新人口论翻案

▲：我们知道，马寅初先生是新中国最先倡导计划生育的学者，在 1957 年 7 月 5 日《人民日报》上发表了《新人口论》，当时影响和争议都很大，您是如何看待马老的观点及这些争议的？

●：自古以来，中国就以地大物博、人口众多著称于世，虽然在历史发展的长河中不乏节制人口的主张，但是众民主义对上策动着统治阶级的人口政策，对下迎合着民众多子多福的心理，从孔子"庶矣哉"、孟子"不孝有三，无后为大"的封建伦理道德，到孙中山的大汉民族"同化论"，无不把人口的多少视为国家兴衰、国力强弱的象征，自觉不自觉地推行旨在鼓励人口增长的政策。

1949 年新中国成立后，这种众民主义思想被传承下来并得到显现，在短短三年国民经济恢复时期，即完成由高出生、高死亡、低增长向着高出生、低死亡、高增长人口再生产类型的转变。1953 年全国人口普查时已达到 6 亿，出生率上升到 37.0‰，死亡率下降到 14.0‰，自然增长率创 23.0‰新高。这种情况为党和国家的一些领导人所关注和警惕，他们或召开座谈会，或成立"节育问题研究小组"，并在"一五"国民经济计划报告中写进"适当地提倡节制生育"字样。人口的快速增长更引起社会有识之士的关注，邵力子先生在第一届全国人大第一、第二次会议上，呼吁宣传避孕知识，放宽对人工流产的限制。马寅初先生利用担任人大代表之便，于 1954～1955 年先后三次视察浙江，形成他对人口问题比较系统的观点，在人大代表浙江小组会上作了"控制人口与科学研究"的发言；1957 年在一届人大四次会议上进一步阐述他的观点，7 月 5 日《人民日报》全文发表他的书面发言，这就是他的《新人口论》。

《新人口论》以 1953 年人口普查数据为依据，分析了人口增长过快同经济、社会发展的矛盾，主张控制人口数量、提高人口质量，并且提出具体的办法和建议，由此引发一轮人口问题讨论和探索的热潮。早在 20 世纪二三十年代就主张节制人口的社会学派节制主义者陈长蘅、陈达、吴景超、费孝通等人，也纷纷发表文章，阐发他们的人口主张。这些文章和建议，有的还受到包括毛泽东在内的中央领导的赞赏。

但是1957年反右派斗争之风一起，上述许多人物纷纷遭到批判，社会学派节制主义代表人物无一例外地被戴上右派分子的帽子。不知是声望过高还是别的什么原因，此次风波中只有马寅初先生得以幸免，依然做他的北大校长、全国人大常委职务；但是挨批是少不了的。

1959年我考进北大经济学系学习，正值第二次批判马寅初新人口论。当时的情景是：大字报铺天盖地，声讨之声不绝于耳——我们都在心里发问：发生了什么事情？我们的老校长怎么了？这使我一有时间就跑到期刊阅览室，找那些刊登马老"我的经济理论、哲学思想和政治立场"文章的《新建设》等杂志，同时也找来《光明日报》等发表的批判文章阅读和思考。越读越觉得马老关于控制人口数量、提高人口质量的论述讲得颇有道理，更为他那种年近八旬不屈不挠、誓死捍卫真理的彻底唯物主义精神所打动。

相反，那些连篇累牍的批判文章却讲不出多少道理，除了标签式的政治口号和扣大帽子之外，便是偷换前提一类的逻辑推演，其目的就是要将《新人口论》批臭，把马寅初先生打下去。特别是康生亲临北大点名并发出"属于哪个马家"的怪论之后，整个燕园的大批判就不断升级，直到最后马老从北大校园、政坛和学坛上"消失"，再没有见到马老的身影。这使我着实困惑了一段时间，留下一个悬念，这场大批判就这样收场了？心中埋下一个学术情结。

1964年毕业后，先是参加两年"四清"，接着便是所谓的十年"文化大革命"和干部下放劳动。除了和我们这一代人大同小异的经历外，作为系统学习过马克思主义经济学和西方经济学说史的学人来说，原来盼望祖国尽快强盛、人民尽快富裕起来的情结受到莫大的伤害。在"四清"同吃、同住、同劳动过程中，亲身体验到新中国成立十五六年后，许多农民依然过着缺吃少穿的清贫日子的情景；城市也好不到哪儿去，直至20世纪70年代每人每月只供应几两油、肉、蛋，自行车、手表等日用工业品都要凭票供应，在饥饿、温饱、小康、富裕和最富裕几个发展阶段中，处在由饥饿向温饱过渡阶段。由此不能不对当时的人民公社以及整个国家的计划经济产生疑问：为什西方市场经济国家忧虑的是生产过剩，而高度集中统一的计划经济国家则被短缺困扰？第二次世界大战结束后二三十年，我们同发达国家的差距不是缩小而是扩大了，国家尽快富强起来的期望跌到了失望的边缘。

▲：中共十一届三中全会的召开，纠正了对马寅初先生的错误批判，听说您起了关键作用？

●：只是尽了一个学者应尽的职责。1978 年底党的十一届三中全会的召开，给我的感觉真的是"忽如一夜春风来，千树万树梨花开"，于是便投身到理论战线上的拨乱反正中去，经过长时间的思索和研究，发表了"调整是目前国民经济全局的关键"、"为社会主义的托拉斯恢复名誉"等几篇经济论文。不过积压多年的最大学术情结，还是 20 世纪 50 年代末 60 年代初那场对马寅初的批判。于是我把多年积累的资料整理出来，写出《为马寅初先生的新人口论翻案》的长篇文章。1979 年 8 月 5 日《光明日报》作为"重头文章"发表并加了"编者按"，算做该报对过去错误批判的清算，自然在学术界和社会上产生了较大影响。

说心里话，当时撰写和发表这样的文章是需要一点勇气的。因为马寅初的新人口论遭到批判之后，人口问题很长时期成为无人敢触动的"禁区"，传统的、权威的观点，是原苏联《政治经济学》教科书"人口不断迅速增长是社会主义人口规律"的教条。对此提出异议，弄不好有可能被戴上马尔萨斯人口论的帽子，马寅初等被批判的情景历历在目。然而 30 年的计划经济不仅没有使人民摆脱贫穷，人口却由 1949 年的 5.42 亿增加到 1979 年的 9.76 亿，净增 4.34 亿人，年平均增长达到 2.0% 的高率，"经济上不去、人口下不来"，也可以说人口的过快增长严重地阻碍着人民生活的改善和国家的富强。事实给了人口越多、劳动力越多、生产越多、发展越快的"人口越多越好"论当头一棒，这样的历史再也不能继续下去了。

为了国家和人民的利益必须挺身而出，拿起笔来为马老翻案，为他的新人口论平反。在此基础上，我将马老其他数篇有关人口的文章汇集到一起，以《新人口论》命名重新出版，三年内连续出了三版。为马寅初新人口论翻案打破了人口不断迅速增长是社会主义人口规律的教条，推翻了"人口越多越好"论的神话，带动了整个人口理论的拨乱反正，也为新人口政策的制定作了必要的理论准备。

二　严格控制人口增长：提倡一对夫妇生育一个孩子

▲：20 世纪 80 年代初，中央是在什么背景下提出"一对夫妇生育一个孩子"的人口政策的？

●：人口变动具有速度比较缓慢和累进增长的特点，短期内变动不很显著，但时间一长增长的效果就异常明显，而且积累的势能很难改变。如果说共和国成立后前一二十年人口增长还容易被人忽视的话，那么进入 20 世纪 70 年代忧虑人口增长的人们日渐增多起来。在这种情况下，1973 年国务院成立计划生育领导小组，标志着将计划生育纳入政府行为，提出"晚、稀、少"。具体要求："晚"指晚婚、晚育。那时算了这样一笔账：如果 20 岁结婚并生育，100 年中就是五代人；如果 25 岁生育，就是四代人；如果 30 岁生育，就是三代人多一点，晚婚、晚育对控制人口增长有着现实的意义。"稀"指生育子女间隔时间要长一些，拉开子女之间的年龄距离，要求间隔 4 年。"少"指生育的数量要少，针对多生多育提出生育二个孩子的数量目标。在以后的实践中，对"晚、稀、少"有所发展，演变为"一个不少，两个正好，三个多了"，表明生育政策有进一步收紧的倾向。

从 1974 年起，国家把人口纳入国民经济发展计划，规定了具体的人口增长总量指标。1978 年新一届国务院计划生育领导小组成立，中央批转该领导小组第一次会议的《报告》，要求全党要从战略意义上提高认识，增强抓好计划生育工作的自觉性。这一年 7 月，河北省出台了计划生育十条规定，第二条为"鼓励一对夫妇生育子女数最好一个，最多两个"。1979 年 1 月国务院计划生育领导小组召开全国计生办主任会议，提出"今后要提倡每对夫妇生育子女数最好一个，最多两个，间隔三年以上；对于只生一胎，不再生第二胎的育龄夫妇，要给予表扬；对于生第三胎以上的，应从经济上加以必要的限制"①。这段期间，有的地方如山东省荣成县等部分群众，已经提出只生一个孩子的口号；在有关领导讲话中，也提出了一对夫妇生育一个孩子和 1985 年人口增长率降低到 5‰、2000 年降低到零的目标。

实现人口零增长，涉及未来的人口变动和发展，需要作出科学的人口预测。当时我国已是将近 10 亿人口的泱泱大国，然而从事人口研究的人却少得可怜，预测手段也不发达，只能大致地计算一下。恰在这时，七机部二院宋健副院长等几人提出他们初步预测的一些结果。他们将自动控制论应用到人口预测中来，一是数据资料需要补充完善，某些参数需要推敲审定；二是需要对预测结果作出分析，得到人口学界和社会的承认，因而需要人口学家参与。包括本人在内的人口科学工作者，当时对计算机还知之甚少，更不可

---

① 杨魁孚、梁济民、张凡编著《中国人口与计划生育大事要览》，中国人口出版社，2001，第 65、67 页。

能应用到人口预测中来，因而需要自然科学工作者介入。正是这种相互需要，1979 年下半年至 1980 年初，宋健、李广元等同志常常利用星期天等业余时间，到月坛北小街中国社会科学院经济研究所来同我一起讨论研究、磋商，最后形成了多种方案的中国百年人口预测结果，并由新华社对外发布。该预测由著名科学家钱学森和经济学家许涤新推荐给当时主管人口工作的陈慕华同志，陈慕华同志回信称转报中央政治局。

1980 年 3～5 月，中央书记处委托中央办公厅召开人口座谈会，对人口问题进行了 5 次规模不等的讨论，最后形成向中央书记处的《报告》，以及致全体共产党员、共青团员的《公开信》。人口座谈会讨论了方方面面的人口问题，特别是提倡一对夫妇生育一个孩子、2000 年人口控制目标、人口零增长等敏感问题。本人参加这样的座谈会深受感动，也很受教育，是一次充分发扬民主、科学决策的会议。所以很不赞同社会上有的人说当初什么都没有考虑，是一个不计后果的错误决策。

以提倡一对夫妇生育一个孩子而论，1980 年中央召开人口座谈会，大家都赞成尽快控制人口增长。但是对于能不能提出一对夫妇只生育一个孩子，一些与会者表示出某种担心。因为此举前无先例，需要认真研究。讨论中提出的头一个问题是，只生育一个孩子会不会引起孩子智商和智能的下降问题。有一位领导同志在发言中列举民间的一种说法，叫做老大憨、老二聪明、老三最机灵、最聪明，俗话说"猴仁儿"、"猴仁的"。是不是这样呢？就要休会一段时间，组织力量查阅资料和进行论证。结果表明，生育孩子次序同聪明不聪明没有必然的联系，无论是"老大憨"，还是"老二聪明"、"猴仁儿"等传说，都缺乏真正的科学依据，最多是有些地区群众中有这样的一些说法而已。群众的说法同过去多生多育相联系，因为生育的子女多，第一个孩子（老大）就担负着协助父母照料其弟弟、妹妹的任务，表现出宽容大度，带有一些憨厚的劲头儿；后边的弟弟、妹妹，也显得要更活跃一些、聪明一些。

同时，虽然 1980 年改革开放尚处在"摸着石头过河"初期，但是过去高度集中统一的计划经济再也不能继续下去了，要发展商品经济在经济学界取得较多共识。而要发展商品经济，交换价值升值，势必冲击人们传统的观念，婚姻和生育观念必然要发生某些改变。可以预料的是，诸如婚前性行为、未婚先孕、离婚率和买卖婚姻等的增多和升高，会改变怀孕和实际生育的孩次。作为"第一个孩子"留下来的"老大"，不是实际所怀的第一个孩子的比例会增多起来。今天看来，这样的估计并不过分，实际情况有过之而无不及。由此得出结论，提倡一对夫妇生育一个孩子，不会降低人口的智商和智能。

▲：那么当时有没有讨论"提倡一对夫妇生育一个孩子"是暂时的人口政策，还是长期的人口政策？

●：当然有讨论，而且是会上讨论的第二个重要问题：提倡一对夫妇生育一个孩子以多长时间为宜？会上气氛热烈，有的主张搞长一些时间，列举苏联、加拿大土地面积比我国大，人口比我国少得多；美国与我国国土面积差不多，人口只有我国的1/4。我国人口过剩严重，应当尽快实现零增长和负增长，生育一个孩子搞上半个世纪、一个世纪也不为过。有的不赞成这样的意见，认为长时间实行生育一个孩子的政策，会带来劳动力短缺、老龄化过于严重、社会负担过重等多种社会问题，不能只顾及控制人口数量一个方面。我在会上力陈并在向书记处的报告中阐述，提倡一对夫妇生育一个孩子主要是要控制一代人的生育率，因为控制住一代人的生育率也就自然地控制了下一代做父母的人口数量，因而主要是未来二三十年特别是20世纪内的事情。故提倡一对夫妇生育一个孩子既非永久之计，半个世纪甚至一个世纪的搞下去不行；也非权宜之计，搞上三年五载就收兵不搞了也难以奏效，随着时间的推移其作用也就自然的消减了。提倡一对夫妇生育一个孩子主要着眼于控制一代人的生育率，这是权衡利弊之后的科学选择，得到与会多数同志的赞同。

▲：提出"提倡一对夫妇生育一个孩子"的人口政策时，有没有考虑到短时间内面临人口老龄化问题呢？

●：当时讨论的第三个重要问题就是人口结构问题，也涉及家庭"四二一"结构问题。即提倡一对夫妇生育一个孩子，会不会造成老年人口为四、成年人口为二、少年人口为一的家庭"四二一"年龄结构。经过论证，提倡一对夫妇生育一个孩子，如果两代人都是这样的"单传"，某些家庭可能出现这种"四二一"结构；但就整个社会范围而言，只有双方都是独生子女并且结婚后全部只生育一个孩子，才具备形成"二一"的条件。因此，只要允许独生子女结婚可以生育两个孩子，总体上就不存在"二一"结构。事实上，从这一政策诞生的第一天起，各省、自治区、直辖市都实行了双方均为独生子女者结婚，可以生育两个子女。而整个社会老年人口的"四"，是不可能形成的。众所周知，老年人口的年龄别死亡率较高，处于结婚生育年龄的育龄人口在其后成长到老年的三四十年中，实际上因为不断死亡其数量在逐步减少，老年人口的"四"是没有办法保持下来的，可能变成"三二一"（假定二一成立），甚至是"二二一"（假定二一成立）。所以，无论是四个老人全部健在，还是双方都是独生子女结婚只生育一个孩子，都是与现行生育政策相违背的，所谓"四二一"结构乃是认识上的一个误区。

座谈会向中央书记处的《报告》和中央的《公开信》，体现了上述基本精神。本人在受命起草向书记处的《报告》时，还按照领导要求，分别撰写以个人署名的几个《附件》，以示对这样的论证负有责任。这两个文件奠定了 20 世纪 80 年代以来我国生育政策的基调，产生了很大影响。今天看来，80 年代初提出的以提倡一对夫妇生育一个孩子为主要标志的生育政策，绝不是"拍脑袋"的结果，而是经过认真的讨论和论证，对其实施后果进行了深入研究，符合国家和民族根本利益的抉择。

三　审时度势：调整 2000 年人口目标

▲：当时提出 2000 年人口控制的目标是多少？

●：开始提出 1985 年自然增长率下降到 5‰、2000 年零增长和总人口控制在 12 亿以内目标，人口政策必须相应跟上。于是 1982 年 2 月《中共中央、国务院关于进一步做好计划生育工作的指示》（中发 ［1982］ 11 号），要求国家干部和职工、城镇居民，除特殊情况经过批准者外，一对夫妇只生育一个孩子。农村普遍提倡一对夫妇只生育一个孩子，某些群众确有实际困难要求生二胎的，经过审批可以有计划地安排。不论哪一种情况都不能生三胎。对于少数民族，也要提倡计划生育，在要求上，可适当放宽一些。具体规定由民族自治地方和有关省、自治区，根据当地实际情况制定，报上一级人大常委会或人民政府批准后执行①。同年中共中央办公厅、国务院办公厅转发《全国计划生育工作会议纪要》，对生育政策作了具体的阐述：普遍提倡一对夫妇只生育一个孩子，严格控制二胎，坚决杜绝多胎。各省、区、市规定了三种情况可以生育二胎：（1）第一个孩子有非遗传性残疾，不能成为正常劳动力的；（2）重新组合的家庭，一方原只有一个孩子，另一方系未婚的；（3）婚后多年不育，抱养一个孩子后又怀孕的。此外，在贯彻执

---

① 参见彭珮云主编《中国计划生育全书》，中国人口出版社，1997，第 19 页。

行中，很多省、区、市还对农村作了若干补充规定，主要有：（1）两代或三代单传的；（2）几兄弟只有一个有生育能力的；（3）男到独女家结婚落户的；（4）独子独女结婚的；（5）残废军人；（6）夫妇均系归国华侨的；（7）边远山区和沿海渔区的特殊困难户[①]。

1981 年 3 月第五届全国人民代表大会常务委员会第十七次会议审议通过设立国家计划生育委员会，国家计划生育委员会正式挂牌成立。1982 年中共十二大报告，强调人口问题始终是现代化建设中的一个极为重要的问题，明确"实行计划生育，是我国的一项基本国策"。这是诸多基本国策中，第一个正式宣布的基本国策。随后在 1982 年的机构改革中，建立了自上而下的计划生育组织机构，为推行计划生育基本国策提供了强有力的组织保证。

▲：您当时是如何看待初步确定的 2000 年人口实现零增长和总人口控制在 12 亿以内的人口调控目标的？

●：在中国社会科学院工作的同志有一条不成文的规定：研究无禁区，宣传有纪律。我本人拥护并身体力行这条原则。对于 2000 年全国人口控制在 12 亿以内的目标，心里存有一定的疑虑；但在公开文章中，还是遵循力争达到的基调。但是研究的任务，则要实事求是地探讨这一目标和相关政策的可行性，在内部刊物发表不同研究结果。机会来了，1981 年 3 月，时任中共中央总书记的胡耀邦同志在同《人民日报》、《红旗》、中国社会科学院部分同志座谈时，讲到要研究 20 世纪末中国将展现出一幅怎样的图像？占世界人口 1/5 的我国人民，那时将过着怎样的物质文化生活？希望通过调查研究绘出具体生动的前景，以激励人民为之奋斗。根据这一指示，中国社会科学院和国务院技术经济研究中心组织部分同志着手《2000 年的中国》研究。该研究是一项大工程，涉及人口、经济、消费、能源、交通、科技、环境、国际等各个方面，要完成系列研究报告，描绘出 2000 年我国经济、社会、科技发展的图像、特征、思路和相应的决策选择。我同另一位领导同志负责《2000 年的中国》首篇《2000 年中国的人口和就业》研究报告。由于是呈送党中央、国务院领导的内部研究报告，适用"研究无禁区"原则，开展实事求是的科学研究。

1984 年该研究完成，提出并论证了 2000 年中国人口和就业发展的 10 个

[①] 参见彭珮云主编《中国计划生育全书》，中国人口出版社，1997，第 22 页。

方面的图像：人口数量得到控制，增长速度放慢；婴儿死亡率不断下降，人口预期寿命不断延长；人口文化素质不断提高；人口由年轻型向成年型过渡；人口的城镇化趋势；经济生产年龄人口比总人口增长为快，就业人口空前膨胀；农业劳动力向非农业转移；工农业物质生产部门劳动力向非物质生产部门转移；总人口就业率上升，经济生产年龄人口就业率下降；就业效益和劳动生产率提高 10 个方面的发展趋势、可能达到的目标和决策选择。关于人口发展战略和 2000 年人口发展目标，《报告》从我国人口以及经济、文化、社会等的实际出发，提出并阐发了实现低位预测 12 亿目标困难极大，要做突破的准备；但一般认为也不会超过 12.8 亿高位预测；最大可能是中位预测的 12.5 亿左右。《报告》给出的 2000 年人口和就业图像最主要之点是：人口数量控制在 12.5 亿人左右，身体和文化素质有较大提高，城乡结构大体上"四六开"的成年型人口。安排比目前多出 2 亿多劳动力，城乡劳动力大致对半开，管理体制比较科学，具有较高效益的就业①。就人口目标而论，在当时已经确定并大力宣传 2000 年全国人口控制在 12 亿以内的情况下，提出并论证控制在 12.5 亿左右，整整多出 5000 万即相当于英国或法国一个国家的人口，是需要有坚定的科学信念和勇气，顶住来自包括学术界在内的某些压力的。

关于 2000 年人口控制在 12 亿以内的目标，学术界存在不同观点，也有同志通过不同方式向上反映过，中央领导同志有过批示。1984 年中央批转国家计生委《关于计划生育情况的汇报》（即 7 号文件），提出"要进一步完善计划生育工作的具体政策"。主要是：对农村继续有控制地把口子开得稍大一些，按照规定的条件，经过批准，可以生二胎；坚决制止开大口子，即严禁生育超计划的二胎和多胎；严禁徇私舞弊，对在生育问题上搞不正之风的干部要坚决予以处分；对少数民族的计划生育问题，要规定适当的政策。可以考虑，人口在 1000 万以下的少数民族，允许一对夫妇生育第二胎，个别的可以生育三胎，不准生四胎。具体规定由民族自治地方的人大和政府、有关的省、自治区，根据当地实际情况制定，报上一级人大常委会或人民政府批准后执行②。结果"大口"没有堵住，"小口"则开得大了，造成 20 世纪 80 年代中期一定程度的生育小高潮。与此同时，国家也将 2000 年全

---

① 参见国务院技术经济研究中心《2000 年的中国》之一《2000 年中国的人口和就业》（研究报告），1984。

② 参见彭珮云主编《中国计划生育全书》，中国人口出版社，1997，第 24 页。

国人口控制在 12 亿以内修改为 12 亿左右，当时国务院领导还作出"左右不过五"的诠释。结果呢？2000 年全国人口普查时为 12.66 亿人，既不是 12亿以内，恐怕也不能称之为 12 亿左右，人口高指标的教训值得认真总结。

四 与时俱进：立足于统筹解决人口问题的政策选择

▲：第十一届全国人民代表大会第二次会议期间，人口政策再次成为讨论的热点，您认为新时期我国人口政策是否应作出调整？如何调整？

●：历史推进到 21 世纪，人口变动与发展面临新的态势。一是人口增长的势能减弱许多，2030 年全国人口增长到 14.65 亿人左右时，即可实现零增长；二是劳动年龄人口增加到临近峰值，2017 年 15～64 岁劳动年龄人口增加到 10 亿将成为由增到减的拐点；三是人口老龄化加速推进，2050 年 65岁以上老年人口比例可上升到 23% 的高水平；四是人口城市化步入 S 形曲线中部，呈加速上升趋势；五是出生性别比持续攀升，与现行生育政策的关系值得重视。如前所述，这些问题早在 20 世纪 80 年代初大力控制人口增长时已经作出大致的估计。但是那时毕竟没有实践检验，现在经过实践人口素质、结构方面的问题日益凸显出来，成为新时期人口发展战略和人口政策必须着力解决的问题。同时随着科学发展观和可持续发展战略的深入贯彻，人口问题的解决也必须纳入其中，纳入和谐社会建设之中。基于这样的认识，提出统筹解决人口问题"三步走"人口发展战略和相应的政策选择。

"三步走"人口发展战略：第一步，把高生育率降下来，降到更替水平以下，实现人口再生产由高出生、低死亡、高增长向低出生、低死亡、低增长类型的转变。1992 年生育率下降到更替水平以下，标志着这一步已经完成。第二步，稳定低生育水平，直至实现人口的零增长；同时注重人口素质的提高、人口结构的合理调整。这一步预计 2030 年前后可以实现。第三步，零增长以后，由于人口的惯性作用将呈一定程度的减少趋势，再依据届时的经济、社会发展状况以及资源、环境状况，作出理想适度人口的抉择。这样理想的适度人口是全方位的，不仅数量是适当的，而且素质是比较高的，年龄、性别等的结构也是合理的。这一步是人口零增长以后的事情，现在能做到的是走好第二步，为第三步战略的实施创造条件。如何走好第二步？其指导思想和基本点，可表述为：在以人为本科学发展观指导下，实现控制人口数量、提高人口素质、调整人口结构相结合，促进"控制"、"提高"、"调整"协调发展，人口与资源、环境、经济、社会可持续发展。

▲：为实现人口发展的第二步战略目标，您有什么建议？

●：为实现这样的人口目标，我提出下述可供选择的生育政策建议：

（1）全国不分城乡，双方均为独生子女者结婚一律允许生育两个孩子。这一步现在即可实施。当前，已婚育龄妇女独生子女领证率在 22% 左右，城镇远远高于农村，实行"双独"结婚生育两个孩子，生育率升高极其有限，可不附加任何条件。

（2）农村一方为独生子女者结婚，允许生育两个孩子，现在也可以开始实施；城镇可暂缓几年，2010 年以后组织实施为宜。对于农村来说，由于独生子女率较低，"一独生二"影响有限；对于城镇说来，由于独生子女率普遍很高，一方为独生子女结婚者比例不会很高，对生育率影响也不会很大，特别是推延到 2010 年，30 岁以下育龄妇女进一步减少后实施。但是实行"一独生二"的生育政策，对于"一独"方的父母家庭养老和改变家庭人口年龄结构说来，有着现实的、不可替代的意义。

（3）在有效制止三孩及以上多孩生育条件下，农村可不分性别普遍生育两个孩子。目前全国农村实际的总和生育率在 2.0 水平上下，如果除人数较少的少数民族外均不得生育三个及以上孩子能够做到，生育率可大体上维持现在的水平。我们的"软着陆"预测方案还留了一点儿微升的余地，只要真正做到"限三生二"，——"限三"是前提，只有确保"限三"才能"生二"——是不会造成农村和整个社会生育率有多大反弹的。

（翟胜明）

不懈追求学术真谛[*]

——记中国社会科学院学部委员、著名人口学家田雪原

今年是我国实行改革开放政策 30 周年。我院学部委员、著名人口学家田雪原研究员的人口学学术研究活动与改革开放的历程相伴，在不懈拼搏、求索之中，播撒学者的正义与良知。

一　少年"立志"与青年"思虑"

综观田雪原的学术研究，我们有一个强烈的感受，这就是，字里行间充满学术激情和社会责任感。它源于什么？因何而生发？我们试图从他的童年和青少年时代的经历中找寻答案。

1938 年 8 月，田雪原出生于"煤铁之城"本溪。在其童年时代，印象最深的是日本鬼子的侵略与奴役。日本帝国主义投降，结束了中国人当牛做马的日子；可是中国人为什么会成为亡国奴呢？这是他幼小心灵中解不开的谜。后来上小学时，作为教师的哥哥给他拿来一本方志敏烈士遗著《可爱的中国》——他将其称为打开自己心灵天窗的第一本启蒙读物，当读到帝国主义列强宰割祖国母亲的身体、吸吮母亲的乳汁时，再也抑制不住夺眶而出的泪水，心头充满悲愤，作为祖国母亲的儿子，立下毕生要为国家富强献身之志。1959 年，抱着这样的志向他走进北京大学殿堂，心中好不欢畅，然而入学后不久便赶上第二次批判马寅初校长的《新人口论》，却使他陷入迷茫。于是便躲在图书馆一隅，找来马老发表的"我的经济理论、哲学思想和政治立场"等文章，同时也找来一大堆批判文章读了起来。越读越觉得马老

---

* 原载《中国社会科学院院报》2008 年 8 月 5 日。

关于控制人口数量、提高人口质量的论述讲得很有道理，更为那种年近八十誓死捍卫真理、直至战死为止的彻底唯物主义精神所感动；相反，那些连篇累牍的批判文章却讲不出多少道理，除了标签式的政治口号和扣大帽子之外，便是偷换前提一类的逻辑推演，其目的就是要将《新人口论》批臭，把马寅初打下去。特别是康生亲临北大点名"属于哪个马家"之后，包括马老居住的燕南园在内的整个燕园，更是大字报铺天盖地，声讨之声不绝于耳，最后马老真的从北大校园、政坛和学坛上"蒸发"了。这使他着实困惑了一段时间，并且隐约地感到，有一天颠倒的历史还会重新颠倒过来的。当时不清楚，正是这种情结和不同认识，埋下后来他为马寅初《新人口论》翻案和走上人口科学研究之路的种子。

1964 年，田雪原从北大经济学系毕业后，先是参加两年"四清"，接着便是所谓的十年"文化大革命"和干部下放劳动。除了和这一代人大同小异的经历外，作为系统学习过马克思主义经济学和西方经济学说史的学人说来，原来盼望祖国尽快强盛、人民尽快富裕起来的情结受到莫大的伤害。在"四清"同吃、同住、同劳动过程中，亲身感受到新中国成立十五六年后，许多农民依然过着缺吃少穿的清贫日子；城市也好不到哪儿去，直至20 世纪 70 年代每人每月只供应几两油、肉、蛋，自行车等日用工业品都要凭票供应，在饥饿、温饱、小康、富裕和最富裕几个发展阶段中，处在由饥饿向温饱过渡阶段。由此不能不对当时的人民公社以及整个国家的计划经济产生疑问：为什么西方市场经济国家忧虑的是生产过剩，而高度集中统一的计划经济国家则被生产短缺困扰？第二次世界大战结束后 30 年，我们同发达国家的差距不是缩小而是更大了。国家尽快富强起来的期望跌到了失望的边缘。1978 年底，党的十一届三中全会的召开，给他的感觉真的是"忽如一夜春风来，千树万树梨花开"，于是便即刻投身到理论上的拨乱反正中去，在《光明日报》等报刊上发表了《调整是目前国民经济全局的关键》、《为社会主义的托拉斯恢复名誉》等几篇经济论文，把憋了多年的经济理论上的情绪呐喊出来。不过积压多年的最大学术情结，还是 1959 年入学后那场对马寅初的批判：于是他把积累的资料整理出来，写出并发表了《为马寅初先生的新人口论翻案》等几篇文章，又将马老其他几篇有关人口的文章汇集到一起，以《新人口论》命名重新出版，三年内连续出版三次，在人口理论界拨乱反正中发挥了显著作用，得到广泛赞誉。自此，他同人口科学结下了不解之缘。

二　壮年宏图大展

田雪原转入人口研究领域后，对中国人口问题的性质、现状、未来变动和发展的趋势研究着力甚多，为全面妥善解决中国人口问题贡献才智。他的人口研究按照这样的路子一步步走下来，大致可分做以下五个阶段。

第一阶段为20世纪70年代后期至80年代初期，重点是人口理论的拨乱反正。中心是以为马寅初先生新人口论平反为契机，破除"人口不断迅速增长是社会主义人口规律"的教条，在论著中提出并论证了中国人口问题的过剩性质，控制人口增长的必要性、可行性和政策建议。

第二阶段重点为中国人口发展战略研究。可分为前后两个时期，前期始于20世纪80年代初。1980年3~5月中央召开5次人口座谈会，共商国家人口大计。他除了用研究结果力陈大力控制人口增长及其政策选择外，受主持会议的中央领导同志委托，还担负会议向中央书记处起草报告的任务；并受命就提倡一对夫妇生育一个孩子会不会导致新生儿智商下降、劳动力供给短缺、老龄化不堪重负、家庭发生四二一年龄结构、人口的城乡和地区分布结构发生逆转等问题，以个人名义写出附件，备领导查询时参阅。现在看来，对这些问题的阐释，至少是实事求是和经得起历史检验的。这也是作为学者最大的满足了。另一项是1984年主持《2000年的中国》首篇《2000年的中国人口和就业》研究，由于是内部研究报告，针对2000年全国人口控制在12亿以内目标，提出12.0亿、12.5亿、12.8亿低、中、高三种方案，阐述倾向于12.5亿左右的决策选择，以及控制人口数量、提高人口质量、调整人口结构相结合，并以数量控制为重点的人口发展战略，对政府决策产生一定影响。后期为步入21世纪以后的人口发展战略研究。

第三阶段为20世纪80年代后期，重点是人口年龄结构变动老龄化以及城市化问题研究。在20世纪80年代前期的人口发展战略研究中，已经注意到控制人口数量增长和生育率持续下降后人口年龄结构老龄化问题；"七五"期间他主持国家社科重点项目"中国老年人口调查与老年社会保障改革研究"，在国家统计局城乡抽样调查队的支持合作下，进行了1987年全国60岁以上老年人口抽样调查，完成老年人口、经济、社会三部专著和报告，提出并阐发了社养、家养、自养"三养"相结合的养老保障体系和相应的对策建议。与老龄化研究同步进行的，是人口流动与城市化研究。分析了改革开放给人口城市化带来新的生机和活力的态势和发展趋势，提出加速推进户籍改革的建议。这两项研究，可视为人口发展战略研究在人口年龄、城乡结构领域的延伸，使战略研究趋于完备。

第四阶段为 20 世纪 90 年代前期，侧重微观的家庭经济与生育并涉及中观社区研究。要落实人口发展战略，除了宏观上要制定科学的人口发展目标和做好发展规划，注意人口老龄化等影响外，还必须取得中观和微观层面上的支持，将战略变为广大群众的自觉行动。为此承担"八五"国家重点和联合国资助项目"中国家庭经济与生育研究"。1992 年进行了中国 10 省市家庭经济与生育抽样调查，出版了抽样调查资料、报告和专著，提出并阐发了孩子社会附加成本—效益理论，给出具体计算方法，取得创新性成果。

第五阶段为 20 世纪 90 年代中期以来，将人口发展战略纳入可持续发展视野。提出并阐发了以人为本的可持续发展战略体系：资源是可持续发展的前提，一切发展都可归结为资源的物质变换；人口是可持续发展的关键，只有人类参与资源的物质变换才称得上发展；环境是可持续发展的终点，可持续发展最终是为了给人的发展创造良好的自然和社会环境；经济和社会发展是可持续发展的调节器，推行可持续发展战略主要依赖经济和社会的协调发展。结合他国实际，重点研究人口与经济——总体人口与生活资料、劳动年龄人口与生产资料、人口老龄化与社会保障、人口城市化与产业结构、人口文化教育素质与科技进步、人口地区分布与生产力布局的可持续发展，受到关注。

田雪原认为，从事学术研究，学术勇气是必不可少的。1979 年他发表文章为马寅初平反，在当时也是有压力的。在他看来，这个问题不解决，人口理论拨乱反正便无法进行，人口研究便无法走上科学的轨道。1980 年公布了 2000 年全国人口控制在 12 亿以内的战略目标，但是他作为人口科学工作者知道它的难度有多大。类似这样的问题还有出生性别比升高、当前生育政策决策选择等。提出和坚持自己的学术观点需要一点儿精神和勇气，当然也需要一点儿艺术。在这方面，老校长马寅初树立了榜样，他坚持真理、宁死不屈，荣辱不重要、唯有真理高的治学精神和气节，永远值得后人学习。

而学术勇气离不开扎实的基础知识作为支撑。田雪原认为，要做好研究工作，最重要的是两方面的知识，一是本专业的基本理论，二是与本专业交叉的相关学科知识。1980 年，院所领导找他谈话，要他做人口研究。"服从分配"是他们那一代人的天职，大学毕业分配表上第一志愿填的就是"服从分配"。不过他十分清楚，虽然经济学同人口学联系紧密，但是"隔行如隔山"，必须补上人口学这一课。他在年过"不惑"之后，于1982年5月至1983年6月到美国东西方中心作访问学者，利用课题研究之余，比较系统地阅读了主要的一些人口学论著，并且结识了前往那里作高级访问学者的美国普林斯顿大学的A.柯尔、芝加哥大学的G.S.贝克尔和F.豪泽、布朗大学的S.哥德斯坦、伦敦大学的布拉斯、日本大学的黑田俊夫、澳大利亚大学的考德维尔等名家。学习他们之所长，进行学术交流，算是补上人口学这一课。人口学是一门比较规范的学科。补上这一课很有必要，打不好基础是很难做出规范化研究的。人口学又是一门属于边缘和交叉性质的学科，人口科学研究不仅需要经济学、社会学、统计学等社会科学知识，而且需要一定的数学、医学、生物学等自然科学知识。可以这样说，人口科学研究差不多可以涉足一切科学领域，哪门科学同人口的变动和发展没有关系？办法就是学习，看书是学习，与这些学科的学者合作研究也是学习，是更有针对性的学习。他在合作研究中，学习受益匪浅。

三 不懈追求学术真谛

用知识和汗水，播撒学者的正义和良知。这是田雪原在学术生涯中对自己始终如一的基本要求。他的童年在半殖民地、半封建的旧中国度过，这使他埋下了深深的爱国情结，立志要报效祖国，报效包括父母亲人在内的人民。用什么报效呢？用知识。学习知识要肯于付出。

田雪原认为，播撒学者正义良知，就要始终站在人民大众立场，坚持不唯书、不唯上、只唯实，坚持学术创新、与时俱进。多年来践行"研究无禁区、宣传有纪律"原则体会颇深。研究工作不能有禁区，若研究有禁区还要我们干什么呢？但宣传有纪律也很必要，因为有些研究如人口政策，随便发表意见会引起错误的导向，造成不应有的损失。随着年龄的增长，他特别告诫自己要警惕思想僵化，要不断接受新事物，研究新问题，还要向青年同志学习。

田雪原在1984～1998年期间担任中国社会科学院人口研究所（中心）所长（主任）。由于该所为新建研究所，作为所领导行政事情占用的时间比较多。当时院领导强调所长要专心致志地治所，同时所长作为学科带头人必须站在学术前沿，这两个方面都不容忽视。没有什么特别好的办法，唯一的办法就是勤奋加上科学安排，向效率要时间，向效率要成果，研究所的工作严格按照院关于所长职责规定行事，几个人分工负责，他主要分管科研。但还是要常到院里所里来，经常是早晚两次上班的感觉：早晨上行政班，到办公室处理公务；下午下班也是回家上班，开始晚上的科研。一般情况下他到家进入科研角色较快，从进门到坐下来开始工作可在 5 分钟之内完成。家人不动他书房、书桌、电脑上的东西，使他在很短时间内就能接着做前面的研究。

田雪原虽年近"古稀"，但给人的印象是精力充沛，甚至可以说很有朝气。他认为，身体健康与心理健康密切相关，最重要的是有一个良好的心态；要勤用脑、多用脑，用脑对健康大有好处；也要进行必要的体育锻炼，每周坚持到就近公园变速跑两三次，每次二三千米。

从田雪原的学术历程中，我们感到，作为学者，学术情结和社会责任感两者都不可缺少。学术情结更多的是执著的治学态度和不懈的求索精神，社会责任则是对社会现实的强烈关注，进而探寻解决问题的途径。将两者结合起来，才有可能做到：当社会问题尚未显露或尚处于初萌状态时，即能敏锐地觉察到它未来的变动走势，开展与时俱进的研究，为国家制定相关政策提供智力支持。只有这样，社会科学家才能无愧时代的要求。

（纪南）